PRESIDENTIAL STUDIES READER

PRESIDENTIAL STUDIES READER

ROBERT P. WATSON
EDITOR
Florida Atlantic University

nova History Publications
New York

Copyright © 2009 by Nova Science Publishers, Inc.

All rights reserved. No part of this book may be reproduced, stored in a retrieval system or transmitted in any form or by any means: electronic, electrostatic, magnetic, tape, mechanical photocopying, recording or otherwise without the written permission of the Publisher.

For permission to use material from this book please contact us:
Telephone 631-231-7269; Fax 631-231-8175
Web Site: http://www.novapublishers.com

NOTICE TO THE READER

The Publisher has taken reasonable care in the preparation of this book, but makes no expressed or implied warranty of any kind and assumes no responsibility for any errors or omissions. No liability is assumed for incidental or consequential damages in connection with or arising out of information contained in this book. The Publisher shall not be liable for any special, consequential, or exemplary damages resulting, in whole or in part, from the readers' use of, or reliance upon, this material. Any parts of this book based on government reports are so indicated and copyright is claimed for those parts to the extent applicable to compilations of such works.

Independent verification should be sought for any data, advice or recommendations contained in this book. In addition, no responsibility is assumed by the publisher for any injury and/or damage to persons or property arising from any methods, products, instructions, ideas or otherwise contained in this publication.

This publication is designed to provide accurate and authoritative information with regard to the subject matter covered herein. It is sold with the clear understanding that the Publisher is not engaged in rendering legal or any other professional services. If legal or any other expert assistance is required, the services of a competent person should be sought. FROM A DECLARATION OF PARTICIPANTS JOINTLY ADOPTED BY A COMMITTEE OF THE AMERICAN BAR ASSOCIATION AND A COMMITTEE OF PUBLISHERS.

LIBRARY OF CONGRESS CATALOGING-IN-PUBLICATION DATA

Presidential studies reader / Robert P. Watson (editor).
   p. cm.
 Includes index.
 ISBN 1-60021-082-1
 1. Presidents--United States--History. 2. Presidents--Study and teaching--United States. 3. United States--Politics and government. 4. United States--Politics and government--Study and teaching. I. Watson, Robert P., 1962-
 E176.1.P897   2006
 973.09'9--dc22   2006007843

Published by Nova Science Publishers, Inc. ✦ *New York*

CONTENTS

Preface   vii

Introduction: Presidential Studies and Presidential Research   ix
    Robert P. Watson

HISTORICAL REASSESSMENTS OF PRESIDENTS   1

Chapter 1   George Washington's Character and Slavery   3
    James P. Pfiffner

Chapter 2   Governing the Devil in Hell: "Bleeding Kansas" and the Destruction of the Franklin Pierce Presidency (1854-1856)   13
    Michael J. C. Taylor

Chapter 3   The Domestic Lincoln: White House Lobbying of the Civil War Congresses   23
    Jon Schaff

Chapter 4   The "Smallest Mistake": Explaining the Failures of the Hayes and Harrison Presidencies   37
    Douglas Steven Gallagher

THE CHALLENGE OF GOVERNING   55

Chapter 5   Separating Rhetoric from Policy: Speechwriting under Gerald Ford and Jimmy Carter   57
    Karen M. Hult and Charles E. Walcott

Chapter 6   The Rhetoric of Presidential Veto Messages   73
    Christopher J. Deering, Lee Sigelman and Jennifer L. Saunders

Chapter 7   A Revisionist View of George Bush and Congress, 1989: Presidential Support, 'Veto Strength,' and Legislative Strategy   93
    Richard S. Conley

Chapter 8	The Politics of Presidential Appointments: A Thorny Business *Colton C. Campbell*	109

RELATIONS WITH CONGRESS AND PUBLIC POLICY   125

Chapter 9	Regime Formation and Maturation in the White House: The Rise of Internationalism during the Administration of Theodore Roosevelt *Tom Lansford*	127
Chapter 10	The Collapse of an Inherited Agenda: George Bush and the Reagan Foreign Policy Legacy *Victoria A. Farrar-Myers*	147
Chapter 11	Debunking the Myth: Carter, Congress, and the Politics of Airline Deregulation *David B. Cohen and Chris J. Dolan*	163
Chapter 12	Clinton's Greatest Legislative Achievement? The Success of the 1993 Budget Reconciliation Bill *Patrick Fisher*	189

RESEARCHING AND EVALUATING THE PRESIDENCY   205

Chapter 13	Ranking and Evaluating Presidents: The Case of Theodore Roosevelt *Max J. Skidmore*	207
Chapter 14	The Emerging Scholarly Consensus on Presidential Leadership: A New Realism, an Old Idealism *Raymond Tatalovich and Thomas S. Engeman*	217
Chapter 15	Research on the Presidency: The Usual Problem of Biographical Accounts *William Cunion*	233
Chapter 16	Presidents after the White House: A Preliminary Study *Max J. Skidmore*	249

Appendix A. The Presidents	263
Appendix B. Article II of the Constitution	265
Appendix C. Constitutional Amendments Pertaining to the Presidency	269
Appendix D. Law of Presidential Succession	273
Appendix E. Sources for Studying the Presidency	275
About The Contributors	281
Index	285

PREFACE

The idea for this book originated in part in the classroom, through my experience teaching undergraduate and graduate courses on the presidency and with input in the form of questions, comments, and feedback from my students over the years. As my colleagues who teach courses on the presidency know, it is often difficult to find just the right types of readings – right in the mix of topics, coverage of pressing issues in the field, level of difficulty for students, and so on – in a single book. More often than not, we assign several books, picking and choosing from the readings, or we are photocopying recent research articles to be put on reserve at the library for our students' use. As such, the idea of producing a single volume containing a wide array of current research on the presidency was appealing to me as an editor, but more importantly, as a scholar who teaches and writes on the presidency.

One of the goals of this project was to offer teachers and readers "one-stop shopping" – an assortment of timely research included conveniently in a single volume. The essays are rigorous and scholarly, yet students will find them readable. There is a lot of important and quality research being produced in presidential studies, but not all of it is approachable for students. Students will not be intimidated by the contents of this book. At the same time, the essays should spark critical thinking and debate on both the topics at hand and other, larger issues relating to the presidency. The readings also reflect a variety of methodologies and approaches to the study of the presidency and are a reflective sample of the types of scholarship being produced today in the field.

The book also offers students an introductory essay that discusses presidential studies and the types of questions presidential scholars ask and attempt to answer. A feature of the book that students, teachers, and scholars should find helpful is the appendix. Handy appendices include a list of the presidents (with basic biographical information), Article II of the Constitution (the Article focusing on the presidency), constitutional amendments that pertain to the presidency, the presidential succession law, and a helpful list of sources (websites, journals, associations, centers, libraries, and books) on the presidency to facilitate further study of the topics in the book.

Of course, such a volume would not be possible if it were not for the contributions of colleagues in the discipline. Indeed, this is a strength of the book. A diverse group of presidential scholars – political scientists and historians, leading voices in the field and junior scholars – contributed to this volume. Another one of the goals of the book was to bring together not only a variety of scholars, but a variety of topics, methods, and approaches to the study of the presidency.

The book is organized into four major sections: Historical Reassessments of Presidents; The Challenge of Governing; Relations with Congress and Public Policy; and Researching and Evaluating the Presidency. It is not possible in a book of this length to cover all the issues, debates, and areas within the discipline. Yet, the sections included in the book represent a compromise between including as many topics as possible and offering a concise and handy reader. Each of the sections is broad-based and contains four readings. The readings are applicable to many of the other issues in the field and are suitable for undergraduate or graduate students.

There are already a handful of solid books containing the "classic" readings in the field penned by such luminaries as Richard Neustadt, Fred Greenstein, James David Barber, and others. This book offers readers a look at *contemporary* research and study being produced by presidential scholars and published in journals dedicated to the study of the presidency. The essays were selected from scholarship appearing in recent issues of the journal *White House Studies*. As editor of the journal, I had the good fortune of being quite familiar with the essays and having the task of selecting essays for inclusion in the book from well over 50 articles in recent issues. Readers will note that, among those selected, are several well-regarded and prominent scholars in the field, including James Pfiffner, Karen Hult, Charles Walcott, Lee Sigelman, Max Skidmore, and Raymond Tatalovich. There are also several junior, "up-and-coming" scholars doing some exciting research that is catching the attention of others in the field. It is a pleasure to work with all of them.

I wish to thank Frank Columbus, President and Editor-in-Chief of Nova Science Publishers, for his receptivity to my proposals as well as his continual outpouring of ideas. The staff of Nova's imprint, Nova History Books, and the team at Nova Science Journals who publish *White House Studies* made the project possible. So, to Frank Columbus, Donna Dennis, Susan Boriotti, Tatiana Shohov, Ave Marie Gonzalez, Nadia Columbus, Jennifer Vogt and Serge Shohov a sincere thanks. Among the contributors to this book are several valued colleagues with whom I frequently collaborate - a special thanks to Tom Lansford, Colton Campbell, Max Skidmore, and Victoria Farrar-Myers. Also, I wish to recognize my in-laws Celeste and Julio Pavone for all their support. As always, thanks to Claudia and Alessandro, as well as Nancy, Bob and Linda and Gustavo for demonstrating much patience with my work hours.

I hope you, the reader, find the book helpful in presenting a rich variety of current scholarship that is both readable and informative.

Robert P. Watson
Boca Raton, Florida

INTRODUCTION: PRESIDENTIAL STUDIES AND PRESIDENTIAL RESEARCH

Robert P. Watson

CHALLENGES FACING THE PRESIDENCY

To many people, the presidency is the most visible aspect of government. The president represents the United States abroad and serves as a symbol of the nation. While this has, to a degree, always been the case – George Washington was the "Father of His Country" – the intensive coverage by the media in recent years has further increased the office's visibility and symbolic importance. Stories on the president lead the evening news broadcast and are found on the front page of the nation's newspapers; the public recognizes the familiar backdrop whenever the press reports live from the White House lawn; and the White House press corps introduces the public to even the most mundane details about the first family. Reagan liked jelly beans. George and Barbara Bush's dog was named Millie. Chelsea Clinton graduated from Stanford. And Gerald Ford apparently had a tendency to trip or fall at the most public and inopportune times. In short, the presidency is a central facet of American politics and the American system of government. To scholars, it is an important sub-field in political science.

Yet, ironically, it is one of the least understood components of American government. As a field of study, it shows signs of intellectual maturity. But, at the same time has suffered from underdeveloped theory, inadequate models to test hypotheses, suspect methodological approaches, and a general lack of reliable data. Indeed, systematic study of the presidency is a challenging endeavor.

Further complicating matters, the presidency is a dynamic institution. Although the presidency has roots firmly planted in the Constitution and many of the traditions and customs of the institution are carried over from president to president, it is at the same time certainly not the same office as the one occupied by George Washington. Washington oversaw five federal agencies and a budget of roughly $250,000. Today, the president's staff numbers in the thousands, the federal government's budget has long surpassed the trillion-dollar mark, and the chief executive oversees fourteen cabinet departments, the homeland security program, and many dozen independent agencies.

The size, roles, and scope of the federal government have ballooned since 1789. They have ballooned since 1933. Even the presidential home has changed. George Washington served from private mansions in New York City and later in Philadelphia while the building now known as the White House was being constructed. Paralleling the institution it houses, the White House has endured times of tragedy (it was burned by the British in 1814 during the War of 1812), experienced great growth (it was enlarged under Theodore Roosevelt and other presidents), and has changed in response to the times and crises (it was gutted and rebuilt under Truman). George Washington, who played a prominent role in its construction but did not live to see it completed, would hardly recognize the White House today.

The first fundamental shift in and growth of the role and scope of the presidency occurred under Franklin D. Roosevelt (1933-1945), and is frequently referred to as the start of the "modern presidency." With assistance from the Brownlow Committee, the organization of federal agencies and the federal government was revamped and, responding to the crisis of the Great Depression, FDR expanded the power of the presidency. In subsequent years, the advent of the mass media would provide presidents with another tool for extending their influence.

By the 1960s and 1970s, presidential power was seen as excessive and problematic. The overextended, "imperial" presidency was seen by some as the reason for the Vietnam War, the Watergate scandal, and other negative actions and behaviors by presidents.[1] Gerald Ford and Jimmy Carter entered the presidency in the mid and late 1970s and attempted to heal the nation, return the office to a sense of normalcy, and renew respect for the institution. Both Ford and Carter were careful not to give the appearance of improperly expanding the president's role and office and were careful not to exceed the constitutional and statutory powers of the office.

But their efforts were apparently not enough. Starting in the 1960s and running through the 1970s public frustration with, even hostility toward, the office grew. The growing cynicism of the public coincided with increasing animosity between the Congress and president, antagonistic relations between the White House and press corps, and divided government – whereby the presidency was in the hands of one party and the Congress controlled by the other party – which seemed to become the norm and result in policy gridlock. Not only were individual presidents challenged by these conditions, but public opinion polls revealed that public faith in the institution itself was eroding.

In the past three decades, the presidency has suffered from major foreign policy crises seemingly beyond the control of the sitting president, a series of foreign policy and political missteps, scandals which were magnified by an adversarial press and an already weakened office – Watergate, the Iran-Contra scandal, the embarrassment of the Lewinsky scandal and a president being brought before the Congress for impeachment – and recessions under Carter in the late 1970s, Reagan in the early 1980s, George Bush in the early 1990s, and George W. Bush in the early 2000s. Media commentators and scholars have been quick to focus on Ronald Reagan's disconnected (even absent) style, George Bush's inability to connect with the public and articulate a vision for the country, Bill Clinton's lack of personal integrity, and George W. Bush's suspect maturity and intellectual abilities to the point where these issues might remain as defining traits of these presidencies.

Scholars are now focusing on such problems as the ungovernability of the office and inability of many recent presidents to lead effectively.[2] Such problems are not new. The Constitution established a weak office with few formal powers. In the blunt words of scholar Forest McDonald, "The presidency is often described as the most powerful office in the world. That is the stuff of nonsense."[3] However, the nature of the political system today is such that it, rather than any inherent weakness of presidents, explains much of the problems with presidential leadership.[4]

Presidential scholar Michael Genovese, for instance, has identified a "variety of built-in roadblocks" in the political system that explain the recent problems with ineffective presidents and low approval ratings. These factors make it difficult for presidents to lead from a position of power and include the following:

- the intention of the Founders to produce a weak office
- the constitutional design of checks and balances
- declining leadership skills
- cynicism in American political culture
- the cyclical nature of politics and national leadership
- weak political parties
- a combative, expensive presidential selection process
- the presence of a strong capitalist economy
- decline in U.S. power abroad[5]

The presidency is arguably the most demanding and challenging office in the country, if not the world, and has changed considerably over its 200-plus-year history. Presidents must contend with an invasive media hungry to fill a 24-hour news cycle, be wary of even the slightest misstep (or perceived misstep), handle the pressure of countless interest groups, find a way to work with a divided Congress, and raise tens of millions of dollars in order to mount a competitive bid for office. This is an exciting time to study the presidency. The office faces emerging challenges and a cadre of systematic "roadblocks" making it difficult for presidents to govern or lead.

At the dawn of the new century, the presidency is an office under assault, in transition, and one in need of further scholarly study. This is the office we seek to better understand.

CHALLENGES TO STUDYING THE PRESIDENCY

Initially, when studying the presidents or presidency, one must consider whether one is studying the person or the institution. All presidents are part of the larger institution. Presidents find themselves both benefiting from the enduring, powerful forces of the institution and functioning in a certain way because of them. For example, the person occupying the office benefits from the public's respect for the office and is viewed, in part, through his or, perhaps one day, *her* predecessors. The president is not completely free to act as he or she deems appropriate, because of precedents and customs forged by previous presidents dating to George Washington. Yet, presidents bring to the office a specific style, unique skills and abilities, and their own policy agenda. The question remains whether one can separate the person from the office or the president's public persona from his private actions. Interestingly, the presidency of Bill Clinton seemed to arm both sides of the debate with ammunition. While some argued that Clinton's policy successes and presidential actions can be viewed apart from his personal indiscretions, others felt that there was no room for such a public-private divide and that his personal behavior harmed his ability to govern.

The most famous work on the presidency continues to be that of Richard Neustadt's *Presidential Power*, over forty years after its initial publication.[6] Neustadt identified the limits to the formal authority of the president and pointed out the need for students of the presidency to understand not only notions of such formal authority in the office, but how the personal communication, bargaining, and political skills of a president serve to shape the presidency. His message that presidential power is defined by the power to persuade has guided presidential studies since the publication of his book in 1960.

In general, the field shows signs of being mature intellectually, but still faces growing pains and problems inherent in studying the office. Such problems as underdeveloped and underutilized theoretical and methodological approaches to the study of the presidency, a lack of reliable data, and other concerns continue to limit the effectiveness of scholarship and, in turn, our understanding of the office.

Methods for Studying the Presidency

The more rigorous, systematic approaches to the study of the presidency found in scholarly journals and textbooks today are relatively new in the history of presidential scholarship. Historically, studies of the presidency and presidents relied largely on anecdotal information. Often this information was subjective, leaving one to question the reliability of the data. To the present day, many first-hand accounts of presidential behavior and decisions from the presidents themselves, their senior aides, and critics from the opposing political party might be tainted by politics. What passes as an autobiography, biography, or study might serve a political agenda to repair, promote, or destroy the reputation of a president or presidential aide. Nearly everything coming out of the modern White House is filtered ("spin control") through the screen of politics. Those interested in studying the presidents must keep this in mind.

Very often, biographical accounts of a presidency by former aides reveal multiple stories and explanations to the extent that it would seem that they were not talking about the same president. While this might very well be a healthy occurrence and offer a diversity of opinion, often it is simply frustrating for scholars. Likewise, different television news shows, networks, newspapers, and news magazines put presidential actions in a different light, depending on their perspectives. Journalists covering the White House are not above personal bias, might not be trained in research methods, or lack an historic understanding of the presidency. The parties have a political agenda in mind when "explaining" presidential behavior. But, there often exists more than one perspective on a particular presidential decision. The problems are complex and presidents must consider a bewildering array of concerns and interests in the political environment within which they act.

An obvious challenge in studying the presidency from a systematic approach is the small number of presidencies with which researchers have to work (n = 43 as of 2002). Those studying congressional voting or voting behavior among the American public have far more cases to consider. Moreover, in presidential studies there is much variation among the cases. There are Abraham Lincolns and there are Warren Hardings. Attempts to quantify and reduce the bias and subjectivity in research are needed, but not easily done. Presidential scholars apply the rules of scientific research and empiricism – experience, experiments, observation, quantifiable data – to the study of the presidency.[7]

One of the earliest empirical approaches to studying the presidents was public opinion. Opinion polling helps us understand the public perceptions of presidents and polls are used by the White House in making decisions. But, it is hard to determine to what extent this latter phenomenon occurs and its exact place in the decision-making process. Polling has become a complex, scientific undertaking with focus groups, thermometer polls, multiple-day tracking polls, and a host of ways of measuring approval, negatives, and so on. In general, presidential studies has moved beyond subjective, descriptive ad hoc assessments and has made strides in embracing more rigorous examinations of the office.

Old and trusted methods are still useful, however. Case studies, despite all the criticism, remain popular and useful tools in all disciplines. Studying an individual president, a single appointment, or a policy produces findings that are limited in their scope. Still, however, case study methods have advanced and, in aggregate, case studies provide important data for understanding the presidency. The narrative approach is also popular among presidential scholars. The lack of data that plagued early studies is also being remedied. Presidential libraries have improved their archival and research services and do an admirable job making information available to scholars. A number of research centers have opened and journals have been founded devoted to the study of the presidency. And books and archives have appeared which provide comprehensive collections of presidential data and statistics.[8]

Conceptual Approaches to Studying the Presidency

A variety of approaches are used to study the presidency. These approaches guide scholars in asking certain questions and influence the type and usefulness of the data produced.

One of the more traditional approaches is to study the ***constitutional and legal*** aspects of the presidency. Such studies examine the Constitution, laws, treaties, executive orders, and executive agreements, while examining the president's formal roles and powers.[9]

Article II of the Constitution focuses on the executive, but does little to empower the president. The Constitution is in this respect noteworthy for saying what the president cannot do and simply not specifying the roles of the office as much as it is for spelling out the president's powers and what the president may do. Scholars using this approach are often interested in studying the system of checks and balances with the legislative branch, limits to formal presidential power, and other questions that help answer concerns about the president's proper role in the constitutional system.

A number of issues lend themselves to this approach such as the line-item veto, former legislative veto, efforts by Richard Nixon to impound funds appropriated by congress, and executive orders of constitutional questionability. Perhaps the main question approached by scholars in this manner has been the issue of war powers. For instance, some of the actions of Presidents Johnson and Nixon during the Vietnam War were carried out without express congressional approval. More recently, President George W. Bush's use of military tribunals in the "war on terror" raises similar questions.

Another popular approach is the study of ***political power***. In such studies, the president is assessed as a person and key political actor within the system capable through political influence and strategy of impacting public policy.[10] Whereas other studies might focus on formal authority in such matters, studies approaching the issue from the perspective of political power consider the president's political skills. There are numerous actors and interests in the U.S.'s pluralistic political environment and to ignore this facet of decision making is problematic. As Neustadt, Samuel Kernell, and others have pointed out, the president must rely on persuasion, political strategy, popularity, and appeals to the public.[11]

In crafting policy, the president works with Congress, the White House staff, the federal bureaucracy, interest groups, the press, and others in advancing the agenda. Students of the presidency might be interested in studying the interactions among them. Relatedly, another approach to studying the presidency considers the ***institutional presidency*** by looking at the institutional aspects of the office such as the structure and organization of the White House, agencies and staff reporting to the presidency, and so on, rather than just examining the person.[12] The White House is a large bureaucracy containing many agencies and a large staff of experts and advisors. It is thus equipped to play a role in presidential decision making. Many presidents, realizing the difficulty of working closely with a large number of agencies and aides, have come to rely on an inner circle of advisors or "kitchen cabinet." The notion of a plural presidency, whereby a number of offices, aides, and even the presidential spouse must be considered to understand presidential behavior is served by this approach.

One of the most interesting and controversial approaches to studying the presidency is ***presidential psychology or character***. Scholars have joined the media, talk-show pundits, and armchair political enthusiasts in considering the personality of the president as a key ingredient to understanding presidential decision making and behavior. This approach seeks to understand the presidency by employing forms of psychoanalysis. Many studies try to assess the fitness of the individual's character for the demands of the office, others formulate psychobiographies, and some studies attempt to place presidents into categories or types based on personality.[13]

Personality influences actions. So, it stands to reason that scholars would be interested in determining why presidents act as they do, how he views himself, and whether the president's character will help or harm their presidency. A basic premise of these studies is that the president has a view of the world and political problems that is a product of a cognitive process. The apparent character flaws in Richard Nixon proved to be fertile ground for psychological studies. Other presidents such as Woodrow Wilson, Lyndon Johnson, Ronald Reagan, and Bill Clinton have also been subject to psychoanalysis because certain personality traits were believed to impact their presidencies.

Although an important and popular approach to studying presidents, such studies have been criticized for over-generalizing findings based on insufficient data. Most scholars, after all, have not met their subject, much less spent considerable amount of time interviewing and psychoanalyzing him. Most political scientists and historians are not trained psychologists and it is always difficult to reduce a behavior to a single personality trait. Still, these concerns have not slowed scholarship in this area, much of which has produced useful biographical information on the presidents.

The field of presidential studies has been slow – slower than most of the other fields within political science – to embrace and then fully harness the tenets of empiricism and scientific research methodology. But, it has simultaneously been wise to not cast aside some of the more traditional approaches to studying the presidents. Also, in presidential studies, there is no preferred or one best method for approaching the subject. All approaches contain strengths and shortcomings. Scholars must match the methodological approach or approaches to the particular question at hand and objectives of their research. Some approaches have as their goal to produce a descriptive account of a presidential action. Others are analytical, seeking to assess why an event happened. Still other studies are prescriptive in nature, with the goal of offering advice. In the essays included in this volume the reader will find a wide variety of approaches and methods for studying the presidency.

QUESTIONS TO CONSIDER

As you read the essays in this book, consider the following questions and issues:

1. Identify the basic research question and goals of the study.
2. What approach or approaches are used to examine the presidency? Institutional, Political Power, Constitutional-Legal, Psychological, or another approach?
3. What methodology does the author(s) use in examining the research question? A case study, quantitative analysis, or another approach?
4. What do other studies (literature review) say about the question at hand? What appear to be some of the strengths and weaknesses of the existing literature base on the issue?
5. What are some of the challenges the author(s) faced in researching the question/topic?
6. What is the significance of the findings presented in the study to the field of presidential studies?

NOTES

[1] Arthur Schlesinger, Jr., *The Imperial Presidency* (Boston: Houghton Mifflin, 1973); Fred I. Greenstein, "Nine Presidents in Search of a Modern Presidency," in Fred I. Greenstein, *Leadership in the Modern Presidency* (Cambridge, Mass.: Harvard University Press, 1988).
[2] Gary L. Rose, *The American Presidency Under Siege* (Albany: SUNY Press, 1997)
[3] Forest McDonald, "Foreword," in Martin L. Fausold and Alan Shank, *The Constitution and the American Presidency* (Albany: SUNY Press, 1991), xi.
[4] Louis W. Koenig, *The Chief Executive*, 5th ed. (New York: Harcourt, Brace, 1986).
[5] Michael A. Genovese, *The Presidential Dilemma* (New York: Harper and Row, 1995).
[6] Richard Neustadt, *Presidential Power: The Politics of Leadership* (New York: Wiley, 1960).
[7] For a good discussion of presidential research and methods, see George C. Edwards, III and Stephen J. Wayne, *Studying the Presidency* (Knoxville: University of Tennesee Press, 1983) and George C. Edwards, III, Bert A. Rockman, and John H. Kessel, *Researching the Presidency* (Pittsburgh: University of Pittsburgh Press, 1993).

[8] See the National Archives and Records Administration (www.nara.gov) for a list of and information on the presidential libraries. See also Lynn Ragsdale, *Vital Statistics on the Presidency* (Washington: Congressional Quarterly Press, 1996).

[9] Louis Fisher's work is a good example of this approach. See, Louis Fisher, *Presidential War Power* (Lawrence: University Press of Kansas, 1995); Louis Fisher, *Constitutional Conflict Between Congress and the President* (Lawrence: University Press of Kansas, 1993).

[10] For a good example of this approach, see Richard Neustadt, *Presidential Power and the Modern Presidents* (New York: Free Press, 1990); Fred I. Greenstein, *The Hidden-Hand Presidency* (New York: Basic Books, 1982).

[11] See Neustadt, *Presidential Power* and Sam Kernell, *Going Public*.

[12] For a good example of this approach, see Karen M. Hult and Charles E. Walcott, *Governing the White House* (Lawrence: University Press of Kansas, 1995).

[13] Perhaps the most famous studies of this nature are Alexander L. George and Juliette L. George, *Woodrow Wilson and Colonel House: A Personality Study* (New York: Dover, 1964); James David Barber, *The Presidential Character*, 4th ed. (Englewood Cliffs, N.J.: Prentice Hall, 1992)

HISTORICAL REASSESSMENTS OF PRESIDENTS

Chapter 1

GEORGE WASHINGTON'S CHARACTER AND SLAVERY

James P. Pfiffner

INTRODUCTION

George Washington's character was recognized as sterling during his lifetime, and the assumption that he would be the first president played a key role in the formulation and adoption of the Constitution. Even during his lifetime he was revered by many, and after his death he was exalted almost to the point of apotheosis. At the dedication of the Washington Monument in 1885, Robert C. Winthrop declared: "Does not that Colossal Unit remind all who gaze at it... that there is one name in American history above all other names, one character more exalted than all other characters, ... one bright particular star in ... our firmament, whose guiding light and peerless lustre are for all men and all ages ... ?"[1]

More recent scholars have also written of Washington's admirable character. Seymour Martin Lipset argues that Washington's character was essential to the founding of the Republic because of his personal prestige, his commitment to the principles of constitutional government, and his key precedent of leaving office after two terms.[2] David Abshire argues that Washington was not perfect, but that he learned from his experience, and his public character was not different from his private behavior.[3] Joseph Epstein writes that Washington's "genius was perhaps the rarest kind of all: a genius for discerning right action so strong that he was utterly incapable of knowingly doing anything wrong." Epstein laments: "Each generation of our politicians today, at the end of their careers, happily peddle their influence in large law firms, or simply set up as straight for causes in which they can have no real belief. Washington would have been aghast..."[4] Perhaps Washington would have been aghast if he knew about modern politicians cashing in on their government experience. But then, modern politicians do not have slaves to provide for their economic well being. The question to be addressed here is: what light does slavery shed on the nature of Washington's character?

WASHINGTON'S CHANGING ATTITUDE ON SLAVERY

George Washington was born into a slave-holding family, and he continued to increase his human property until late in his life. When he was eleven years old in 1743, Washington's father died and left him ten slaves. When Washington's half-brother died in 1752, he inherited a larger number of slaves. In an agreement with his half-brother's widow, Washington acquired Mount Vernon along with 18 more Negro slaves; he eventually added 5,600 acres of land to Mount Vernon. In 1759, when Washington married the widow, Martha Dandridge Custis, she brought with her several hundred more slaves. The slaves who came with Martha were legally "dower slaves," and Washington kept them separate in his financial accounting, though for practical purposes they were used as Washington's property in the running of Mount Vernon. Although the counts may not be exact due to conflicting records, Washington's slave holdings steadily increased during his lifetime, from 49 in 1760, to 87 in 1770, to 135 in 1774, to 317 when he died in 1799.[5]

Through most of Washington's life up to the Revolutionary War, his attitude toward slavery was much like that of most slave owners in the American South. He fed them adequately as important components of the operation of his plantation at Mount Vernon.[6] Though Washington did not encourage whipping of slaves by his overseers, he did condone it when deemed necessary for discipline.[7] He bought and sold slaves and threatened to sell disruptive slaves to owners in the West Indies as the ultimate enforcement of discipline. Conditions in the West Indies were even harsher than in the mainland colonies and later United States, and the tropical climate and probability of disease made the threat a serious one. For instance, in 1766 Washington wrote to Captain Joseph Thompson, a slave trader, that:

> With this Letter comes a Negro (Tom) which I beg the favour of you to sell... for whatever he will fetch... This Fellow is both a Rogue & Runaway... [though] he is exceedingly healthy, strong, and good at the Hoe... and [I] must beg the favour of you (least he should [sic] attempt his escape) to keep him handcuffd till you get to Sea...[8]

Nor did Washington hesitate to pursue slaves who escaped his plantation.

It appears that Washington's attitude toward slavery, though not his public position, began to change during the Revolutionary War when he left Mount Vernon to lead the Continental Army.[9] Washington's change of perspective may have stemmed from the necessity of extending to slaves the opportunity to enlist in the Continental Army. Initially, when Washington went to Massachusetts to lead the Continental Army in 1775, he removed the free Negro soldiers from the Army.[10] Southern slave owners did not want to take the risk of allowing slaves to join the army and bear arms. But, in 1775, Lord Dunmore, the royal governor of Virginia, issued a proclamation that any Negro who joined the British forces would be granted freedom. Washington thus felt compelled to allow the free blacks to reenlist and fight with the revolutionary forces, lest they constitute an effective force for the British against their former owners.[11] During the War, with blacks constituting 20 percent of his army, Washington treated Negroes as human beings and with the respect due to any soldier.[12] He also witnessed their willingness to fight and die for the revolutionary cause. After the War, perhaps because of his experience, Washington's attitude toward slavery began to change, though his public position did not.

In the winter of 1778-1779, Washington considered selling his slaves and investing the capital, in part because he did not want to "traffic in the human species," but he did not seriously pursue the idea.[13] In 1783, the Marquis de Lafayette proposed that he and Washington establish a small estate and work it with free Negroes as tenants rather than slaves, and added that "Such an example as yours might render it a general practice..."[14] Washington praised Lafayette's character, but nothing ever came of the proposal. In 1786, Washington wrote to Robert Morris, "I can only say that no man living wishes more sincerely than I do to see the abolition of [slavery]... by slow, sure, and imperceptible degrees."[15] Washington's contemporary, David Humphreys, quoted Washington as regretting the institution of slavery: "The unfortunate condition of the persons whose labors I in part employed has been the only unavoidable subject of regret."[16] Though Washington had resolved not to sell his slaves, when he returned to Mount Vernon after the War, he continued to manage his estate, fully utilizing the slave labor that was essential to its economic viability.

When Washington went to Philadelphia to preside over the Constitutional Convention, it was widely known that he was one of the largest slave holders in Virginia. At the Convention, his prestige and reputation was second to none, and he weighed his actions and words carefully because he was aware of their political effect. His acceptance of the institution of slavery and refusal to make any public statement against it, undoubtedly influenced the deliberations of the delegates against taking any steps against slavery, despite some strong arguments to do so.[17] But it is also probably that if the Constitution had contained proscriptions on slavery that the southern states would not have ratified it.

As president, Washington was careful to stay neutral on the slavery issue. His only official act on the issue was to sign the Fugitive Slave Law, which was passed by Congress in February 1793. In 1791, in Philadelphia, President Washington feared that if he was considered legally a resident, his household slaves might be automatically freed. He ordered Tobias Lear, his aide, to take some of his slaves back to Mount Vernon. "I wish to have it accomplished under a pretext that may deceive both them and the public... I request that these sentiments and this advice may be known to none but *yourself* and *Mrs. Washington*."[18]

In 1793, Washington "entertained serious thoughts" of dividing his Mount Vernon estate and renting the land to English farmers who would employ his slaves as free laborers. Washington could thus live off of the rent. His purpose was "to liberate a certain species of property which I possess very repugnantly to my own feelings, but which imperious necessity compels, and until I can substitute some other expedient by which expenses not in my power to avoid (however well disposed I may be to do it) can be defrayed."[19] Washington was not able to find suitable English farmers to rent Mount Vernon.

Despite Washington's private reservation about slavery, as late as 1796 when he was president, he sought the return of Oney Judge, a slave who had escaped to New Hampshire. Denouncing "the ingratitude of the girl," he wrote in a letter that she "ought not to escape with impunity if it can be avoided."[20] On the day in 1797 that Washington departed Philadelphia after his presidency to return to Mount Vernon, one of his other slaves escaped rather than return to work on the plantation. Washington sought this slave's return, but feared he had to replace him by buying another slave. He wrote to Major George Lewis, "The running off of my cook has been a most inconvenient thing to this family, and what renders it more disagreeable, is, that I had resolved never to become the master of another slave by *purchase*, but this resolution I fear I must break."[21] He continued to seek the return of his property into 1798, the year before his death, though he did not purchase another slave.

How General was the Acceptance of Slavery?

It has been argued that Washington grew up in an era and in a part of the country where slavery was taken for granted and widely accepted by the white population, and thus he should not be held to account for his behavior with respect to owning slaves. This perspective maintains that we should not impose twentieth century values on eighteenth century people and blame them for violating what are only recently accepted as human rights. While this argument might be accepted with respect to some aspects of changing attitudes toward human rights, such as economic and political rights, the issue of slavery is much more basic. The owning and disposition as property of other human beings, despite various precedents in human history[22], is such a basic breach of human values that it is hard to excuse. Other forms of economic or social exploitation pale in comparison with the evil of slavery. Thus, we must acknowledge that Washington, even though he was more humane than some other slave owners, may have had a character flaw in his behavior with respect to slavery.

His culpability for his behavior might be mitigated if slavery was so universally accepted that no one was speaking out against it. But from the earliest days of the European colonization of North America, voice had been raised against slavery by religious groups such as the Methodists, Puritans, Quakers, and Mennonites, and by prominent individuals such as James Oglethorpe, William Penn, and Roger Williams. In 1785, for instance, a Virginia Quaker, Robert Pleasants, wrote a letter to Washington saying, in part:

> How strange then must it appear to impartial thinking men, to be informed, that many who were warm advocates for that noble cause during the War, are now siting [sic] down in a state of ease, dissipation and extravigance [sic] on the labour of Slaves? ... It seems highly probable to me, that thy example & influence at this time, towards a general emancipation, would be as productive of real happiness to mankind, as thy Sword may have been: I can but wish therefore, that thou may not loose the opertunity [sic] of Crowing the great Actions of thy Life, with the sattisfaction [sic] of, "doing to Others as thou would (in the like Situation) be done by," and finally transmit to future ages a Character, equally Famous for thy Christian Virtues, as thy wordly achievements...[23]

There is no record that Washington ever responded to the letter.[24]

Washington's unwillingness to abandon slavery or even speak out against it can be contrasted with some other Founders at the Constitutional Convention, such as Luther Martin and Gouverneur Morris, both of whom denounced slavery at the Convention. John Adams was a consistent opponent of slavery.[25] George Mason, a slave owner who was a close friend and neighbor of Washington, sought the end of trading in slaves, declaring: "This infernal traffic originated in the avarice of British Merchants... Every master of slaves is born a petty tyrant... By an inevitable chain of cause & effects providence punishes national sins, by national calamities... the Genl. Govt. Should have the power to prevent the increase of slavery."[26] But Mason's position against the slave trade did not mean that he favored giving the national government the authority to abolish slavery. Virginians had an economic interest in the continuation of slavery, and their own slave property would multiply naturally; thus they would benefit from the ending of the slave trade in the United States, but did not want their own slaves to be freed.[27]

Yet, not all Virginians accepted slavery as natural and inevitable. The Commonwealth of Virginia passed a law in 1782 providing that owners of slaves could grant them freedom if they wished; by 1790, more than 12,000 slaves had been freed, and by 1800, there were 20,000 free blacks in Virginia.[28] Most of the northern states had declared slavery illegal in the late 1770s and early 1780s, and had abolished it by 1804.[29] A number of anti-slavery motions were introduced in the U.S. Congress as well as in the Virginia legislature. In 1790, Benjamin Franklin, who was president of the Pennsylvania Society for Promoting the Abolition of Slavery, signed an anti-slavery document brought to the House of Representatives.[30] Though Franklin had owned and traded slaves in the 1730s, he came to see slavery as unwise as well as immoral. He wrote and spoke out on the evils of slavery from the 1750s until his death.[31]

While many of the abolitionists did not benefit from slavery personally and had little to lose in advocating its abolition, such was not the case with Robert Carter III, grandson of the notorious Robert "King" Carter who "seasoned" his newly arrived slaves from Africa by a "minor dismemberment – perhaps a finger or a toe."[32] The grandson was a correspondent of Jefferson, Madison, Mason, Patrick Henry, and neighbor of Washington. He was a significant member of the landed gentry who owned more land and slaves and books than either Washington or Jefferson. He lent money to Jefferson and hesitated to allow his daughter to marry into the Washington family.[33] In 1791, Carter decided that: "... Slavery is contrary to the true Principles of Religion and Justice, and that therefor it was my duty to manumit them."[34] Over a period of years, Carter proceeded to free his slaves, at least 280 and probably many more, possibly as many as 500.[35]

Thus, slavery was not universally accepted in Washington's time, even by southern landholders, and many voices were raised against it, some of them directed personally at Washington.

WASHINGTON FACES THE SLAVERY ISSUE

Toward the end of his life, Washington privately expressed opinions critical of slavery. In 1797, in a letter to his nephew, Washington confided: "I wish from my soul that the Legislature of the State could see the policy of a gradual Abolition of Slavery; it would prevt. much future mischief."[36] John Bernard talked with Washington about slavery in the summer of 1798 and quoted Washington as saying that the end of slavery was:

> an event, sir, which, you may believe me, no man desires more heartily than I do. Not only do I pray for it, on the score of human dignity, but I can clearly foresee that nothing but the rooting out of slavery can perpetuate the existence of our union, by consolidating it in a common bond of principle.[37]

Finally, at the end of his life, Washington fully faced the implications of his changed attitude toward slavery. When he was drawing up his will in the summer of 1799, he made "the first and only tangible commitment... to the emancipation of the slaves."[38] Washington decided to free those slaves belonging completely to him at the death of his wife, Martha. The dower slaves that she had brought to the marriage would remain in her estate. His will provided:

> Item Upon the decease of my wife, it is my Will & desire that all the Slaves which I hold in my own right, shall receive their freedom... it not being in my power, under the tenure by which the Dower Negroes are held, to manumit them... they... shall be comfortably cloathed & fed by my heirs while they live... taught to read & write; and to be brought up to some useful occupation... And I do hereby expressly forbid the Sale, or transportation out of the said Commonwealth, of any Slave I may die possessed of... [39]

Washington set up a fund for their support as long as they lived. Martha Custis Washington, however, decided to free his slaves after a year, rather than waiting until her death, fearing that there might be too much motive on the part of some to speed their own freedom by quickening her demise. But Martha still possessed about 150 dower slaves in her own right that she left, along with Mount Vernon, to her own heirs.[40]

How then should we evaluate Washington's character with respect to slavery? His motives for freeing his slaves at the end of his life probably ranged from guilt to a recognition that abolition was inevitable if the United States was to survive, to an act of personal generosity toward those who had served him during his life.[41] But the deeper reality was that Washington benefitted from his slaves all of his life. It was slavery that made his great wealth possible, and he was unwilling to make the serious economic sacrifice of freeing his slaves as long as he depended on their work for his own income.

His public silence on the issue, along with his own slave holdings, given his reputation, must have had an important effect on the willingness of others to go along and not question the status quo. Washington's reputation was so great that even a small public gesture or statement might have made a large difference. Joseph Ellis argues that regarding slavery, Washington, "perhaps alone, possessed the stature to have altered the political context if he had chose to do so." Observing that Washington had what Adams called "the gift of silence," Ellis concludes, "... this was one occasion when one could only have wished that the gift had failed him."[42] Thus, Washington's vice, as well as his virtues, had important public effects.

The most persuasive argument that Washington's lack of public opposition to slavery was based on admirable motives might be the argument that any sudden move to abolish slavery would have alienated the southern states so much that the union would have been in peril. At the time of the Constitutional Convention, any public move by Washington in the direction of emancipation might have jeopardized the willingness of the southern states to join the union and ratify the Constitution. His silence as President, particularly in his Farewell Address in which he spoke out against sectionalism generally, might be attributed to a prudential judgment that a public statement hostile to slavery might have inflamed sectionalism enough to put the union in jeopardy.[43]

But this explanation for his failure to speak out is more persuasive when applied to the time Washington was in public office than it is about the time after he retired from the presidency, when he refused to favor publicly even a gradual phasing out of slavery. The argument in this article is that Washington's character was flawed in that he failed to speak out publicly against slavery after leaving the presidency at the end of his life. His private statements clearly demonstrate that he knew slavery was wrong, yet he was unwilling to associate his personal prestige to public criticisms of slavery. The argument that Washington had a character defect with respect to slavery does not vitiate all of the other admirable aspects of Washington's character. Despite his public attitude toward slavery, Washington was still a great president and a great man. We must admit, however, that Washington's greatness existed along side his buying and selling of human beings.

Historian, Pulitzer Prize winner, and civil rights activist, Roger Wilkins, argues that Washington's ownership of slaves was understandable, because it was only the work of the slaves that enabled Washington to have the time to become a statesman and to lead the United States in its founding period.[44] "Washington became the indispensable man" necessary to the survival of the early Republic, and the success of the new Republic played an important role in the expansion of human freedom over the past two centuries. Wilkins continues, "Isn't it a wonderful coincidence that he was present and out front each step of the way." Wilkins concludes, "The founding slave owners were more than good men; they were great men. But... myth presents them as secular saints, and ... whitewash[es] their ownership of slaves and the deep legacy of racism that they helped to institutionalize..."[45]

In an article in *The New York Times* in 1998, historian Robert F. Dalzell, Jr. implicitly contrasted Washington with more recent presidents.[46] The question being publicly discussed was how could President Bill Clinton act effectively as president at the same time that he was engaging in unbecoming conduct with Monica Lewinsky. The explanation of being able to do these seemingly incompatible things at the same time (sometimes simultaneously) was that Clinton could "compartmentalize" in his mind the contrasting aspects of his personality and thus be capable of contradictory behavior.

Dalzell argued that, in deciding to free his slaves in his will, Washington was giving up a lot. "Washington had no talent for compartmentalizing the separate parts of his life. Nor did he wish to."[47] This is an argument that Washington's character was seamless, with no disjuncture between his private and public life. But the fact that Washington's slaves would not be freed until after he was dead proves just the opposite point from Dalzell's claim. Washington had to be capable of extreme compartmentalization in order to continue owning slaves at the same time as fighting for the ideals expressed in the Declaration of Independence and presiding over the newly created Republic. Especially toward the end of his life when he began to reflect more seriously about the implications of slavery and privately express his distaste for it, his source of economic support must have weighed heavily on his mind.

Dalzell also makes the point that, in freeing his slaves, Washington was giving up a lot, since it necessarily implied the break up of his beloved Mount Vernon. But the fact that Washington had no children of his own may have played a role in his final decision. If he had biological heirs, would he have dissipated their patrimony on the principle of the injustice of slavery? Neither Thomas Jefferson nor George Mason, both of whom spoke out publicly against slavery, freed their slaves when they died.

CONCLUSION

George Washington was born into a slave holding family and accepted slavery without question. As he grew to maturity, he had too much at stake to risk his economic well being and reject slavery. At some point, probably during the Revolutionary War, Washington came to realize that slavery was inconsistent with the ideals of the emerging Republic. Yet, he refused to speak out openly against slavery. Acceptance of slavery was not universal in the new Republic or even in its southern states. Washington may have refused to speak out on the slavery issue while he was president because he feared that the union would be torn apart, although he did not articulate this reasoning into his writings.

It can thus reasonably be concluded that Washington's failure to speak out publicly against slavery late in his life was a character flaw. But he must be given some credit for freeing his slaves and providing for them after his death, an action that some other, more outspoken founders, failed to take. But, if we are to be honest with ourselves, we must accept the negative dimensions of Washington's decision to embrace slavery (until after his death) along with his many accomplishments that were essential to the founding and establishment of the United States. The point here is not that Washington was a bad person or president, merely that his character was complex and not seamless.

ACKNOWLEDGMENTS

For comments and counsel on this article, the author would like to thank the following friends and colleagues: Al Felzenberg, Booth Fowler, Michael Genovese, Hugh Helco, Matthew Holden, Lois Horton, Peter Henriques, Mark Kann, Robert Pool, Matthew Spalding, Fred Timm, Toni Travis, and Roger Wilkins. It must be noted that the author rejected some of the advice of these valued colleagues and that it should not be assumed that they agree with the author's conclusions in this article.

NOTES

[1] Quoted by Marcus Cunliffe, *George Washington: Man and Monument* (New York: New American Library, 1982), p.1.

[2] Seymour Martin Lipset, "The Conditions for Democracy in the United States and the Greatness of George Washington," typescript draft, second from the last page in manuscript. For an argument that Washington was more honored in his own time than recently, see Colleen J. Shogan, "George Washington: Can Aristotle Recapture What His Countrymen have Forgotten?" in Mark Rozell and William Pederson (New York: Praeger Press, 2000).

[3] David Abshire, "The Character of George Washington and the Challenges of the Modern Presidency," pamphlet (Washington: Center for the Study of the Presidency, 1998).

[4] Joseph Epstein, "George Washington, An Amateur's View," *The Hudson Review* LI (Spring 1998), p. 39.

[5] Fritz Herschfeld, *George Washington and Slavery: A Documentary Portrayal* (Columbia: University of Missouri Press, 1997), pp. 11-12, 20, 212, 220. Hirschfeld's book is an impressive collection of documents and analysis. Much of the analysis in this section is based on the book. For a similar account of Washington's slave holdings, see James Thomas Flexner, *George Washington: Anguish and Farewell, 1793-1799*, (Boston: Little Brown, 1969, 1972), p. 113.

[6] Washington was a "kind master," as slave owners went. But, as Roger Wilkins points out: "There were kind masters, though kindness in the context of such a heinous criminal enterprise as American slavery must necessarily have a rather shallow meaning." *Jefferson's Pillow* (Boston: Beacon Press, 2001).

[7] Hirschfeld, p. 37.

[8] Letter from Washington to Captain Joseph Thompson of the schooner, Swift, dated July 2d, 1766. Reproduced in Hirschfeld, pp. 67-68. The letter is also printed in part in Flexner, pp. 113-114.

[9] However, as early as 1774 Washington wrote that if the Americans submitted to British domination, then "custom and use shall make us tame and abject slaves, as the blacks we rule over in such an arbitrary way." Quoted in Flexner, p. 114. Note that the words "custom and use" imply that blacks are not inherently inferior to whites, but that any perceived inferiority came from "custom and use" rather than race.

[10] Flexner, p. 115.

[11] Hirschfeld, pp. 21-29.

[12] Roger Wilkins, pp. 44-45.

[13] Flexner, p. 118.

[14] Flexner, p. 118.

[15] Flexner, p. 121.

[16] Flexner, p. 121.

[17] Hirschfeld, pp. 172-178.

[18] Quoted in Flexner, p. 122 (italics in original).

[19] Quoted in Flexner, p. 113.

[20] Letter from Washington to Oliver Wolcott, Jr., dated September 1, [1796]. Reproduced in Hirschfeld, p. 113. See also, Wilkins, pp. 82-83.

[21] Letter from Washington to Major George Lewis, dated November 13, 1797. Quoted in Hirschfeld, p. 70.

[22] See Flexner, p. 115.

[23] Hirschfeld, p. 200.

[24] Letter from Robert Pleasants to George Washington, dated "Curles 12mo. [Dec.] 11th 1785," reprinted in Hirschfeld, pp. 193-195.

[25] See David McCullough, *John Adams* (New York: Simon and Schuster, 2001), pp. 132-134, 330-331, and passim.

[26] Max Farrand, ed. *The Records of the Federal Convention of 1787*, 2:364, 369, 370. Quoted in Hirschfeld, p. 174.

[27] See Flexner, p. 115; see also Joseph J. Ellis, *Founding Brothers: The Revolutionary Generation* (New York: Alfred A. Knopf, 2000), p. 96. Ellis argues that Madison, like Jefferson and others of the Virginia dynasty "regarded any explicit defense of slavery in the mode of South Carolina and Georgia as a moral embarrassment. On the other hand, he regarded any effort to end slavery as premature, politically impractical, and counterproductive." Ellis refers to this position as the "Virginia straddle." See Ellis, pp. 113-114.

[28] Ellis, p. 90; Andrew Levy, "The Anti-Jefferson," *The American Scholar* 70 (Spring 2001), p. 19.

[29] Ellis, pp. 89-90; see also Gordon S. Wood, "The Greatest Generation," *The New York Review of Books* (29 March 2001), pp. 17-22. Wood states: "Not only were there more anti-slave societies created in the South than in the North, but manumissions in the upper South grew rapidly in the years immediately following the end of the War for Independence."(p. 21)

[30] Hirschfeld, p. 182.

[31] On Benjamin Franklin and slavery, see Carl Van Foren, *Benjamin Franklin* (New York: Garden City Publishing, 1941), pp. 128-129, 774-775; John C. Van Horne, "Collective Benevolence and the Common Good in Franklin's Philanthropy," in J. A. Leo Lemay, *Reappraising Benjamin Franklin* (Newark: University of Delaware Press, 1993), pp. 431-439; Claude-Anne Lopez, *My Life with Benjamin Franklin* (New Haven, CT: Yale University Press, 2000), pp. 205-211.

[32] Wilkins, pp. 90-91.

[33] Levy, p. 16.

[34] Levy, p. 24.
[35] Levy, p. 25; See also "The Deed of Gift," Letter from the editor of *The American Scholar*, p. 2.
[36] Hirschfeld, p. 79.
[37] John Bernard's memoirs, Retrospections of America, 1797-1811, quoted in Hirschfeld, p. 73.
[38] Hirschfeld, p. 209.
[39] Hirschfeld, pp. 209-211.
[40] Hirschfeld, pp. 213-222. John Adams' wife, Abigail, wrote to her sister Mary on December 21, 1800: "... she [Martha Washington] did not feel as tho (sic) her life was safe in their Hands, many of whom would be told that it was [in] their (sic) interest to get rid of her – She therefore was advised to set them all free at the close of the year." Quoted in Hirschfeld, p. 214.
[41] Hirschfeld, p. 6.
[42] Ellis, p. 263.
[43] See Matthew Spalding and Patrick J. Garrity, *A Sacred Union of Citizens: George Washington's Farewell Address and the American Character* (Lanham, MD: Rowman & Littlefield, 1996), p. 71.
[44] See Wilkins.
[45] See Wilkins, pp. 128, 138-139.
[46] Robert F. Dalzell, Jr., "George Washington, Slaveholder," *The New York Times* (20 February 2000), p. A27.
[47] Ibid.

Chapter 2

GOVERNING THE DEVIL IN HELL: "BLEEDING KANSAS" AND THE DESTRUCTION OF THE FRANKLIN PIERCE PRESIDENCY (1854-1856)

Michael J. C. Taylor

BACKGROUND

On 2 November 1852 Democrat Franklin Pierce was elected the fourteenth president of the United States. His slogan had been a powerful one: "In Union is strength–the Union now and forever." But there was more to Pierce's victory than mere political tactics and strategy. By this time the nation had sectionally divided against itself and seemed prepared to cut asunder the political, social, economic, theological, and philosophical ties that had bound regions together during the War for American Independence. Debates over the 1850 compromise exhibited the potent divisions that emerged during this period; thus, the nation had placed its hopes for a cessation of these hostilities in the candidate who embodied Union first and foremost. The question that lay before Pierce was whether his formidable talents as a politician could bridge the great sectional crevasse in American political culture and avoid a seemingly inevitable civil war.

Few men have been as uniquely qualified to be president of the United States as Franklin Pierce in 1853. Pierce's father Benjamin was a veteran of the American Revolution whose political career had culminated with his twice being elected Governor of New Hampshire.[1] Following study at Bowdoin College young Franklin served his legal apprenticeship under the tutelage of future Supreme Court justice Levi Woodbury. Pierce was admitted to the bar in 1827 at age 22. Thereafter, his ascent in politics was meteoritic: elected to the House of Representatives at 27 and selected as a Senator at 32–the youngest man in the body at the time. After the Whig takeover of Congress in 1840–and jaded by his diluted role and aspiring to earn more money–Pierce resigned his seat and engaged in a lucrative private law practice.[2]

Pierce remained a popular political figure–twice offered the nomination for governor; elected to a further Senate term; and, extended the position of Attorney General by President

James Polk–all of which he refused. When war with Mexico was declared in 1846, Pierce enlisted as a private, but was soon promoted to brigadier general by President Polk and was injured at the battles of Contreras and Churubusco. Upon his return home the general received a hero's welcome and his popularity rose steadily throughout New England. Upon the death of Justice Woodbury in 1851, Pierce became New Hampshire's favorite son presidential candidate. Though he was chosen as the compromise nominee of a deadlocked convention, Pierce won both a popular and electoral landslide against Whig candidate Winfield Scott.

In his inaugural address, Pierce did not allude to a grand vision. Instead, the President presented a specific set of practical goals: Further expansion of American territory, increasing free trade, restructuring the armed forces, and civil service reform. In its initial 14 months, the Pierce administration negotiated the nation's first free trade agreements and completed the continental borders of the United States. Pierce instituted civil service initiatives and made full enforcement a precondition for appointment to a cabinet post. His fiscal management provided the only period in which deficit reduction occurred in consecutive years of a presidential term prior to the Truman administration. Newspaper columnist Benjamin Perely Poore remarked that Pierce was "the man of the time, his cabinet–an aggregation of the wisdom of the country, his policy the very perfection of statesmanship."[3]

Franklin Pierce held the belief that the Constitution was "sacred in the eye of honor and indispensable for the great experiment of civil liberty."[4] Though the President did not condone slavery, he conceded that the Constitution protected the practice, as evidenced by Article IV section 2. Pierce was a strict constructionist who supported the proposition that those states, which recognized slavery as legitimate, were subject to the protections of the Full Faith clause. Thus, the fourteenth president placed the law above his private opinions, much to the chagrin of the leaders of both political parties. For reasons that Pierce's personal origins were in a northern state that held strong abolitionist convictions it was assumed by southerners that the President's views were compatible with his constituency, though many in the North viewed him as being beholden to the pro-slavery faction. On the other hand, the Southern congressional delegation were in agreement that when push came to shove the free-soil factions of his home state would have more influence than any personal convictions.[5]

THE KANSAS-NEBRASKA ACT

With the introduction of the Kansas-Nebraska Act the President faced a complex political dilemma: To embrace one side of the "popular sovereignty" question was the equivalent of disavowing the other and either choice carried with it dire political consequences. Illinois Senator Stephen Douglas, the powerful chairman of the territorial committee, was aware that the only was to preserve party unity was to force the President's endorsement and then bring it to the floor as an administration proposal. To secure Pierce's sanction, however, the senator acceded to the President's demand to compose the language of the clause that repealed the long-standing boundaries between slave and free states. The Missouri Compromise was in effect "inoperative and void," but all questions of legality were the unchallenged domain of the Supreme Court. Though all Democrats were not elated with the arrangement, they ultimately agreed to the compromise.

When the Nebraska bill came up for reconsideration, Kentucky's Senator Archibald Dixon introduced the amendment written by the President. To avoid further divisiveness,

Senator Douglas negotiated an agreement that divided Nebraska into two territories and which left the popular sovereignty clauses intact. When the bill was passed in both houses of congress, Pierce found himself in a political corner: to sign the bill meant estrangement from the North, while a veto meant the possible secession of the South. The quandary left to the President was to side with the faction that could do him the most political damage. Pierce signed the Kansas-Nebraska Act into law at his desk in the Executive Office on 30 may 1854.

The debates over the Kansas-Nebraska Act churned with vitriol over the extension of slavery into territories, which the 1820 Missouri Compromise had previously prohibited. New York Senator William Seward chided his Southern colleagues during one such debate that "We will engage in competition for the virgin soil of Kansas, and God give the victory petition to the side which is stronger in numbers." With the passing of the legislation, activists such as Henry Ward Beecher, Amos Lawrence, Eli Thayer, and Gerrit Smith established the New England Emigrant Aid Society to bring together abolitionists willing to settle in Kansas. Their goal was to place 20,000 abolitionist settlers in the new territory and by sheer numbers claim it as a free state.[6]

Once the news was published of the Emigrant Aid Society's existence, Senator David Rice Atchison published a series of newspaper articles throughout the South and the Midwest calling for Southerners to drive the abolitionists out of Kansas. Southern political leaders criticized northern emigration efforts as having "scraped the very off-scourings of their cities and sent them to this Territory."[7] In response, the pro-slavery opposition created cabals such as the "Society of Missourians for Mutual Protection" based in the Missouri border town of Westport. At a speech in Weston in 1854, Atchison voiced the rallying cry that he "would sooner see the whole of Nebraska in the bottom of hell than see it a Free State."[8]

President Franklin Pierce appointed Andrew Reeder, a popular sovereignty Democrat from Pennsylvania, as the first governor of the Kansas Territory.[9] Reeder's primary function, according to the President's handwritten guidelines, was to establish a "just administration of the organic law;" to avert the "interposition of [the] immigrant aid society to force a solution on one side," as well as the "reactionary interpretation of citizens of Missouri to force a solution on the other side."[10] The governor divided the territory into 17 electoral districts and called elections for a legislature and a representative to the national congress. "The election was bound to be irregular in any case, for the loosely phrased law permitted any resident to vote, however recently he had arrived." According to historian David M. Potter, writing of the March 1855 canvas, "[t]his encouraged both sides to deploy all the last-minute residents they could muster."[11] The 1855 Territory of Kansas Census demonstrated that many settlers were counted twice simply because their lands straddled district voting lines and there was no procedures in place to guard against it.

According to Kansas State historian William Zornow, form his 1957 book Kansas: A History of the Jayhawk State, there "were enough bona fide pro-slavery residents in Kansas at this time that such intervention would not have been necessary."[12] Within the entire territory, only 34 percent of the population came from "free" states from Maine to Iowa. Outside of the concentration of immigrants within the twenty-mile radius of Lawrence–which represented 65 percent of all of the total Free-Soil population–the bulk of Kansas residents came from Missouri, Arkansas, and Virginia. But this did not stop Missouri pro-slavery proponents led by Senator Atchison, Samuel Young, and Claiborne Jackson from instigating an invasion from Westport and Platte City.[13] The result was that 6,307 cast ballots in the elections where only 2,905 were qualified to do so.[14] When the election frauds were brought to his attention

Reeder refused to certify pro-slavery members and called for new caucuses in those districts. By December 1854 Senator Atchison began lobbying the President for Reeder's removal, citing his inability to bring stable government to the territory.

The Kansas territorial legislature enacted statutes calling for severe penalties for anti-slavery agitation and a test oath for office holding. Reeder vetoed every bill. The legislature responded by passing every bill over the governor's objections. Within a few weeks the legislature also petitioned the President to remove Reeder. Convinced this mutual animosity could not promote his aims in the territory, Pierce sought to alleviate the problem by offering Reeder a federal position, which he refused. After the President fired him, Reeder made overtures to free-soil factions in Lawrence. Pierce then appointed Ohio congressman Wilson Shannon to the governor's post–a man noted in political circles as "genial, compassionate, [whose] sympathies naturally gravitating towards whatever is just and honorable."[15]

Supreme Court Justice Samuel Chase wrote that once that rule of law was subverted, "there must soon be an end to all government in this country."[16] According to Justice Chase, when a citizen recants his allegiance to the political authority of his society he has committed treason against his sovereign state. As Governor Shannon arrived at his post in September 1855, 100 anti-slavery settlers had gathered at a four-cabin trading post named Big Springs to launch a government that would culminate in the territory being admitted to the union as a free state. The resulting resolutions repudiated all allegiance to the Kansas territorial government, an entity established, empowered, and recognized by the Federal government in the same manner South Carolina had during the Nullification Crisis. At that time, President Andrew Jackson had stated that "[t]reason is an offense against sovereignty, and sovereignty must reside with the power to punish it."[17] Reeder made this point succinctly at the Big Springs meeting when he said: "We owe no allegiance or obedience to the tyrannical enactments of this spurious legislature."[18] Though the abolitionists acted upon what they viewed as a higher law, their conduct was nonetheless in opposition to the jurisdiction of the United States government. Therefore, President Pierce was correct when he stated in a special message to Congress on 24 January 1856 that the free-soilers–by extolling the Big Springs Resolutions–had involved themselves in acts of "organized resistance by force to the fundamental or any other Federal law and to the authority of the General Government."[19]

Between 23 October and 2 November 1855, free-soil delegates met at Topeka to draft a constitution based on the Big Springs resolutions. During the previous summer, due to the ongoing threat of violence at the hands of Missouri border ruffians, the conventioneers had appealed to the federal government to protect them–a plea Pierce ignored. In the President's opinion their positions were illegal and he vowed not to reward their efforts with any action that could be interpreted as a sanction:

> [I]f the obstruction be to the laws of the Territory, and it be duly presented to him as a case of insurrection, he may employ for its suppression the same object the militia of any State or the land or naval force of the United States.[20]

BLEEDING KANSAS

The initial confrontation in what became known as "Bleeding Kansas" occurred ten miles south of Lawrence in a grove of hardwood known as Hickory Point on 21 November 1855. It had nothing whatsoever to do with slavery: it was a squatter's dispute between pro-slaver Franklin Coleman and abolitionist Charles Dow. During an argument over which settler had the right to jump the land claim of an Indiana lumber company, Coleman shot Dow in the back. Though such squatter disputes were common, the tumultuous state of the territorial government allowed circumstances to escalate to the brink of war. Coleman was granted protective custody by the governor. Dow's cabin-mate, Jacob Branson, a 40-year-old Iowa farmer, organized a militia and destroyed the homes of pro-slavery settlers along the eastern Kansas countryside. Within a few short hours all public order in Kansas degenerated.

Shannon wired the President from Kansas City and requested command of the federal troops at Fort Leavenworth in order preserve order. Upon receiving the governor's telegram Pierce granted Shannon's request. Though Pierce's orders were sent to the War Department they were never received by either the governor or Colonel Edwin Sumner, the commander of Fort Leavenworth. Shannon traveled to the militia camp on the Wakarusa River only to learn that the Federal troops had not been dispatched, and that Colonel Sumner had refused to order his men into a potentially bloody fracas. Forced to negotiate, the governor gained a settlement that guaranteed the release of all free-soil prisoners and fair trials before a Federal Court. Despite the bitter cold of a prairie winter, free-soil delegates made their way to Topeka to approve their constitution and elect an extra-legal legislature and a territorial governor, the local chief of the Emigrant Aid Society, Charles Robinson.

In his third State of the Union Message, President Pierce warned both sides to either cease their discord or the result would be civil war. He reaffirmed his support of the territorial government and denounced the Emigrant Aid Society as venturing "in offensive and hopeless undertakings of reforming domestic institutions of other states, wholly beyond their control and authority."[21] Within the text of this message, he gave his position as such:

> If one state ceases to respect the rights of another and obtrusively intermeddles with its local interests; if a portion of the states assume to impose their institutions on the others or refuse to fulfill their obligations for them, we are no longer united, friendly states, but distracted, hostile ones, with little capacity left of common advantage, but abundant means of reciprocal injury and mischief.[22]

Most importantly, the President reassured southern leaders–who held most of the committee chairmanships thwarting his reform legislation–that a firm hand would resolve the crisis: "The storm of frenzy and fraction must inevitably dash itself in vain against the unshaken rack of the Constitution."[23] Pierce's third State of the Union message bolstered his support among the southern delegation. The President had taken a definitive stand and in the opinion of Southern legislators such as Clement Clay, he had dealt a firm blow "to the sectionalists and fanatics."[24]

As the violence escalated in Kansas, Pierce issued a proclamation on 24 January 1856 that became the defining moment of his presidency. Prepared as a concise legal brief, Pierce defended the Kansas-Nebraska law and carefully explained how its good intentions had been circumvented by "local maladministration and the unjustifiable interference of the inhabitants of some of the states, foreign by residence, interests, and rights to the Territory."[25] He reasoned that the election of both the territorial legislature and the congressional representative had not been "determined before conflicting passions had become inflamed by time, and before an opportunity could have been afforded for the systematic interference of the people of individual states."[26] Pierce was inflamed by citizens who "toil[ed] with misdirected zeal in the attempt to propagate their social theories by the perversion and abuse of the powers of Congress."[27]

The Emigrant Aid Society settlers were, in Pierce's opinion, guilty of treason and he announced to the nation that he was no longer tolerant of their interference in the legitimate affairs of State: No principle of public law, no practice or precedent under the Constitution of the United States, no rule of reason, right, or common sense, confers any such power as that now claimed by a mere party in the Territory. In fact what has been done is of a revolutionary character. It is avowedly so in motive and in aim as respects the local law of the Territory. It will become treasonable insurrection if it reaches the length or organized resistance by force to the fundamental or any other Federal law and to the authority of the General Government.[28]

It was the most forceful statement made by President Pierce on the violence in Kansas. However, the President issued a further proclamation on 11 February in which he pledged to, if necessary, intervene with "the whole power of the General Government."[29] President Pierce had publicly assured Governor Shannon that he had incontrovertible control of the troops at Fort Leavenworth. Abolitionist William Lloyd Garrison commented that Pierce was "ready to do all that the Slave Power demands at his hands."[30] The following month, Senator Douglas' territorial committee denounced the Topeka legislature as illegal and recognized the territorial government at Lecompton as the seat of legal authority in Kansas, thus reinforcing the President's position. Afterwards, abolitionist Senator William Seward offered a bill that provided for the immediate admission of Kansas under the Topeka constitution that passed handily in the House, but was effectively killed by Southerners in the Senate.

The Emigrant Aid Society had utilized much of its resources to establish Lawrence as an abolitionist stronghold in Kansas. Thus, it was an obvious target for pro-slavery forces and of concern to the government in Lecompton who were, according to free-soil settler Richard Cordley, "watching for an opportunity to bring on a collision which would compel the citizens either to recognize or resist the laws of the bogus legislature."[31] Many pro-slavery activists from Missouri had claimed much of the land by preemption adjacent to the town. Pro-slavery forces mobilized in spring 1856 and arrested free-soil leaders, sacked abolitionist farms, and then descended upon Lawrence and set the town ablaze. Northern newspapers claimed, "Shannon has not scrupled to take such steps as have given these pro-slavery fighting rowdies and Missourians possession of public arm belonging to Kansas."[32]

The free-soilers regrouped in Topeka and vowed to retaliate. The governor reacted by transferring Federal troops from Fort Leavenworth to protect Lawrence "with as little delay as possible."[33] But Marshall Israel Donelson replied to the governor that he could not protect the town unless all arms were surrendered and the residents "pledge themselves to obey the present enactments of Kansas."[34] A hundred free-soil troops were dispatched from Manhattan and Van Bonsa to reinforce Topeka and defend Lawrence. "Civil War is upon us," wrote the editor of the *New York Daily Times*, "we pray the Almighty God avert these dreadful evils."[35]

The worst of the retaliatory actions by free-soilers occurred during the twilight hours of 24-25 May 1856. Anti-slavery activist John Brown led an armed party from Osawatomie into the pro-slavery community of Dutch Henry's Crossing at Pottawatomie Creek. Though the settlement was inhabited by Southern emigrants none of the citizens owned slaves. This fact, however, did not deer Brown. He ordered five male citizens be taken from their homes to the banks of the creek and hacked to death with sabers. Shannon denounced the massacre as but the "regular system which the Free-state party had adopted toward their opponents."[36] Two days later, the governor ordered the forces that had secured Lawrence to move to Franklin, which left the former defenseless.

RENOMINATION

Prior to the sacking of Lawrence, the President's chances for renomination were realizable. Throughout the past six months, Pierce had gained political ground with the Southern leaders of his party. Though he had estranged many Northerners, several delegates to the Cincinnati convention harbored strong support for the President. Supporters of Buchanan and Douglas sought to take political advantage of the Kansas tragedy; but at the convention Pierce delegates effectively swayed their counterparts when they pointed out that the President's renomination meant continuity and a "reendorsement by the party of its declared principles and authentic history."[37] As the floor votes began, Douglas delegates withheld their support in favor of Pierce.

The results of the first ballot were unanticipated. Expected to capture the nomination on the initial roll call, Buchanan received a bare numerical majority of twelve-and-one-half votes over Pierce. The south held firm for Pierce, along with the northern states of Vermont, Rhode Island, and New Hampshire. Despite the fact the New York delegation–led by Secretary of State William Marcy–had refused to support Pierce because he had removed a Tammany Hall appointee from his post as Collector of the Port of New York, the President carried a large majority of the New York delegates. Though the initial balloting was no knockout punch to Buchanan, it was a devastating defeat for Pierce. By the fifteenth ballot Pierce's delegates had switched their support to Senator Douglas. Two ballots later, Buchanan was nominated by acclamation. Many delegates left the convention in disgust, including David Rice Atchison who remarked to the press: "The nomination is not exactly what I had desired. I should have preferred either Pierce or Douglas, because he and Douglas both so thoroughly identified with our cause."[38]

In a speech before 5,000 supporters gathered at the Executive Mansion, the President voiced his support for Buchanan: "Men become insignificant, except as instruments, when great principles and the vast interests of a country like ours are involved."[39] In his acceptance letter, Buchanan upheld Pierce's position on Kansas: "Not to legislate slavery into any territory or state, nor to exclude if therefrom, but to leave the people thereof perfectly free to form and regulate their domestic institutions in their own way."[40] But afterwards, at his desk in the Executive Mansion, Pierce capitulated on his resolve to refrain from drinking. The President slumped cheerlessly into the leather-clad chair facing his desk. "There's nothing left to do," he said to his aide Sidney Webster, "but to get drunk." As the painful reality of his nomination defeat confronted him, Franklin Pierce sought his solace in a bottle of Jamaican rum.[41]

Conclusion

Until 1854, federal government had relied upon a body of legal precedent to determine the ideological design of a territorial government in every instance from the Northwest Ordinance of 1787 onwards. Under the provisions of popular sovereignty this authority was forfeited in favor of an edict from a volatile numerical majority. This created an environment in which rancorous partisanship made constructing a political order, according to Governor Wilson Shannon, the equivalent of "govern[ing] the devil in Hell."[42] When all local leverage was exhausted, federal authority was hopeless in its charge to restore order–in much the same manner as the confederation government during Shays' Rebellion in 1786.

Thus, the turmoil of Pierce's presidency had less to do with his actions than the simple fact that no one leader could have bound the nation together at this juncture in its history, for the political atmosphere was too partisan. In his initial State of the Union address, president Jackson proclaimed a new political era of popular democracy in which "the majority is to govern."[43] With the advent of Jacksonianism a more democratic model of politics was established, in which violent confrontations between political parties with opposing ideologies was not only accepted, but also actively encouraged. At the onset of the Second Great Awakening, religious conviction became inextricably interwoven into political issues and invigorated a strictly secular motif with the fervor of a moral crusade. As suffrage expanded, contentious issues proliferated at an alarming rate without the benefit of a compromised solution. As the political parties sectionalized into representatives of either northern communitarian industrialists or southern individualistic agrarians, the slavery issue was absorbed into the political ideology of each major party.

Franklin Pierce personified many of these ideological inconsistencies and was, in turn, the conduit for the turmoil ahead caused by them. Yet, in his oath of office, Pierce affirmed an his charge to "preserve, protect, and defend the Constitution." As the chief executive of the country, he was required to administer the law regardless of his own personal preferences until such time as the people either amended or changed it. The Kansas-Nebraska Act did not conflict with either of those tenets–had they done so, Pierce would have vetoed it. This was evidence in March 1854 by his veto of a land grant bill that he personally favored, but could not find a legal justification for within the text of the constitution–as evidenced by nine page explanation that accompanied his veto. The President supported the repeal of the Missouri Compromise because it authorized an extra constitutional power that limited a constitutionally protected practice. Such actions are demonstrative of a man who sought to place the law at the center of his decision-making process through careful, deliberate reflection.

Rather than supporting the rule of law, as Pierce had envisioned, the Kansas-Nebraska Act unleashed all of the sectional animosity that were simmering since the territorial disputes of the 1780's, and chaos ensued. The sovereignty of the federal government was shoved aside and the people were allowed to decide the slavery question for themselves, albeit with disastrous results. When it became clear to President Pierce that local authority had completely broken down, and federal intervention was necessary, he issued a proclamation that placed federal troops at the immediate disposal of the governor. Later, when Governor Shannon resigned, Pierce appointed John White Geary to the Post–the highly respected law enforcement officer who had brought order to San Francisco during the height of the California Gold Rush.

The Civil War was the historical moment when the failure of politics led to military force, and the culmination of political dysfunction. It began not with the first roar of cannons at Fort Sumter in April 1861, but in June 1856 with the destruction of the potentially productive Pierce presidency. Though the fourteenth president admirably sought to rectify the problem without overstepping constitutional authority, he has endured the brunt of violence and bloodshed born in the name of democracy and, as a result, suffered the affront of historical indifference.

NOTES

[1] According to New Hampshire State historian Everett Stackpole, Benjamin Pierce was "one of the most popular chief magistrates the State ever had." Everett Stackpole, *A History of New Hampshire* (New York: The American Historical Society, 1901), 4:86. His mother Anna Kendrick Pierce's background was as rich as her husbands, one of her ancestors being John Rogers, the first protestant martyr of Queen Mary. Roy Franklin Nichols, *Franklin Pierce: Young Hickory of the Granite Hills* (Philadelphia: University of Pennsylvania, 1931), 10.

[2] Pierce, Letter to James Knox Polk, 18 Sep. 1846, in The Franklin Pierce Papers, Manuscript Division, Library of Congress, Washington, D. C.

[3] Poore, quoted in William Seale, *The President's House: A History* (Washington, D. C.: White House Historical Society, 1986), 322.

[4] *A Compilation of the Messages and Papers of the Presidents*, ed. James D. Richardson (Washington, D. C.: Bureau of National Literature and Art, 1907), 5:222.

[5] These men misjudged the President's resolve. While serving in the Senate, Pierce received word that his elder brother, State Legislator Benjamin Kendrick Pierce, intended to vote for an anti-slavery initiative. Franklin promptly traveled by train from the Capitol to Concord to warn his brother that should he carry through his plans, "you are no brother of mine, I will never speak to you again." Paul F. Boller, Jr. *Presidential Anecdotes* (New York: Penguin Books, 1982), 115. Yet, it is also clearly stated in his inaugural address that he believed slavery, though protected by the Constitution, should be contained to where "it exists in the different states of this confederacy." *The Inaugural Addresses of the Presidents*, ed. John Gabriel Hunt (New York: Grammercy Books, 1995), 171.

[6] Richard Cordley, *A History of Lawrence, Kansas From the First Settlement to the Close of the Rebellion* (Bowie, MD: Heritage Books, Inc., 1991), 2.

[7] Roy D. Bird and Douglas W. Wallace, *Witness of the Times: A History of Shawnee County* (Topeka, KS: H. M. Ives and Sons, 1976), 9.

[8] Atchison, quoted in William E. Connelly, *A History of Kansas: State and People* (New York: American Historical Society, Inc., 1928), 306. He claimed "American citizens should be privileged to go where they pleased and carry their property with them, whether that property was furniture, mules, or niggers." Ibid. This was the same line of reasoning Chief Justice Roger Brooke Taney would use in his 1857 majority decision in Dred Scott v. Sandford.

[9] Reeder was "doughface–a northerner who held an affinity toward positions that were pro-southern–who had campaigned for Pierce during the 1852 campaign and was recommended for an appointment by former Pennsylvania congressman Ely Moore. In his 1990 book Kansas Governors, Historian Homer E. Socolofsky claims that Pennsylvania Democrats Asa Packer and John Forney recommended Reeder to Pierce. Socolofsky, 33.

[10] Franklin Pierce, Letter to Andrew H. Reeder, June 1854; in Pierce Papers.

[11] David M. Potter, *The Impending Crisis 1848-1861* (New York: Harper & Row Publishers, 1976), 201.

[12] William F. Zornow, *Kansas: A History of the Jayhawk State* (Norman: University of Oklahoma Press, 1957), 70.
[13] *The Census of the Territory of Kansas, 1855* (Overland Park: Kansas Statistical Publications Co., 1985), 57; 69.
[14] Zornow, 70.
[15] Alice Nichols, *Bleeding Kansas* (New York: Oxford University Press, 1954), 48.
[16] Chase, quoted in Kermit L. Hall, *The Magic Mirror: Law in American History* (New York: Oxford University Press, 1989), 77.
[17] Andrew Jackson, Proclamation, 10 December 1832, in Richardson, 650.
[18] Bleeding Kansas, 44.
[19] Franklin Pierce, Message to Congress on Kansas, 24 January 1856; Pierce Papers.
[20] Ibid.
[21] Richardson, 5:908.
[22] Ibid., 911.
[23] Ibid., 917.
[24] Clement Claiborne Clay, Letter to C. Comer Clay, 3 January 1856, in The Clement Claiborne Clay Papers Manuscript Division, Duke University Collection.
[25] Franklin Pierce, Message to Congress on Kansas, 24 January 1856; in Pierce Papers.
[26] Ibid.
[27] Ibid.
[28] Ibid.
[29] Franklin Pierce, Message on Kansas, 11 Feb. 1856; in Pierce Papers.
[30] *The Letters of William Lloyd Garrison: Volume IV, From Disunionism to the Brink of War*, ed. Louis Ruchames (Cambridge, MA: The Belknap Press of Harvard University Press, 1975), 4:390.
[31] Cordley, 35.
[32] Ibid., 45.
[33] Wilson Shannon, Letter to Col. Edwin V. Sumner, 21 May 1856, in Kansas Territorial Papers, Manuscript Division, Kansas State Historical Society Collection.
[34] *New York Daily Times*, 26 May 1856, 1.
[35] Ibid.
[36] Wilson Shannon, Letter to Col. Edwin V. Sumner, in Kansas Territorial Papers, Manuscript Division, Kansas State Historical Society Collection.
[37] Murat Halstead, *Trimmers, Trucklers, and Temporizers: Notes of Murat Halstead from the Political Convention of 1856.* William B. Hesseltine and Rex G. Fisher, eds. (Madison: University of Wisconsin Press, 1971), 23.
[38] *New York Daily Times*, 8 September 1856, 2.
[39] "Remarks of President Pierce." *New York Daily Times*, 9 June 1856, 1.
[40] Moore, 10:99.
[41] Harry Barnard, *Rutherford Hayes and His America* (Indianapolis: University of Indiana Press, 1954), 503.
[42] Homer E. Socolofsky, *Kansas Governors* (Lawrence: University of Kansas Press, 1990), 48.
[43] Jackson, "First Annual Address on the State of the Union," 8 Dec. 1829, in Richardson, 2:448.

Chapter 3

THE DOMESTIC LINCOLN: WHITE HOUSE LOBBYING OF THE CIVIL WAR CONGRESSES

Jon Schaff

THE DOMESTIC LINCOLN AND CONGRESSIONAL GOVERNMENT

One of the foremost scholars of the modern presidency, Theodore J. Lowi, argues that the American political system was a 'Congress-centered' regime that supported distributive policies, with presidents acting as marginal figures. This is in contrast to 20th Century regulatory and redistributive policies, which feature a much more active president in the policy making process. Most leading presidential scholars share Lowi's assessment of the weak 19th Century presidency.

Fred Greenstein argues that Franklin D. Roosevelt set a new paradigm for presidential activity that sharply deviates from the "traditional presidency."[1] Previous to Roosevelt there had been small shifts in power from president to president, but with Roosevelt there was a "general increase in the size and impact of American government" and "the presidency began to undergo not a shift but rather a metamorphosis."[2] In the 19th Century, Greenstein contends, Congress was disturbed by any presidential attempts at leadership, but by the conclusion of FDR's tenure presidential legislative leadership became commonplace.[3]

An important work of modern presidency scholarship by Richard Neustadt explains how the constitutional powers of the presidency are inadequate to the tasks that face the president in the post-FDR era.[4] The president is central to our system, the "focal point of politics and policy."[5] This is a central theme to modern presidency scholarship. In the past, the president was a mere clerk who simply did the bidding of a dominant Congress. Only crisis, such as a war, might elevate the president to equal footing with the legislature. The power of the presidency in modern times, Neustadt argues, is not "acquired or employed on the same terms befitting Calvin Coolidge, or Theodore Roosevelt, or Grover Cleveland, or James Polk."[6] The post-World War II era represents a break with the past that brings unique problems and powers to the president.

Another presidency scholar, Bert Rockman, has written that the 19th Century was a time when "Congress itself played a larger initiating role (over a much smaller government of course), and when presidents, for the most part, kept a much lower profile than they have grown accustomed to in recent times. Until the New Deal realignment, presidents were not always the principal political directors behind surges of political movement."[7] Rockman is typical of modern presidency scholars in thinking that Franklin D. Roosevelt represented a sharp break with the past, creating a completely new model of presidential activity.

Theodore Lowi believes that the alleged presidential deference to Congress in the 19th Century may have resulted from of the type of public policy being considered by Congress. The legislative branch dominates this distributive type of policy, especially the standing committees with programmatic jurisdiction.[8] Unlike distributive policy, which simply requires Congress to appropriate money or land, regulatory policies, which seek to control certain sectors of the economy, tend to need constant administration by a bureaucracy within the executive branch. The bureaucratic oversight of these more complex policies increases the power of the executive. The delegation of power to the executive branch gives the executive extra power in devising, implementing, and revising regulatory policies. Further, bureaucrats are specialists in these areas who have a monopoly on information Congress needs when creating or reforming these policies. As will be shown, contrary to what Lowi would expect, Lincoln's policy positions were not all distributive, as banking and currency legislation would certainly qualify as regulatory policy.

Lincoln's presidential secretaries, John Hay and John Nicolay, suggest Lincoln was an active participant in creating and promoting vital parts of his administration's domestic agenda. They write that Lincoln "sometimes made suggestions of financial measures . . . and when the Secretary [of Treasury] needed his powerful assistance with Congress he always gave it ungrudgingly." During "frequent and informal conferences at the Executive Mansion he exerted all his powers of influence and persuasion to assist the Secretary in obtaining what legislation was needed."[9] Hay wrote in is diary that bank legislation was one issue that Lincoln and Chase talked about frequently. "He had generally delegated to [Chase] exclusive control of those matters falling within purview of his department. This matter he had shared in."[10] It is also worthwhile to note that Lincoln was the first president to have a personal staff whose primarily loyalty was to him. Like contemporary presidents, Lincoln chose a cabinet to please various factions of his party, which meant choosing people with their own constituencies and their own agendas. But Hay, Nicolay, and Lincoln's other aide, William Stoddard, were first and foremost loyal to Lincoln.

James McPherson argues that legislation passed by the 37th Congress during the Lincoln presidency constitutes a "second American Revolution." This legislation includes the Homestead Act, the Land-Grant College act, the Pacific Railroad act, the creation of an income tax, and national banking and legal tender acts.[11] This paper explores whether the Lincoln administration attempted to influence Congress on the non-war legislation that made its way through Congress during those tumultuous times. If Lowi's policy thesis is correct, then the Lincoln administration should have been passive in regards to distributive legislation like the Homestead Act, the Land-Grant College Act, and the Pacific Railroad Act. To the contrary, policies such as those regarding legal tender, national banking, and internal revenue may have been regulatory enough to demand presidential leadership.

The findings of this paper have deep implications for the "modern presidency." Modern presidency scholars believe that an important change occurred in the presidency with the massive power given to the executive office during the administration of Franklin D. Roosevelt. This power was both formal and informal. It was formal in that the great delegation of power to the executive enhanced his power vis-à-vis Congress. It was informal in that Roosevelt used modern technology such as radio and polling to speak over the head of Congress and directly to the people. This paper looks at the formal side of this equation and asks whether there were not modern components to the Lincoln administration. If there were, than this should lead us to begin to question significant portions of the modern presidency thesis.

LAND LEGISLATION

In one of his few policy statements between his election and inauguration, on February 12, 1861 in Cincinnati, Lincoln said that he favored improving the conditions of man and ameliorating the position of the poor. He stated that the Homestead Act would help accomplish both ends.[12] Homestead legislation had been a crucial component of the Republican platform of 1860, as it attracted westerners into the Republican fold. Homestead proposals had been enacted in previous Congresses only to see them vetoed by Democratic presidents, most recently by James Buchanan in the summer of 1860.[13] With a westerner like Lincoln in the White House, victory seemed inevitable.

In reality it was not so simple, as Republicans themselves were split over the legislation. This was despite the fact that the 1860 Republican platform demanded "the passage by Congress of the complete and satisfactory homestead measure which has already passed the House."[14] As debate on the bill began in winter 1861, among the leaders of the opposition was Justin Morrill (R-VT), sponsor of the land-grant college proposal. Morrill feared that homestead legislation would expropriate land he needed for his college bill. Morrill's opinion was that the Homestead Act represented a give-away of land much needed to buttress the nation's credit. His college bill, he argued, would actually increase the value of the land.[15] George Julian (R-IN) countered by saying the western lands no longer brought any revenue to the government. The government should let people improve the land, he argued, to make money and expand the tax base. Julian stated that if the lands were "cut up into small farms, to be tilled by there occupants, who will build villages, school houses, and churches . . . and organize civil communities in the wilderness" the whole country "will share in the blessing and benefits" of public lands.[16] This sentiment was echoed by Speaker Galusha Grow (R-PA), who stepped down from the chair to state that the "real wealth" of the nation was not in "the sums of money paid into the Treasury, but in its flocks, its herds, and cultivated fields, and above all in the comfort of its laboring classes; not in its mass of wealth, but its diffusion."[17]

The Homestead Act was finally signed into law May 20, 1862 (An Act to secure Homesteads to actual Settlers on the Public Domain 1862). Besides Lincoln's remark in early 1861 regarding the concept of a homestead bill, there does not seem to have been much administration agitation for such legislation. The congressional debate barely even mentioned the executive branch, and only once to cite an Interior Department report proving Rep. Julian's point that public lands had ceased yielding revenue to the government.[18]

In the end, the Homestead Act was relatively uncontroversial. The bill first passed the House by a 107 to 16 margin, and the Senate 33 to 7.[19] After a conference committee ironed out some differences, both chambers passed the final version of the bill without with a recorded vote.[20]

The proposed land grants for colleges and universities provided each state with 30,000 acres of public land for each representative and senator. For western states with large tracts of federally owned land, the state would select actual parcels of land. Other states would receive scrip, which they would sell. The proceeds from the sale of land scrip would then be invested in a fund to pay "the endowment, support, and maintenance of at least one college" in each state.[21]

Like homestead legislation, Buchanan had vetoed a previous land-grant college act. The bill, a pet project of Representative Justin Morrill (R-VT) to democratize education and promote agricultural education, had passed the 36th Congress by a 25 to 22 margin in the Senate and 148 to 95 in the House. But unlike the homestead proposal, the 1860 Republican platform did not endorse any land-grant college schemes. Still, the act had broad support among Republicans. The only opposition came from western state congressmen concerned about eastern states acting as absentee owners of land within their own states. This was the only objection to the bill as it worked its way through the Senate. After passing the Senate, it passed the House with virtually no debate. In fact the bill was so well known, because it had been proposed in the previous Congress, that it did not even go to committee for consideration.[22] As was the case with the Homestead Act, the Land-Grant College Act, or Morrill Act as it is sometimes called, had such overwhelming support that the administration needed to provide no pressure for passage. The bill passed the House 90 to 25 and the Senate 32 to 7, significantly higher margins than in the previous Congress.[23]

It cannot be said that the Pacific Railroad bill lacked controversy. While it could be said that support for the bill was localized in western states, opposition heeded no section. Despite the fact that the Republican platform of 1860 and both the Douglas and Breckenridge Democratic platforms supported a Pacific Railroad, there was significant opposition to the new railway. The Republican platform called for the federal government to give "immediate and efficient aid in [the] construction [of a Pacific Railroad]."[24] The Douglas Democratic platform supported "such Constitutional Government aid as will insure the construction of a Railroad to the Pacific coast," while the Breckenridge wing called for the passage of a bill to build "at the earliest practicable moment" a railroad from the Mississippi to the Pacific Ocean.[25]

Debated from January to June in 1862, the major defense of the railroad legislation was on military grounds. This justification allowed for executive influence, as the military power was indisputably under executive influence. In the House, James Campbell (R-CA) cited a report from Secretary of War Edward Stanton stipulating that troops and supplies could be moved much more efficiently using railways rather than waterways or overland methods. Secretary of War Gideon Welles reported, Campbell said, that defending the West coast would be much easier if a railroad were in place.[26] Another Californian Republican, Aaron Sargent, mentioned that the "minister at the Court of St. James," Charles Adams, reported that trade and military needs required a Pacific Railroad connecting coasts.[27] Sargent noted that the President himself, in a message to the Senate, had passed along a report from the State Department regarding the advanced state of the French railway system. The letter concluded that the Pacific Railroad was "such a direct national concern that the government must charge itself with the execution of it without delay."[28]

Sargent was also one who appealed to loyalty to the people. Noting that both party platforms endorsed the bill, Sargent asked whether promises made before a presidential election should later be discarded. A party must keep its "pledges to the people."[29] Justin Morrill opposed the bill, stating that he would rather forgo a party plank rather than "knock out my brains" against it. Samuel Fessenden (R-ME) rejoined, "I think by passing this bill is the only way to keep the brains in the Republican party."[30]

Senator Lyman Trumball (R-IL) typified the opposition to the plan. While some thought the act was merely a payoff to railway interests, Trumball's argument was constitutional.[31] His contention was that federal government had power to build railroads through territories but not through states.[32] He also disputed the military nature of the bill. Perhaps if this was a case of military necessity the federal government could build across states, but there was no necessity. Trumball pointed out that by the time the railroad was completed the current war would almost certainly be over (and he was correct).[33] Trumball offered a poison pill amendment changing the eastern terminus of the railroad so as to render eastern lines unprofitable, but the amendment failed.[34] The Railroad bill passed the Senate by a 35 to 5 vote, and the House 104 to 21.[35] The large margin of victory on final passage belies the conflict in Congress over the Railroad bill.

Unlike the Homestead Act and the Land-Grant College Act, no Pacific Railroad legislation had ever passed Congress. With so large financial interests affected by this huge undertaking, it is not surprising that such legislation was difficult to pass. Perhaps it is no coincidence that the Lincoln administration, and even Lincoln himself to some extent, acted as advocates for the measure, and the bill did pass. It was advantageous that there was some military connection to justify administration involvement in the legislative process, but it cannot be said that the administration "lobbied" Congress on the bill. However, they did put information in the hands of known supporters.

CURRENCY AND BANKING

There can be no doubt, on both the Legal Tender Act of 1862 and the National Bank Act of 1863 that Salmon Chase and Congress worked hand in hand. Chase himself believed that one principle of the Republican Party should be a national bank system with the federal government furnishing the bank notes.[36]

On January 23, 1862 John Alley (R-MA) stated on the floor of Congress three things needed to buttress the economy. First, he felt that the government needed to issue $100 million in treasury notes. Second, a tax of $150 million needed to be levied. "Thirdly, [the government should] provide a uniform currency, by adopting the recommendation in the report of the Secretary of the Treasury."[37] The next month Congress spent much of its time debating a bill to allow the issue of treasury notes to be used as legal tender for all debts public and private. These notes would become the famous "greenback" and constitute the introduction of paper money into the American economy.

One of the key players in the house supporting passage of the Legal Tender Act was Elbridge Spaulding (R-NY). Spaulding was considered the finance expert on the Ways and Means Committee. Like many members of Congress, Spaulding used Chase's annual report to Congress as the basis for his support of the bill. In his initial speech on the House floor regarding the bill, Spaulding cited liberally from Chase's report, using Chase's own numbers on the financial condition of the government.[38] He remarked that Chase had two plans to buttress the nation's finances:

> first, the issue of demand Treasury notes; and second, a national currency secured by a pledge of United States stocks, to be issued by banks and associations, with proper regulation for their redemption by the banks themselves.[39]

In this report Chase maintained:

> [I]t is too clear to be reasonably disputed that Congress, under its constitutional powers to lay taxed, to regulate commerce, and to regulate the value of coin, possesses ample authority to control the credit circulation which enters so largely into the transactions of commerce, and affects in so many ways the value of coin.[40]

Chase went on to make a case for a sound currency, and the dangers of uncertainty in the value of money. He then proceeded to present his plan for the easy circulation of a stable currency:

> Two plans for effecting this object were suggested. The first contemplated the gradual withdrawal from circulation of the notes of private corporations, and for the issue, in their stead, of United States notes, payable in coin on demand, in amounts sufficient for the useful ends of a representative currency. The second, contemplated the preparation and delivery, to institutions and associations, of notes prepared for circulation under national direction, and to be secured as to prompt convertibility into coin by the pledge of United States bonds and other needful regulations.[41]
> Chase claimed, "In this plan the people, in their ordinary business, would find the advantages of uniformity in currency; of uniformity in security; of effectual safeguard...against depreciation; and protection from losses in discounts and exchange."[42] Chase continued to say, "A further important advantage to the people may be reasonably expected in the increased security of the Union, springing from the common interest in its preservation, created by the distribution of its stocks to associations throughout the country."[43]

Spaulding further mentioned that he had solicited the Attorney General's opinion on the constitutionality of the bill. Not surprisingly, Attorney General Edward Bates had reported back positively on Congress' power to issue paper money. Bates wrote to Spaulding:

> Certainly the Constitution contains no direct prohibition [of a national currency], and I think it contains no inferential prohibition that can be fairly dawn from its express terms. The first article of the Constitution, section eight, grants to Congress specifically a great mass of powers."

In regards to the "necessary and proper" clause of Article 1, Section 8, Bates drew on Story's Commentaries, writing:

> If the word necessary were used in the strict rigorous sense, it would be an extraordinary departure from the usual course of the human mind, as exhibited in solemn instruments,

to add another word, the only possible effect of which is to qualify the strict and rigorous meaning, and to present clearly the idea of a choice of means in the course of legislation. If no means are to be resorted to but such as are indispensably necessary, there can be neither sense or utility in adding the word 'proper' for the indispensable necessity would shut out from view of all consideration of the propriety of means.[44]

On January 29, Roscoe Conkling (R-NY) inquired on the floor of the House into Chase's constitutional opinion of the matter. Spaulding asked for and got Chase's opinion. Chase replied to Spaulding and Congress in general that, in his opinion, the war required the extreme measure of paper money. He was supportive of Congress' efforts to put his requests into law.[45]

Both opponents and supporters of the currency measure referenced Chase during the discussion of the bill. John Bingham (R-Ohio) cited the Chase annual report against the likes of F.A. Conkling (R-NY) and Justin Morrill. Bingham, citing Chase, argues that some "persons and institutions" were refusing Treasury notes. Making the notes legal tender for all debts would solve that problem.[46] On the other hand, William Sheffield (U-RI) referred to the legal tender bill as a "financial scheme presented to this House by the Secretary of the Treasury."[47] Valentine Horton (R-Ohio) insisted though he respected the knowledge of the Treasury Secretary, that he did not think Chase had made a strong enough case the necessity of introduction of paper money.

> I know perfectly well that the Secretary of Treasury thinks that it is necessary, and I have the utmost confidence in his ability and zeal. I think he is mistaken. At any rate, whether he is mistaken or not, he has not furnished the proof of the correctness of his opinion.[48]

President Lincoln did not go unmentioned in the congressional debate on this matter. Frederick Pike (R-ME) quoted from Lincoln's July 4, 1861 message to Congress to defend as necessary for the defense of the government the extreme measure of introducing a paper currency. Pike stated:

> Upon the consideration of every finical measure there might well present itself anew the same question fitly put by President Lincoln in is message to Congress in July. 'Is it better to assume powers, the exercise of which shall violate a portion of the Constitution, rather than allow the whole to be destroyed?' And country came to the paradoxical conclusion that it was his duty, as president, to violate the Constitution to preserve it.[49]

The implication of his statement is, of course, that under ordinary circumstances this legislation would be unconstitutional. Given the dire straights that the country faced, however, the passage of the legal tender bill was as important as the controversial military measures Lincoln had made the previous year.

The Senate debate included more references to Chase, often mentioning Chase's opinion as gospel. Sen. John Sherman (R-Ohio) avowed that Chase's annual report had a significant effect on his thinking.[50] On a particular amendment, Sen. John Hale (R-New Hampshire) opposed the amendment, but said, "As the committee on finance and the Secretary of the Treasury seem to insist upon it, I will not make a noise about it."[51] Sherman opposed a separate amendment, but he said, "I do not pretend now to call for a division [on the amendment] because the Secretary of the Treasury earnestly desires this."[52] On an amendment concerning different types of bonds to be issued by the Treasury, Sherman and Finance Committee chairman Fessenden politely argued over Chase's position. Fessenden argued that Sherman had Chase's general opinion correct, but the Secretary had indicated support for a particular amendment that differed with that general position. Fessenden indicated, "on matters of detail . . . I am much more inclined to trust the judgment of the Secretary of the Treasury than my own."[53] There was also some question as to what kind of notation would appear on the back of the proposed legal tender notes. Fessenden stated that "in an interview with the Secretary of Treasury this morning," the Secretary indicated that Congress should not act on the matter, leaving Chase with discretion.[54] Finally, Fessenden proposed an amendment allowing the Treasury to issue certificates of deposit for not less that $500 for 5 percent per annum. James McDougall of California spoke up and said that he wanted to offer an amendment making $100 the minimum deposit. "I was at the Treasury Department this morning," he stated, "and the Secretary himself said . . . the amendment would be a just and wise one." Fessenden acquiesced, stating, "I accept the modification if the Secretary amends it."[55] In every single one of these matters, the position of the Secretary Chase won the day.

McDougall's mention of his early morning trip to the Secretary of the Treasury indicates that there was some behind the scenes politicking done by Chase. One the floor of the Senate John Sherman indicated that Chase was involved in "private intercourse" with members on important matters.[56] Chase's own diary indicates that giving dinners for congressmen was not atypical. His entry for January 8, 1862 states that he "gave the usual dinner to committees of finance of the Houses." Senators present were Fessenden, Sherman, William Howe (R-WI), James Simmons (R-RI), and James Pearce (D-MD). House members were Stevens, Morrill, Spaulding, Horton, Samuel Hooper, Horace Maynard, and John Stratton.[57] Eventually the bill passed the Senate 30-7 and the House 97-22.[58]

One senses in early 1863, as Congress debated the bill to create a national banking system to compliment the national currency, much the same influence of Chase was evident on the bank bill as on the currency initiative. The matter of a national bank system, however, drew some direct involvement from President Lincoln. In his Annual Message of December 3, 1862, Lincoln advocated the "organization of bank associations, under a general act of Congress." The creation of these banks would augment the issuing of paper money, as the national banks would be furnished "circulating notes, on the security of the United States bonds deposited in the treasury." These national banks could control the issuing of paper money, and thus keep inflation in check.[59] In a subsequent letter to Congress in January of 1863, Lincoln digressed from the point of the letter to make these same points in favor of national bank association.[60]

These efforts by Lincoln were not lost on Congress during the debate on a national bank system in early 1863. Elbridge Spaulding noted how the president had advocated such a measure in his annual address. Lincoln stated in his 1862 annual address:

> I know of [no way of guaranteeing a stable currency] which promises so certain results, and is, at the same time, so unobjectionable, as the organization of banking associations, under a general act of Congress, well guarded in its provisions. To such associations the government might furnish circulating notes, on the security of the United States bonds deposited in the treasury. These notes, prepared under the supervision of the proper

officers, being uniform in appearance and security, and convertible always into coin, would at once protect labor against the evils of a vicious currency, and facilitate commerce by cheap and safe exchanges.[61]

Lincoln also took advantage of his signing a bill providing for immediate payment of the military to lobby for the National Bank Act. He argued that "Congress has power to regulate the currency of the country," and it was important to do just that so as to keep inflation down. "To that end, a uniform currency…is almost, if not quite indispensable." Further, "Such currency can be furnished by banking associations, organized under a general act of Congress." The Secretary of the Treasury made the same argument in his annual report. In fact Spaulding referred to the bill as the "national bank bill proposed by the Secretary of the Treasury.[62] Reuben Fenton (R-NY) called it "substantially the scheme of the Secretary of the Treasury," and he supported the bill because Chase considered action necessary.[63]

In the Senate, John Sherman once again drew heavily from Chase to defend the bank act. He mentioned liberally Chase's support of such a bill in his annual reports of 1861 and 1862 and Sherman used those reports to rebut his opponents.[64] After Charles Sumner (R-MA) noticed that the amount of treasury notes circulated under the act had been changed, Sherman said that after "consultation" with Chase both thought the change should be made.[65] Sherman even quoted the *London Times* saying "the bill promoted by Mr. Chase" would provide order to a confused system where so many different bank could issue their own notes.[66]

Sherman's constant defense of Chase and the administration eventually offended some turf conscious congressmen. Jacob Collamer (R-VT) castigated Sherman for insinuating that Senators should support the bank bill simply because the administration desired it:

We are told in the Senate that the whole cabinet are in [the bill's] favor . . . [I]t is not many years since a man would have been called to order for using an expression of that kind in the Senate . . . Legislation is to be left to the House of Representatives and the Senate; it is the exercise of their judgment, not the authority of others, which it to give currency and support to measures.

Collamer asserted that any implication that the administration might exert influence on congressional deliberation suggested "subserviency" on the part of the Senate. Collamer pointed out that, unlike Great Britain, the United States does not have ministers of the government sitting in on the legislature.[67]

Sherman responded to this criticism by saying that he mere wanted to point out that the Secretary of the Treasury, the cabinet, and "a great body of the people," supported the bill. If Collamer was able to cite opinions of people who thought the bill would bring ruin upon local banks, than he could cite "the opinions of grave and honorable men who are charged with the responsibilities of administering the Executive Departments of the Government." Sherman assured Collamer that this was not done to "influence our feeling," but simply to show that these men "gave this bill their hearty approbation."[68] Of course one can hardly believe that Sherman mentioned the strong support of the administration only to put that support on record. Indeed, Chase's annual report and Lincoln's Annual Message were public documents. Common sense dictates that Sherman hoped appeals to executive authority would sway votes, but the conventions of his time required him to deny that.

As the vote on final passage neared in the Senate, an anticipated close vote had the administration lobbying specific senators in an attempt to sway their votes. Chase had discussed the act with Sen. Benjamin Wade (R-OH), and "a good many callers" from Congress convinced him that there "seems an increasing disposition to favoring the bill for banking."[69] Secretary Chase brought pressure upon Henry Anthony (R-RI) to vote for the measure. Anthony exclaimed that "he believed it to be his duty to vote for the bill, although it would be the end of his political career."[70] Chase, Interior Secretary John Usher and Lincoln personal Secretary William Stoddard lobbied Timothy Howe (R-WI) and Jacob Howard (R-MI), both of whom switched votes based upon this pressure.[71] This proved crucial as the bill barely passed the Senate by a scant 23 to 21 margin. The bill passed the House by a slim margin of 78 to 64.[72]

The National Bank Act provides the clearest examples of widespread administration influence on the legislative process. Chase's statement that he perceived and "increasing disposition" towards the act suggests that he was counting votes. It is clear that the administration was not averse to twisting arms when the vote became extremely close in the Senate. In announcing his support for the bill in two messages to Congress, President Lincoln put his stamp of approval on the effort. In gaining enactment of a national bank system, the Lincoln administration looks almost modern in its efforts.

With all this activity on the Legal Tender Act and the National Bank Act, it surprising that an examination of the congressional debate on the revenue measures of 1861 and the Internal Revenue Act of 1862 show little administration involvement. Senator James Simmons (R-RI) did make some adjustments to his tariff proposal in July, 1861 upon the request of the Secretary of the Treasury.[73] Later Chase sent a letter to Finance Committee chairman Fessenden asking for a joint resolution exempting from new tariff duties goods that were already in the warehouse when the duties became operative.[74] This resolution did end up passing.[75] But by and large the references to Chase and the administration are perfunctory remarks regarding fact and figures.[76] The revenue measures of the special congressional session of 1861 included the creation of the first income tax in the history of the nation. But still, this seems to have been largely a congressional initiative. Perhaps the task of raising revenue was considered ordinary business that Congress could do on its own, while innovations such as a national currency and national banking system required more administration involvement.

CONCLUSION

The Lincoln administration clearly attempted to influence the passage of important pieces of domestic legislation. It had the most profound influence on economic measures, the Legal Tender Act and the National Bank Act. On other legislation--the Homestead Act, the Land Grant College Act, the Pacific Railroad Act, and the Revenue Acts of 1861 and 1862 – the administration was largely on the outside looking in.

It cannot be denied that these lesser enactments were significant in their own right. The Homestead Act helped settle the West, and the Pacific Railroad Act helped make the West prosperous. The Land-Grant College Act helped democratize higher education. The Revenue acts, while subsequently amended or outright repealed in parts, did set precedent for the future. But they were all part of the prototypical distributionist public policy of the 19th

Century. They may have been larger examples of distributive policy, but not so much that they were different in kind.

On the contrary, the Legal Tender Act and the National Bank Act altered the relationship between the national government and the nation's monetary system. As Lowi would predict, the executive did have a much larger role to play in the formation of this regulatory legislation than it did in the congressionally dominated distributionist legislation. This is the important distinction between the distributionist land policies and the regulatory banking and currency policies. Considering both types of policy in the Lincoln administration allows us to see how policy typology was influencing presidential power long before the modern presidency. The Legal Tender Act and the following acts taxing rival currency out of existence made national treasury notes the only currency of the nation, eventually supplanting specie as the medium of economic activity. This represented a huge increase in the government's power to regulate currency. The bank system supplemented the act of the previous year by increasing the nation's power over the banking system. These are legitimately seen as regulatory policies of the type that would become more commonplace in the late 19th and early 20th Centuries. Like the policy theory that suggests the executive has a larger role to play in the formation of regulatory policy, the Lincoln Administration was indispensable to the creation and passage of these two significant pieces of legislation. This represented a break from the past and precedent for the future. The massive new regulation of banking and currency drastically altered the economy and perhaps even set the stage for the industrialization of America.[77]

The evidence indicates that the Lincoln Administration was not as hermetically sealed from Congress as many historians and presidential scholars would have us believe. Chase, with Lincoln's support, was crucial to the passage of this legislation. There is every reason to believe that the Republican party, made up of almost as many former Democrats as Whigs (Speaker of the House Grow is an obvious example), would be wary of this nationalistic move by the administration. Given the close vote on the National Bank matter, it appears that the administration's influence may have been decisive.

It seems fair to say that Chase was to Lincoln as Alexander Hamilton was to George Washington, and perhaps even more so. Besides his reports to Congress, the evidence is clear that Chase was taking positions on particular amendments and personally lobbying individual members of Congress. Further, unlike Washington, Lincoln's own views on the subject of banking in particular were made public. Lincoln's personal secretaries report that Lincoln and Chase worked together on these important policy proposals, so it is not unreasonable to assume that Lincoln knew of and endorsed Chase's activities. Surely Lincoln and Chase did not have the personal attachment Washington and Hamilton had. It is well known that Chase was highly critical of Lincoln's pursuit of war aims and on these matters sought to undermine Lincoln with Congress. The volatility between the two men reached such a fever pitch that, under pressure from Lincoln, Chase resigned as Secretary of Treasury in 1864. But it should be noted that Chase's difficulties with Lincoln stemmed from Chase's radicalism on the slavery question and a large ego that could not accept the fact that Lincoln was president instead of him. On matters of finance the two were in basic agreement, and to the extent that the bank and currency proposals helped the war effort, it brought the two into relative harmony.

Modern presidency scholars should take note of the lengths the Lincoln administration went to in order to pass the Legal Tender Act and the National Bank Act. Nonetheless, it should be noted that Lincoln did not use a "going public strategy, which has so characterized the modern presidency. Lincoln was always careful about the words he used and did little public speaking not related to the war. He felt he was on far firmer constitutional footing as Commander-in-Chief than as legislative leader. Lincoln was not a modern president. But the actions of his administration on historic legislation should make us give pause before we breezily accept the modern presidency thesis in whole cloth.

NOTES

[1] Greenstein, Fred. 1978. "Change and continuity in the modern presidency." In *The New American Political System*. Ed. Anthony King. Washington, D.C.: American Enterprise Institute.
[2] Greenstein, p. 45.
[3] Greenstein, p. 48.
[4] Neustadt, Richard. 1960. *Presidential Power: The Politics of Leadership*. New York: Wiley and Sons.
[5] Neustadt, p. 1.
[6] Neustadt, p. 3.
[7] Rockman, Bert A. 1984. *The Leadership Question: The Presidency and the American System*. New York: Praeger, p. 103.
[8] Lowi, Theodore J. 1985. *The Personal President: Power Invested, Promise Unfulfilled*. Ithaca, NY: Cornell University Press.
[9] Nicolay, John, and John Hay. 1890. *Abraham Lincoln: A History*. 10 vls. New York: The Century Co.
[10] Hay, John. 1997. *Inside Lincoln's White House: the Complete Civil War Diary of John Hay*. Carbondale : Southern Illinois University Press.
[11] McPherson, James M. 1991. *Abraham Lincoln and the Second American Revolution*. New York: Oxford University Press.
[12] Basler, Roy. 1953. *The Collected Works of Abraham Lincoln*. New Brunswick, NJ: Rutgers University Press.
[13] Curry, Leonard.1968. *Blueprint for Modern America; Non-military Legislation of the First Civil War Congress*. Nashville: Vanderbilt University Press.
[14] Porter, Kirk H. and Donald Bruce Johnson. 1956. *National Party Platforms 1840-1956*. Urbana, IL: University of Illinois Press.
[15] Cong. Globe, 37th Cong. 2nd Session, 136.
[16] Ibid.
[17] Ibid., p. 910.
[18] Ibid., p. 1938.
[19] Ibid., pp. 1951 & 1035.
[20] Ibid., pp. 2147-2148.
[21] Cross, Coy F. 1999. *Justin Smith Morill: Father of the Land-Grant Colleges*. East Lansing, MI: Michigan State University Press.
[22] Curry, pp. 111-112; Cong. Globe, 37th 2nd Session, pp. 2275-2277.
[23] Cong. Globe, 37th 2nd Session, pp. 2769-2770.
[24] Ibid., pp. 2634 & 2770.
[25] Porter & Johnson, p. 33.
[26] Ibid., p. 31.
[27] Cong. Globe, 37th 2nd Session, pp. 1578-1579.
[28] Ibid., p. 1596.

29 Basler, pp. 5: 156-157; Cong. Globe, 37th 2nd Session, p. 1590.
30 Ibid., p. 599.
31 Ibid., p. 1708.
32 Ibid., pp. 1698-1711.
33 Ibid., pp. 2654-2655.
34 Ibid., p. 2655.
35 Ibid., p. 2906; Curry, p. 131.
36 Cong. Globe, 37th 2nd Session, pp. 2840 & 2906.
37 Chase, p. I: 423.
38 Cong. Globe, 37th 2nd Session, p. 458.
39 Ibid., pp. 523-524.
40 Ibid., p. 524.
41 Ibid., Appendix 25.
42 Ibid.
43 Ibid., Appendix 26.
44 Ibid.
45 Ibid., p. 525.
46 Ibid.
47 Ibid., p. 639.
48 Ibid., p. 640.
49 Ibid., pp. 664-665.
50 Ibid., p. 657.
51 Sherman, John. 1895. *John Sherman's Recollections of Forty Years in the House, Senate and Cabinet*. Chicago: The Werner Company, p. 271.
52 Cong. Globe, 37th 2nd Session, p. 772.
53 Ibid.
54 Ibid., p. 774.
55 Ibid., pp. 774-775.
56 Ibid., p. 802.
57 Ibid., p. 789.
58 Chase, pp. 322-323.
59 Cong. Globe, 37th 2nd Session, pp. 804 & 939.
60 Basler, pp. V: 522-523.
61 Ibid., pp. VI: 60-61.
62 Ibid., PP. V: 522-523.
63 Cong. Globe, 37th 2nd Session, p. 1114.
64 Ibid., p. 1117.
65 Ibid., pp. 840-841.
66 Ibid., p. 821.
67 Ibid., p. 842.
68 Ibid., p. 874.
69 Ibid.
70 Chase, pp. 425-426.
71 Sherman, pp. 298-299.
72 Boritt, Gabor. 1994. *Lincoln and the Politics of the American Dream*. Urbana, IL: University of Illinois Press.
73 Cong. Globe, 37th 2nd Session, pp. 897 & 1148.
74 Cong. Globe, 37th 1st Session, p. 315.
75 Cong. Globe, 37th 2nd Session, p. 221.
76 Curry, p. 160.
77 Cong. Globe, 37th 2nd Session, pp. 1217-1218, 1412 & 2446.

Chapter 4

THE "SMALLEST MISTAKE": EXPLAINING THE FAILURES OF THE HAYES AND HARRISON PRESIDENCIES

Douglas Steven Gallagher

INTRODUCTION

Charles O. Jones's *Passages to the Presidency* notes a particular peculiarity in the American political system. Unlike Great Britain, where the transfer of power from Conservative prime minister John Major to Labour leader Tony Blair took less than 24 hours, the United States Constitution provides for approximately 75 days between the election of a president and the taking of the office. The "transition" is a unique opportunity with perils for the new president and his staff, and Jones outlines those many promises and pitfalls in his study of four transitions which entailed a switch between political parties as well as presidents.[1] The transition, along with the separate election of presidents and congressional representatives and the separation of powers, make the American system interesting.

This study will concern the plight of two presidents (and a situation) Jones overlooks in his research: Rutherford B. Hayes and Benjamin Harrison. Each of these "minority" presidents, elected with fewer popular votes than the candidate they defeated, pressed ahead and dealt with issues they considered important to America's future.

Hayes's first priority was an end to sectional divisiveness that had existed since the Civil War, and he did much to accomplish that goal in his first weeks. He appointed a southern Democrat to his cabinet, pulled federal troops out of Florida and South Carolina (in accordance with the deal struck to award him the presidency), and spoke in soothing tones about moving past the war. He also signaled his intention to carry out civil-service reform, much to the dismay of many other Republicans. In doing all of this, Hayes appears far stronger than future generations would assert. The trouble would come because he tried to promise all things to all people: he claimed that reconciliation with the South would not hurt black voters, when Democratic rule did just that. Few would forget that "His Fraudulency" did not keep all of his promises, and his historical reputation would suffer as a result.

Benjamin Harrison faced less onerous tests in his first days: these controversies were limited to party squabbles over appointments to cabinet positions and ambassadorships. However, they were no less important to his political future. In each early decision he made, Harrison unwittingly antagonized a certain faction of the party to which he owed his election, be it civil-service reformers or politicians more committed to the "spoils" system. It appears with hindsight that he was an effective president that could manage important legislation well and act as a spokesman (in some ways) for blacks and other minorities. However, his early mistakes earned him some lasting enemies that would hurt him in his unsuccessful re-election bid.

The clearest lesson from this study will be that, in American politics, first impressions count for a great deal. These impressions are especially important since, as Paul Light has noted, presidents encounter what he calls a "cycle of decreasing influence" during their terms. A president must "spend increasing capital just trying to unclog the legislative calendar," forego the pursuit of major policy initiatives, and do so with the knowledge that their power relative to Congress and the bureaucracy declines as time passes. They also lose support in Congress and lose popularity with voters over the years, so they must act quickly if they wish to effect real changes.[2]

Light's insights are particularly important to presidents like Hayes and Harrison, since they arrive without the popular mandate that greets other leaders. Mistakes, however minor they may appear, are far more costly for minority presidents than for those who have been elected with majorities of the popular vote. James P. Pfiffner's *The Strategic Presidency* states that the first months of a president's terms are crucial to success or failure in the office. "[The new administration] want[s] to take advantage of the 'mandate' from the voters and create a 'honeymoon' with Congress," they want to move fast, and they understand that this period "is also a time of danger."[3] Each of these statements is particularly true of Hayes and Harrison. Failing to protect the rights of a certain constituency or antagonizing a powerful senator in one's own party is never a good idea, but there is no margin for error if a president does so without even the slightest mandate. This paper will detail how first Hayes, then Harrison, failed to consolidate the power they possessed with small mistakes that became magnified under the intense scrutiny of the press, politicians and voters.

BACKGROUND: HOW DID HAYES AND HARRISON WIN?

Charles O. Jones's research claims that American presidents can be originated (elected for the first time), regenerated (re-elected or, in some cases, presidents who inherited the office and won a term of their own), or received (vice-presidents who assume the office upon the death or resignation of the president).[4] His categorization, which covers presidents elected between 1896 and 1992, neglects the "minority" president, one elected while earning fewer popular votes than the defeated candidate.[5] Since Andrew Jackson's Democratic Party extended the franchise to most white males in the 1830s, only two elections prior to 2000 had featured such a result. In 1876, a dispute similar (though not identical) to the Bush-Gore contest propelled Republican Rutherford B. Hayes into the White House over Samuel Tilden.[6] The other such election occurred in 1888, when Republican Benjamin Harrison scored a solid and undisputed electoral majority over Democrat Grover Cleveland, though Cleveland's large popular majorities in the South gave him a 100,000-vote advantage.[7] Each of these elections bears some resemblance to the Bush victory, especially that of Hayes. His victory came because a panel of five House members, five Senators, and five Supreme Court justices voted along party lines and awarded a set of disputed electors, including those of Florida, to Hayes. There are some important differences, however. For example, the electorate Hayes and Harrison faced in the late 1800s did not include women in most states and actively discouraged black men from voting. There was also virtually no support for Republicans in the South, particularly in 1888. Neither Republican candidate garnered much support in this Democratic stronghold, while the contests in these states were far closer in 2000 (though the South went solidly for Bush in this case).

Jones's consideration of presidential transitions does not account for these elections. The problem for minority presidents, no matter the circumstances surrounding their elections, remains the same: how does a president transition to power and govern when he knows that a good portion of the country probably considers him an illegitimate leader in the first weeks of his administration? The verdict in the two previous examples of minority presidents does not bode well for Bush. Hayes declared that he would not seek a second term in the White House even before he won the office in 1876, and many in Washington referred to him as "His Fraudulency" throughout his term.[8] Harrison did not make such a campaign promise and ran again in 1892. Grover Cleveland ran again for the Democrats and won another term as president with a 2-to-1 electoral majority and a 400,000-vote popular margin.[9] It remains to be seen how George W. Bush does as a minority president, but past examples are not encouraging.

RUTHERFORD B. HAYES: BALANCING BLACK RIGHTS AND SOUTHERN RECONCILIATION

Of course, the demise of the Hayes and Harrison administrations did not come about in their first few weeks in office. Still, each of them knew that if they were to succeed as presidents, they had to deal with the knowledge that a cloud hung over their respective elections. For Hayes, the transition was non-existent, since the commission that awarded Hayes the White House rendered its final decision only two days before the inauguration. In fact, "Hayes had [originally] thought that no invitation from Washington would move him from Columbus [Ohio, where he had been governor] until the result of the election was declared."[10] He was attempting to act "presidential" at a time when no reasonable politician would declare that he wanted to be president. Therefore, the new president had to deal with the office-seekers and Cabinet headaches of previous administrations with little time to prepare.

Inaugural

He also had to prepare for his inaugural address. It would be the first opportunity Hayes would have to address the people as their leader and set a tone for the new administration, and he knew that his words would be especially important because of the dispute that had been settled just forty-eight hours earlier. Despite the pressure, "of all the throng gathered on and around the platform on the east portico of the Capitol [on 5 March 1877], he seemed the least tense." (Perhaps this was because Hayes had already declared he would not seek re-election in 1880.) This calm came despite rumors that assassins lurked in the shadows. Nevertheless, Hayes's taking of the oath of office passed without incident, as did his address. It would turn out to be quite important because, as Harry Barnard notes, "problems not stated in his inaugural he largely ignored, or he was satisfied merely to define."[11]

He touched on five topics in the speech, which reiterated points he had made in accepting the Republican nomination. Four concerned specific policy issues: the South, reform of the civil service, the end of "greenbacks" (fiat paper money), and non-interference in foreign affairs. The fifth topic, however, was perhaps the most important. He made a statement concerning the election dispute. Hayes called the peaceful end to the controversy a "reason for rejoicing," saying that the United States had given the world "the first example in history of a great Nation, in the midst of a struggle of opposing parties for power, hushing its party tumults, to yield the issue of the contest to adjustment according to forms of law."[12] This inaugural was thus a clear attempt to calm passions, especially among embittered Democrats who considered the election stolen.[13]

Selecting a Cabinet

Another sign of how Hayes would govern came from his selection of cabinet secretaries and other officeholders. He faced a major problem: the president did not have the kind of discretion in selecting his advisors that modern presidents now enjoy. There was a small group of Republican senators, led by Roscoe H. Conkling of New York and James G. Blaine of Maine, who formed an "oligarchy" in Congress. The group had led the fight to impeach Andrew Johnson, and it had been responsible for many of the scandals of the Grant administration. They had "accepted the Ohioan most ungraciously," though they had worked on Hayes's behalf during the campaign. Now they sought to control his appointments. Nevertheless, Hayes had a reputation as a civil-service reformer, so he fought the oligarchs. He filled most of the seats in his cabinet according to his own preferences. For example, his choice of Ohio's John Sherman to head the Treasury Department met with little resistance.[14]

He made two other appointments, however, that caused far more controversy with some Republican senators, signaling that any thought of controlling President Hayes as completely as they had Grant would have to be set aside. He selected Missouri Senator Carl Schurz to head the Interior Department. Schurz had been one of the leaders of the Liberal Republican revolt of 1872 and was "the most picturesque and unbiased public man of the day." In short, he symbolized "the reformer in politics," everything the oligarchs did not want in the government. Nevertheless, Schurz's nomination had little trouble in passing the Senate, however, and his inclusion in the Hayes Cabinet "was an advertisement that the corruption of Grant's reign had come to an end."[15]

The other controversial appointment was an even stronger indication that Hayes was trying to reconcile those who had voted against him and strengthen his own legitimacy. His platform and inaugural address had indicated that reconciliation with the defeated South was a top priority for the new administration, and he thought that the symbolic gesture of placing a southern Democrat in the Cabinet would go a long way toward his goal. He had originally wanted former Confederate general Joseph E. Johnston to head the War Department, but objections from the oligarchs and, more importantly, General William T. Sherman put an end to that notion. He then turned to lesser-known Confederate colonel David M. Key of Tennessee and appointed him as postmaster general. One optimistic observer claimed that Hayes's decision would bring conservative southerners around to supporting the administration, and Hayes liked to think of this action in romantic terms. In his diary, he said that "I was ready to resort to unusual measure and to risk my own standing and reputation with my party and my country" to end sectionalism in the badly-divided nation.[16]

Many of his early public statements also concentrated on the subject of the South and how best to bring it back into the Union. Though the circumstances of the Presidency in the 19th century were far different than those of modern times, this can be construed as an example of the president "going public," as Samuel Kernell has famously explained it. Kernell cites rare cases of past presidents who had taken their cases directly to the people, but "the emergence of presidents who *routinely* do so to promote their policies in Washington awaited the development of modern systems of transportation and mass communications."[17] The examples he cites include Theodore Roosevelt's "bully pulpit" and Franklin Roosevelt's "fireside chats," but Hayes's advocacy of his southern policy could be considered a primitive example of such a strategy. His goals were twofold. He genuinely wanted to move past the divisiveness of the bloody Civil War, and he wanted to cement his legacy as President.

The South as His First Test

The first weeks of Hayes's administration provided fodder for the president's strategy that went beyond any potential controversy over the appointment of Postmaster Key. Much of the news of the day was about this new Southern policy. Groups of North Carolina and Tennessee Republicans weighed in on Hayes's efforts, hoping they would succeed and help both country and party. More importantly for the president, businessmen in Memphis met at that city's Cotton Exchange and endorsed his reconciliation efforts as a "broad departure" from past administrations. The *Richmond Dispatch* weighed in, calling his ideas "as agreeable as [they are] surprising." His actions during his initial days in office, according to the Virginia paper, "manifested enough steadiness of purpose to create a strong inclination toward confidence in his sincerity."[18] Each of these testimonials, which appeared during his first week as president, gave Hayes confidence that he was doing the right thing.

His efforts at reaching out to Democrats did worry some constituents, however. The most nervous groups were blacks in the South, who knew the fate that likely awaited them if Democrats regained control of state governments. To assuage their fears, Hayes held two public meetings with black leaders. One such meeting took place on 14 March. The leader of the delegation, John F. Quarles, expressed his "surprise" at the new administration's policy and urged the appointment of a prominent black Washingtonian, John Langston, as Commissioner of Agriculture to ease their fears. The president replied that southern blacks "need have no fear" because of his ideas: "if it should be found that through [reconciliation] it should be found that through it the rights of any man, white or black, were curtailed in any way, it would be changed at once."[19] A similar meeting with ministers of the African Methodist Episcopal Church contained soothing words for blacks, who had overwhelmingly voted for Hayes in 1876. "It shall be my purpose in the discharge of my official duties to care equally for all out people, and I assure you that the race represented by you will never be neglected by my Administration."[20] The president was, in this case, "going public" with assurances that his presidency would protect southern blacks. The media covered these events with some interest, since the black population was an important reason Hayes had been elected in the first place.[21]

How well did he succeed in keeping his promise of protection to black Republicans? Hayes's pledges contrasted with the expressed platform of his party, which counseled reconciliation but said little on supporting black aspirations in the South. The test for Hayes's "moderate" policy began on 5 March when a special session of Congress met to resolve a dispute over what to do about the two remaining Republican governors left in the South, Louisiana's Stephen B. Packard and South Carolina's Daniel H. Chamberlain. It is obvious that Hayes's sympathies leaned toward these embattled men, but economic and military considerations did not help their chances. The army was as small as it had been before the Civil War, and the Democrat-controlled House had threatened to cut off federal money to the armed forces if the Packard and Chamberlain governments were sustained. Hayes's larger problem with keeping troops in Louisiana and South Carolina, however, was public opinion, which had turned heavily against radical Reconstruction and considered it a "failed experiment." "With force no longer an option, he decided that only 'peaceful methods' could achieve 'safety and harmony for the colored people' and 'restore harmony and good feeling between Sections and races.'"[22] In other words, he hoped his moderate policy toward the South would protect the civil rights of blacks *and* restoring the southern states to equilibrium in the Union.

The policy turned out to be a success in one regard while being a miserable failure in the other. One biographer states that it could have been no other way: "if the ex-Confederates had not shown the spirit of reconciliation they did, the president's course would have been much the same."[23] He attempted to mollify more radical elements of Republican opinion, particularly the highly critical *New York Times*, by consulting his cabinet, sending a commission to Louisiana, and inviting the rival governors of South Carolina to Washington for talks. In the end, both Republican governors yielded their posts, ostensibly "for the present." All involved, however, knew that Democrats were back in control of these states permanently. The pledges of Democrats on behalf of black civil rights, which included stringent enforcement of civil rights laws and constitutional amendments, were conveniently forgotten.[24]

Public reaction to the removal of troops from Louisiana and South Carolina was largely positive at the time. *International Review* assessed his southern policy and lamented that "certain acts of the present Chief Executive . . . have been the occasion of some party dissatisfaction and some individual complaint, for neither of which, in the light of the supreme law of the land, does there appear to be any just occasion." Walter Allen of the *Atlantic Monthly* noted that Hayes's sympathies likely lay with Packard and Chamberlain, but his decisions were positive nevertheless. After all, "during the past two years the Southern States have been more peaceful, more prosperous, and on the whole more tolerant" than they had been during Reconstruction. Another columnist for that magazine, Theodore Bacon, proclaimed the end of the war, saying "the greatest revolution in history has been accomplished" and Hayes deserved credit for finishing it.[25]

Of course, not all Americans were satisfied with the end of Reconstruction, especially after southern Democrats repeatedly broke their political promises. How much culpability did Rutherford B. Hayes deserve for the unsatisfying end of the Reconstruction experiment? Many Americans thought he deserved quite a bit; the whispers about "His Fraudulency" lasted his entire presidency and survived into the history of his administration. There can be little doubt that Hayes merely submitted to an inevitable outcome: "the Civil War period in American history was definitely ended," and the president had "executed the national will" in ending federal occupation of the South. He also faced the considerable problem of having to deal with Grant's legacy: the former President's actions on this matter had left him little room to maneuver.[26]

Summary

Hayes's record during this period was thus decidedly mixed. He had had great success in organizing his government: his selections of a liberal Republican and a southern Democrat to fill key posts were important gestures to a party and a nation that needed healing in the days following such a contested election. However, his efforts at reassuring African-American constituents in the White House of his good intentions were an abject failure, and it did not speak well of his intentions in keeping promises for other important Republican groups. Hayes spoke of his commitment to black civil rights in several remarks during his first days in office, but he ended up ceding power in the South to groups that had no intention of protecting these vulnerable citizens. Jeffrey Tulis notes that Hayes made more speeches than any of his presidential predecessors, but he rarely if ever spoke on important policy matters.[27] Perhaps his experience with the South convinced him that making policy statements would be a bad idea, since such speeches remained on the public record.

Above all, Hayes profoundly misjudged southern Democrats: they had promised him certain actions would be taken, and he naively "had come to associate with and expect from Southern gentlemen" a certain "chivalry and high honor" they would never show to blacks. "Hayes was a victim of his own antebellum education and inherited beliefs. He had a passion for social harmony at a time when fierce regional, partisan, religious, ethnic, class, and racial tensions bitterly divided Americans."[28] Rutherford B. Hayes was a good man in a bad situation, and this problem affected his entire presidency.

HARRISON: THE PRICE OF BEING A REPUBLICAN MAVERICK

One positive that would come from Hayes's decisions regarding the South would greet Benjamin Harrison on his election to the presidency. The end of Reconstruction ended debate on this issue, precluding such a problem from facing Harrison as he took office. Another important difference was that Harrison faced no official challenge to his presidential credentials. The far different atmosphere of Washington in 1888-1889 can best be seen in an anecdote from the Harrison inauguration. While the Republican took the oath of office in a driving rainstorm on the Capitol, outgoing Democrat Grover Cleveland "good-naturedly held his umbrella over the bared head of his successor." There were also warning signs present. Republicans controlled both chambers of Congress by small margins, but House members still "complained bitterly of the insolence with which they were treated by the employees of the Senate." In addition, the procession to the east portico of the Capitol became "an unseemly scramble" because of poor planning.[29] Harrison did not face a bitterly divided country, but all was not perfect as he became president.

His political philosophy was clear from the start, and it showed how different government in the 1800s was from its modern counterpart. Because he thought that the people should be allowed to make their own laws, "he based his political philosophy on the premise that: 'to govern best is to govern least.'" He was, and set out to be, the perfect example of Tulis's "old way" of presidential governance and rhetoric. Some of his political foes, of course, played up his silence on many issues, noting that "Senators call and say their say to him, and he stands silent. . . . As one Senator says: 'It's like talking to a hitching post.'" However, he also made 296 speeches during his term, *more* than any other previous president. As was the norm, most of those speeches were delivered on three tours he made of the country, but he nevertheless "attempted to introduce policy discussion into the tour," no matter how bad he may have been at doing so.[30] How did this new, yet still conservative, style of leadership emerge in Harrison's transition and first weeks as President?

Early Talk of Nominations

The focus of the news media and the politicians, as always, turned to his nominations for offices, both at the cabinet level and for other federal offices. As had long been the case, Republican senators and state party bosses expected to control the selection of their president's top advisors, since they had been so instrumental in electing him. However, as with Hayes, the new party leader showed surprising backbone and bucked much of the pressure he received from those men, choosing to "drive the elephant" himself.[31]

This did not mean that he would ignore the various factions of his party. In fact, an uproar came early in the transition when word leaked to the press that Harrison had nominated of Senator James G. Blaine of Maine as secretary of state. Blaine had barely lost the presidency to Cleveland in 1884, and his support had been a crucial factor in Harrison's securing of the nomination four years later. In the days following the 26 January leak, the press launched "an avalanche of criticism" at the president-elect, calling Blaine the "Premier" of the new administration and lamenting the possibility that he might corrupt Harrison's judgment.[32]

Another appointment that caused a good bit of controversy for Harrison came when he tapped wealthy Pennsylvania businessman John Wanamaker to be Postmaster General. He had raised a great deal of money for the Republican ticket in 1888, both from his private funds and donations from fellow manufacturers. Some of his money had gone for somewhat questionable purposes, and his political opponents cried that there had been a *quid pro quo* in the new administration.[33] Despite such vehement criticism, Harrison stood firm, and the Senate quickly confirmed all of Harrison's Cabinet appointments before it adjourned for the summer. Wanamaker became a non-descript postmaster whose eccentricities provided gossip for the newspapers, while Blaine became a distinguished leader of the State Department. No matter the merits of his selections, however, Harrison managed to ignore "almost every prominent Republican" in making his choices. By doing so, "he alienated those leaders who had hoped to be in the cabinet" and upset those who had hoped to give advice to the president-elect. He had not even been inaugurated, but Benjamin Harrison had sown the seeds of his demise in 1892.[34]

Setting a Tone

Harrison's Cabinet selections marked him as a man that would be independent from traditional Republican factions. In addition, he had ample opportunity during his transition, particularly at scheduled events, to make his views on numerous subjects known. Charles O. Jones's study of transitions notes that modern presidents have often thought of the press as a "mouthpiece" or "window" that the president-elect can use to make his voice heard on policy matters. Harrison's experience shows that these are not new ideas. For example, he hosted a New Year's party in Indianapolis at which 2,000 people greeted him and his wife. The media covered the event, and though the gathering was not "public" in the strictest sense, the President-elect still used the occasion to champion the voting rights of southern blacks. He particularly wanted a "bugle-call throughout the land demanding a pure ballot."[35] His words aroused a negative reaction from some Republicans (and most Democrats), but he did not retract them. It was a good example of a president-elect putting an item on the national agenda through the media. No one was entirely sure what Harrison's commitment to black suffrage in the South truly meant, but his words stirred debate nevertheless.

As part of this debate, black ministers called on Harrison in Indianapolis several times in January 1889; though the president-elect gave the men no guarantees, he did give "an attentive hearing to their impassioned plea" for black rights. Of course, they were not the only people to call on the next president. Applicants for federal jobs, Civil War veterans, and businessmen besieged his office and home, as they did with any incoming administration, particularly since the White House was passing from a Democrat to a Republican. In these meetings, he had much less to say to his callers, which left "the public unable to focus its views."[36]

A Strong Inaugural

Clarification of his views would come only when President Harrison delivered his inaugural address on 4 March. His public-speaking skills were quite considerable, according to those that heard him speak. "His oratory was marked by ease and finish, and a certain geniality of tone which by no means belonged to his ordinary conversation." His first speech as President combined that understated, polished style with discussion of serious policy matters. He would not initiate legislation, though; his political philosophy was too Whiggish to allow for that. What he did indicate were some of his presidential preferences, including the development of a stronger navy, a high protective tariff to encourage domestic manufacturing, and stricter enforcement of present regulatory laws. Harrison also advocated a moderate position on civil-service reform: party men would not be disqualified from government positions, but they had to perform well in doing their jobs. It was a fine speech according to all who heard it, thus getting the Harrison administration off to a fine start and proving what one close friend said about the president's oratory: "Harrison can make a speech to ten thousand men, and every man of them will go away his friend. Let him meet the same ten thousand men in private, and every one will go away his enemy."[37]

Dealing with the "Bosses"

Harrison had delivered his inaugural address and formed his cabinet with the approval of the Senate, but there was still controversy that lay ahead, for many ambassadorships, ministries, and other government jobs had yet to be filled. Advice came from all corners about what to do. (It should be noted that because of his deference to legislative superiority on domestic policy, such matters could monopolize Harrison's time in the first weeks of the administration.) During his first months in the White House, Harrison spent most of his time dealing with mail and visits concerning the civil service, and he "considered the political implications of each and every appointment." The clamor for offices was especially bad from states that Harrison had carried narrowly in the 1888 election. New York, for example, had voted for Harrison by a margin of 13,002 votes out of 1,315,409 cast.[38] The bosses of that state, therefore, thought their claims for offices should be especially important to the president.

President Harrison, however, made it clear in his first Cabinet meeting on 7 March that he intended to stay in control of his administration and "would reserve to himself the final decision as to the character and fitness of every appointee." In other words, there would be no informal advisers acting as "gatekeepers" for the president, and "machine" considerations would not enter into his thinking. Senators used to the old spoils system "decided to test the President's sincerity" by presenting him with lists of prospective appointees that he was expected to approve. The Republican senators from Pennsylvania, Matt Quay and J. Donald Cameron, were the first to probe the president's weaknesses, but Harrison stood firm. His reasoning was particularly interesting: he claimed that "no matter whom senators might recommend or what the Senate might do in the way of confirmation, if an appointee turned out badly, the President, not the senators or the Senate, would be held responsible."[39] In short, Harrison claimed to be the sole representative of the entire American population, and he would not let forces beyond his control run his presidency.

Harrison's negative response to Cameron and Quay can be considered in a success or a failure, depending on one's perspective. It was an impressive display of presidential mettle and a surprisingly modern view of the president's representative powers, especially considering that Harrison had earned fewer popular votes than the Democratic candidate had in 1888. On the other hand, it was dangerous for the president to antagonize powerful party men as he did. The nomination and campaign systems of the 19th century were not conducive to men who tried to buck convention and change the system. It would have been hard enough for presidents who had won landslide victories to challenge the civil-service system, but Harrison had no margin for error as he began his administration. His responses to powerful seekers of patronage, therefore, were either admirable or suicidal.

The Halstead Affair

Other nominations were contentious for similar reasons. The Senate's implacable hostility to the president's ideas on the civil service affected those close to Harrison, and this were never more apparent than when Harrison selected Murat Halstead to become minister plenipotentiary to Germany. Halstead was the editor of Cincinnati's *Commercial Gazette*, the city's major Republican newspaper, and Harrison considered him a particularly close friend and loyal supporter. There were also more concrete policy objectives at work for the president. German Prime Minister Otto von Bismarck had wanted to make the Samoan Islands, in which the United States had commercial interests, into a protectorate, and a threat of war was in the air as a conference on the matter was set to begin in Berlin on 29 April. Harrison wanted "a strong and implacable fighter" for American interests in Germany, and he thought Halstead to be that man. Unfortunately for the President, the Senate thought differently. Differences on policy matters were not the problem with Halstead, however.

Halstead had been a vocal critic of corruption in politics, especially in the case of Ohio Senator Henry B. Payne. The legislature had sent Payne to the Senate several years earlier, and a subsequent investigation revealed that Standard Oil had bribed a number of legislators to secure Payne's Senate seat. A new legislature in Columbus sent evidence from this investigation to Washington in hopes of starting a full inquiry and eventually unseating Payne. Senatorial courtesy and matters of honor dictated that Payne should welcome such an inquiry, but he did not, and the Senate refused to investigate. Halstead's *Commercial Gazette* had been a vocal critic of the Senate in the Payne affair, and many senators remembered his barbs. They took this opportunity to send a message to Halstead (and the president) by rejecting the editor for the ministry to Germany.[40]

The Senate's action in this case touched off a firestorm of criticism in the press, as editors stood up for their rejected colleague. Democrat Henry Watterson of Louisville's *Courier-Journal* supported his Republican counterpart, stating that the fate of the Halstead appointment "carries with it primarily a warning from the Senate to the press of the country to look to its utterances when dealing with that body or any of its members." Senator John C. Spooner of Wisconsin, who had supported Halstead, made a similar point in his speeches on the Senate floor. Had Harrison wanted to appoint Halstead to the post in Germany without the Senate's approval, he could have done so. Public sentiment was with the president. However, as much as the rejection hurt the President personally, he dropped the Halstead matter. For one, he knew that Halstead was an excitable man whose presence in Berlin might not help the already tense situation between the two countries. More importantly, however, "he preferred to hold to the rule that Executive appointments be made by and with the advice and consent of the Senate, which was responsible for judging a nominee's competency, fitness, and character."[41] Harrison strongly supported the limited, conservative presidency of the Founders, and he quietly appointed former Representative William Walter Phelps to the German ministry after Phelps helped the United States score a major victory for American interests at the Berlin conference on Samoa.

Summary

In short, Harrison pressed his tough stance on the civil service only to a point. Because of his support for the strong legislature and weak executive that reigned at this time in the American system, Harrison could not afford to have problems with Congress. He was therefore flexible enough to allow the Senate to reject a less qualified choice for an especially important diplomatic post. He needed to be flexible particularly because the American populace was so evenly divided at the time of his election. The Republicans held a small majority in the House and a somewhat larger advantage in the Senate, and Harrison's presence in the White House allowed congressional leaders to make the 51st Congress one of the most active to date. Nor was Harrison's influence limited to signing bills like the McKinley Tariff Act or the Sherman Antitrust Act. His ability to get along with congressional leaders allowed the president to use informal dinners or receptions to "let them know about specific items that he would need in order for him to sign certain bills. He [even] used a threat of veto on some measures, although his actual vetoes were few."[42]

The Republicans' ability to pass most of the major planks of their 1888 platform should have given Harrison a solid record on which to stand in 1892. Indeed, he easily won renomination in 1892 at the Republican convention in Minneapolis. There were signs of trouble for Harrison, however, and they could be traced back to his first days in office and his impolitic stance on civil service appointments. One of the major party leaders who opposed his nomination was Matthew Quay of Pennsylvania, who controlled the party in that state and was determined to use the power of the national party against the incumbent president. Harrison had to recognize trouble in the vote on his renomination, since 364 convention votes were cast for either Blaine (who had resigned his post as Secretary of State to run for the nomination) or Governor (and later president) William McKinley of Ohio. New York, Pennsylvania, and Ohio delegates had gone against President Harrison strongly, and their defection signaled major political trouble in the 1892 campaign. Despite Harrison's success on several important foreign and domestic issues, his antagonism toward the party bosses caused him major problems in the campaign, and he lost his bid for re-election to Cleveland by a margin of over 400,000 popular votes and a 277-145 electoral count.[43]

CONCLUSION: LESSONS LEARNED?

How do these examples from the distant past of the American political system matter to the present? The answer is simple: the current occupant of the White House has much in common with his predecessors. George W. Bush became the forty-third President of the United States in January 2001 with 271 electoral votes, compared with 267 for Democrat Al Gore. This win came despite the fact that Bush polled 400,000 fewer votes than Gore. The outcome hinged on popular-vote totals in the state of Florida, with the U.S. Supreme Court halting Democratic efforts to include a set of disputed ballots in the final tally. This electoral contest (and the closeness of the election itself) was the result of many factors, but one factor has particular resonance for historical and political scientists. The United States is unique among Western nations in that the indirect mechanism of the Electoral College, not direct popular sentiment, determines who the nation's leader will be. Changes to this system are unlikely, but the 2000 presidential election has caused Americans to realize that this system, and not necessarily their votes, elects our presidents.

With this admittedly cursory examination of the two minority presidents who preceded this nation's most recent example, it is clear that comparisons between Rutherford B. Hayes and George W. Bush are tough to make. Hayes's situation was far more contentious than that which faces President Bush. Not only did Hayes have the specter of the Electoral Commission's decision weighing on him, but his administration had committed itself to the difficult task of ending Reconstruction policies on terms with which North and South could live. His success in these matters was ambiguous at best: American troops were removed from the South without incident, but policies that protected blacks in Louisiana and South Carolina also ended. The problem for Hayes was that he had been quoted in the press saying that the rights of southern blacks would be an important priority during his presidency. Such a public contradiction of principle was not good for a president who needed to convince the American people that his administration was legitimate. It also overshadowed the effect his appointment of political opponents, both from his own party and the opposition, to high offices was intended to have.

President Bush's situation does not resemble Hayes's dilemma in any significant way. There are more noticeable parallels, however, with Benjamin Harrison's presidency. Like Bush, Harrison faced a deeply divided electorate that had given Republicans the White House and both houses of Congress by narrow majorities. Like Bush, some of Harrison's earliest appointments caused some serious controversy because of the complaints of certain powerful interest groups. (One must note here, however, that the comparison is not completely valid. The interests in Harrison's case worried little about the policy consequences of their actions, and each of Bush's cabinet appointments, even controversial Attorney General John Ashcroft, was eventually confirmed.) Finally, both Harrison and Bush did not let the narrow nature of their victories prevent them from acting boldly on issues about which they cared deeply. For Harrison, continued emphasis on reform of the civil service was essential, despite opposition from powerful senators and party leaders. Bush indicated that the dispensation of the federal surplus for tax cuts is a top priority, and much of the nation seems to agree with him, despite his minority status.

One aspect of the Harrison example is a cautionary tale: despite the government's strong legislative agenda, Harrison's antagonistic attitude toward party leaders cost him their support (and eventually the White House) in his bid for reelection. The comparison is not strict: major changes in the process of selecting candidates for the presidency have made the process far more popularly centered. Incumbent presidents generally do not face primary challenges in reelection campaigns, and they command the full cooperation of their parties. Bush, therefore, is not likely to face a major uprising among Republican leaders in 2004 unless a major economic recession faces the country at the time of the campaign. However, Harrison's example does show that minority presidents have no margin for error in the American political system. The chances that their electoral status will be used against them are high, so any mistakes the president makes will be magnified, particularly as media coverage has become more intense. President Bush's margin of victory was so small (and controversial) that he cannot afford the bold sort of move that Harrison made in attacking civil-service conventions. If such moves backfire, the minority president is in trouble.

How has President Bush dealt with these problems in his early days? He appears to have heeded the advice of political scientists like James P. Pfiffner, who cautions that a new president should "hit the ground running," fairly well. His plan for cutting taxes has not escaped from Congress without changes, but he has fundamentally changed the nature of the debate, persuading Democrats to accept far deeper cuts than they had previously wanted. Like Harrison, he has made a concerted effort to forge personal relationships with influential congressional leaders of both parties. Bush has also weathered the first major international crisis of his presidency with positive results. Some caution that Bush sacrificed too much to secure the return of twenty-four crew members from a U.S. spy plane that landed in China in March 2001, but such criticism is fairly small-scale. It remains to be seen whether Bush's actions on smaller issues, like the easing of environmental restrictions, will prove to be political mistakes. However, an early assessment of Bush's record indicates strong performance on important issues.

Lyn Ragsdale has forlornly noted that "on occasion, historians remind presidents about what past chief executives have accomplished," while political scientists have largely been ignored.[44] The circumstances surrounding the election of the newest president show that if George W. Bush is to succeed, he must consult both groups of scholars. The cases of the two most recent minority presidents show that his chances for success, historically and politically, are not great. Rutherford B. Hayes and Benjamin Harrison each served only one term in office, and polls that rank American chief executives place these two men near the bottom of the list.[45]

The similarity between historical assessments of these minority presidents could call for a more sophisticated distinction between "mistakes" that a president can make. One type, the "historical mistake," is not necessarily costly for the president politically, but is instead a bad long-term decision for the country that brings about problems for his successors. Hayes made such a mistake in selling out his southern black constituency. He may have won praise from politicians, but this decision led (directly or indirectly) to decades of racial strife with which Americans still deal today. Harrison's mistakes, on the other hand, were "political." He was a good steward of the nation, and his leadership allowed a number of important laws to come to fruition. However, he was a political failure in antagonizing much of his own party's leadership during his term. This caused his re-election bid to be doomed almost from the outset. Perhaps such a distinction between "historical" and "political" mistakes can explain why these different politicians are each regarded as presidential failures.

No matter how one explains these different administrations, first impressions certainly count, and analyzing what these men did in their transitions and first days in office can reveal a great deal about why they are not remembered well. The comparisons one draws between Hayes, Harrison, and Bush cannot be precise for several reasons, the most important being the nature of the office in modern times. The American people in general (and the Congress in particular) expect a modern President to do far more than the electorate expected of a late 19th-century President. However, each has "gone public" in their first days as chief executive to express their positions on important issues. The cautionary examples of Hayes and Harrison can still be of use to America's most recent minority chief executive and those that want him to succeed.

POSTSCRIPT: IS *BUSH V. GORE* MOOT?

The research for this paper was completed in April 2001. Since this paper was first written, much has changed, both in the political arena and in the wider world. First, many legal scholars, reporters, and political pundits published an avalanche of material on matters great and small concerning the 2000 campaign. The most important group of books, for our purposes, either supported or criticized the Supreme Court's decision on 12 December 2000, ruling in favor of the Bush campaign and, in effect, ending the contested presidential election. The pro-Gore forces, in particular, included many prominent commentators and were particularly vehement in their views, calling *Bush v. Gore* a "criminal" and reckless decision.[46] There was by no means any consensus on this matter. American University law professor Jamin Raskin compared *Bush v. Gore* unfavorably with the Dred Scott decision of 1857. George Mason University law professor Peter Berkowitz and journalist Benjamin Wittes countered Raskin's scathing remarks, criticizing many liberal law academics for overly hyperbolic claims about the validity of the Supreme Court's decision in what was, they claim, a very tough decision.[47]

This debate might have captured the nation's attention and sparked a great deal of controversy, had the events of 11 September 2001 not intervened and cast a pall over any such arguments. The collapse of the World Trade Center, the destruction of parts of the Pentagon, and the war against Afghanistan have since dominated news coverage of the President, and his approval ratings have gone from 50 or 55 percent before the tragedy to 85 or 90 percent after it. There has been no talk of the President as an "illegitimate" leader. In fact, some supporters of the vanquished Vice President have expressed surprising sentiments as events have unfolded throughout the world. *Newsweek/MSNBC* reporter Howard Fineman, in talking with some unnamed (yet highly-placed) Gore operatives from the election, reveals that most of these Democrats are secretly pleased their candidate is not the current occupant of the White House. Some express pleasure with the president's performance, while others "have realized that Bush has far more political room to maneuver at home than Al Gore would have had. With his reasonably good ties to the conservative, pro-military wing of his party, the president has been able to both talk tough and take his time." The most important reason for their relief, however, is more basic. Because the likely perpetrator of the 11 September attacks, Osama bin Laden, was a threat to the United States during the Clinton-Gore administration, "former Gore lieutenants think their man might have been seriously hampered as a war leader, at least in this war at this time, by the controversies and personalities of the past. . . . The papers these days are full of stories from the Clinton era about what was, or was not, done to make the country more secure—or to capture or kill bin Laden and his terrorist cells."[48]

Obviously, the terms of the debate over the election and the legitimacy of the current President have taken a turn that the presidencies of Rutherford B. Hayes and Benjamin Harrison never took. These men never faced such a crisis, nor did they have the approval numbers Bush now has. However, the relief of Gore supporters does not mean there will not continue to be a debate over *Bush v. Gore*. The debate may become more academic in nature now, though. Legal scholar Jeffrey Toobin may have inadvertently created the new paradigm for this argument with his book *Too Close to Call*. After reviewing the same evidence as other scholars, he concludes that Gore should have been elected if each voter going to the polls in Florida on 7 November had voted as they wanted to vote that day. He does *not* say that one side or the other "stole" the election or that Bush is an "illegitimate" ruler. He does say that "the wrong man was inaugurated on January 20, 2001, and that is no small thing in our nation's history."[49] Whatever one thinks of the conclusion, it is a far cry from the virulent, passionate conclusions of observers prior to 11 September. If a debate about Bush's "legitimacy" is to continue in the future, it will likely do so in a far less polarized environment.

NOTES

[1] Charles O. Jones, *Passages to the Presidency: From Campaigning to Governing* (Washington: Brookings Institution Press, 1998): 7.

[2] Paul Light, *The President's Agenda: Domestic Policy Choice from Kennedy to Reagan*, rev. ed. (Baltimore: Johns Hopkins UP, 1991): 36-37.

[3] James P. Pfiffner, *The Strategic Presidency: Hitting the Ground Running*, rev. 2nd ed. (Lawrence: University Press of Kansas, 1996): 6-7.

[4] Jones: 15.

[5] One other example of a "minority" president existed in the nineteenth century: in 1824, John Qunicy Adams defeated Andrew Jackson and two other candidates for the presidency in an election that the House of Representatives decided when none of the candidates received a majority of the electoral vote. The parallels with the situation of George W. Bush are striking: both Adams and Bush followed their fathers into the White House, and each dealt with charges of impropriety in their elections (in Adams's case, many Jackson supporters thought House Speaker Henry Clay had unfairly thrown his support to Adams in exchange for a promise to appoint Clay Secretary of State after the election). However, there are two striking differences that make comparison on this basis difficult. First, in 1876 and 1888, the popular vote in each state was the determining factor for awarding all of that state's electoral votes to one candidate or another. This was the culmination of a trend toward giving this power to a state's voters; in 1824, that process had yet to be completed, and several states (most prominently South Carolina) cast their electoral votes via the state legislature or other indirect balloting. Second, not all white males in the United States were eligible to vote in 1824, as they would be in future elections. Therefore, saying that Adams received fewer popular votes than Andrew Jackson does not mean what it would in the Hayes and Harrison examples.

[6] For a comprehensive history of the 1876 election and the contests that followed, see Paul Leland Haworth, *The Hayes-Tilden Disputed Presidential Election of 1876* (Cleveland: Burrows Brothers Press, 1906); and C. Vann Woodward, *Reunion and Reaction: The Compromise of 1877 and the End of Reconstruction* (Garden City, NY: Doubleday Anchor Books, 1956).

[7] For an account of the 1888 election, see Harry Thurston Peck, *Twenty Years of the Republic: 1885-1905* (New York: Dodd, Mead and Company, 1907): 152-164.

[8] Haworth: 38.

[9] Peck: 304.

[10] H.J. Eckenrode, *Rutherford B. Hayes: Statesman of Reunion* (Port Washington, N.Y.: Kennikat Press, 1930): 236.

[11] Harry Barnard, *Rutherford B. Hayes and His America* (Indianapolis: The Bobbs-Merrill Company, 1954): 399, 407.

[12] Ibid., 413.

[13] There was no better indication of the continued bitterness of many Democrats over Hayes's election than the action of party leaders in Ohio, Hayes's home state. Democrats in the state legislature passed a resolution condemning his accession to the presidency, and (in a more

amusing vein) there was great excitement in Columbus when it appeared Samuel Tilden would pay them a visit. He did not make the visit, however; the crowd that had gathered listened to a speech from a House member who had attempted to block Hayes's election instead. "Indecency of Ohio Democrats," *New York Times* 4 March 1877: 1, 4th column; "Ohio Democrats Disgusted," *NYT* 8 March 1877: 5, 2nd column.

[14] Eckenrode: 241; Ari Hoogenboom, *Rutherford B. Hayes: Warrior and President* (Lawrence: University Press of Kansas, 1995): 296.

[15] Barnard: 414; Eckenrode: 244.

[16] Barnard: 417-418; Hoogenboom: 296.

[17] Samuel Kernell, *Going Public: New Strategies of Presidential Leadership*, 3rd ed. (Washington: Congressional Quarterly Press, 1997): 2.

[18] "The President Sustained By the Republicans of North Carolina—Meeting of Citizens of Schenectady," *NYT* 11 March 1877: 1, 3rd column; "Democrats of Memphis Indorsing the President's Southern Policy—Meeting of Business Men at the Cotton Exchange," *NYT* 11 March 1877: 1, 3rd column; "Standing By Hayes, ," *NYT* 11 March 1877: 7, 5th column.

[19] "The Southern Question: Policy of the Administration," *NYT* 15 March 1877: 4, 7th column.

[20] "Colored Men at the White House," *NYT* 24 March 1877: 1, 2nd column.

[21] Nor was this the only case in which the President transmitted his message to the American people through coverage of public meetings with constituents. He thanked a group of German citizens who visited him on 20 March for their kind words on the appointment of Interior Secretary Schurz and noted that "a great portion of my life was spent among people of your nationality" as Ohio's governor. "The President and the Germans," *NYT* 21 March 1877: 1, 2nd column.

[22] Hoogenboom: 307.

[23] Eckenrode: 247.

[24] Barnard: 432.

[25] "The Southern Policy of the President," *International Review* 4.38 (September 1877): 686; Walter Allen, "Two Years of President Hayes," *Atlantic Monthly* 44.262 (August 1879): 192-194 (quote on 194); Theodore Bacon, "The End of the War," *Atlantic Monthly* 47.281 (March 1881): 400.

[26] Barnard: 432.

[27] Jeffrey K. Tulis, *The Rhetorical Presidency*. (Princeton: Princeton UP, 1987): 66, 84.

[28] Hoogenboom: 310-318; Kenneth E. Davison, *The Presidency of Rutherford B. Hayes* (Westport, CT: Greenwood Press, 1972): 143.

[29] Peck: 167.

[30] Tulis: 66, 86; Harry J. Sievers, *Benjamin Harrison, Hoosier President: The White House and After, 1889-1901* (Indianapolis: The Bobbs-Merrill Company, 1968): 43.

[31] Sievers: 6.

[32] Ibid.: 9-12. Not all observers thought Harrison's choice of Blaine was one which Harrison wished to make. Harry Thurston Peck states that "the President had practically no choice in the matter; and therefore, as it appeared, with reluctance and somewhat sullenly, he offered the portfolio of State to Mr. Blaine." Peck: 173.

[33] Peck: 175.

[34] Homer E. Socolofsky and Allen B. Spetter, *The Presidency of Benjamin Harrison* (Lawrence, KS: University Press of Kansas, 1987): 23, 29.

[35] Jones: 135; Sievers: 27.

[36] Sievers: 29.

[37] Peck: 166-168, 170; Sievers: 34-36; Socolofsky and Spetter: 47; "Under a New President," *NYT* 5 March 1889: 3, 7th column.

[38] Socolofsky and Spetter: 15.

[39] Sievers: 41, 42.

[40] Ibid.: 47; Peck: 194-195.

[41] Sievers: 47-48.
[42] Socolofsky and Spetter: 48.
[43] Ibid.: 195-198.
[44] Lyn Ragsdale, "Studying the Presidency: Why Presidents Need Political Scientists," in Michael Nelson, ed., *The Presidency and the Political System*, 5th ed. (Washington: Congressional Quarterly Press, 1996): 29.
[45] Donald McCoy, "Chicago Sun-Times Poll," *Presidential Studies Quarterly* 26 (1996): 281-283. Hayes ranked 27th in the poll McCoy studies, while Harrison placed 31st.
[46] For pro-Gore books, see Vincent Bugliosi, *The Betrayal of America: How the Supreme Court Undermined our Constitution and Chose Our President* (New York: Nation Books, 2001); Jake Tapper, *Down and Dirty: The Plot to Steal the Presidency* (Boston: Little, Brown, 2001); Alan M. Dershowitz, *Supreme Injustice: How the High Court Hijacked Election 2000* (Oxford: Oxford UP: 2001). For pro-Bush books, see Bill Sammon, *At Any Cost: How Al Gore Tried to Steal the Election* (Washington: Regenry Publishing, 2001); Timothy Montrose, *Democracy's Biggest Test: The 2000 Presidential Election* (n.p.: iUniverse.com, 2001); Richard A. Posner, *Breaking the Deadlock: The 2000 Election, the Constitution, and the Courts* (Princeton, NJ: Princeton UP, 2001). The sheer volume of articles on the 2000 election preclude selecting a representative sample that does any justice to the spectrum of opinion.
[47] Jamin Raskin, "Bandits in Black Robes: Why you should still be angry about *Bush v. Gore*," *Washington Monthly* 32.3 (March 2001): http://www.washingtonmonthly.com/features/2001/0103.raskin.html; Peter Berkowitz, "The Professors and *Bush v. Gore*," *Wilson Quarterly* 25.4 (Autumn 2001): http://wwics.si.edu/outreach/wq/wqselect/berk.htm.
[48] Howard Fineman, "Gore Loyalists are Relieved that Bush is the Man," *Newsweek* 5 November 2001: 51.
[49] Jeffrey Toobin, *Too Close to Call: The Thirty-six Day Battle to Decide the 2000 Election* (New York: Random House, 2001): 265.

The Challenge of Governing

Chapter 5

SEPARATING RHETORIC FROM POLICY: SPEECHWRITING UNDER GERALD FORD AND JIMMY CARTER

Karen M. Hult and Charles E. Walcott

INTRODUCTION

Much of the modern presidency is about words. From major and minor speeches to messages and remarks, presidents must govern in part by communicating. Inspirational speeches can help galvanize the public behind the president's program. Inept speeches can raise doubts about an administration's purposes or competence. In many cases, these communications are intended not just as attractive rhetoric, but also as statements of policy, settled or proposed. Accurate and compelling articulation of policy ideas is critical to presidential leadership. This means that speeches must not only sound good, but must reflect the president's substantive goals and political purposes. Thus the crafting of the president's words and the deciding of policy and political strategy are intimately intertwined – or at least they ought to be. One of the ongoing challenges in structuring the White House during the modern presidency has been how exactly to join these strands, words and policy, in a timely and effective manner.[1]

The sheer volume of rhetorical demand forced presidents, starting with Lyndon Johnson, to incorporate full-time speechwriters in the White House Office staff. But this posed new problems for the integration of policy and strategy into presidential speeches, since now the writers and decision-makers were seldom the same people. Beginning in the Johnson administration, a gap emerged between the two.[2] Writers too often felt inadequately informed about policy, and their speeches sometimes showed it. Communication between writers and policy-makers, including the President, failed to consistently bridge the gap. The challenge, at least in part, was to organize the White House for this new task, and LBJ's people never quite succeeded. But Johnson was reluctant to fully confront the need for structural reform of his White House organization.[3]

Richard Nixon, by contrast, initially seemed aware of the need to fit words and policies together. During his first term, he crafted and sustained a productive relationship among himself, his top policy and political advisers, and his staff of speechwriters. To some extent, this reflected the President's sensitivity to issues of organization, developed in large part during his service in the Eisenhower administration. Communication between Nixon and writers such as William Safire, Ray Price, and Pat Buchanan was effective, and no substantial gap between policy and rhetoric surfaced. But in Nixon's second term, most of the writers became more remote both from the President and from his senior aides. As Watergate obsessed the White House and the top writers left or took on specialized assignments, the writing operation began to show the pathologies that had plagued its predecessor.[4]

The discussion here examines the legacy of Johnson and Nixon for the structuring of presidential speechwriting by looking at both the Ford and Carter White Houses.[5] Gerald Ford inherited the basic structures of the Nixon White House along with some of its personnel, but he also arrived with a mandate to operate his White House differently from his predecessor. Jimmy Carter was at great pains to assure that his White House avoided the perceived pathologies of both the Nixon and Ford staffs. For Presidents Ford and Carter, the crucial matter of relating writing to policy turned out to be problematic.

This analysis will focus upon the consequences of three clusters of independent variables: the external environment of the White House, its internal organizational dynamics, and presidential choice.[6] First, aiming at description, we will examine the manner in which Ford and Carter structured their writing staffs. Second, pursuing both normative and analytic goals, we will assess and try to account for the extent to which they succeeded at integrating policy and associated political strategy with presidential rhetoric.

The first two sections sketch the structuring of speechwriting in the Ford and Carter White Houses, highlighting the difficulties each administration confronted as it struggled to assure that presidential rhetoric accurately reflected presidential policy goals and political strategy. This provides the basis for a more theoretical comparison of the two administrations. Discussion concludes by suggesting some of the broader implications of the analysis.

WRITING FOR GERALD R. FORD

The Ford administration inherited Nixon's writing unit, but rather quickly replaced almost all of its members. It also inherited the basic structural design of the Nixon White House, and, despite protestations to the contrary, left it mostly unchanged.

In the writing, or "editorial" area, Ford's main innovation was to charge one of his closest advisors, Counselor to the President Robert T. Hartmann, with overseeing the writing staff. This approach created a new level of hierarchy between the head of that staff – David Gergen, soon to be replaced by Paul Theis – and the President, yet it seemed to promise more rather than less access to political and policy decision-making due to Hartmann's stature. Beyond that, Ford maintained Nixon's "editorial office" structure, grouping writers with researchers, and typically assigning one of each per speech.

Hartmann, a former journalist and chief of Ford's congressional and vice-presidential staffs, was an accomplished speechwriter whose most memorable contribution to the presidency may well have been the phrase, "Our long, national nightmare is over." Yet his duties as Counselor were not limited to writing – which he did only on major speeches – or supervision of the Editorial Department staff of about a half-dozen writers and a supporting cast of researchers and others. Hartmann also inherited a general "politics" portfolio from outgoing Counselor Dean Burch (which mainly involved liaison with, for example, governors and the Republican National Committee) as well as the general expectation that he would be one of Ford's closest confidants on most matters.

Hartmann had the responsibility "to approve every single word that went out of the White House in the President's name[7] – with the exception of statements [Ford] authorized the Press Secretary to make."[8] This reinforced the notion that Hartmann's relationship to Ford would bridge the gap that had opened between writers and top policy people during Nixon's second term. Indeed, Hartmann instituted precisely the sort of communication that had been lacking. Most importantly, he routinely involved the writers in meetings with the President prior to the writers' work on particular speeches.[9] Hartmann or, often, Theis in his stead, attended daily Senior Staff meetings, and occasionally a writer was invited along.[10] If access to policy-makers had been the central problem for writers under Johnson and Nixon, the Ford administration seemed to have solved it.

Despite the apparent congruence of the Ford writing structure and the task at hand, the actual product, the President's speeches, drew constant and increasing criticism throughout his tenure. A number of explanations for this have been offered, including Ford's woodenness as a speaker and, possibly, less than sterling writing. Richard Reeves has suggested that Ford's bland speech style reflected his years in the congressional minority: he simply was not used to being widely heard, and therefore "did not understand the power of his presidential words."[11] Still, the complaints involved more than style – Ford's speeches too often lacked clear policy direction as well.[12] To account for this one must go beyond issues of writing talent. A key is to recognize that any single set of structural arrangements exists amidst a diversity of other, interacting structures.

Ford's structure for speechwriting existed in the context of an attempted "spokes of the wheel" White House organization. Multiple advisors would have roughly equal access to the Chief Executive, unimpeded by a strong, gatekeeping chief of staff. Environmental pressures probably left Ford little choice in this because of negative public and media reaction to Nixon's system and to his long-time chief of staff, H.R. Haldeman. Also relevant was Ford's own predilection. As a career legislator, Ford had little experience with or interest in leading a highly centralized staff. Yet the "spokes" approach, however compatible with Ford's preference for dealing with people rather than paper, and however responsive to calls for openness in the Administration, ultimately did not serve the President well.

The primary problem that emerged in the Ford White House involved organizational politics. Fierce rivalry erupted at the top, much of it between Hartmann and Donald Rumsfeld, Ford's "staff coordinator" and the closest thing to a chief of staff in the White House. Rumsfeld's efforts to control paper flow and harmonize the activities of the various staff units inevitably led to friction with Hartmann, who resisted any attempt to constrain his access to or influence over Ford. Moreover, Hartmann quickly grew to despise the numerous Nixon holdovers operating Rumsfeld's staff system as manipulative, power-hungry "Praetorians."[13] Early in the Administration, these conflicts resulted in Rumsfeld seeking to compete with Hartmann's staff in preparing and influencing major speeches, sometimes calling upon David Gergen (then in the Treasury Department) for assistance with alternative drafts.[14]

Hartmann fought back, using everything from his relationship with Ford to his newspaper contacts. But the acrimony helped distract Hartmann from his task of assuring that a relationship existed between writers and policy-makers. His attendance at Senior Staff meetings turned spotty, limiting his ability to provide policy guidance to the writers. For his part, Rumsfeld made no effort to work with the writing staff.

Even though the clash between Rumsfeld, the organizationally-minded, ambitious Nixon holdover, and the freewheeling, cantankerous Hartmann may have been inevitable, President Ford did little to help. Indeed, Hartmann versus Rumsfeld was only one of numerous White House rivalries; yet Ford seemed to permit them. Accustomed to conflict and compromise from his legislative days, Ford failed to keep rivalry within boundaries more appropriate to an administrative setting, where the premium placed on decision closure and conflict resolution typically is higher.

Staff tensions were not the only flaw in the Ford writing effort. A related problem – one that would surface regularly in succeeding White Houses – was the "staffing" of speeches. Early in the Ford administration, Rumsfeld had complained of inadequate staffing, that is, circulation of speech drafts to all persons concerned with the substance or impact of the speech. This failure, Rumsfeld argued, had produced "errors of fact and conflicts with previous presidential statements . . ."[15] Weak staffing had led to such things as Hartmann's insertion of the WIN ("Whip Inflation Now") slogan into a Ford speech that no one else saw before it was delivered.[16] After that episode, at Rumsfeld's behest, a formal system was instituted, with clearance forms attached routinely to drafts, requiring checkoffs by numerous aides. In essence, the system of staffing speeches used in the Nixon White House had resurfaced. Orderly staffing was a reasonable response to a real problem. In this case, though, the cure may have been worse than the disease. Staffing of speeches grew like a weed, sometimes involving as many as sixteen different advisors. A minor speech like Ford's remarks at a Christmas party for the White House press corps was cleared by eight different offices.[17] Not surprisingly, the staffing procedure generated multiple drafts filled with internal compromises. Speechwriter Pat Butler recalled the result:

> Ford and his staff assistants were being so careful that they just took everything controversial and politically upbeat out of his speeches. A bureaucracy had been established that did not serve the President's best interests.[18]

Casserly agreed that Ford's speeches were overstaffed. He described his feeling when sitting in a meeting where rival aides fought over language:

> I feel like a man watching an old tree being cut down. However weatherbeaten and battered, it seems to me that it has more integrity than the two men axing it down . . . Declarative sentences, filled with ifs, buts and maybes, become dishwater. The ringing pronunciations of a President become hollow sixty-word sentences, dangling with participles. [The staffers] have done their jobs -- protected their rear ends. In service to their President and their country, they have failed to communicate.[19]

Significantly, rhetorical analysis by Roderick Hart comports fully with the writers' assessment of Ford's speeches. Using a computerized language analysis program, Hart concluded that Ford's rhetoric was generally ineffective. Looking for an explanation beyond

Ford's limited rhetorical skills, Hart attributed the problem in part to the "lack of coordination" in the White House speechwriting process.[20]

Although excessive staffing has proven in more than one administration to be the speechwriters' bane, it need not be. Whatever the difficulties in the Nixon White House, no veteran of that organization has held up the speech staffing system for blame.[21] The problem in the Ford case was an underlying factor: policy dissensus. The writing of a speech is often an occasion for policy debate and crystallization. If the president has to articulate policy, he had better know what the policy is. Thus, the process of writing and editing speeches must either reflect a prior consensus on policy or be arranged in such a way as to produce one. It is here that the Ford administration most conspicuously failed.

Part of the problem, of course, stemmed from the continued jealousies and rivalries among top staff and cabinet officials. The staffing of a speech became an invitation to renewed argumentation and maneuvering. On major speeches, such as the 1976 State of the Union address, the battles could involve much of the White House. In this instance, Hartmann and his aides confronted Richard Cheney (Rumsfeld's successor), David Gergen, and the rest of the "Praetorians." Yet even on lesser speeches, the difficulty that the Ford administration had in finally resolving disputes and reaching closure on decisions caused problems for the writers. Kaye Pullen, exhausted from her battles over a July 1975 Ford speech to the NAACP, summed up the situation: "I am rewriting this thing because no one can make up his mind what we're supposed to say."[22] Obviously, such a process was unlikely to lead to crisp, compelling declarations of policy and purpose. Meanwhile, in the face of such ambiguity, writers frequently wound up as the unwilling fabricators of policy, simply to fill the voids caused by conflict and uncertainty.[23]

The key to the writing process was Hartmann. But staff tensions clearly took their toll on him as a manager. Although he met fairly routinely with the writing staffers, they tended to find the meetings unproductive. Regular sessions with department head Paul Theis were no more satisfactory.[24] Even the institution of regular meetings between writers and the President, presided over by Hartmann, were unhelpful. Gergen has attributed this to lack of advance preparation on the part of all concerned.[25] As Hartmann increasingly participated in staff infighting, and as policy decisions proved more difficult to make, he simply could not perform the task of linking his writers to policy in a way that would permit them to articulate it clearly.

As the 1976 campaign drew near and staff perceptions that the writing situation simply would not do crystallized, Hartmann's rival, Cheney, resolved to do something about it. Cheney had assured Hartmann that "wildcat" speechwriting in competition with Hartmann's staff would cease.[26] But Cheney now acted to legitimize the production of alternative speech drafts. He brought David Gergen back to the White House from the Treasury Department in December 1975 as his assistant with a mandate to write speeches.

At about the same time, responding both to similar dissatisfaction with Ford's speeches and to friction within the now thoroughly demoralized writing staff, Hartmann reorganized the editorial office. He replaced Theis with former joke writer Robert Orben, put the researchers in a separate unit under "political" aide Jack Calkins, and replaced most of the writers, including Pullen and Casserly.[27] Hartmann also resolved to take a more active role in the writing process himself.[28]

The effect of these changes is difficult to assess. According to Hartmann, the struggle over the 1976 State of the Union message, in which he for the most part prevailed, signaled a clear victory for Hartmann, if not for his staff. The next major task for the writers, in March 1976, was preparation of the President's Bicentennial speeches. Here, Hartmann clearly functioned as the head of a hierarchical writing structure, collecting many drafts, including one from Gergen, seeking additional input from sources outside the White House, and presenting the alternative drafts and ideas to Ford.

Three days later they came back with his unconditional surrender: "I have read – many good. I believe *you* should use your own judgment and have drafts prepared." ... After two years the President had learned by experience that one subordinate must be given sufficient authority to produce a speech . . .[29]

For his part, Gergen continued to write speeches and to press for better organization of overall campaign planning.[30] His presence at least produced a certain redundancy. Pat Butler, who eventually became second in command in the speech office under Orben, recalled meetings in which speeches would be reviewed by a group of about six, including the President, who spent an unusually large amount of time reviewing the details of these speeches. Usually there would be a draft from Gergen and another from our shop. The President would review the drafts and take what he wanted. He seemed to find some way to take something from both drafts. He always found a compromise that made all of the principals feel that their work was being appreciated.[31]

Nevertheless, Butler reported tension during the campaign. Once on a campaign plane Hartmann fired Butler and Cheney immediately rehired him.[32] At the same time, Gergen complained of disorganization and inadequate staffing on speeches.[33] Still, the pressure of the campaign allowed the Ford team to avoid some of the excessive staffing and editing that had characterized the earlier period.

In general, the structuring for speech in the Ford White House never succeeded in systematically linking the writers to those charged with setting and pursuing the Administration's policy objectives and political strategies. Such ties were difficult to forge and to sustain in a White House riven by disagreement and uncertainty, with few structural arrangements for debating and then resolving policy priorities and directions. Only toward the end of the Administration, during the campaign, did the President become consistently involved in adjudicating disputes and trying to rein in staff conflict.

WRITING FOR JIMMY CARTER

Jimmy Carter's White House organization did not differ fundamentally from that of his predecessor, since many White House units had become permanent parts of the institutional landscape, present at least since Nixon and often long before. Congressional relations, public liaison, the press office, the foreign and domestic policy staffs, and the counsel's office, for instance, had predictable structures and functions inherited from Carter's predecessors. Still, other elements of the White House still tended to vary from one administration to the next, largely as a result of perceived problems with previous versions.

Speechwriting was in the latter category. Ford's improvisation on Nixon's approach had not worked well, and Carter's people knew it. Indeed, the Carter transition team recommended not only abolishing the Hartmann role, which was done, but also cutting the writing staff to as few as three.[34] The unit finally was pruned to a normal complement of five or six writers and no researchers. Meanwhile, the political environment was demanding more, not less, rhetorical activity from the President and his administration than it had from its predecessors. Nonetheless, Carter chose to resist these demands by reducing his capacity to respond. Structurally, the major change was placing the writers in a hierarchy lodged in the press office, reporting to the President through Press Secretary Jody Powell.

Reducing the size of the writing staff reflected President Carter's relative indifference to (or perhaps even "suspicion" of) the process of having speeches written for him to deliver.[35] Prior to his presidential campaign, Carter had written his own speeches. Once he entered the White House and could no longer do that, he proved reluctant to expend much in the way of resources, including his own time and energy, on speeches. Predictably, the Carter speechwriting process began to show some of the pathologies familiar during the Ford era, including writers detached from policy-making and a lack of effective communication between the President and his writers.[36]

Placing the writing staff under one of Carter's closest aides, Powell, did not provide a workable mechanism for dealing with the problems that arose. Powell, as both press secretary and close confidant to the President, simply had too much else to do. He was considerably less attentive to the writers and their problems than Hartmann had been. As Powell put it, the writers "were and weren't the responsibility of the press office as we went along, depending on who you talked to and how people felt at the moment."[37] Upon reflection, the Press Secretary conceded that placing the writers under him was "not the correct decision," blaming the arrangement on both his desire to keep control of things and his experience in the campaign.[38] This decision, then, seems to have been born more of Powell's than of Carter's preference.

Without an effective conduit to the President, the writers concluded early on that their central problem was lack of access to both the policy process and Carter himself. Head speechwriter James Fallows had asked as early as January 1977 to be included in senior staff and cabinet meetings, and was met with a grudging reply from Carter: "OK - don't overdo it."[39] That response was optimistic: Fallows seldom saw the President and was largely isolated from policy decision settings. Indeed, congressional relations chief and Carter intimate Frank Moore guessed that "Fallows spent maybe an hour with the President all told."[40] For his part, Fallows complained that on those occasions he did meet with Carter, the advice he received was usually "vague."[41] The rest of the writers saw the President even less, if at all.

Given prior administrations' experiences, the result of this gap between policy and writing was predictable. As writer Caryl Conner put it in a memo to Fallows in August 1978:

> . . . it is difficult to write in a vacuum. Speechwriters should sit in on policy discussions related to the substance of their assignments. This eliminates the problem of "writing blind," and of loaded or incomplete reporting by one party to the meeting. More important, the exposure makes the writer familiar with the thinking behind the decisions.[42]

Conner, who had written speeches for corporate executives as well as for Senator Hubert Humphrey, lamented the lack of access to the President, arguing:

> Ghostwriting is an esoteric art requiring psychological transference as well as subject-matter expertise. I can't get into the head of Jimmy Carter because I've never met Jimmy Carter.[43]

To remedy these failures, Conner proposed an arrangement in which writers would regularly sit in on policy discussions and have meetings with the President prior to drafting speeches. Fallows himself had made a similar recommendation the previous November.[44] Despite formal endorsement of these ideas from Powell and both domestic policy chief Stuart Eizenstat and national security aide Zbigniew Brzezinski, little or nothing came of it.

For the balance of the Administration, according to writer Chris Matthews, the best the writers normally could do to overcome "writing blind" was to read *Why Not the Best?* and old Carter speeches and proclamations "like . . . biblical scholar[s]."[45] A perverse result was that writers sometimes wound up taking an off-the-cuff Carter pronouncement, like his promise to cut the number of government agencies, as virtual prophecy, even if it was not truly a serious or useful idea. Writer Gordon Stewart later estimated that there had been perhaps 10-12 examples throughout the Administration of close collaboration between writers and Carter.[46] That is not many when one considers the writers usually drafted about 25 speeches per week.

The decision to dispense with researchers, who had worked closely with the writers in administrations since Nixon, also hampered the writing effort. As early as the second month of the Carter term, Fallows had complained that his staff was overburdened and had specifically asked for research help.[47] Conner later seconded this in her memo to Fallows, again to no effect.[48] Until the end of the Administration, the combination of Carter's relative indifference to the writing process and his determination to keep the White House Office arbitrarily small (limited to 351 total staff) prevented the hiring of researchers and kept the speechwriting operation chronically understaffed.[49]

A final problem that surfaced in the early years of the Carter speechwriting experience was strongly reminiscent of Ford's initial troubles: speech staffing was erratic. In the relatively collegial Carter White House, this clearance process did not have the implications for factional politics that it had under Ford. Still, correctable errors of fact could creep into speeches because they had not gone past the proper people in a timely fashion.[50] Later, the "Too Many Cooks Syndrome" of overstaffing, seen under Ford, resurfaced and became a concern to the writers under Carter.[51] Hart likewise cites "too many hands" on the writing process as partial explanation for what he finds to be Carter's lack of rhetorical success.[52]

In the area of foreign affairs, where competition between Brzezinski and Secretary of State Cyrus Vance often was intense, the problem could be most severe. The tendency of Brzezinski to keep Vance out of the drafting and clearance processes had to be countered informally by the writers themselves until late in the Administration when an orderly staffing system was implemented.[53] This rivalry – the Carter White House's closest approximation to the kind of strife commonplace under Ford – produced the notorious struggle over the President's Naval Academy speech on U.S. policy toward the Soviet Union, as revealed by Fallows soon after he left the White House.[54] Nor did the President act as adjudicator. Instead, he "assembled the speech essentially by stapling Vance's memo to Brzezinski's, without examining the tensions between them."[55]

Faced with these sorts of problems, plus the generally lukewarm public and press reaction to his speeches, Carter's first response was to restructure marginally, taking the writers out of the press unit and putting them in Gerald Rafshoon's Communications Office in mid-1978.

By the writers' account, Rafshoon changed little, though there was a tightening of the timetable for getting press conference briefings to the President.[56] Rafshoon took more interest in the substance of Carter's speeches than in the process of producing them. He stressed the need to emphasize particular themes. But, the writers complained, Rafshoon's enthusiasm for a theme rarely lasted more than a few days. As writer Achsah Nesmith recalled, if a writer stuck to a theme any longer than that, Rafshoon would send speeches back, saying "I can't use this."[57]

Rafshoon departed the White House for the campaign staff in the late summer of 1979. After some uncertainty over where to lodge the writers, it was decided that they would be placed under deputy chief of staff Alonzo McDonald. New to the White House, McDonald was a management expert recruited from the consulting firm McKinsey & Co. He set out to solve the structural difficulties plaguing the writing process. Hendrik Hertzberg, now chief speechwriter, identified the central problems: limited access to Carter and lack of "clout." Access was needed to find out what the President wanted. Greater clout would help prevent speeches from being watered down through overstaffing.[58]

McDonald responded by instituting a more orderly speech planning process, routinizing the staffing and policy meetings associated with each speech, and assuring that cleared speeches would move up the writing hierarchy to the President on time. He developed a monthly planning calendar and instituted standardized staffing forms.[59] The writers regarded these efforts as successful as far as they went, with Hertzberg even labeling the new system "a roaring success."[60] At the same time, the chief writer highlighted "one ironic, unintended result": bringing more people into the process resulted in speeches becoming even more the products of committees, albeit better ones than before. There still was "almost never the opportunity for the kind of intimate give-and-take that makes for creative interaction" with the President.[61] In other words, neither of the two problems Hertzberg had initially identified – access and clout – had been satisfactorily addressed. Hertzberg later summarized the situation: McDonald and his two deputies ("who we used to call R2D2 and C3PO") produced a good system, given the basic flaw "of having speeches written by people who were not in close contact with the person giving them . . ."[62]

Unlike the period of Rafshoon's leadership, a genuine structural reform was attempted, prompted largely by McDonald, but ultimately flowing from the external and internal criticism of the Carter staff that had led to bringing McDonald on board in the first place. But the organizational fix proved superficial. It made business-as-usual more efficient, but it did not address the problems inherent in the way that "business" was conducted.

The writers' central concern was with speech quality and fidelity to the President's views. Of equal importance was the use of the writing process as a forum for airing competing points of view and settling policy. Here, the difficulties experienced under Powell and Rafshoon persisted. The basic problem, at least from the writers' point of view, was the "compartmentalization" of the White House, where each unit tended to view matters exclusively from its own perspective. Gordon Stewart observed that three groups in the White House tended to operate independently: one (including the writers) worried about words, public image and rhetoric; another about politics and political tactics; and a third about policy substance. "You have three tracks, just going off on their own. When they all come together, watch out."[63] Few structural mechanisms were available to bring these divergent perspectives together. The McDonald reforms gave the writers better control of the overall process. But they failed to fully solve the problems of resolving inconsistencies and conflicts, and integrating words, tactics, and policy.

Looking back, Hertzberg tended to put the blame for the problems of writing in the Carter White House on the loss of the approach that had worked so well for Richard Nixon. He noted that in Nixon's first four years, the top writers were just outside the inner circles of the White House, in close contact with policy makers and unafraid to take policy positions themselves. Carter's arrangements did not imitate this, but instead came close to emulating Ford's, with the writers connected to policy through an additional level of hierarchy occupied by a Powell, a Rafshoon, or a McDonald – a "rabbi," in the writers' vernacular. In the Carter White House, as in Ford's (and in Nixon's abbreviated second term), the specialized job of "speechwriter" came to replace fully the position of writer-policy maker.[64]

From the perspective of the Carter writers, then, the problems were largely structural, although the remedies that were attempted helped marginally at best. One might wonder why other solutions were not attempted, such as bringing in at least one high-status writer who would participate in both policy and politics discussions in the way the writing staff never did. Chris Matthews even lamented that they never had someone to play this role in the way David Gergen did in the early Reagan Administration.[65] Perhaps the most persuasive explanation was suggested by Gordon Stewart, who observed that organizations "band together to resist bringing in highly competent people."[66] Carter's own organizational preferences, including surrounding himself primarily with people whom he knew and trusted from his campaign, may have contributed to problems in the area of writing.

CONCLUSIONS AND IMPLICATIONS

The Johnson and Nixon administrations "marked the death of the old system of writing presidential speeches and initiated a groping toward something new."[67] The Ford and Carter administrations, on the one hand, can be said to represent the institutionalization of a new system: full-time writers working in a separate unit became an established and predictable part of the White House Office. Yet, on the other hand, neither Ford nor Carter was especially successful at making this new system work.

The first dependent variable, broadly defined, that we examined here was how presidential writing was *structured*. Both Ford and Carter attempted to rely on a type of structuring that had been problematic in Nixon's second term: a hierarchy in which one designated aide served as a conduit between policy processes at the top and speechwriting at a lower level. Whereas Nixon's last writing chief, David Gergen, was not a top-level staffer, Ford's aide, Robert Hartmann, was. Arguably, he was a throwback to the writer/senior advisor model of earlier years. Ford, however, actually added a layer of hierarchy in assigning the writers to Hartmann, since Paul Theis took over the editorial office headship that had been Gergen's. Later, another level – a deputy to Theis (and his successor, Robert Orben) – was added.

Carter approximated the same hierarchical arrangement as Ford. Jody Powell and Gerald Rafshoon were not writers like Hartmann, but they had considerable stature within the White House. Similar to the Nixon/Ford design, one of the writers – first James Fallows, then Hendrik Hertzberg – was in charge of the writing staff. Carter's principal innovation was to eliminate the job of researcher. The only major structural change came when Al McDonald replaced Rafshoon, dropping the status of the writers' emissary to top policy circles down one level.

The most straightforward explanation for structuring in both administrations is that they essentially adopted the model left to them by their immediate predecessors. This design, featuring full-time writing specialists, was congruent with a political environment that demanded an ever-expanding torrent of presidential words. Particular presidential preferences had little impact on the basic model, although there is evidence that Carter's White House economies and his discomfort with speechwriting kept the staff smaller than optimal throughout the Administration.[68]

The heart of the matter, however, lies in the second dependent variable: how presidential writing was *linked* to the policy processes (including both substantive decision-making and political strategizing) of the White House. Here the story is one of continued groping without a satisfactory resolution. Based on the evidence of the writers' constant complaints (during their tenure and in retrospect), the evident dissatisfaction with speechwriting at the top of each White House, and the judgments of contemporaneous media and later rhetorical criticism, neither the Ford nor the Carter White House was able to produce writing that compellingly explained and justified presidential priorities and actions. For the writers in both cases, the core reason was essentially structural: access to the policy process and to the president himself, and enough "clout" to maintain the integrity of a speech in the face of the "Too Many Cooks Syndrome." Neither Ford nor Carter solved these problems.

Compared to Nixon's first term efforts, the most promising experiment performed in both White Houses was elevating the position in the overall White House hierarchy of the individual who was charged with linking writers and policy (Hartmann, Powell, Rafshoon). Yet clearly the status of the writers' "rabbi" was not the solution to the puzzle. In fact, the Carter effort improved under McDonald, who was not a top staffer. Likewise, the Ford staff may have achieved better results when a competitive arrangement, pitting the Hartmann/Orben staff against David Gergen, surfaced.

The continuing difficulties in linking writing to policy require a layered explanation. At one level, they simply represent the persistence of a problem that Nixon had during his last year-and-a-half in office. To the extent that Ford and Carter copied the system that produced those problems, one may look to organizational inertia (or, more positively, "institutionalization") for the explanation.

Then, however, one must ask: why the copying? Here the preferences of each president evidently made at least some contribution. In the case of Ford, the influence was marginal, since circumstances permitted him little time or opportunity to comprehensively reorganize the structures of the Nixon White House. Yet one can still note that he did open up access to himself and to policy debate in a way that generated intense staff rivalry, but elected neither to put a damper on the contentiousness nor to become routinely involved in adjudicating the disputes. This highly competitive staff system, allowed if not crafted by Ford, hurt the writing operation considerably.

In Carter's case, the president's contribution is even clearer. His apparent aversion to the speechwriting process led him to give the whole matter relatively little thought. The Carter administration largely took the writing structures of the Ford White House as given. That might have been less of a problem had not Carter put writing in Jody Powell's portfolio. Although this happened more as an afterthought than as a plan, it added to the Press Secretary's already too numerous responsibilities as head of the press office and senior presidential advisor. Such neglect, coupled with Carter's determined and arguably unwise decision to control the perceived problem of White House staff size by keeping units lean – whatever the seeming demands upon them – laid the groundwork for the troubles the writers experienced.

Moreover, it is obvious that the individual characteristics of presidents critically affect rhetorical success in ways that go beyond the nature of the writing-policy linkage. Ford's preference for rather bland rhetoric is a case in point. Jimmy Carter's preference for policy details over conceptual structure is another.[69] The best speechwriting cannot make a great orator out of a person of severely limited talent or interest. As Dwight Eisenhower famously put it, "(o)rganization cannot make a genius out of an incompetent."[70] But as Eisenhower went on to say, "disorganization can scarcely fail to result in inefficiency."[71] In the cases of Ford and Carter, the result is better characterized as ineffectiveness in the articulation of policy.

Ford and Carter did not make their decisions in a vacuum. When Ford adopted a "spokes-of-the-wheel" White House form that encouraged staff rivalry, he was responding in part to demands from the press, public, political officials, and some scholars for more White House "openness" in the aftermath of Watergate. Likewise Carter's enthusiasm for staff reduction responded to fears that the sheer size (and thus power) of the White House had somehow contributed to Nixon's downfall. This post-Watergate environment, then, at least constrained the choices these two presidents could make in their staffing.

More generally, these experiences also suggest that arranging a satisfactory response to the demand placed upon the modern presidency for rhetoric is not apt to be a matter of following a simple formula. The success of the writing staff is likely to be contingent upon the success of other aspects of White House organization. Particularly in the Ford White House, the failure of basic policy-determination routines left the writers unable to explain what could not be explained to them. But even in a White House where all else works smoothly, speechwriting will not prosper unless the gap between policy and speechwriting that first arose under LBJ is satisfactorily bridged. This bridging can be facilitated through effective liaison by one or more senior aides, who may or may not be writers. It likewise can be addressed by providing writers with personal access to the president. Or, it can come about as a result of ideological consensus, as existed in Ronald Reagan's first term. There is no "one best way" in an internal milieu that is as varied and as complex as in contemporary White Houses.

What is clearer is that the traditional use of the occasion of a speech as a vehicle for catalyzing policy deliberation, debate, and clarification is something that became, and has largely remained, detached from the actual writing of that speech. The Ford and Carter speechwriters were hardly demanding to participate in policy-making. To the extent that they influenced policy, it was often because they guessed at policy in the absence of good information -- something that nobody believed was desirable. In the contemporary presidency it appears that the key to an effective speechwriting process is merely to convey the policy and its justifications to the writing specialists, whose job it will be to present the policy as compellingly as possible. Which policies are selected for emphasis and how they are formulated have become matters with which others must grapple.

NOTES

1. See, for instance, Jeffrey Tulis, *The Rhetorical Presidency* (Princeton, NJ: Princeton University Press, 1987); Mary E. Stuckey, *The President as Interpreter in Chief* (New York: Seven Bridges Press, 1991); Meena Bose, *Shaping and Signaling Presidential Policy: The National Security Decision Making of Eisenhower and Kennedy* (College Station TX: Texas A&M University Press, 1998).
2. Karen M. Hult and Charles E. Walcott, "Policymakers and Wordsmiths: Writing for the President under Johnson and Nixon," *Polity* 30 (1998): 465-487; Carol W. Gelderman, *All the President's Words: The Bully Pulpit and the Creation of the Virtual Presidency* (New York: Walker and Company, 1997).
3. Hult & Walcott, 1998. Gelderman (1997, 63-194), whose focus on a few major speeches leads her to overlook the full-time writing staff in the Johnson White House, traces the problem to Nixon. The same focus also tends to lead her away from an organizational analysis of the writing process under Nixon and his successors.
4. Hult & Walcott, 1998.
5. It should be noted that White House writers are, strictly speaking, more than "speechwriters." They write, for instance, messages to Congress that are not delivered orally, and speeches for administration figures other than the president. Nonetheless, the term "speechwriter" is commonly used, not least by the writers themselves, and will be employed here.
6. See Charles E. Walcott and Karen M. Hult, *Governing the White House: From Hoover Through LBJ* (Lawrence, KS: University Press of Kansas, 1995), ch. 1.
7. The number would eventually exceed three million. See Robert T. Hartmann, *Palace Politics: An Inside Account of the Ford Years* (New York: McGraw-Hill, 1980), p. 404.
8. Hartmann, 1980, p. 278.
9. Hartmann, 1980, pp. 343-5; John J. Casserly, *The Ford White House: The Diary of a Speechwriter* (Boulder, CO: Colorado Associated University Press, 1977), pp. 49, 69.
10. Casserly, 1977, p. 100.
11. Roderick P. Hart, *Verbal Style and the Presidency: A Computer-Based Analysis* (New York: Academic Press, 1984), p. 151.
12. See Pat Butler, Interview with William A. Syers, 1985. Syers Papers, "Files, 1985 – Interviews," Ford Library; Casserly, 1977, pp. 114, 154, 158; Hart, 1984, p. 151.
13. Hartmann, 1980, especially chapters 1 & 9.
14. See, e.g., Casserly, 1977, p. 201; Gelderman, 1997, pp. 121-127.
15. Donald Rumsfeld, Memorandum to President Ford, October 15, 1974. Jerry H. Jones Files, Box 15, "White House Operations – Paperwork Flow," Ford Library.
16. Robert Goldwin, Interview with A. James Reichley, 1978. Reichley Transcripts, Box 1, "Ford White House Interviews," Ford Library.
17. Paul Theis, Memorandum to President Ford via Robert Hartmann, n.d. Ronald H. Nessen Files, Box 45, "Theis, Paul," Ford Library.
18. Butler, 1985, p. 1.
19. Casserly, 1977, p. 51.
20. Hart, 1984, p. 167.
21. In contrast to ex-staffers from other White Houses, Nixon writers tend to praise the writing process they experienced. See, for example, Ray Price, *With Nixon* (New York: Viking Press, 1977); William Safire, *Before the Fall: An Inside View of the Pre-Watergate White House* (Garden City, NY: Doubleday, 1975).
22. Casserly, 1977, p. 114.
23. Cf. Casserly, 1977, pp. 32, 144, 192-6.
24. Casserly, 1977, pp. 58, 177.

25 David Gergen, *Eyewitness to Power: The Essence of Leadership, Nixon to Clinton* (New York: Simon & Schuster, 2000).
26 Hartmann, 1980, p. 393.
27 Robert T. Hartmann, Memorandum to President Ford, *circa* March, 1976. Robert T. Hartmann Files, Box 13, "Office – Organization," Ford Library.
28 Casserly, 1977, p. 239.
29 Hartmann, 1980, p. 397.
30 David Gergen, Memorandum to Richard Cheney, January 31, 1976. Jerry H. Jones Files, Box 19, "Communications (campaign related)," Ford Library.
31 Butler, 1985, p. 3.
32 Ibid.
33 David Gergen, Memorandum to Richard Cheney, August 10, 1976. James E. Connor Files, Box 7, "Campaign – Planning 1976," Ford Library.
34 White House Study Project, December 7, 1976, "Analysis of Present White House Office, Counselor to the President (Hartmann)," Report No. 1, Ford Library.
35 Hendrik Hertzberg, Miller Center Interview, December 3-4, 1981, Carter Library. Interviewees also included Christopher Matthews, Achsah Nesmith, and Gordon Stewart.
36 James Fallows, Memorandum to Jody Powell, December 2, 1977. Jody Powell Files, Box 42, "Memoranda: Fallows, Jim 7/5/77-12/14/77," Carter Library. Caryl Conner, Memorandum to James Fallows, August 22 1978. Staff Offices, Speechwriters Subject File, Box 29, "Speechwriting Organization, 8/78 JF," Carter Library.
37 Jody Powell, Miller Center Interview, December 17-18, 1981, Carter Library, p. 3. Interviewees also included Patricia Bario, Al Friendly, Rex Granum, Dale Leibach, and Claudia Townsend.
38 Powell, 1981, p. 5.
39 James Fallows, Memorandum to President Carter, January 21, 1977. Jody Powell Files, Box 42, "Memoranda: Fallows, Jim 1/21/77-5/20/77," Carter Library.
40 Frank Moore, Miller Center Interview, September 18-19, 1981, Carter Library. Interviewees also included William Cable, Dan Tate, and Robert Thomson.
41 James Fallows, Memorandum to Jody Powell and Richard Harden, February 1, 1977. Domestic Policy Staff: Eizenstat Files, Box. 253, "Personnel," Carter Library.
42 Conner to Fallows, 1978.
43 Ibid.
44 James Fallows, Memorandum to President Carter, November 10, 1977. Jody Powell Files, Box 42, "Memoranda: Fallows, Jim 7/5/77-12/14/77," Carter Library.
45 Matthews in Hertzberg, 1981, p. 114.
46 Stewart in Hertzberg, 1981, p. 115.
47 Fallows to Powell and Harden, 1977.
48 Conner to Fallows, 1978.
49 See Hertzberg, 1981, p. 112.
50 James Fallows, Memorandum to President Carter, February 1, 1978. Jody Powell Files, Box 42, "Memoranda: Granum, Rex 2/1/78-12/13/78," Carter Library.
51 Hendrik Hertzberg, Memorandum to Hamilton Jordan, August 20, 1979. Staff Offices, Speechwriters – Administrative File, Box 3, "Personnel, 12/31/77-6/9/80," Carter Library.
52 Hart, 1984, p. 193.
53 See Hertzberg, 1981, pp. 48-53.
54 James Fallows, "The Passionless Presidency: The Trouble with Jimmy Carter's Administration," *Atlantic Monthly* 243 (1979): 33-48. Vance's memo to Carter about this speech -- and his position more generally -- emphasized the need to explain to the public the importance of negotiating a SALT agreement with the USSR; Brzezinski's stance, in contrast, favored a harder line toward the Soviets.
55 Ibid., p. 43.

[56] Memorandum to Gerald Rafshoon, n.a., n.d. Staff Offices, Speechwriters, Fallows, Box 10, "Press Conference Briefing Book Format – 1978," Carter Library.
[57] Nesmith, in Hertzberg, 1981, p. 133.
[58] Hertzberg, 1979.
[59] Alonzo McDonald, Memorandum to Hendrik Hertzberg, October 2, 1979. Hugh Carter Files, Box 42, "McDonald, Alonzo L. [2]," Carter Library.
[60] Hendrik Hertzberg, Memorandum to Alonzo McDonald, February 18, 1980. Staff Offices, Speechwriters – Administrative File, Box 3, "Personnel, 12/30/77-6/9/80," Carter Library.
[61] Ibid.
[62] Hertzberg, 1981, p. 46.
[63] Stewart, in Hertzberg, 1981, p. 86.
[64] Hertzberg, 1981, pp. 46-49.
[65] Matthews, in Hertzberg, 1981, p. 133.
[66] Stewart, in Hertzberg, 1981, p. 131.
[67] Hult and Walcott, 1998, p. 484.
[68] See Charles E. Walcott and Karen M. Hult, "White House Staff Size: Explanations and Implications," *Presidential Studies Quarterly* 29 (1999): 638-656.
[69] Hart, 1984, pp. 193-4.
[70] Quoted in Stephen Hess, *Organizing the Presidency*, 2nd ed. (Washington, DC: Brookings), p. 70.
[71] Ibid.

Chapter 6

THE RHETORIC OF PRESIDENTIAL VETO MESSAGES

Christopher J. Deering, Lee Sigelman and Jennifer L. Saunders

OVERVIEW

On April 5, 1792, George Washington issued the first presidential veto of an act of Congress. According to Washington, the bill, which would have apportioned the House of Representatives pursuant to the 1790 census, violated the Constitution because no single "proportion or divisor" would have yielded the number of representatives allotted to each state and because eight states would have had more than one representative for every 30,000 people. Five years later, Washington issued his only other veto, indicating that portions of the offending act would be "inconvenient and injurious to the public" and did "not seem to comport with economy." Making no mention of constitutional prescriptions or proscriptions, the need to protect presidential prerogatives, or other lofty principles, he simply presented his "opinion," which, he said, was based upon "the best information [he had] been able to obtain." When amended versions of the two bills reached him, a few days later in both instances, he promptly signed them.

In each case, Washington submitted his objections to Congress in a brief veto message, thereby fulfilling a constitutional requirement:

> Every bill which shall have passed the House of Representatives and the Senate, shall, before it become a law, be presented to the President of the United States; if he approves he shall sign it, but if not he shall return it, *with his objections*, to that House in which it shall have originated... (Article I, Section 7, emphasis ours).

Subsequent presidents have used the veto power far less sparingly. Since 1792, presidents have issued 1,471 regular vetoes, each attended by the requisite message.[1] These messages have varied greatly in length, form, and tone. Washington's first veto contained only 150 words, but in 1832 Andrew Jackson used more than 8,000 words in vetoing a bill incorporating subscribers to the Bank of the United States.

Outwardly at least, most veto messages have been conciliatory in tone and solicitous of congressional cooperation, qualities especially prominent in Woodrow Wilson's 1915 veto of an immigration bill:

> It is with unaffected regret that I find myself constrained by clear conviction to return this bill...without my signature. Not only do I feel it to be a very serious matter to exercise the power of veto in any case, because it involves opposing the single judgment of the President to the judgment of the majority of both the Houses of the Congress, a step which no man who realizes his own liability to error can take without great hesitation, but also because this particular bill is in so many important respects admirable, well conceived, and desirable. Its enactment into law would undoubtedly enhance the efficiency and improve the methods of handling the important branch of the public service to which it relates. But candor and a sense of duty with regard to the responsibility so clearly imposed upon me by the Constitution in matters of legislation leave me no choice but to dissent.

Although far less florid, Washington's veto messages, like this one by Wilson, betrayed neither anger, animosity, nor indignation. They were businesslike and, though not in so many words, invited Congress to alter the portions of the bill he considered objectionable, in which case the implication was that he would sign the legislation into law. Accordingly, Washington's use of the veto was well in keeping with the idea that the veto power is an extension, rather than the termination, of the legislative process.[2]

On the other hand, vetoes and veto messages can be contentious. In March 1834, an angry Senate censured President Andrew Jackson after his 1832 veto of the bank bill.[3] By itself Jackson's veto was not novel; Madison had rejected similar legislation in 1815. But the attending message was described by one scholar as "a regime-builder's manifesto" and by another as an attack that "bordered on class warfare."[4] In 1841, John Tyler's second veto of a bank bill sparked resignations by all but one member of his cabinet,[5] and a year later, his veto of a tariff bill became headline news and led one member of the House to cite Tyler's refusal to "assent to laws" as a major charge in articles of impeachment.[6] Even so, Tyler's veto messages remained conciliatory and regretful in tone. More generally, in the two centuries that presidents have been entrusted with the veto power, only rarely have they used language as provocative as that invoked by Herbert Hoover when he rejected emergency relief and reconstruction legislation in 1932: "This proposal violates every sound principle of public finance and of government. Never before has so dangerous a suggestion been seriously made to our country."

If a conciliatory veto message could do Tyler so much political damage while Hoover's much harsher message caused barely a ripple, questions arise about the nature and purpose of these messages. Veto messages are public communications between the branches, but they have received little attention in the press, from the public, or from scholars interested in presidential rhetoric. Why? A reasonable speculation would be that, since the Jackson Administration, presidential signaling of veto threats has taken place during rather than at the conclusion of the legislative process.[7] Rather than conveying news from president to Congress, therefore, veto messages transmit an "I told you so" message. Even so, they communicate (or reiterate) potentially important political information across a constitutional divide. We focus on veto messages as a medium of presidential communication, analyzing them as a unique form of presidential "speech." Given their function, we might well expect these messages to be negative in tone, hostile in theme. Then again, they might be popularized, intended for public consumption, and full of jabs at congressional ineptitude or intransigence. Or veto messages may be filled with boring technical matter — sober messages from one part of the government to another. Or, finally, they may be cautiously written as gentle reminders to a Congress that has simply lost its way.

Although veto messages are little studied, several scholars have taken a fairly close look at this rhetorical genre. We begin by reviewing these earlier efforts. Next, we present a method of stylistic analysis that permits rigorous comparison of veto message texts across presidential administrations. This stylistic analysis uses a series of "dictionaries" to characterize and compare important characteristics displayed by these texts. We find that veto texts are a distinct but stable element of what Campbell and Jamieson call the "discourse of government."[8] The messages also appear more emblematic of the institutional presidency than what has recently been called the public presidency.

THE VETO MESSAGE AS A RHETORICAL GENRE

Studies of the presidential use of language have contrasted the "old" and "new" rhetoric.[9] Two aspects of this body of research bear mentioning: it focuses on public rather than private language, and on the spoken rather than the written word. Fields, for example, has characterized presidential speechmaking as a series of distinct "oratorical occasions that define a presidential career."[10] According to Campbell and Jamieson, presidential rhetoric consists of a set of identifiable sub-genres that include inaugural addresses, state of the union messages, the rhetoric of war, veto messages, and farewell addresses, which collectively define a discourse of governance that transcends the idiosyncrasies of any particular president.[11] Of these distinct "occasions" and "sub-genres," veto messages are one of the few presented in written rather than spoken form.[12]

Like the president's speeches and other public pronouncements, veto messages hardly ever convey the "president's own words."[13] Beginning with George Washington's very first veto, these messages routinely have been drafted, not by the president, but by personnel in the departments and agencies to which the enrolled bills are sent.[14] Unlike other subgenres of presidential rhetoric, though, which are increasingly aimed at the general public,[15] the subgenre of veto messages seems outwardly to have retained more of its traditional function and form. That is, it is written communication of a public, but not a popular, character, and because of its institutional origins, it is typically bureaucratic or lawyerly in form. Although the use and effects of vetoes have been studied frequently, with three exceptions the language of veto messages has been ignored.

In one of the three exceptions, Ringelstein categorized the vetoes of presidents Eisenhower, Kennedy, Johnson, Ford, Carter, and Reagan according to their policy domain and explicit rationale.[16] After distinguishing among three broad types of rationale (protection of the office, ideology, and unconstitutionality or defective drafting), Ringelstein used keywords within the messages to develop a more detailed set of ten categories. This exercise led him to conclude that, with few exceptions, the six presidents differed little in their publicly stated motives for vetoing legislation.

In a study of broader historical sweep, Campbell and Jamieson examined veto messages as one of several sub-genres of presidential rhetoric.[17] In their view, veto messages generally state objections based on either constitutionality or expediency, with most being of the latter variety, and the typical veto message is deferential and conciliatory, expressing regret, reluctance, praise for Congress, and hope for a resolution of differences. There are, according to Campbell and Jamieson, some circumstances in which veto messages do not display these traits or display them less abundantly. For example, partisan discourse is said to increase during periods of divided government, while vetoes on constitutional or ideological grounds are thought to have a more uncompromising tone; similarly, activist presidents are more likely to embellish their messages with rhetorical flourishes—ceremony, patriotism, optimism.

Finally, Gleiber and Shull used veto messages to measure the degree of presidential opposition to a bill, using the length of a message and the number of discrete justifications contained therein as measures of opposition.[18] Active presidents with legislative orientations, they found, have produced longer messages with fewer discrete objections, whereas presidents with "delegate" orientations have sent shorter messages with more objections. Because there has been a high level of idiosyncracy across presidents, Gleiber and Shull concluded that the number of justifications may be largely a function of the president's audience, while the length of the message is a function of the president's personality.[19]

The primary questions that remain are whether any clear trends in the language of presidential vetoes have emerged over the course of the twentieth century; whether twentieth-century veto messages have differed appreciably from those of the nation's earliest presidents; whether the language of twentieth-century veto messages has differed appreciably from other forms of twentieth-century presidential rhetoric; and whether certain types of chief executives (those presiding over divided rather than unified governments, and Republicans rather than Democrats) have differed in their veto language. Our goal is to answer these questions for a longer period of time and in a more systematic fashion than has previously been done.

DATA, HYPOTHESES AND MEASURES

Our primary focus is upon the messages attached to vetoes of public bills issued by the twentieth-century presidents, Theodore Roosevelt through Bill Clinton.[20] To provide historical perspective, we supplement these messages with the veto messages the first four presidents who used the regular veto; because John Adams, Thomas Jefferson, and John Quincy Adams vetoed no public bills, the supplementary messages examined here are those of George Washington, James Madison, James Monroe, and Andrew Jackson. Veto messages, by their nature, are a negative, even if conciliatory, form of rhetoric. To provide a base for comparison to another, more intentionally positive, form of presidential rhetoric, we also analyze the inaugural addresses of these same early and twentieth-century presidents.

We do not consider the enormous number of messages attached to vetoes of private ("relief") legislation because of their marginal political significance during the period studied here.[21] We obtained the texts of veto messages for the 1789-1837 period from *Veto Messages of the Presidents of the United States*[22]; those for the twentieth century are from the *Congressional Record* or *Public Papers of the Presidents of the United States*. Where possible, we also include memorandum pocket vetoes on the grounds that they clearly belong to the sub-genre of veto messages. Thus, we are working with a very sizable text base: The twentieth-century veto messages—697 in all—total approximately 450,000 words, and the supplementary file of veto messages by early presidents—17 messages—accounts for another 30,000 words. The texts of the twentieth-century inaugural addresses[23] add about 50,000 more words. Overall, then, the textual database analyzed here totals more than half a million words.

As noted above, prior studies of presidential rhetoric in general and veto messages in particular provide the basis for a series of expectations about the style and substance of veto messages. To test these expectations, we employ a combination of measures that have been introduced in earlier research or developed especially for the present study. (Our methods and measures are described in greater detail in the Appendix.)

Accessibility

Because veto messages are written to be read, not spoken, and because their primary intended audience is Congress, not the general public, there is reason to expect them to be relatively inaccessible by the standards of presidential rhetoric. According to Sigelman, over the course of two centuries inaugural addresses have become much more accessible, and studies cited earlier reveal that presidential rhetoric in general has become more popular over the years.[24] Because veto messages are drafted by bureaucrats rather than speechwriters, they should be expected to be less accessible than other forms of presidential rhetoric. Similarly, because veto messages are not aimed at a general audience, they might be expected to have been relatively immune to the "dumbing down" that Sigelman finds characteristic of presidential rhetoric in other subgenres. To test these expectations, we apply a standard accessibility measure, the Flesch readability formula, to the twentieth-century veto messages and, for good measure, to the veto messages of presidents Washington through Jackson and to the inaugural addresses of the twentieth-century presidents.[25]

Forcefulness

According to Campbell and Jamieson, the generic veto message expresses "reluctance and regret…, praises the Congress for its efforts, [and] indicates agreement with specific parts of the legislation."[26] That is, veto messages are thought to be deferential and conciliatory rather than strident and partisan. Although they stress the generic or common elements of veto messages, Campbell and Jamieson do assert that under certain conditions vetoes are likely to come across as especially uncompromising or strident. To examine these propositions, we adapt Martindale and Martindale's two-dimensional approach to measuring the forcefulness of a text.[27] According to this approach, temperament can be evaluated along two dimensions extrovert-introvert and stable-neurotic—each of which is composed of two of the "four basic human temperaments."[28] Forcefulness is associated with extroversion—the sanguinic and choleric temperaments—and restraint with introversion—the phlegmatic and melancholic temperaments. Joint consideration of the two dimensions—choleric versus phlegmatic, and sanguinic versus melancholic—yields a measure of forcefulness or its opposite, restraint; the basic idea is that forceful language is at once choleric and sanguinic. If Campbell and Jamieson are correct, on the whole, veto messages should be more restrained than forceful. On the other hand, how restrained these messages are could well vary across presidencies and according to circumstances; for example, activist presidents may approach vetoes more assertively, as may presidents facing a Congress dominated by members of the opposition party. Moreover, veto messages seem likely to outscore inaugural addresses on the choleric versus phlegmatic dimension, for, as Sigelman has shown, presidents heavily season their inaugural addresses with calm, reassuring, peaceful language. By contrast, veto messages by their very nature involve disagreement and may, in some instances at least, slip over into contentiousness.

Constitutionality

In *Federalist 78*, Alexander Hamilton defended the veto power as a necessary tool to protect the executive against the "depredations" of the legislative branch. From his words, other popular commentary at the time, and the actions of the earliest presidents, an image of the veto emerged as a constitutional tool intended for rare use.[29] Even Jackson, who is credited with "going public" and preemptively announcing his veto intentions, put forward vetoes that followed closely the precedents established by Washington, Madison, and Monroe. Indeed, Spitzer argues that Jackson's vetoes, though more numerous, were not unique in form. Moreover, like his predecessors, Jackson based his veto messages on constitutional grounds and "relied on the logic and precedent of similar Madison and Monroe vetoes."[30] Thus, whatever precedents might have been set in Jackson's "popular" presidency, his veto messages, though occasionally adorned with populist rhetoric, are not regarded as a sharp break from those of his predecessors.

After the hotly contested Tyler administration, the veto power fell by the wayside as subject of political debate, though particular vetoes could still spark controversy. Campbell and Jamieson, among others, have suggested that after the earliest administrations the rationales presented in veto messages focused on expediency, i.e., on issues of policy and economy, rather than on constitutionality or the powers of the legislative and executive branches, and Ringelstein categorizes only about eight percent of post-World War II vetoes as defended on constitutional grounds. Based on these indications, we did not expect our pool of veto messages to contain many references to the constitutionality of legislation being returned to Congress. However, our constitutionality measure casts a wider net capable of capturing references not only to the Constitution itself and the issue of constitutionality, but also to the several branches and to inter-branch relations. (See the Appendix for a listing of the terms in the constitutionality dictionary.)

Partisanship

As noted at the outset, the earliest vetoes betrayed little concern for partisan or ideological disputation. However, events surrounding congressional debates about the veto power and, in recent decades, partisan battles during periods of divided party government reveal clear partisan antagonisms. Jackson's veto of the bank bill was followed closely by bitter partisan debate and the introduction of several constitutional amendments designed to make it easier for Congress to override a veto. Tyler's bitter relations with Congress and his vetoes provoked a lengthy floor debate pitting Calhoun against Clay and, later, the introduction of articles of impeachment. More recently, partisan intransigence was at the heart of President Clinton's vetoes of stop-gap spending bills in 1995 and early 1996. Notwithstanding these partisan flare-ups, neither Ringelstein nor Campbell and Jamieson detect much partisanship in veto messages, though Campbell and Jamieson assert that partisan language tends to increase during periods of divided government.[31] To tap the use of partisan language in veto messages, we rely on a dictionary of "partisanship" terms that draws heavily on the list of party and election keywords that Hinckley (1990) compiled for her analysis of presidential addresses.

Economy

Both Campbell and Jamieson and Ringelstein have described expediency and economy as the principal rationales that presidents offer when they use the veto power; more than a third of the veto messages Ringelstein categorized were in his "economic" category — more, by a wide margin, than in any other category. Accordingly, we developed an "economy" dictionary aimed at ferreting out such references.[32]

Unity

According to Sigelman, the use of language evoking a sense of national unity and inclusiveness has increased steadily in inaugural addresses throughout the nation's history. Indeed, in contrast to Washington's first inaugural address, which contained only about 15 "unity" symbols per 1,000 words, Clinton invoked nearly 100 such symbols per 1,000 words in his first inaugural. We anticipate no such outpouring of unification symbolism in veto messages. To determine whether that expectation is accurate, we employ the same unity dictionary that Sigelman used to analyze inaugural addresses.

FINDINGS

As Table 1 reveals, the language that twentieth-century presidents employed in their veto messages was pitched, on average, at a comprehension level for which 16 to 17 years of formal education would be appropriate. The inaccessibility of these messages varied from president to president, with Lyndon Johnson (14.3) and Woodrow Wilson (19.6) defining the extremes; in general, though, the veto language of twentieth-century presidents produced Flesch scores within fairly close proximity to the overall mean of 16.6 (s.d. = 1.5).

Table 1. The Language of Veto Messages, 20th Century versus Earliest Presidents (Independent Sample t-tests for Mean Differences)

	20th Century Presidents	Earliest Presidents	t-value
Accessibility	16.6	19.0	-0.8
Forcefulness			
Choleric/Phlegmatic	-1.2	-2.1	1.0
Sanguinic/Melancholic	-2.9	-3.0	0.2
Constitutionality	10.6	19.4	-1.9
Partisanship	1.5	0.3	3.6*
Economy	14.2	11.8	0.7
Unity	12.9	9.9	0.9
N	17	4	

Note: Accessibility entries—years of education; forcefulness entries—difference in words per thousand; remaining entries—words per thousand.
*$p < .01$.

The mean scores on the two forcefulness dimensions convey the impression that, on average, twentieth-century veto messages were more phlegmatic than choleric and more melancholic than sanguinic, for each mean has a negative sign. Both of these, it will be recalled, are associated with restraint or forcefulness. The imbalance between sanguinity and melancholia was greater than the choleric/phlegmatic imbalance, as indicated by the greater distance of the former from 0. Of every 1,000 words in these messages, roughly 11, on average, evoked constitutionality, another 13 evoked unity, and 14 evoked economy. By contrast, words evocative of partisanship were much less prominently featured in these messages, where they appeared at a rate of less than two per 1,000.

Having said this, we must immediately sound a caution against dwelling on the absolute values of these scores or even, in the case of the forcefulness dimensions, on their sign. In constructing a given dictionary, we may have failed to include some particularly important term or terms, thereby inadvertently altering the observed balance among themes. For example, even though the unity dictionary contains only 18 elements, words from it appeared much more often in twentieth-century veto messages than did words from the much more extensive partisanship dictionary; if the unity dictionary had been more comprehensive, this imbalance could have been even more pronounced. More generally, the two forcefulness scores and the four thematic scores are intended to be relative and indicative rather than absolute and comprehensive. Thus, it is best to compare, for example, one unity score or one set of unity scores with another unity score or set of unity scores, rather than with a score or set of scores associated with a different theme.

Did any clear trends in these messages evolve during the twentieth century? Our answer to this question is generally negative. Of the seven time-lines charted in Figure 1, five are either flat or fluctuate erratically over time. Only constitutionality and accessibility followed a more or less consistent course, the former by steadily increasing since Warren Harding was president; as we shall presently see, this trend marks, to some extent, a reversion to the tendency of the nation's earliest presidents to discuss institutional arrangements in their veto messages. As for accessibility, the linguistic difficulty of veto messages steadily declined during the twentieth century, but at a leisurely pace, averaging only -0.24 per president.

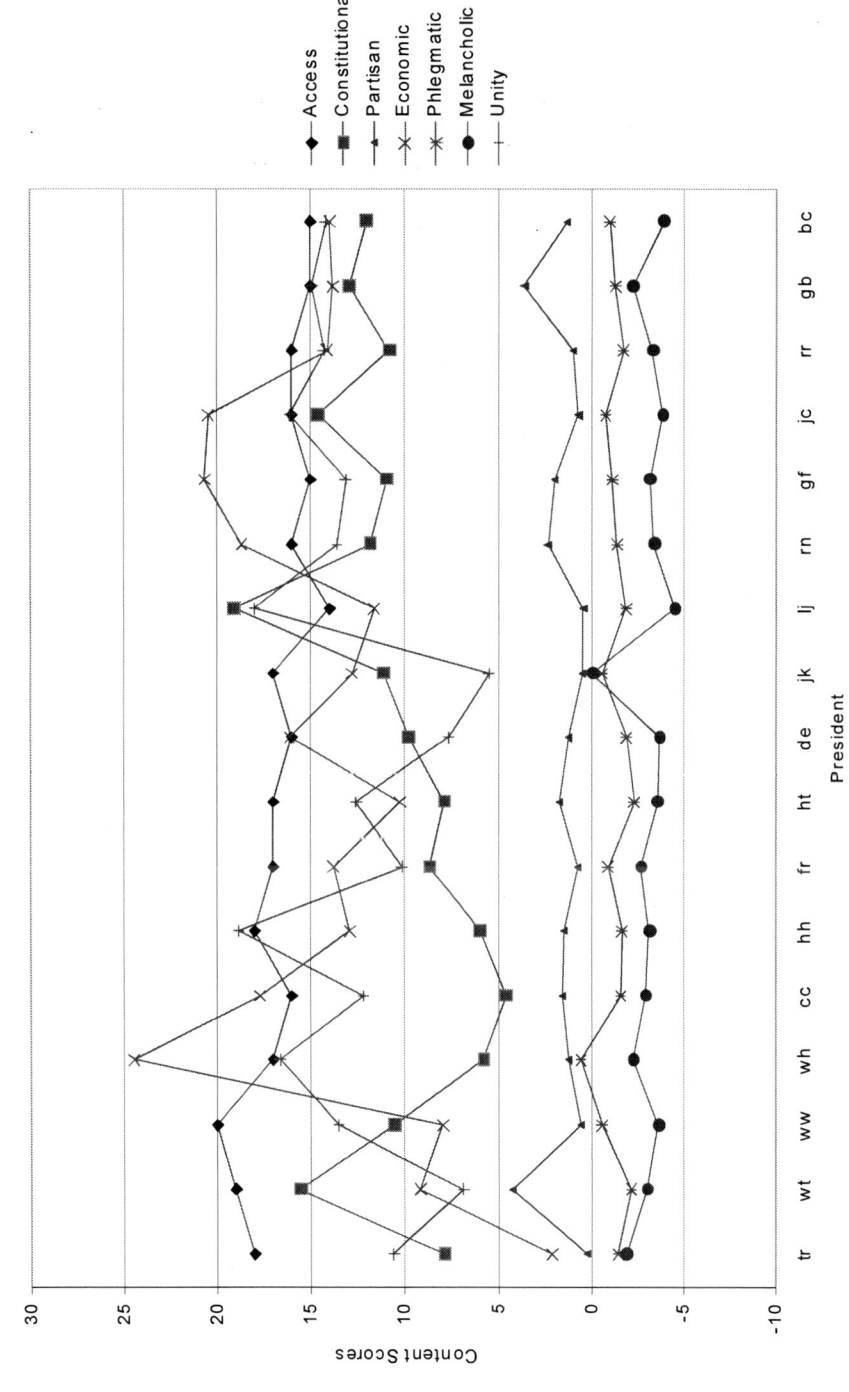

This brings us to the question of whether twentieth-century presidents as a group struck off in new directions in their veto messages, or whether they stayed on the course set by the nation's earliest presidents. The answer is that in most instances veto messages did not evolve during the twentieth century in ways that would have been considered at all unusual during the nation's formative era. (See Table 1.) Overall, these messages became neither more nor less accessible or forceful during the twentieth century, nor were twentieth-century presidents significantly more likely to work the themes of economy or unity into their messages.

On the other hand, in the earliest veto messages, the theme of constitutionality was somewhat more prevalent—though not significantly so—than it was during the twentieth century, reflecting Madison's (29.9) and Monroe's (24.0) unusually frequent references to institutional arrangements; the other two early presidents (Washington with 9.7 constitutional words per 1,000 and Jackson with 14.0) were unexceptional in this respect.[33] A more notable, and statistically significant, difference involved partisan language. Partisan references, which appeared only in trace amounts in the veto messages of any president, were almost entirely absent from the messages of Washington, Madison, Monroe, and Jackson. By no means did such references dominate the veto messages of twentieth-century presidents, but they were significantly more common, especially after the 1970s (though with the conspicuous exception of Jimmy Carter).

Overall, then, twentieth-century veto messages differed relatively little from their earliest predecessors; that is, over the course of two centuries, veto messages underwent minimal evolution as a sub-genre of presidential rhetoric. By contrast, some striking differences do emerge between veto messages and another sub-genre of presidential rhetoric, inaugural addresses. These differences come through clearly in Table 2, where we compare the words that 16 of the 17 twentieth-century presidents used in their veto messages to what the same presidents said immediately after being administered the oath of office.[34] These presidents obviously pitched their inaugural addresses much more to the mass audience, as indicated by the wide gap in Flesch formula scores between their veto messages (16.7) and their inaugural addresses (13.3). Veto messages, which, after all, are occasioned by disagreement with Congress, were also more forcefully stated (significantly so on the choleric/phlegmatic dimension) than inaugural addresses, which tended to be full of bland reassurances and soaring platitudes. Thematically, too, veto messages differed markedly from inaugural addresses: Of the 16 presidents, only one, Calvin Coolidge, used constitutional symbols more in his inaugural address than in his veto messages, a result more attributable to his disuse of such symbols in veto messages than to an embrace of such symbols in inaugurals. On average, the theme of constitutionality was more than three times as prominent in veto messages as in inaugural addresses. Virtually the same pattern held for the theme of economy. Only Taft had a greater proportion of economic symbols in his inaugural address than in his veto messages, and on average words pertaining to the economy were almost three times as prevalent in veto messages. As for unity symbols, as expected, these were far less abundant in the predominantly businesslike veto messages than in the highly ceremonial inaugural addresses, as indicated by the fact that on average, only 12.9 words per thousand in the veto messages but fully 100 words per thousand in the inaugural addresses came from our unity dictionary. The only real point of convergence between veto messages and inaugural addresses is their mutual eschewal of partisan language.

Table 2. The Language of 20th Century Veto Messages versus Inaugural Addresses (Paired t-tests for Mean Differences)

	Veto Messages	Inaugural Addresses	t-value
Accessibility	16.7	13.3	7.6**
Forcefulness			
Choleric/Phlegmatic	-1.2	-3.0	3.4*
Sanguinic/Melancholic	-3.0	-3.6	1.2
Constitutionality	10.6	3.2	6.7**
Partisanship	1.5	2.1	-1.3
Economy	13.8	4.9	5.9**
Unity	12.9	100.0	-4.2**
N	16	16	

Note: Accessibility entries—years of education; forcefulness entries—difference in words per thousand; remaining entries—words per thousand.
*p < .01. **p < .001.

The sense that veto messages are an altogether different mode of communication than inaugural addresses is strengthened by the fact that, with a single exception, knowing the score a president achieved on a given measure in his inaugural address(es) tells us essentially nothing about his score on the same measure in his veto messages. On a president-by-president basis, the correlation, averaged across six of the seven measures, between veto message scores and inaugural address scores is only .08. The exception is accessibility: The (in)accessibility of presidential language seems to transcend considerations of audience, with presidents who were more long-winded or more laconic in their inaugural addresses tending to demonstrate the same tendencies in their veto messages (r = .71). Of course, this is not to say that veto messages were as accessible as inaugural addresses, for Table 2 indicates that that was not the case.

Finally, are there any observable differences in language use across different types of presidents? If Gleiber and Shull's data on overall length and number of justifications are indicative, then we have no reason to think that Republican and Democratic presidents might have used distinctive language in their veto messages.[35] Our data give us little reason to rethink that expectation. (See Table 3.) The sole exception was on the partisanship theme, which Republicans sounded more than twice as frequently as Democrats—though, as noted above, no president made very frequent partisan references in his veto messages. Closer examination reveals that this difference stems largely from the pronounced partisanship of the veto messages of one Republican president in particular (Taft), and the above-average partisanship of the messages of three more recent Republican presidents (Nixon, Ford, and Bush). The identities of these presidents, each of whom confronted a Congress dominated by the partisan opposition for some (Taft) or all of his years in office (Nixon, Ford, and Bush) made us suspicious that the observed partisan difference was less between Republican and Democratic presidents per se than it was between those presiding over a divided government and those who did not bear this burden.

Table 3. The Language of 20th Century Veto Messages: Republican versus Democratic Presidents (Independent Sample t-tests for Mean Differences)

	Republicans	Democrats	t-value
Accessibility	16.7	16.5	0.3
Forcefulness			
Choleric/Phlegmatic	-1.3	-1.1	-0.7
Sanguinic/Melancholic	-2.8	-3.1	0.5
Constitutionality	9.7	12.0	-1.3
Partisanship	1.9	0.9	2.4*
Economy	15.0	13.0	0.8
Unity	12.9	12.9	0.0
N	10	7	

Note: Accessibility entries—years of education; forcefulness entries—difference in words per thousand; remaining entries—words per thousand.
*p < .01.

As we anticipated, in the veto messages of the seven twentieth-century presidents who never had the luxury of working with a Congress controlled by their own party, partisanship was more than twice as common (2.1 words per thousand) as it was in the messages of the five who never presided over a divided government–the only significant difference between such presidents.[36] (See Table 4.) This left five presidents (Taft, Wilson, Hoover, Truman, and Eisenhower) who each headed a combination of unified and divided governments. For them, we subdivided veto messages according to the composition of Congress at the time the vetoes were issued. The results indicate that a given president was significantly more likely to state his case forcefully when dealing with a Congress dominated by the partisan opposition, and was significantly more likely to cite economic factors when vetoing legislation passed by a Congress controlled by members of his own party. (See Table 5.) With only five presidents to consider, the difference on the partisanship theme falls short of statistical significance, but the magnitude of the difference (3.8 versus 1.8) is very similar to that of the significant difference shown in Table 4.

Table 4. The Language of 20th Century Veto Messages: Presidents under Unified versus Divided Government (Independent Sample t-tests for Mean Differences)

	Unified Government	Divided Government	t-value
Accessibility	16.6	15.4	2.3
Forcefulness			
Choleric/Phlegmatic	-0.9	-1.3	1.1
Sanguinic/Melancholic	-2.6	-3.1	1.0
Constitutionality	10.3	11.7	-0.7
Partisanship	0.8	2.1	-2.5*
Economy	14.7	16.3	-0.5
Unity	12.8	14.0	-0.8
N	7	5	

Note: Accessibility entries—years of education; forcefulness entries—difference in words per thousand; remaining entries—words per thousand.
*p < .01.

Table 5. The Language of 20th Century Veto Messages: Presidents Who Served Under Both Unified and Divided Government (Paired t-tests for Mean Differences)

	Unified Government	Divided Government	t-value
Accessibility	18.0	17.9	0.2
Forcefulness			
Choleric/Phlegmatic	-1.7	-1.5	-1.0
Sanguinic/Melancholic	-3.6	-2.9	-11.4**
Constitutionality	10.4	6.7	1.2
Partisanship	1.8	3.8	-1.0
Economy	12.8	8.5	4.9**
Unity	12.1	11.2	1.0
N	5	5	

Note: Accessibility entries—years of education; forcefulness entries—difference in words per thousand; remaining entries—words per thousand.
**$p < .001$.

CONCLUSION

Our analysis yields two clear conclusions. First, for the most part the language of the veto messages of the twentieth century differed little from that of the veto messages of the earliest presidents. With the exception of a greater proportion of partisan language, which appears attributable, at least in part, to the increased incidence of divided government, none of our stylistic or content measures differs substantially from the pattern established by the nation's earliest presidents. This finding confirms Campbell and Jamieson's and Spitzer's assertions that the basic form of veto messages was set as early as the Madison Administration. It further confirms our own suspicion that the production of veto messages has become institutionalized in a way that is resistant to radical changes. In large part, we think, this is due to the bureaucratic nature of the messages, and to the fact that they are generally drafted by department and agency personnel rather than by the president and his close advisors. The same factor also may account for the minimal differences we observed among the veto messages of different presidents, as the department and agency personnel drafting the veto messages may well carry over from one administration to another. Therefore, although presidents have come and gone, and although they have varied somewhat in their use of economic and unity symbols, they have been remarkably stable on the other measures employed here.

Second, the language of veto messages is considerably different than the language of inaugural addresses. Given the different audiences for the two forms of communication, this is perhaps unsurprising. Presidents have become more likely to use language accessible to a wider audience in their inaugural addresses, as Sigelman found, but the limited audience for veto messages imposes no such requirement. As a class, veto messages are less accessible, less partisan, and employ far fewer unity symbols than inaugural addresses, but more constitutional and economic language. Although the differences are slight, veto messages are also delivered with greater force. If inaugural messages—a form of public *and* popular rhetoric—can be treated as reasonably representative of other forms of public presidential rhetoric, then it would appear that veto messages occupy a unique and fairly stable niche in the taxonomy of presidential communications.

With the exception of partisan language, we have observed little systematic variation in veto messages that can be attributed to political circumstances. Partisan language is employed with greater frequency by presidents facing an opposition Congress, and by Republicans, but even these differences are relatively slight, reflecting only a few words in every thousand. That said, questions remain that are worthy of future research. For example, do a president's rhetorical devices vary by subject matter? Are there differences, for example, between the language used to reject foreign policy legislation and domestic policy bills? Another avenue for inquiry, hinted at above but not pursued here, is echoed by the literature on veto success and failure specifically and by notions of the "administrative" or "unilateral" presidency.[37] Do presidents use the language of veto messages strategically? Do they strengthen the language when prospects of an override are slim or when alternative mechanisms for policymaking are available? Alternatively, as was the case with Jackson's veto of the bank bill, do presidents use those opportunities to "go public" with their appeals, crafting messages for a wider audience than just Congress?

Campbell and Jamieson characterize the sub-genres of presidential rhetoric as the discourse of governance. Based on the evidence reported here, veto messages constitute a stable element of that discourse. They clearly belong more to the institutional presidency than to the public presidency. They are driven by the substantive (i.e., policy) interests of the departments and agencies that produce them, and as such seem to bear many of the marks of other public but largely non-popular forms of presidential rhetoric, such as executive orders, presidential decision memoranda, and presidential signing statements–comparisons to which offer another avenue for future research. Each of these has a specific institutional or official target rather than a popular one. As such, they constitute an integral, and highly stylized, component of the language of governance.

APPENDIX

The research reported in this paper is based upon our content analysis of the veto messages and inaugural addresses of the presidents of the twentieth century (Theodore Roosevelt through Bill Clinton) and, for purposes of comparison, the four early presidents (George Washington, James Madison, James Monroe, and Andrew Jackson) who vetoed public bills. The analysis focuses upon our measures of accessibility, forcefulness, unity, partisanship, constitutionality, and economy. We measure accessibility and forcefulness by adapting or applying measures employed in prior research. We use measures based upon dictionaries developed especially for the present study to tap the other four themes.

Accessibility

We used *PC-STYLE*,[38] a personal computer program that measures the readability of a text formula in terms of the mean number of syllables per word and the mean number of words per sentence–an adaptation of the conventional formula developed by Rudolph Flesch. On this measure, readability is expressed in terms of grade level; thus, whereas a score of 10 would signify that a person with 10 years of formal schooling could understand what is being said, it would take someone who had completed 15 years of school to achieve adequate comprehension of a text with a score of 15.

Forcefulness

Our measure of forcefulness was created by Martindale and Martindale and further developed by Sigelman, Martindale, and McKenzie.[39] The measure is based upon four basic temperaments: sanguinic (enthusiastic, optimistic, sociable, impersistent and irresponsible), melancholic (conservative, responsible, pessimistic, and anxious), choleric (impetuous, egocentric, active, and proud), and phlegmatic (calm, controlled, reasonable, and apathetic). These four temperaments combine to form two dimensions, with each temperament anchoring one of the poles: A sanguinic v. melancholic dimension and a choleric v. phlegmatic dimension. These in turn indicate forcefulness and its opposite, restraint. The dictionary contains over 1,000 words that are indicative of each temperament. Sample words for each of the categories are as follows: melancholic (anxious, concerned, critical, pessimistic, worried), sanguinic (carefree, contented, enthusiastic, hopeful), choleric (active, ambitious, greedy, impulsive, irritable), phlegmatic (apathetic, calm, inactive, slow, steadfast). For additional details on the measure, its derivation, and its adaptation see Sigelman, Martindale, and McKenzie. These dictionaries are implemented in the computer program *ALEXIS PC 1.4* (McKenzie, Martindale, Hogenraad, Stone, Kabanoff, Dunphy, West, Sigelman, and Clarke, 1996), which we employed here. The two dimensional scores were obtained by subtracting the number of phlegmatic words per thousand from the number of choleric words per thousand, and the number of melancholic words per thousand from the number of sanguinic words per thousand.

Unity

The frequency of presidential invocations of the unity theme was measured by counting the number of times a president used words from the unity dictionary per thousand words used. Word frequency counts for unity and all the remaining themes were conducted in the *WordCount* program (Sigelman, 1994). The unity dictionary, first used in Sigelman's analysis of inaugural addresses, contains the following elements: America, American, Americans, citizens, citizenry, country, nation, national, our, a people, the people, the public, together, union, United States, unity, us, we.

Partisanship

Our partisanship dictionary began with the coding scheme Hinckley (1990) devised for analyzing presidential addresses. Unfortunately, many terms that can be tabulated human coders using contextual cues, such as "1984" when used to refer to an election (but not, for example, to a novel), cannot be employed in context-free computerized word counts. Consequently, we dropped certain items from Hinckley's list and added some of our own. The frequency of presidential invocations of the partisanship theme was measured by counting the number of times a president used words from the partisanship dictionary per thousand words used. The partisanship dictionary contains the following elements: aisle, ballot, balloting, ballots, campaign, campaigning, campaigned, campaigns, convention, convention's, democrat, democrat's, democrats, democrats', democratic party, elect, elected, electing, election, election's, elections, elections', electoral, electorate, electorate's, electorates, electorates', elects, faction, factional, factions, factions', majority, majority's, majorities, majorities', nominate nominated, nominates, nominating, nomination, nominations, opposition, opposition's, the other side, party, party's, parties, parties', partisan, partisanship, political, politically, politician, politician's, politicians, politicians', politics, reelect, re-elect, reelected, re-elected, reelection, re-election, reelecting, re-electing, reelects, re-elects, republican, republicans, vote, voted, voter, voter's, voters, voters', votes, voting.

Constitutionality

The frequency of presidential invocations of the constitutionality theme was measured by counting the number of times a president used words from the constitutionality dictionary per thousand words used. The partisanship dictionary contains the following elements: according to law, appeals court, appeals courts, appellate court, appellate courts, articles of confederation, associate justice, bill of rights, chartered, checks and balances, chief executive, chief justice circuit court, circuit courts, clause, commander in chief, commander-in-chief, commerce clause, congress, congresses, congressional, constitution, constitutional, constitutions, court, court of appeal, court of appeals, courts of appeal, courts of appeals, department, departmental, departments, district court, district courts, enumerated power, enumerated powers, executive, executives, illegal, implied power, implied powers, judicial, judiciary, judge, judges, jurisdiction, justices, lawful, legal, legalized, legislative, legislator, legislatorial, legislators, legislature, necessary and proper, presidency, president, presidential, regulate, regulated, regulates, regulatory, separation of powers, sovereign, sovereignty, statute, statutory, supremacy, supreme court, unconstitutional, unlawful, vested.

Economy

The frequency of presidential invocations of the economy theme was measured by counting the number of times a president used words from the economy dictionary per thousand words used. The economy dictionary contains the following elements: appropriating, appropriation, appropriations, arrears, bonds, borrow, borrower, borrowed, borrowing, borrows, budget, budgetary, budgets, burden, burdening, burdens, burdensome, capital, cost, costing, costly, costs, credit, creditor, creditors, credits, currency, debit, debited, debitor, debitors, debits, debt, debted, debtor, debts, default, defaulted, defaulter, defaulting, defaults, deficit, deficits, economic, economical, economics, economies, economies', economize, economy, economy's, expend, expended, expending, expenditure, expenditures, expends, expense, expenses, expensive, export, exported, exporting, exports, floating capital, frugal, frugality, full employment, import, imported, importing, imports, indebt, indebtment, indebtments, indebted, inflating, inflation, inflationary, insolvent, insolvency, liabilities, liability, nonpayment, non-payment, notes, paid, parity, parsimonious, pay, paying, pays, premium, premiums, profligate, prudence, prudent, retrench, retrenched, retrenches, retrenching, retrenchment, retrenchments, revenue, revenues, save, save-all, saved, saves, saving, savings, specie, spend, spending, spends, spent, stock, stocks, surplus, surpluses, tariff, tariffs, tax, taxed, taxes, taxing, taxpayer, tax payer, tax payers, taxpayers, thrift, thriftiness, thrifty, treasury, unemployment, usury, waste, wasted, wasteful, wastes, wasting.

NOTES

Authors' note: The authors are grateful for the assistance and comments of Steve Balla, Paul Brewer, Andrew Barrett, Gregory Harness, James Pfiffner, Robert Watson, and anonymous reviewers for *White House Studies*.

[1] This total is as of the end of the 105th Congress. Through 1998, presidents had also pocket vetoed 1,065 bills, for a total of 2,536 vetoes. Nothing prevents presidents from stating their opposition to bills they pocket veto, but they are not required to do so since Congress cannot receive messages officially or react to the president's rejections. In fact, Presidents Madison through Andrew Johnson generally did provide Congress with their reasons for pocket vetoing bills. See Clement Vose, "The Memorandum Pocket Veto." *Journal of Politics* 26 (May 1964): 397-405. The practice fell into disuse during the Grant Administration and was not recommened until June 26, 1934, when the following White House statement announced that President Roosevelt was instituting the memorandum pocket veto: "In the past it has been customary in most cases involving [pocket] vetoes for the President to withhold his signature, thereby, in effect, allowing the bill to die without becoming a law. The President has desired, however, to take a more affirmative position than this, feeling that in the case of most legislation reasons for definite disapproval should be given. Therefore, he has written on the copy of each bill the words 'Disapproved and signature withheld,' and has appended in every case a brief statement giving the reason or reasons for disapproval." This practice was formalized during the Truman administration and has been in practice since.

[2] On this notion see Robert A. Spitzer, *The Presidential Veto: Touchstone of the American Presidency*. Albany, NY: State University of New York Press, 1988; and Karlyn Kohrs Campbell and Kathleen Hall Jamieson, *Deeds Done in Words: Presidential Rhetoric and the Genres of Governance*. Chicago: University of Chicago Press, 1990.

[3] Oddly enough, Jackson's lengthy and heated retort to the censure resolution is included in Veto Messages of the Presidents of the United States: 1792-1886, although it was not really a veto; a simple Senate resolution is not a public law and is thus not subject to veto.

[4] The former point can be found in Steven Skowronek, "Presidential Leadership in Political Time." The Presidency and the Political System, Michael Nelson, ed. Washington, DC: CQ Press, 1984, p. 94. The latter in Donald B. Cole, The Presidency of Andrew Jackson. Lawrence, KA: University Press of Kansas, 1993, p. 104. That said, Cole also points out that those who highlight the colorful language commencing and concluding the message tend to ignore the body of the message, which is largely a constitutional argument against the bank and modeled on Jefferson's objections offered more the fifteen years earlier.

[5] Spitzer, p. 51. Ironically, the only member of Tyler's cabinet who did not resign was Daniel Webster, who had been a vocal critic of Jackson's use of the veto during the debate that preceded the Senate's 1834 censure.

[6] A motion to refer the articles of impeachment to committee was defeated. Tyler vetoed ten bills in all, and on March 3, 1845, became the first president to have a veto overridden by Congress.

[7] Spitzer credits Jackson with being the first president to announce his veto intentions prior to the passage of legislation (p. 33).

[8] Campbell and Jamieson, p. 4.
[9] See, for example, Campbell and Jamieson, 1990; Roderick P. Hart, Verbal Style and the Presidency: A Computer-Based Analysis. Orlando, Florida: Academic Press, 1990; and Jeffrey K. Tulis, The Rhetorical Presidency. Princeton: Princeton University Press, 1987.
[10] Wayne Fields, Union of Words: A History of Presidential Eloquence. New York: Free Press, 1996, p. 24. Also see Richard J. Ellis, ed., Speaking to the People: The Rhetorical Presidency in Perspective. Amherst: University of Massachusetts Press, 1998.
[11] Campbell and Jamieson, p. 4.
[12] An alert reviewer correctly points out that presidential signing statements, though having the opposite message, also are prepared to be read rather than spoken and, further, that they are the product of bureaucratic hands. Both chambers of Congress have long-standing mechanisms for receiving messages (both positive and negative) from the president, entering them on the Journal, publishing them in the Record, and further disposing of them. See House Rule XII and Senate Rules 7 and 9 on receipt of messages. Procedures for considering the messages and voting to override the veto are contained in the precedents of the two chambers. Although contrary examples exist, the actual reading of the veto message is set aside by unanimous consent in the Senate. In the House, veto messages are "laid before the House" (but not read) by the speaker prior to disposition. In both chambers, "disposition" (which may mean an immediate vote, tabling, postponing to a date certain, or referral to committee) is considered to fulfill the mandate of the Constitution.
[13] See Carol Gelderman, All the Presidents' Words: The Bully Pulpit and the Creation of the Virtual Presidency. New York: Walker, 1997; and James C. Humes, Confessions of a White House Ghostwriter: Five Presidents and Other Adventures. Washington, DC: Regnery, 1997.
[14] See Spitzer, p. 28; Steven J. Wayne, The Legislative Presidency. New York: Haper & Row, 1978; and Steven J. Wayne, Richard L. Cole, and James F.C. Hyde, "Advising the President on Enrolled Legislation: Patterns of Executive Influence." Political Science Quarterly 94 (Summer 1979): 303-317.
[15] See Campbell and Jamieson; Hart; and Tulis.
[16] Albert Ringelstein, "Presidential Vetoes: Motivations and Classifications." Congress & the Presidency 12 (Spring 1985): 43-55.
[17] See Campbell and Jamieson.
[18] See Dennis W. Gleiber and Steven A. Shull, "Justifying Presidential Decisions: The Scope of Veto Messages." Congress & the Presidency 26 (Spring 1999): 41-59.
[19] Gleiber and Shull, p. 56.
[20] Strictly speaking, William McKinley also was a twentieth-century president. Re-elected in 1900, the last year of the nineteenth century, he served for less than a year of the new century before dying on September 14, 1901. We include all Clinton vetoes through the end of the 104th Congress.
[21] Pension vetoes by Cleveland did, in fact, excite considerable sectional stress. See Richard F. Bensel, Sectionalism and American Political Development. Madison: University of Wisconsin Press, 1984, p. 63. Our focus on the twentieth century, however, makes the exclusion of private bills reasonable. This exclusion eliminates all "relief" bills for private citizens, corporations, and other entities. Also excluded are bills (essentially private in nature) seeking to establish federal jurisdiction in court cases involving specifically named individuals, organizations, or groups. Because such bills are intended to aid the financial claims of specific parties, we treat them as private.
[22] U.S. Congress, Senate. Veto Messages of the Presidents of the United States, With the Action of Congress thereon. 49th Congress, 2d. Sess, Mis. Doc. No. 53. Washington, DC: U.S. Government Printing Office, 1886.
[23] We obtained the texts of the inaugural addresses from Inaugural Addresses of the Presidents of the United States from George Washington 1789 to George Bush 1989. Washington, DC: U.S. Government Printing Office, 1989; and, for 1993 and 1997, from the Washington Post.

24. See Lee Sigelman, "Presidential Inaugurals: The Modernization of a Genre." Political Communication 13 (January-March, 1996): 81-92.
25. A synopsis of the measure appears under "Accessibility" in our appendix. For a complete discussion see Rudolf Flesch. The Art of Readable Writing. New York: Harper & Row, 1974.
26. Campbell and Jamieson, p. 86.
27. Anne E. Martindale and Colin Martindale, "Metaphorical Equivalence of Elements and Temperaments: Empirical Studies of Bachelard's Theory of Imagination." Journal of Personality and Social Psychology. 55 (1988): 836-848. See also Lee Sigelman, Colin Martindale, and Dean McKenzie, "The Common Style of Common Sense." Computers and the Humanities. 30 (No. 5): 373-379.
28. Sigelman, Martindale, and McKenzie, p. 376.
29. Louis Fisher, The Constitution Between Friends: Congress, the President, and the Law. New York: St. Martin's, 1978.
30. Spitzer, Presidential Veto, p. 33. See also Cole, The Presidency of Andrew Jackson, p. 103-105. Jackson twelve vetoes, five regular and seven pocket, stood as the high-water mark until the administration of Andrew Johnson. But Madison's total of seven vetoes, a collection that included the first veto of a private bill and the first two pocket vetoes, wasn't dramatically different.
31. Campbell and Jamieson, p. 90.
32. Unfortunately, Ringelstein provided little information about his method of identifying keywords and did not list the keywords themselves, so we developed our own dictionary.
33. Washington produced two, brief, veto messages. The first offered a constitutional objection but without lengthy elaboration. The second, as noted at the outset, was purely on the grounds of economy and good sense. Thus his low level of constitutional language is not surprising. Jackson's veto messages had constitutional reasoning at their core but were leavened with populist appeals. As a result, his constitutional "score" is below two of his three predecessors but higher than the average for twentieth-century presidents–additional evidence, perhaps, for his status as a transition president.
34. Ford is omitted from this table, because, as an unelected president, he never delivered an inaugural address.
35. Gleiber and Shull, p. 46.
36. We include Bill Clinton in the group of seven. Although the Democrats controlled Congress during Clinton's first two years in office, 1993 and 1994, he vetoed no public bills in those years.
37. On the administrative presidency see Richard Nathan, The Administrative Presidency. New York: Wiley, 1983. For a more formalized and recent rendition, see Terry M. Moe and William G. Howell, "The Presidential Power of Unilateral Action." Journal of Law, Economics, and Organization.15 (March 1999): 132-179.
38. Jim Button, PC-STYLE [computer program] Bellevue, WA: ButtonWare, 1986.
39. Martindale and Martindale, "Metaphorical Equivalence..." and Sigelman, Martindale, and McKenzie, "The Common Style of Common Sense."

Chapter 7

A REVISIONIST VIEW OF GEORGE BUSH AND CONGRESS, 1989: PRESIDENTIAL SUPPORT, 'VETO STRENGTH,' AND LEGISLATIVE STRATEGY

Richard S. Conley[*]

INTRODUCTION

Assessments of George Bush's legislative presidency have been sharply critical. In the absence of an active, first-year agenda in 1989 many observers chided his first one hundred days as "'lagging,' 'faltering,' 'wasting time,' 'playing a losing hand,' and 'hitting the ground crawling'."[1] To the chagrin of liberals, his steadfast commitment to maintaining Reagan's policy legacy allegedly held the country "marching in place" for four years.[2] Some scholars have typecast Bush's successful use of the veto as "negative achievement,"[3] even as his exceptional ability to sustain his vetoes when challenged by the Democratic majority has now come to puzzle others.[4]

Application of several measures of presidential success — from positions on roll-calls to individual-level support in Congress — seemingly confirmed Bush's failure to meet expectations for his legislative presidency. His 54 percent roll-call success rate in 1989 was the lowest first-year figure recorded by *Congressional Quarterly* since the organization began keeping track of presidential position votes in 1953. Presidential scholars Jon Bond and Richard Fleisher found that congressional support of the president in the House of Representatives was much lower than anticipated by a baseline model, particularly among Bush's co-partisans.[5] Although later analysis suggested that Bush's legislative support was roughly what might be expected in the post-reform era,[6] conventional views of his putative shortcomings in the legislative arena have been difficult to dislodge.

This research challenges some of the prevailing wisdom about Bush's legislative presidency in 1989 by introducing different criteria for presidential success — *the*

---

[*] Author gratefully acknowledges funding provided by the College of Liberal Arts and Sciences, University of Florida, for this research.

benchmarks used by the administration itself. Prior studies have not fully come to grips with Bush's strategic adaptation to opposition party control of Congress. With the aid of primary data culled from the Bush Presidential Library in College Station, Texas, a more subtle analysis of floor votes prioritized by the White House in 1989 reveals that Bush did far better in terms of individual legislative support than scholars' baseline models have predicted. And such support was pivotal in Bush's ability to manage legislative outcomes through the veto power — a linkage scholars have overlooked.

Archival records reveal much about White House legislative strategy. Bush's "success" was in controlling the policymaking process, not getting legislation passed. He emphasized maintaining "veto strength" on priority floor votes, most of which were connected to the Democratic majority's agenda, rather than prevailing necessarily on the immediate roll-call outcome. The strategy was aimed at ensuring that initial roll-calls on select bills evidenced enough support — 33 percent or more of legislators — to foreclose the possibility of a successful override by the Democratic leadership. Grasping the administration's focus on partisan and cross-partisan support on floor votes, frequently under the veil of veto threats, sheds new light on the foundation for Bush's highly successful veto record.

The analysis is organized in three sections. The first section places Bush's legislative presidency into context by examining agenda magnitude between the branches and characteristics of voting alignments on the president's positions. The empirical analysis presented in the second section reconstitutes prior studies' forecasts of Bush's first-year congressional support among party factions in the House of Representatives using bills identified by the White House as a priority. A comparison of predicted and actual legislative support rates on this subset of White House "key votes" shows that Bush did far better than expected, particularly among his Republican party base, even if he lost on the roll-call outcome. Tracing the legislative histories of the priority legislation underscores how Bush's successful effort to maintain veto strength aided his ability to extract policy concessions from the Democratic leadership or halt objectionable legislation. The final section considers the significance of these findings for the larger question of presidential legislative success in recent periods of divided government.

STEERING THE LEGISLATIVE AGENDA: BUSH OR THE DEMOCRATS?

When pressure for governmental action recedes, divided partisan control of national institutions is far more likely to yield policy conflict between the president and Congress.[7] George Bush's election in 1988 with a solid majority of Democrats in charge of both houses of Congress yielded little consensus on the electorate's preferred course of action on the domestic front. Bush's lack of coattails — House Republicans lost three seats and Senate Republicans one — bolstered Democrats' argument that the president had no mandate.[8] But widespread split-ticket voting also robbed the Democratic majority of any claims to a mandate. The penultimate challenge for Bush in 1989 was to manage a more cohesive and activist Democratic majority that had responded to Reagan's early legislative victories and confrontational approach by strengthening organizational resources and party cohesion to advance its policy objectives.[9]

Bush's legislative leadership defied the "FDR" model that has become ingrained in popular expectations of the modern presidency.[10] The president's objective was to maintain the status quo and lower public expectations of the federal government.[11] Bush promised to guard against encroachments on Reagan's policy legacy. His leadership appeal "was not that he had an agenda for the future," Dean C. Hammer maintains, "but that he was better able to handle whatever situation arose."[12] Moreover, in light of the federal budget deficits that carried over from the Reagan years and the partisan disadvantage he faced in Congress, Bush did not seek to advance a far-reaching agenda in 1989.[13]

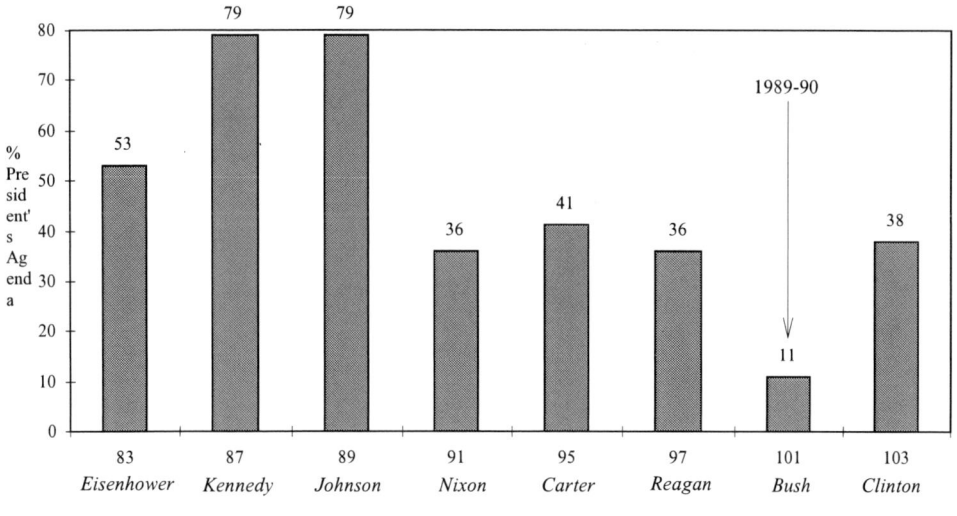

Figure 1 First-Term Presidents' Agenda as a Percentage of the Total Legislative Agenda in Congress

Source: adapted by author from Andrew J. Taylor, "Domestic Agenda Setting, 1947-1994," *Legislative Studies Quarterly* 23 (1998), 373-97.

Congressional Democrats set the basic contours of legislative business and Bush's lack of an agenda placed him in a defensive role on much legislation that emerged. Figure 1 shows the proportion of the total legislative agenda set by first-term presidents during their initial two years from 1953-1994.[14] The share of legislation connected to Bush's agenda (11%) was the lowest for all presidents. Only five of 45 measures reflected Administration priorities. Although there is a noticeable decline in presidential agenda-setting since Kennedy and Johnson in an era of greater resource constraints, Nixon, Carter, Reagan, and Clinton all set more than a third of the congressional docket in their first two years.

The key for Bush was that he wound up opposing the lion's share of bills that made it to the floor, particularly in the realm of domestic policy. House Democrats used the organizational perquisites of majority control to push legislation spanning budget issues, social policy, labor, and the environment. Of the 86 positions he took on roll-calls in the House of Representatives in 1989, Bush opposed 54 of the bills (63%). On average, Democrats supported the president's position less than two-fifths of the time. Party-unity voting was the rule, not the exception. Nearly two-thirds of Bush's policy positions pitted a majority of Republicans against a majority of Democrats.

Bush adapted his legislative strategy to the institutional constraints he met in Congress. Often unable to control roll-call outcomes through cross-party coalition-building and with only 175 Republicans in the House, the president turned party-unity to his advantage in conjunction with implied and applied use of the veto. Veto signals on legislation adopted on partisan grounds, or occasionally with the support of the remaining contingent of conservative Democrats enabled Bush to force policy negotiation. Otherwise, the Democratic leadership was compelled to engage in "blame-game" politics[15] by attempting overrides that were doomed to failure. A closer examination of congressional support for Bush, and the emphasis on "veto strength" on votes prioritized by the White House, suggests how the president was more successful in the legislative realm in a way that scholars have missed.

DATA AND ANALYSIS

Scholars confront a fundamental problem in the attempt to evaluate presidential success and congressional support for the president on the basis of roll-call outcomes: Which votes should be used? Since 1953, *Congressional Quarterly* has recorded all public positions presidents take on pending legislation. This pool of position votes comprises routine legislation, votes on amendments, as well as priorities of the administration and congressional leaders. Scholars have suggested a variety of ways to ferret out issues of greatest significance to gauge executive influence, including a focus on *Congressional Quarterly's* "key votes" and "conflictual votes" that exclude lopsided outcomes.[16] All of these measures are aimed at tapping elements of the president's agenda and/or high-profile issues of national importance that are tests of presidential power.

Rarely do scholars have the ideal list of bills *actually prioritized by the White House*.

The exception is the discovery of such lists in the archival holdings of the presidential library system managed by the National Archives and Records Administration. Covington found "headcount" data of members' positions kept by the Office of Congressional Relations for Presidents Kennedy and Johnson, including some issues on which the president chose not to take a public stand.[17] Conley discovered whip-check data and White House lobbying records detailing Gerald Ford's efforts to sustain key veto override votes.[18]

Records uncovered at the George Bush Presidential Library in College Station, Texas, offer a unique, "insider" view of which votes were considered critical to the White House in 1989. In January of 1990, Frederick D. McClure, Assistant to the President for Legislative Affairs, compiled a list of 24 House roll-call votes prioritized by the administration during the first session of the 101st Congress.[19] McClure believed that his analysis of individual members' support of Bush in 1989 was more useful than *Congressional Quarterly's* measure, which was based on all recorded votes on which the administration expressed a preference. "By comparison," he wrote to the president, "our analysis is based on selected key votes — those in which a clear Presidential position was taken *and* the vote was treated as a priority by the administration."[20] Eighteen of the 24 votes concerned domestic policy and budget issues. Six votes concerned foreign affairs and defense. Appendix 1 provides a detailed listing of the votes.

The advantage of using this subset of votes to measure Bush's legislative success and congressional support for his positions is twofold. First, roll-call success and individual members' support scores reflect the administration's own standards of bills with priority status. Comparing congressional support scores on this pool of bills to scholars' baseline model predictions on all position votes offers an alternative test of presidential influence. Second, McClure's analysis casts light on the White House's legislative strategy for dealing with the Democratic agenda. McClure noted that Bush's position prevailed outright on only 13 of the 24 votes (54%). But he took pains to note that "Significantly, we had veto strength (146 or more votes) on all of the 24 key votes."[21] The statement is a straightforward acknowledgment that the administration approached building legislative support in Congress in anticipation of using implied use of the veto power to influence policy outcomes. It is thus possible to examine more closely how veto strength on the roll-call outcomes that Bush lost did — or did not — work to his advantage in conjunction with veto threats.

BUSH'S ROLL-CALL SUCCESS ON WHITE HOUSE KEY VOTES, 1989

Bush's 54 percent win-loss ratio on priority votes in the House of Representatives paralleled his success rate for *Congressional Quarterly's* overall measure (Table 1). Six of his 13 victories came with the support of a majority of Democrats. In other cases the president was able to cobble together winning coalitions on the basis of Republican unity and the support of moderate-to-conservative Democrats. Several of his immediate victories were in the realm of foreign policy. Bush prevailed on a bipartisan accord on Central America. Aid to Central America had been one of the most contentious issues to carry over from Reagan's presidency. Bush also beat back several amendments, including one proposal to de-fund "Star Wars" (the Strategic Defense Initiative) in favor of drug interdiction and another restricting military aid to El Salvador. On the domestic front Bush's victories included the savings and loan bailout plan, foiling amendments on emergency supplemental aid and budget reconciliation legislation, and two failed veto override attempts — one on an increase in the minimum wage and the other for appropriations for the Department of Labor that contained provisions to lift some abortion restrictions.

Table 1* Bush's Victory Ratio on White House Key Votes, 1989

	N = 24
Overall	13
	(54%)
Democrats	6
	(25%)
Republicans	24
	(100%)

* Votes on which the president won a majority of members overall and by party

All eleven of Bush's losses were party-unity votes: A majority of Democrats voted against a majority of Republicans. On the domestic side the losses ranged from legislation charging the president to set up a congressional panel to investigate a labor dispute at Eastern Airlines, two amendments targeting the minimum wage bill, and oil pollution liability. On foreign and defense policy Bush lost votes on a resolution of disapproval on the co-development of the FS-X aircraft with Japan and several amendments on a defense bill (HR 2461).

Bush's success rate on White House key vote roll-calls begs several important questions. How did the support the president received from his co-partisans and conservative Democrats on priority votes compare to forecasts of congressional support? How did "veto strength" on the bills Bush lost bolster his negotiating position with the House Democratic leadership? The next two subsections take up these questions in turn.

INDIVIDUAL LEGISLATIVE SUPPORT: BASELINES FOR COMPARISON

A comparison of members' actual support of the president on White House key votes to levels of support forecast by regression models based on partisanship, ideology, and the president's job approval tests Bush's legislative influence and success in 1989 from the vantage point of the Administration's issue priorities. Forecast errors may be used to ascertain whether partisan and opposition members supported the president more or less often than expected on this subset of issues compared to all position votes.

Presidential scholars Jon Bond and Richard Fleisher were the first to develop a baseline model of congressional support of the president through regression analysis.[22] They drew a random sample of 500 House members' presidential support scores from 1959-1974. Using party affiliation, the president's mean year public approval, and the absolute difference between members' and the president's support for the *conservative coalition* as an indicator of ideological conflict,[23] Bond and Fleisher were able to explain 52 percent of the variance in presidential support scores. The model estimation is as follows:

$$PSS = 59.99 + .27PPs - .35ICs + 7.67Xo - .16PPo - .27ICo + e$$

Where:
- PSS = presidential support score
- PPs = presidential popularity and House member is of the president's party, 0 otherwise;
- ICs = ideological conflict between the president and member of the president's party, 0 otherwise;
- Xo = 1 if member is of the opposition party, 0 otherwise;
- PPo = presidential popularity and the House member is of the opposition party, 0 otherwise;
- ICo = ideological conflict between the president and member of the opposition party, 0 otherwise;

The Bond and Fleisher model suggests that ideological conflict between the branches drives down legislative support at roughly the same rate for members of both parties. Presidential popularity is positively associated with partisan support but shows an inverse relationship for members of the opposition.[24] As the positive sign for the dummy variable for partisanship (Xo) shows, members of the opposition party are *not* automatically predisposed to support the president less often.

Bond and Fleisher's baseline estimation has been critiqued in light of institutional and electoral changes that post-date the sample period 1959-1974. Mark Joslyn argues persuasively that increasing partisanship in the House of Representatives, greater ideological conflict between the parties in Congress, particularly on budget issues, and the strengthening of party leadership structures in the post-reform era have diminished presidential support.[25] Drawing inferences about presidential support from data ending in the mid-1970s, he argues, is problematic. Joslyn re-estimates the Bond and Fleisher model using sample data for the period 1977-1988 to show how structural change in the House has had a pronounced impact on presidential support. The parameter estimates for the "post-reform" sample period were as follows:

$PSS = 71.66 + .039PPs - .52IC - 26.75Xo + .18PPo - .396ICo + e$

Joslyn's model explains a larger proportion of the variance in support scores (76%) and shows that ideological conflict between the branches has come to play a much larger role in conditioning presidential support. Opposition members also appear far less supportive compared to the Bond and Fleisher data. Members of the opposition are expected to support the president nearly 27 percent less than the president's co-partisans. This finding dovetails with evidence of increasing partisanship in the House in recent decades.[26] Public approval is positively related to support for both parties, but the impact is much greater for members of the opposition. Joslyn concludes that presidents' legislative fortunes in the opposition party may be much more contingent upon the public's evaluation of their job performance in the post-reform era.

Table 2 Forecast Errors of Bush's First-Year Legislative Support by Party Factions, *Congressional Quarterly* Position Votes and White House Key Votes Analysis

Party Faction	CQ Position Votes, 1989	CQ Position Votes, 1989	White House Key Votes Analysis, 1989	White House Key Votes Analysis, 1989
	Mean Forecast Error *Bond and Fleisher Model*	Mean Forecast Error *Joslyn Model*	Mean Forecast Error *Bond and Fleisher Model*	Mean Forecast Error *Joslyn Model*
Republican Party base	-9.23	3.50	10.61	15.93
Cross-pressured Republicans	-20.08	-1.92	-6.87	5.90
Cross-pressured Democrats	9.40	4.91	8.73	11.74
Democratic Party base	1.91	4.24	-11.68	-1.53
Mean Forecast Error (all legislators)	*-1.77*	*3.85*	*-.31*	*7.10*

Bond and Fleisher and Joslyn test George Bush's legislative support with their respective models based on *all presidential position votes in 1989*. They come to very different conclusions about Bush's legislative strategy and success. Examining the columns to the left in Table 2, the forecast errors for the Bond and Fleisher model show that Bush received less support from Republicans than expected. Under-support was most pronounced among cross-pressured Republicans (members of the GOP with ideological scores closer to the Democratic party). Bond and Fleisher attribute the lower levels of support from Bush's GOP base and moderate Republicans to a strategy of reaching out to Democrats. By contrast, Joslyn's model shows far less error in forecasts of congressional support.[27] Joslyn concludes that congressional support for Bush was on par with expected levels in the post-reform era. Conservative Democrats were somewhat more supportive overall, but Bush's average support among the opposition hovered around 37 percent. At a time of greater intra-party cohesion, the average Republican's support score of 69 percent is very close to the model's forecast.

The goal of the data presented in Table 2 is not to reconcile the debate over the Bond and Fleisher and Joslyn models. Rather, the objective is to show that when either model is applied to congressional support on White House key votes in 1989, *Bush did better generally than expected, particularly among his partisan base*. The two right hand columns of Table 2 present forecast errors derived from the support scores from McClure's analysis of 24 key votes and the parameters of the Bond and Fleisher and Joslyn regression models, respectively. Thus, the data in the two right-hand columns are estimates from these existing baseline models, not from a "new" model of the author's creation.

The right-hand columns show better-than-expected congressional support of Bush's positions on priority bills, substantiating the Administration's efforts to marshal veto strength with the aid of GOP stalwarts and moderate-to-conservative Democrats. The "all legislators" row in Table 2 shows the mean forecast error for all 435 members. Using the parameter estimates of the Bond and Fleisher model, Bush's overall support was almost right on par with expectations — his overall support was less than half a percent lower than anticipated. Employing the Joslyn model, Bush's overall support was about 7 percent greater than expected. Let us examine support across sub-groupings of legislators in more detail.

On the issues of greatest importance to the White House, Bush's overtures to the Democratic majority are less evident and his strategy appears far more partisan than Bond and Fleisher posit. Bush drew the most support from his co-partisans and legislators to the right of the ideological spectrum in both parties. Support of Bush among members of the Republican party base averaged 83 percent (std. dev. = 10.5%). This level of support was 10 to nearly 16 percent greater than predicted by the Bond and Fleisher and Joslyn models, respectively. Moreover, Bush did better among more conservative Democrats—by nearly 12 percent over the Joslyn model forecast and nearly nine percent better than the Bond and Fleisher model. The average southern Democrat supported Bush about 50 percent of the time (std. dev. = 22.9%), some eight percentage points higher than Joslyn's model forecasts. Support from the liberal Democratic base was far less, by about 12 percent, than the Bond and Fleisher model forecasts — but approximately what could be expected according to Joslyn's parameters. Liberal Democrats supported Bush's key vote positions only 26 percent of the time (std. dev. = 9.8%), reflecting the substantial inter-branch conflict that developed around the majority's policy agenda.

Results of separate analysis of other sub-groups are consistent with Bush's emphasis on building support among congressional conservatives and his party base on key votes.

Members of the extended Republican leadership supported the president, on average, 84 percent of the time on key votes (std. dev. = 10.8%).[28] This level of support is 11 and 17 percent greater than predicted by the Bond and Fleisher and Joslyn models, respectively. Bush relied steadily on the Republican leadership to shore up party-unity. Democratic leaders, mirroring the party's liberal base, were less supportive. The average leader's support score of 33 percent (std. dev. = 16.6%) was nearly 7 percent less than forecast by the Bond and Fleisher model but consistent with expectations of the Joslyn model.

The central point of the reconstituted support score predictions using White House key votes is that *not all position votes carry the same weight from the perspective of the White House*. On the votes the White House viewed as critical, Bush garnered stronger partisan support and backing from cross-pressured Democrats than scholars' models forecast. The lion's share of this support was in opposition to the Democratic leadership's agenda. Because the payoff of such support was not always immediate for Bush — he lost 11 of the 24 roll-calls — the subtleties of his legislative strategy have drawn inadequate attention.

Bush's veto threats on losing roll-calls, and the appearance of strong partisanship and occasionally conservative Democrats' backing of his positions, facilitated negotiations with Democratic leaders to drop objectionable provisions on some bills. In several cases Bush forced the majority leadership in Congress to engage in "strategic disagreement"[29] as Democrats attempted override votes that were doomed to fail. In several such cases Democratic leaders' bid to win public sympathy was abortive, and Bush won policy concessions on the next round of negotiations.

"VETO STRENGTH" AND VETO THREATS: A CLOSER ANALYSIS

Bush's emphasis on veto strength on losing roll-calls in the House of Representatives yielded success most visibly on measures that were vetoed and subject to override attempts. Bush's ability to withstand challenges to his vetoes halted the legislation on Eastern Airlines and the FS-X aircraft and won compromises from the Democratic leadership on minimum wage and labor appropriations following failed override attempts. Bush had threatened to veto each of these bills save SJR 113, which was a resolution of disapproval of an executive agreement the president had reached with Japan on the co-production of the FS-X fighter jet.

The president forced the hand of the Democratic leadership on several override attempts that were clearly subject to "blame-game" tactics. Democratic leaders chose to ignore the president's veto threats and retain objectionable provisions in bills. After Bush cast a veto, the leadership knew in advance that the overrides would fail because of the veto strength demonstrated on the roll-call outcome — but they pushed forth anyway to publicly demonstrate their resolve. These failed override attempts were a kind of position-taking aimed at building electoral support and posturing for future negotiations rather than affecting immediate legislative outcomes.[30] However, it was Bush who won key concessions in subsequent bargaining.

The minimum wage bill (HR 2) passed in Spring of 1989 was exemplary. Bush rejected Democrats' efforts to increase the wage floor past $4.25 per hour and favored the inclusion of a sub-minimum training wage. The majority used its procedural advantages in the House to foreclose passage of the president's proposal, sponsored by Republican Bill Goodling. The Rules Committee employed a "king-of-the-hill" tool to ensure that the president's proposal would be considered first and that the last measure to win approval — favored by the Democratic leadership — would be adopted.[31] The Goodling amendment went down to defeat 198-218, and the Democrats' plan for a more generous wage increase to $4.55 per hour (the Murphy amendment), was adopted 240-179. Both White House key votes evidenced strong partisanship and veto strength. Bush vetoed the measure after the Senate approved the bill, calling the increase "excessive."[32]

Democrats had tried to dissuade Bush from vetoing the measure by putting public pressure on the White House. Tony Coelho, the House Democratic whip, argued that "If Bush vetoes this, the American people will have to judge whether he is being kinder and gentler toward working people or some other group of Americans."[33] Senate majority leader George Mitchell called Bush's veto "particularly offensive to millions of poor working Americans."[34] The House leadership then launched an override effort to embarrass the president. But Bush and House Republicans viewed the budgetary implications of the increase in the minimum wage as an issue on which to stand firm and show resolve. The symbolic override attempt was defeated by roughly the same margin of votes that won passage of the Murphy amendment. The impasse ultimately compelled negotiations between the branches that produced a compromise agreement some six months later. Bush won both a cap on an increase in the minimum wage of $4.25 and the training wage he had proposed.[35]

In a similar vein, Bush made good on a threat to veto appropriations for the Department of Labor over the issue of abortion funding (HR 2990). The House agreed to a Senate provision allowing Medicaid funding of abortions in cases involving rape and incest, reversing a long-standing rule that provided for abortions only if the life of the mother was in peril. The conference report was passed by a large margin (364-56), as many who supported the bill despite the abortion provisions did so to avoid jeopardizing other programs.[36] Bush took a firm position against the Senate amendment, and a separate roll-call passed by only five votes in the House. Despite losing the roll-call the president won strong Republican support and marshaled 71 Democrats behind his stand.

Democrats pressed the issue for political gain. The majority hoped to portray Bush's stand against the Medicaid provision as inconsistent with campaign promises to support an exception for rape and incest.[37] Bush was undeterred and after casting his veto, made the case to sustain his decision based on the narrowness of the abortion amendment vote. The Democratic leadership recognized that the votes did not exist to trump the president's veto pen, but wanted to draw attention to increased support of 50 votes for the Medicaid exception compared to the last attempt under President Reagan in 1988.[38] Pro-abortion groups and some Democrats endeavored to paint Bush and Republicans as out of step with public opinion on the issue. The executive director of the National Abortion Rights Action League (NARAL) contended that the override vote would "galvanize America's pro-choice majority and help identify political targets in 1990 and 1992" while Oregon Democrat Les AuCoin called Bush's veto "a sellout to the extreme right."[39] Nonetheless, the president converted back 82 Republicans and 57 Democrats who had voted for the conference report — the vast majority of whom had voted *against* the Senate amendment on abortion funding — and the override was foiled by a comfortable margin. A continuing resolution kept the Department of Labor funded temporarily. A month later Democrats sent Bush a $157 billion appropriations bill void of the abortion language, which he promptly signed.

Bush carried through on his veto threat of legislation (HR 1231) directing him to set up a bipartisan congressional committee to investigate an eight-month old strike by pilots and machinists at Eastern Airlines. The White House key vote on passage of the measure evidenced strong party-unity and was thirty votes shy of the threshold to override. Bush vetoed the bill on the grounds that the matter belonged in federal bankruptcy court and Congress had no basis to intervene in such labor-management disputes. But as California Democrat Douglas Bosco contended, "Democrats see political advantage simply in pressing Bush to reject it. The practical reality is that this is going to be the first opportunity to show that George Bush is anti-labor."[40] House leaders brought up an override some five months after Bush's veto as the strike lingered, in large part to show solidarity with union organizations that had lobbied intensely for the bill.[41] As in the case of the minimum wage legislation and appropriations for the Labor Department, the override vote largely paralleled the passage margin of the original legislation and the president's veto was sustained. The thwarted override "handed Bush an easy victory" in his second veto showdown with Congress in 1990.[42]

Veto strength in the House also aided Bush's drive to stave off congressional efforts to impose restrictions on co-production of the FS-X fighter jet with Japan (SJR 113). The resolution was introduced by Democratic Senator Alan Dixon, who led forces opposed to the agreement. A separate House resolution (HJRes 254) never emerged from the Foreign Affairs Committee. The White House contended that sensitive technology was protected under the agreement, which administration officials forecast to bring $2.5 billion into the U.S. economy. Critics argued that protections in the "memorandum of understanding" between the two nations were insufficient and that the trade deficit with Japan would only expand.[43]

While passage of the resolution in the Senate did not include a record vote, the measure was adopted largely along party lines in the House and some 50 votes below the threshold to override a veto. Bush vetoed the measure on the grounds that the resolution infringed on the president's constitutional authority in foreign affairs. His argument held water with the Senate, where an override attempt failed by one vote. Regardless, had the Senate succeeded with the override, House Democratic leaders would have had to surmount a formidable margin of support for Bush's position.

CONCLUSIONS

This analysis of key votes prioritized by the White House in 1989 offers a fresh perspective on George Bush's first-year legislative strategy. The results challenge some of the criteria scholars routinely employ to evaluate presidential "success." Archival records emphasize the linkage between congressional support for Bush, veto strength on roll-call outcomes, veto threats on pending legislation, and policy negotiation. Bush's frequent losses on immediate roll-call outcomes belied a more complex strategy for dealing with the opposition majority in Congress. Support from his party base and from moderate-to-conservative Democrats on priority legislation was better than scholars' baseline models predicted. Such support was pivotal in conjunction with vetoes threatened and vetoes cast, even if the payoff was not instantaneous. Grasping this strategy solves some of the mystery surrounding Bush's mastery of the veto power over the course of his term, despite frequent override challenges by the Democratic leadership.

This research raises several broad issues for the study of presidential-congressional relations. The debate about which votes best reflect presidential priorities for evaluations of legislative success should be reexamined. Clearly, not all position votes receive the same level of attention and priority status by the White House. Archival records have the potential to clarify presidential priorities. In the absence of archival records, scholars might examine presidents' public activities (State of the Union, speeches, press conferences, etc.) to glean which issues appear most important to the Administration — whether the president or the governing majority in Congress is the driving force behind legislative outcomes. It then becomes vital to look beyond immediate roll-call outcomes in our evaluations of presidential success.

A multifaceted approach that embraces the linkage between roll-calls, individual legislative support, vetoes threatened and applied, and the degree to which policy outcomes ultimately coincide with the president's preferences furnishes a more comprehensive basis to assess presidential strategy and engagement in the legislative realm. These points are particularly critical in evaluating presidents' relative success under conditions of divided party control in recent decades. Presidents' emphasis on halting legislation, or forcing negotiation with opposition majorities through the veto power, entails a different notion of presidential success than the type valorized by the "textbook presidency." Yet the strategy is quite consistent with rise of stronger institutional parties in Congress and more assertive opposition majorities in the 1980s and 1990s that have limited presidents' room to maneuver to build winning legislative coalitions.

This analysis highlights the paradox of Bush's presidency. Archival records suggest that by the yardstick the administration used to assess legislative success, the president's ability to halt or modify elements of the Democratic party's agenda in Congress was superior. Scholarly evaluations of Bush's legislative presidency, however, posit a mediocre — if not failed — legacy on the domestic front. Recriminations include his alleged missed opportunity to use extraordinarily high job approval following the Gulf War to advance a comprehensive agenda,[44] despite few indications that the Democratic majority was willing to follow the president's policy lead in foreign or domestic affairs.[45] Perceptions of Bush's shortcomings may stem from his inability to preempt the congressional majority and use the bully pulpit effectively to reframe the policy debate through the implied and applied use of the veto power in the way that his successor, Bill Clinton, did so successfully from 1995-1996. This may be the lesson, then, of Bush's legislative presidency for future occupants of the Oval Office who face divided government and are forced to rely heavily on the veto power.

APPENDIX 1 WHITE HOUSE "KEY VOTES" ANALYSIS, 1989

Bill No.	Date	White House Position	Outcome	Democrats	Republicans	Win/Loss	Subject
HR 1231	3/15/89	Nay	252-167	232-15	20-152	Loss	Eastern Airlines Dispute
HR 2	3/23/89	Yea	198-218	44-102	154-16	Loss	Goodling amendment/minimum wage
HR 2	3/23/89	Nay	240-179	221-28	19-151	Loss	Murphy amendment/minimum wage

Bill	Date	Position	Total Vote	Dem Vote	Rep Vote	Result	Description
HR 2	3/23/89	Nay	248-171	226-24	22-147	Loss	Passage of HR 2/minimum wage
HR 1750	4/13/89	Yea	309-110	152-99	157-11	Win	Bipartisan Accord on Central America
HR 2072	4/26/89	Nay	172-252	163-92	9-160	Win	Foley amendment/Dire Emergency Supplemental Appropriations
HCR 106	5/4/89	Yea	263-157	157-96	106-61	Win	Budget Resolution
HR 2072	5/24/89	Nay	227-197	219-33	8-164	Loss	Dire Emergency Supplemental Appropriations/Passage
HR 2442	5/24/89	Nay	205-213	201-47	4-166	Win	Star Wars for Drug Wars Act of 1989
SJR 113	6/7/89	Nay	241-168	205-37	36-131	Loss	FSX Weapon System Development with Japan
HR 2	6/14/89	Nay	247-178	227-28	20-150	Win	Veto override attempt of HR 2/minimum wage
HR 1278	6/15/89	Yea	320-97	196-51	124-46	Win	Financial Institutions Reform, Recovery, and Enforcement Act
HR 2655	6/28/89	Nay	185-233	178-68	7-165	Win	McHugh amendment/El Salvador military aid
HR 2461	7/26/89	Yea	176-244	53-194	123-50	Loss	Skelton amendment/Stealth bomber
HR 2461	7/27/89	Nay	223-201	204-48	19-153	Loss	Stenholm amendment/Davis-Bacon provisions
HR 1278	8/3/89	Yea	221-199	182-67	39-132	Win	Conference Report/Financial Institutions Reform, Recovery, Enforcement Act
HR 3299	9/28/89	Nay	190-239	189-64	1-175	Win	Rostenkowski Amendment/Budget Reconciliation
HR 3299	10/5/89	Yea	195-230	36-214	159-16	Loss	Stenholm amendment/Head Start/Social Services
HR 2990	10/11/89	Nay	212-207	173-71	39-136	Loss	Department of Labor Appropriations
HR 2990	10/25/89	Nay	231-191	189-59	42-132	Win	Override attempt of HR 2990/Department of Labor Appropriations
HR 2710	11/1/89	Yea	382-37	247-2	135-35	Win	Minimum wage
HR 1465	11/8/89	Nay	213-207	173-75	40-132	Loss	Miller amendment/Oil Pollution Liability and Compensation Act
HR 1465	11/9/89	Nay	185-197	150-71	35-126	Win	Miller amendment/Oil Pollution Liability and Compensation Act
HR 3299	11/21/89	Yea	272-128	186-47	86-81	Win	Conference Report/Budget Reconciliation

NOTES

[1] Barbara Kellerman, "Beware the Rush to Judge a New President," *Christian Science Monitor*, March 17, 1989, p. 19.

[2] Michael Duffy and Dan Goodgame, *Marching in Place: The Status Quo Presidency of George Bush* (New York: Simon and Shuster, 1992).

[3] Michael Foley, "The President and Congress," in Dilys M. Hill and Phil Williams, eds., *The Bush Presidency: Triumphs and Adversities* (New York: St. Martin's Press, 1994).

[4] Charles Cameron, *Veto Bargaining: Presidents and the Politics of Negative Power* (New York: Cambridge University Press, 2000).

[5] Jon Bond and Richard Fleisher, "Assessing Presidential Support in the House II: Lessons from George Bush," *American Journal of Political Science* 36 (1992), pp. 525-41.

[6] Mark R. Joslyn, "Institutional Change and House Support: Assessing George Bush in the Postreform Era," *American Politics Quarterly* 23 (1995), pp. 62-80.

[7] Paul J. Quirk and Bruce Nesmith, "Divided Government and Policy Making: Negotiating the Laws," in Michael Nelson, ed., *The Presidency and the Political System* (Washington, D.C.: Congressional Quarterly, 1995).

[8] Colin Campbell, "Presidential Leadership," in Gilliam Peele, Christopher J. Baily, and Bruce Cain, eds., *Developments in American Politics* (New York: St. Martin's Press, 1992), p. 103.

[9] David W. Rohde, *Parties and Leaders in the Postreform House* (Chicago: University of Chicago Press, 1991); Barbara Sinclair, "The Emergence of Strong Leadership in the 1980s House of Representatives," *Journal of Politics* 54 (1992), pp. 657-84; Paul S. Herrnson and Kelly D. Patterson, "Toward a More Programmatic Democratic Party? Agenda-Setting and Coalition Building in the House of Representatives," *Polity* 27 (1995), pp. 607-28.

[10] William E. Leuchtenburg, *In the Shadow of FDR: From Harry Truman to Bill Clinton* (Ithaca, NY: Cornell University Press, 1993).

[11] Henry C. Kenski, "A Man for All Seasons? The Guardian President and His Public," in Ryan J. Barilleaux and Mary E. Stuckey, eds., *Leadership and the Bush Presidency: Prudence or Drift in an Era of Change?* (Westport, CT: Praeger, 1991).

[12] Dean C. Hammer, "The Oakeshottian President: George Bush and the Politics of the Present," *Presidential Studies Quarterly* 25 (1995), p. 301.

[13] See *Congressional Quarterly Weekly Report*, December 30, 1989. David Mayhew's analysis parallels this interpretation in *Divided We Govern: Party Control, Lawmaking, and Investigations, 1946-1990* (New Haven: Yale University Press, 1992). Mayhew counted only two "significant" measures for 1989: the savings and loan industry bailout and the increase in the minimum wage. The only first-term president with fewer significant bills passed his first year was Dwight Eisenhower in 1953 (tidelands oil legislation).

[14] Data are from Andrew Taylor, "Domestic Agenda Setting, 1947-1994," *Legislative Studies Quarterly* 23 (1998), pp. 373-97. Taylor researched *Congressional Quarterly's* annual listing of "major" legislation on domestic policy alongside presidents' State of the Union addresses and congressional leaders' speeches to determine whether initiatives were linked to the president's agenda or that of the majority party in Congress. The definition of the national legislative agenda is consequently limited to either the president or Congress. To qualify for inclusion initiatives did not have to pass, but only receive attention by Congress.

[15] Time Groseclose and Nolan McCarty, "The Politics of Blame: Bargaining Before an Audience," *American Journal of Political Science* 45 (2001), pp. 100-120.

[16] Steven A. Shull and James Vanderleeuw, "What Do Key Votes Measure?" *Legislative Studies Quarterly* 12 (1987), pp. 573-82; Jon Bond and Richard Fleisher, *The President in the Legislative Arena* (Chicago: University of Chicago Press, 1990); for a detailed review see George Edwards, "Measuring Presidential Success in Congress: Alternative Approaches," *Journal of Politics* 47 (1985), pp. 667-85.

[17] Cary R. Covington, "'Staying Private': Gaining Congressional Support for Unpublicized Presidential Preferences on Roll Call Votes," *Journal of Politics* 49 (1987), pp. 737-55; see also Terry Sullivan, "Presidential Leadership in Congress: Securing Commitments," in Matthew D. McCubbins and Terry Sullivan, eds., *Congress: Structure and Policy* (New York: Cambridge University Press, 1987).

[18] Richard S. Conley, "Presidential Influence and Minority Party Liaison on Veto Overrides: New Evidence from the Ford Presidency," *American Politics Research* 30 (2002), pp. 34-65.

[19] Frederick D. McClure, memorandum for the President, "Analysis of Key Votes in the 101st Congress, First Session," January 10, 1990, White House Office of Records Management, Subject File-General, Box LE 2, George Bush Presidential Library, College Station, Texas. The McClure memo was subject to a P-5 restriction of the Presidential Records Act (confidential advice between the President and his advisors). Access to the memo was appealed by author and granted. However, elements of the two-page memo to President Bush that accompanied McClure's support score analysis were redacted by archivists at the Bush Presidential Library. This redacted information cannot be accessed until the congressionally-sanctioned moratorium on the disclosure of confidential advice ends in 2005.

[20] Ibid., emphasis in original.

[21] Ibid.

[22] Richard Fleisher and Jon R. Bond, "Assessing Presidential Support in the House: Lessons from Reagan and Carter," *Journal of Politics* 45 (1983), pp. 745-758; Jon R. Bond and Richard Fleisher, "Assessing Presidential Support in the House II: Lessons from George Bush," *American Journal of Political Science* 36 (1992), pp. 525-41.

[23] The *conservative coalition* is defined as a majority of Republicans voting with a majority of southern Democrats.

[24] This finding is not unprecedented. George Edwards discovered that the relation between presidential prestige and Republican support in Democratic presidential years was negative; see Edwards, *Presidential Influence in Congress* (San Francisco: W.H. Freeman and Company, 1980), pp. 96-98.

[25] Mark R. Joslyn, "Institutional Change and House Support: Assessing George Bush in the Postreform Era," *American Politics Quarterly* 23 (1995), pp. 62-80.

[26] Rohde, Parties and Leaders in the Postreform House; Jon R. Bond and Richard Fleisher, eds., Polarized Politics: Congress and the President in a Partisan Era (Washington, DC: Congressional Quarterly, 2000).

[27] Joslyn did not divide out his analysis according to the "four-party" politics of Fleisher and Bond. The coefficients in Table 2 for Joslyn's parameters were replicated by the author.

[28] Members of the leadership in each party include majority/minority leaders and members of the extended whip system.

[29] John B. Gilmour, *Strategic Disagreement: Stalemate in American Politics* (Pittsburgh: University of Pittsburgh Press, 1995).

[30] Richard S. Conley and Amie D. Kreppel, "Toward a New Typology of Vetoes and Overrides," *Political Research Quarterly* 54 (2001), pp. 831-52.

[31] Macon Morehouse, "House Defies Threatened Veto, Passes Minimum-Wage Bill," *Congressional Quarterly Weekly Report*, March 25, 1989, p. 641.

[32] Ann Devroy and Helen Dewar, "Bush Vetoes 'Excessive' Rise in Minimum Wage," *Washington Post*, June 14, 1989, p. A1.

[33] Susan F. Rasky, "House, Defying Threat of a Veto, Backs Increase in Minimum Wage," *New York Times*, March 24, 1989, p. A1.

[34] Devroy and Dewar, "Bush Vetoes 'Excessive' Rise in Minimum Wage."

[35] Robert D. Hershey, "House, 382-37, Approves bill to Raise the Minimum Wage," *New York Times*, November 2, 1989, p. A26.

[36] Ethan Bronner, "House Failes to Void Veto on Abortion; Medicaid Funding Remains Limited," *Boston Globe*, October 26, 1989, p. 1.

[37] Julie Rovner, "Congress Puts Bush on Spot Over Funding of Abortion," *Congressional Quarterly Weekly Report*, October 14, 1989, p. 2708.
[38] Ibid.; also see *Congressional Quarterly Almanac* 1988, pp. 706 and 96-H.
[39] William J. Eaton, "Bid to Override Veto of Eastern Probe Fails," *Los Angeles Times*, October 25, 1989, p. A1.
[40] Paul Starobin, "Lawmakers Pursue Efforts to Halt Eastern Strike," *Congressional Quarterly Weekly Report*, March 18, 1989, p. 573.
[41] *Los Angeles Times*, "Lorenzo Lauds Bush for Strike Probe Veto," November 22, 1989, p. P3.
[42] Eaton, "Bid to Override Veto of Eastern Probe Fails."
[43] Barry S. Surman, "Bush Administration Officials Defend Accord with Japan," *Congressional Quarterly Weekly Report*, May 6, 1989, p. 1058.
[44] Sidney M. Milkis and Michael Nelson, *The American Presidency: Origins & Development, 1776-1993* (Washington, DC: Congressional Quarterly, 1994), p. 393.
[45] It is important to recall that majorities of Democrats in the House and the Senate voted *against* the Gulf War Resolution.

Chapter 8

THE POLITICS OF PRESIDENTIAL APPOINTMENTS: A THORNY BUSINESS

Colton C. Campbell

OVERVIEW

The framers of the Constitution debated over whether the power to make appointments should be lodged in the entire legislature or just in the Senate, wholly with the executive, or in some hybrid of legislative and executive responsibility. Some delegates argued that the president, as chief executive, should appoint all public officials because it would be easier to hold one person accountable for any bad appointment.[1] The supposed senatorial saucer was more capable for James Madison in Federalist No. 62 since it would embody enlightened citizens, whose small number and firmness might fairly interpose against rash councils.[2] Eventually, a proposal for shared responsibility was adopted, calling for nomination by the president but leaving to the Senate the right of confirmation, an informal term for the Senate giving advice and consent to a presidential nomination for an executive or judicial position. Writing in support of this proposal, Alexander Hamilton in Federalist No. 76 commented that such an approach recognized "that one man of discernment is better fitted to analyze and estimate the peculiar qualities" for appointments, while also being mindful that "it would be an excellent check upon a spirit of favoritism in the President."[3]

The debate over the roles of the respective branches and the various interpretations of "advice and consent" has continued over more than two centuries. Some suggest the Senate was denied formal responsibility in the nomination process and given essentially a pro forma role in the confirmation process.[4] According to this view, the president is entrusted with the obligation to nominate those individuals who are confirmable, and the Senate is to refuse such choice only in the gravest and most compelling circumstances.[5] Others argue that the Founders sought to vest senators with an equally shared responsibility in the selection process.[6]

Article II, Section 2 of the Constitution empowers the president to nominate. However, with the exception of "recess appointees" no political appointees to a federal agency can execute federal laws and regulations, no ambassador can represent the United States abroad, and no federal judge can be seated without having been confirmed by a majority vote of the Senate. Although congressional cooperation in presidential appointments is more the rule than the exception, senators are increasingly prepared to exploit their prerogatives.[7] Some senators routinely take advantage of their leverage to thwart presidential nominations if they consider the nominees to be out of step with existing congressional majorities.[8] Others regard advice and consent not as a mere formality but as an important constitutional weapon guarding the independence of the Senate from the executive branch.[9]

The confirmation hearings for President George W. Bush's cabinet nominees demonstrated the potential clout the Senate and large grass-roots constituencies exert over administration policies and appointments, including the Supreme Court, federal judgeships, and pivotal sub-Cabinet-level positions. For the president, the hearings served as an important early window on his skill at navigating a divided Senate and murky political terrain on Capitol Hill, and drawing broad political support even for controversial decisions.[10] For the Senate, the confirmation process rendered the first clue as to how the evenly divided Senate would function under its fledgling power-sharing agreement between the two polarized parties.

POLITICAL NATURE OF THE APPOINTMENT PROCESS

In 1925 the Senate rejected President Calvin Coolidge's nominee for attorney general, Charles Warren, by one vote because his vice president was napping. At the time lawmakers were still smarting from the Teapot Dome investigations into government corruption, and senators were weary of Warren's close relationship with those involved in the sugar trust.[11] Warren's confirmation ended in a tie, but by the time Vice President Charles Dawes wiped the sleep from his eyes and raced to the Capitol, one senator had switched his vote and the confirmation went down in defeat.

Today's presidential appointment process is still defined by these sorts of politics and, occasionally, surprises, although it scarcely resembles its original design and intent. The growth of presidential appointments (nearly 6,000) and the increased specialization required of appointees, have dramatically altered how presidents make appointments. Senatorial prerogatives to block action apply to nominations as well as to legislation, but there was a certain presumption of success when the Senate received a presidential nomination.[12] A collage of factors account for such change with two notable contributions. Senators today are elected largely as representatives of their constituents and carry out the instructions received from their electors. They are increasingly becoming permanent candidates pulled by a geographically defined community with an expectation that the representative protects the interests of constituents and others he or she represents. Second, increased party polarization in the Senate has made the confirmation process more prolonged and contentious. Over the past two decades an intensifying partisan atmosphere has developed in the Senate.[13] This polarization has been effectively explained in terms of the greater ideological homogeneity of the two parties,[14] and indicates the extent to which the number of "centrists" in the chamber–so important for moderating compromise–have declined.[15]

Routine Confirmation or Detailed Inquiry

Two distinct stages mark the appointment process: nomination and confirmation. In the nomination stage, the president selects nominees and sends his or her name to the Senate. The Constitution does not require the president to justify why he makes a particular nomination, nor does it obligate the Senate to explain why it refuses to confirm a nomination. Politics and patronage have often influenced such decisions, a product of nineteenth century politics in which Jacksonian Senator William Learned Marcy of New York, who served from 1831 to 1833, coined the phrase, "To the victor belongs the spoils." Modern presidents look for a blend of comfort, ideology, loyalty, competence, long-time service, and integrity.[16] Identifying these qualities in people is a major challenge that every new president faces. Recent presidents, especially Bill Clinton, have placed a premium on ethnic, gender, and often geographical diversity (see Table 1, for example).

Table 1. Presidential Teams (Senior Administrative Positions Requiring Senate Confirmation)

	Total Appointments	Total Women	Percentage Women
Jimmy Carter	1,087	191	17.6%
Ronald Reagan	2,349	277	11.8%
George Bush	1,079	215	19.9%
Bill Clinton	1,257	528	42%

Source: Adapted from Karen O'Connor and Larry J. Sabato, *American Government: Continuity and Change*, 2000 ed. (New York: Longman, 2000), 271.

While by tradition, presidents are afforded greater latitude over appointments than over legislation, presidents do often consult key senators before sending nominations to Capitol Hill.[17] A nomination to a position does not afford the nominee legal authority to assume the duties and responsibilities of the position. That authority comes only after the nominee is confirmed and appointed.[18] While awaiting confirmation, a nominee often is hired as a consultant and may act only in an advisory capacity.[19]

In the confirmation or second stage, the Senate alone determines whether to approve or disapprove a nomination. Not until 1955 did testimony by a nominee at a hearing effectively become a mandatory part of the Senate's exercise of advice and consent.[20] Before then all Senate discussions about nominees and the votes themselves were held behind closed doors, away from public eyes, keeping under wraps any scandals the inquiries might unearth–as a courtesy to the nominees. But the details of the proceedings inevitably wound up in newspapers, and the clandestine meetings were repeatedly criticized as undemocratic. The Senate then decided to open them to the public, a move that occasionally spawned character assassinations.[21]

The confirmation hearings themselves, along with interest group lobbying and media coverage, are all part of today's political landscape. According to Katzmann over the last seventy-five years Senate confirmations have evolved in roughly three stages.[22] Between 1922-55, senators infrequently questioned nominees. From 1955 to 1967, nominees' appearances before the Senate Judiciary Committee became a routine part of the confirmation process. And from 1987 to the present, confirmation hearings have become occasions for conflict and grandstanding.

In determining the acceptability of presidential nominees, a number of recurring concerns have historically influenced Senate action. Many senators are routinely concerned with the nominee's policy and philosophical views, and his or her approach to statutes and effect on public policy.[23] Senators are particularly displeased with legal reasoning that disregards legislative history.[24] The confirmation process is dominated by policy and constituency considerations because they have become important concerns of the Senate and because the confirmation process provides useful and often unique opportunities for expressing and implementing those concerns.[25] Senator Joseph Lieberman (D-Conn.) outlined this consideration in the confirmation of attorney general Ashcroft:

> Throughout my tenure in the Senate, I have voted on hundreds of Presidential nominees. In each case, I have adhered to a broadly deferential standard of review. As I explained in my first speech on the Senate floor–in which I offered my reasons for opposing the nomination of John Tower to serve as Defense Secretary–the history of the debates at the Constitution Convention make clear that the President is entitled to the benefit of the doubt in his appointments. The question, I concluded, I should ask myself in considering nominees is not whether I would have chosen the nominee, but rather whether the President's choice is acceptable for the job in question.
>
> That does not mean that the Senate should serve merely as a rubber stamp. Were that the case, the Framers would have given the Senate no role in the appointments process. Instead, the Senate's constitutional advice and consent mandate obliges it to serve as a check on the President's appointment power. As I put it in my statement on Senator Tower's nomination, I believe this requires Senators to onsider several things: First, the knowledge, experience, and qualifications of the nominee for the position; second, the nominee's judgment, as evidenced by his conduct and decisions, as well as his personal behavior; and third, the nominee's ethics, including current or prior conflicts of interest. In unusual circumstances, Senators can also consider fundamental and potentially irreconcilable policy differences between the nominee and the mission of the agency he or she is to serve.[26]

Lieberman later noted, ". . . although I believe that the Constitution casts the Senate's advice role as a limited one and counsels Senators to be cautious in withholding their consent, I nevertheless have opposed nominees where their policy positions, statements, or actions made me question whether they would be able to administer the agency they had been nominated to head in a credible and adequate manner."[27]

Some hearings during confirmations for President George W. Bush's Cabinet turned into policy seminars as Democrats used the forums to probe for specifics on issues that the president emphasized during the campaign. When secretary of state designate, Colin L. Powell, appeared before the Senate Foreign Relations Committee, for example, it was the first opportunity for committee members to see what the Bush administration's foreign policy would entail in areas such as missile defense, nuclear proliferation, and the Middle East.[28] As for executive branch positions, presidents should expect that those they nominate to execute their policies will be scrutinized by the Senate with the presumption of confirmability.[29] In fact, one study found that of 1,464 important nominations from 1965 to 1994, fewer than five percent failed.[30]

Setting Standards of Judgment and Evaluation

Senators have three direct means of affecting appointments: the power to suggest candidates for executive and judicial posts; their actual votes on confirmations; and the "holds" they might place on scheduling confirmation votes. The custom called "senatorial courtesy" gives senators influence over presidential nominations to federal positions within their own states. Dating from 1789, the custom holds that senators may call upon the courtesy of their colleagues to reject nominees for positions within the senator's state-for example, federal district judges, U.S. attorneys, and U.S. marshalls.[31] In practice, this means that senators can directly influence the naming of certain officeholders, often selecting their own candidates in the hope that the president will nominate them. Nowhere mentioned in Senate rules or precedents, and only linked to the Senate's tradition of extended debate, "holds" permit a single senator or any number of senators to delay–sometimes temporarily, sometimes permanently–action on a measure or other matter, such as the confirmation vote on a nominee.

Nearly all presidents have faced confirmation fights with the Senate. Rejections of presidential nominees can have a major impact on the course of a new administration. Rejections leave a president without first choices, have a chilling effect on other potential nominees, affect a president's relationship with the Senate, and affect how the president is perceived by the public.[32] Unsuccessful nominations fall into three categories: those voted on and rejected, those not acted on, and those withdrawn.[33] Of the 15 Cabinet nominations that failed to be confirmed, nine were rejected on the floor of the Senate and two were killed intentionally in committee. Additionally, one died in committee because of insufficient time to process the nomination and three were withdrawn for personal reasons not because of Senate opposition. Of the 11 Cabinet nominations that were formally rejected, seven failed because of policy and philosophical differences that senators had with the nominee and the president. The other four failed for a variety of reasons, including conflict of interest, character flaws, incompetence, and perceived disregard and disdain for the Senate.[34]

Only once has the Senate spurned a current or former member. In 1989, it rejected President George Bush's nomination of former Senator John G. Tower (R-Texas) for secretary of defense. Tower's rocky relationship with fellow senators as well as his tarnished personal behavior involving alcohol, women, and cozy relationships with defense contractors eventually derailed his nomination. Many of the senators evaluating Tower had known him for years, especially as chairman of the Armed Services Committee, and were well aware of these problems. Even so, Senators trooped over to a secure room on the fourth floor of the Capitol to read his Federal Bureau of Investigation (FBI) report, which contained evidence about personal indiscretions.[35] In the end the vote was divided along party lines. Senator Nancy Kassebaum of Kansas was the only Republican to vote against Tower, but with a Democratic majority his appointment was rejected 53-47.

Since Tower's nomination, presidents have been particularly meticulous about rooting out skeletons before they publicly name nominees. Although President George W. Bush nominated Cabinet picks at breakneck speed because of the drawn-out presidential election (all but one of his Cabinet seats were filled just ten days after his inauguration) the internal grilling process included an extensive line of questioning about personal problems that could be embarrassing if made public.[36] Shortcuts in probing nominees' backgrounds or nominees intentionally withholding information may incur irreparable political damage, or loss of confidence by the president, thus grounding a nomination. Calling the confirmation process a "game of search and destroy," Bush's initial choice for Labor secretary, Linda Chavez, withdrew from consideration amid controversy over an illegal Guatemalan immigrant who once lived in her home and was paid for odd jobs around the house.[37] But Chavez was not entirely forthcoming to the Bush transition team. Chavez's situation was comparable with that of Zoe Baird, President Clinton's nominee for attorney general in 1993 who withdrew her name from Senate consideration after it became known that she had not paid Social Security taxes for her nanny and other household help. Lani Guinier's nomination to head the Civil Rights Division of the Department of Justice was withdrawn by Clinton after he decided he could not support her views on race-based remedies.

Nominations to high executive posts today are subject to standards and evaluation that go beyond questions of competence or conflict or interest; personal lives and morality are scrutinized as well. This shift in standards, according to Davidson and Oleszek, stems in part from a shift in attitudes by both the press and public.[38] The press now reports more aggressively than in years past the private activities of public officials.[39] Many nominees lament the intrusion in the confirmation process of ideological interest groups that organize "attack campaigns" to defeat nominees who appear unsupportive of their agenda.[40]

Even if no glaring personal problems exist, nominees must nonetheless walk a fine line and remain extremely cautious and deferential when they are going through the delicate confirmation process. A divided Senate Judiciary Committee endorsed the nomination of attorney general-designate, former Senator Ashcroft of Missouri, but only after Democrats grilled him on a wide range of sensitive issues. Committee members dwelled on their former colleague's record on race relations, gun control, and opposition to abortion, focusing heavily on whether he would enforce laws with which he disagreed. Senator Edward M. Kennedy (D-Mass.) spearheaded the fight, lambasting Ashcroft for what he said was his record of using litigation and legislation to advance his personal right-wing views. "When a president nominates a person to serve in his cabinet, the presumption is rightly in favor of the nominee," said Kennedy.[41] "But Senator Ashcroft has a long and detailed record of relentless opposition on fundamental issues of civil rights and other basic rights of virtual importance to all the people of America, and the people of this country deserve better than that."

Liberal Democrats then maximized opposition to Ashcroft during floor debate to discourage President Bush from choosing similarly contentious nominees for other high posts. "It would be a strong statement, I think, as we could make . . . that 41 of us stand together," declared Minority Leader Thomas A. Daschle (D-S.D.). Forty-one senators are needed to sustain a filibuster, and while Democrats decided not to use the tactic against Ashcroft, their ability to muster 42 votes in a 50-50 Senate sent a clear signal to the president: a readiness to thwart action on future nominations, should the Democrats choose to do so. Senator Charles E. Schumer (D-N.Y.) called the vote a "shot across the bow."[42]

Prolonging the Nomination Process

Today's appointment process is much more formal and structured, longer (often many months longer), and more visible and consistently contentious than ever.[43] When recently surveyed, two-fifths of 435 Reagan, Bush, and Clinton administration nominees called the prolonged process confusing and one-fourth called it embarrassing.[44] More than half of the appointees confirmed from 1984 to 1999 said the appointment process, from the first White House contact to Senate confirmation, has become too long, lasting at least five months.[45] Nominees are now required to file financial disclosure statements under the Ethics in Government Act of 1978, as well as committee-sponsored financial and personal questionnaires. Additionally, most committees require the White House to submit a report on the background investigation conducted by the FBI on each nominee. Consequently, committees now must devote substantial time to reviewing and evaluating the numerous documents associated with each nomination.[46] For instance, during the first session of the 106th Congress (1999-2001), on average, the Senate took 58.5 days to confirm a nomination.[47]

Table 2. Average Number of Days to Fill Positions

Dept	1981			1993			Difference
	Days to nominate	Days to confirm	Days to fill	Days to nominate	Days to confirm	Days to fill	
Agriculture	82	28	110	125	20	145	+35
Commerce	137	34	171	189	72	261	+90
Defense	126	12	138	177	42	219	+81
Education	133	44	177	99	43	142	-35
Energy	125	38	163	163	42	205	+42
HHS	130	24	154	133	51	184	+30
HUD	80	39	119	117	29	146	+27
Interior	129	37	166	110	36	146	-20
Justice	138	30	168	135	56	191	+23
Labor(a)	152	24	176	162	47	209	+33
State(b)	78	37	115	86	31	117	+02
Transp.	66	18	84	155	47	202	+16
Treasury	79	20	99	92	29	121	+22
VA	NA	NA	0	122	30	152	+152
Overall aver.	**112**	**30**	**142**	**133**	**41**	**174**	**+32**

NOTE:
(a) Does not include U.S. attorney and U.S. marshal positions.
(b) Does not include most ambassador positions overseas.
Source: Adapted from Rogelio Garcia, *Filling Policy Positions in Executive Departments: Average Time Required Through Confirmation, 1981 and 1993* (Congressional Research Service Report No. 98-641 GOV, July 28, 1998).

The average time required through Senate confirmation to fill policy positions in executive departments has increased in the last decade. In 1981, President Ronald Reagan took nearly five months, on average, to fill a full-time position requiring Senate confirmation. In 1993, President Clinton took nearly six months longer, on average, to fill such a position. Both Reagan and Clinton faced a similar appointment process: the search for a candidate; investigation and clearance of the candidate before being nominated; completion of committee questionnaires and other possible forms before a hearing could be held; and full Senate consideration of the nomination.[48] Additionally, both presidents had the presumed benefit of a Senate controlled by their own party. Table 2 indicates that from 1981 to 1993, the overall time for presidents to nominate candidates for appointment increased by 21 days; the average time to confirm appointees increased by 11 days; and the average time to fill executive positions increased by 32 days.

ASSERTING SENATORIAL PREROGATIVE

Passed in 1868, the Vacancies Act was intended to hamper the president from delaying sending forth nominations for advice and consent positions that could dodge the Senate's confirmation prerogative, and to grant the exclusive means for temporarily filling vacancies in covered positions unless Congress explicitly provided a superseding mechanism. Only two options were available under the statute: either a first assistant or a presidential designee who had previously received Senate confirmation would serve for a strictly defined and limited period. Prior to 1988, the limitation period was 10 days and then 30 days. In that year it was increased to 120 days.[49] However, the Department of Justice has taken the position that any executive department or agency whose authorizing legislation vests all powers and functions of the agency in its head and allows the head to delegate such powers and functions to subordinates in his or her discretion, does not have to comply with the Vacancies Act. As a consequence, during 1998 some 20 percent of the 320 advice and consent positions in departments were being filled by temporary designees, most of whom had served beyond the 120-day limitation period of the Act without presidential submissions of nominations.[50] Table 3 summarizes, by department, the number of full-time positions requiring Senate confirmation, the number and percentage of acting officials in those positions, and the number and percentage of officials who were apparently serving beyond the 120-day limit imposed by the Vacancies Act.

The appointment in December 1997 of Bill Lann Lee by Attorney General Janet Reno as Acting Assistant Attorney General for Civil Rights in the Department of Justice precipitated congressional hearings and the introduction of legislation to remedy a longstanding inter-branch controversy over the legal propriety of the failure of executive department and agencies to comply consistently with the provisions of the Vacancies Act.

Underscoring the importance preserving the Senate's duty to advise and consent on presidential nominees, Senator Fred Thompson (R-Tenn) declared in his introductory statement concerning S. 2176, the Federal Vacancies Reform Act:

> Mr. President, the Framers established a system for appointing important officials in which the President and the Senate would each play a role. Not only did the Framers wish to ensure that more than one person's wisdom was brought to the appointment process, but that the President, in selecting nominees, would be aware that they would face scrutiny. When a vacancy occurs in such an office, it is important to establish a process

that permits the routine operation of the government to continue, but that will not allow the evasion of the Senate's constitutional authority to advise and consent to nominations.[51]

Table 3. Acting Officials in Positions Requiring Senate Confirmation in Executive Depts., 1998

Department	Positions requiring Senate confirmation			Acting officials apparently serving beyond 120-day limit	
	All officials	Acting officials	% acting	#	%
Agriculture	15	2	13%	1	50%
Commerce	29	9	31%	7	78%
Defense	45	8	18%	5	63%
Education	18	6	33%	3	50%
Energy	18	5	28%	3	60%
HHS	20	1	5%	1	100%
HUD	15	2	13%	1	50%
Interior	18	3	17%	2	67%
Justice	28	5	18%	4	80%
Labor	18	6	33%	6	100%
State	38	4	11%	1	25%
Transportation	20	6	30%	5	83%
Treasury	24	1	4%	1	100%
VA	14	6	43%	3	50%
Total	**320**	**64**	**20%**	**43**	**67%**

Source: Adapted from Rogelio Garcia, *Acting Officials in Positions Requiring Senate Confirmation in Executive Departments, As of February 1998* (Congressional Research Service Report No. 98-641 GOV, March 11, 1998).

Under Thompson's guidance, the Senate Governmental Affairs Committee reported S 2176 on July 15, 1998. Although the measure failed to survive a cloture vote on the floor, a compromise version was included in the FY 1999 Omnibus Consolidated and Emergency Supplemental Appropriations Act. The new Vacancies Act rejects the Justice Department's position and makes it the exclusive vehicle for temporarily filling vacant advice and consent positions and prevents undue delay in the president's submission of nominees for Senate consideration.

THE POLITICS OF JUDICIAL APPOINTMENTS

Judicial appointments are a special type of senatorial confirmation. Judges are extensions of neither the executive nor the legislature, which means that both branches exercise equivalent influence. Such shared responsibility, according to Katzmann, "holds the promise of increasing the commitment of each to maintaining a strong and independent branch."[52] For most of this century the confirmation process for the courts was distinguished by a strong presumption in favor of deference to presidential prerogative to fill vacancies on the Supreme Court. "So long as the nominee exhibited a basic level of competence and his political views fit within the narrow confines of acceptable American political discourse," writes Silverstein, the president's choices were typically confirmed by a voice vote, with no opposition on record.[53] "I have made a practice of setting a different standard for approval of persons nominated to serve in the president's cabinet and those the president has chosen for federal judgeships," comments Senator Bob Graham (D-Fla.). "In the former instance, there is a very strong presumption that the president should have the right to choose whomever he feels would effectively carry out his administration's policies. With a federal judge nominee, that presumption is lessened. Federal judges serve not at the pleasure of the president, but rather for a lifetime and represent the third, equal branch of government."[54]

Senators increasingly use their advice and consent power to be heard, sometimes pressing for their own political objectives and to assert senatorial independence from the executive branch.[55] During the Reagan and Bush senior administrations, Democrats blocked judicial nominees that they considered too conservative; in the second half of the 1990s, Republicans blocked many of President Clinton's nominees because they believed them too liberal.[56] In a number of these cases, the nominations never reached the floor. Judicial appointees are queried about their legal qualifications, their private backgrounds, and their earlier actions as public or private figures.[57] Other questions focus on social and political issues, the Constitution, particular Court rulings, current constitutional controversies, constitutional values, judicial philosophy, the analytical approach a nominee might use in deciding issues and cases, and partisan considerations.[58] Whereas nominees in the past tended to keep their distance from the appointment process, they are now active participants. During considerations of Supreme Court nominations, for example, the nominee's demeanor, responsiveness, and knowledge of the law may be crucial in influencing senators' votes on confirmation.[59]

A recurring issue at recent confirmation hearings has been whether a nominee should decline to answer questions that are posed by members of the Judiciary Committee.[60] Senators often try to elicit forthright views from nominees on various legal or constitutional issues. However, nominees cannot compromise their future judicial independence by appearing to make commitments on issues that could later come before the Court.[61] Nominees also worry that frank responses to certain queries might displease some senators and thus jeopardize their confirmation.[62] Protracted questioning, occurring over several days of hearings, is likely when the nominee is relatively controversial or is perceived by committee members to be evasive or insincere in responding to certain questions.[63]

Judicial Fitness

Aside from shedding light on the fitness of the nominee to serve, confirmation hearings are a vehicle for senators to press constitutional or other values upon the nominee, in the hope of influencing how he or she later might approach issues.[64] President Ronald Reagan's 1987 nomination of Robert Bork to the Supreme Court underscored this role. Members of the Senate Judiciary Committee publicly probed Bork's constitutional and philosophical views in minute detail. The Senate rejected the nomination because his views were perceived as too conservative and controversial by many senators concerned with the ideological balance of the Supreme Court. Since 1992, the Senate Judiciary Committee has instituted the practice of conducting a closed-door session with each Supreme Court nominee to address any questions about the nominee's background which confidential investigations might have brought to the committee's attention.[65] In announcing this procedure, then-chairman of the committee, Senator Joseph R. Biden (D-Del.), explained that such hearings would be conducted "in all cases, even when there are no major investigative issues to be resolved so that the holding of such a hearing cannot be taken to demonstrate that the committee has received adverse confidential information about the nomination."[66]

In considering judicial nominees, senators enjoy even greater leverage than in handling executive-branch positions. First, as already noted, the presumption in favor of the president is weaker than it is for executive appointments. Although presidents are expected to seek nominees who share their general approach to the law, senators have come to take seriously their right to reach independent judgments concerning such matters as judicial fitness and judicial philosophy. Second, the tradition of senatorial courtesy applies more broadly to judicial posts than to executive ones. Few executive posts considered by the Senate involve primarily a single state, whereas many judicial ones do–including federal district judgeships and some circuit judgeships, not to mention U.S. attorneys and marshals.

In practice, this means that an administration will generally draw a majority of its nominees from the ranks of its political party and its traditional supporters, but that they will include moderates from the opposing party and a few individuals sponsored by key senators.[67] The politics of judicial appointments was transformed in the 1980s and 1990s, however. According to O'Brien, the politics of rewarding party faithful and institutional accommodation between the White House and the Senate gave way to a more intensely ideological and conservative interest-group driven politics of appointing federal judges,[68] in part the product of an increasingly polarized Congress.[69]

As of mid 2000 the Senate had failed to confirm twenty-six nominations to the Supreme Court, either through an adverse vote or through a refusal to act. According to one study, these twenty-six cases constituted about one-sixth of the nominations that the Senate considered.[70] This proportion of defeats is higher than for any other position to which the president makes appointments. For instance, presidents have made substantially more nominations of cabinet members, but only nine were defeated.[71]

DIPLOMATIC AND OTHER NOMINATIONS

Major diplomatic nominations usually encounter little congressional opposition, largely because the president has been allowed wide discretion in his selection of ambassadors and other persons to assist him in the conduct of foreign relations. Table 4 indicates that from 1987 to 1996, 91 percent of the persons named to ambassadorial positions were confirmed by the Senate. Of the 54 not confirmed (about nine percent of the total), 37 had no hearings on their nominations. Many of these were instances where the nomination was submitted late in the session or where consideration was delayed for other reasons.[72]

Nominations to sub-cabinet positions are treated much like cabinet nominations, although the president is expected to consult in advance with key members of Congress on appointments in which they have a particular interest. Sub-cabinet posts frequently are used to reward various party factions. Presidents have given different directives to those assisting them in staffing an administration. Some allow Cabinet officers to pick their principal aides and staff their departments; often, they later complained that the political appointees owed their primary allegiance to people other than the president.[73] Other presidents choose to control all non-civil service hiring from the White House to ensure that their appointees function as a team.[74]

Table 4. Senate Action on Ambassadorial Nominees, 1987-1996

	100th Cong 1987-8	101st Cong 1989-90	102nd Cong 1991-2	103rd Cong 1993-4	104th Cong 1995-6	Total
Total Nominations	91	145	124	152	106	618
Those Confirmed	82	137	102	148	95	564
with hearings	73	133	100	148	93	547
without hearings	9	4	2	0	2	17
Those Not Confirmed	9	8	22	4	11	54
with hearings	3	3	3	2	6	17
without hearings, submitted in last two months of session	3	1	10	1	1	16
without hearings, submitted earlier	3	4	9	1	4	21
Those Not Confirmed Who were Confirmed in Next Congress	4	2	11	1	7	25
hearings in prior Congress	0	2	1	0	6	9
no hearings in prior Congress	0	10	1	1	16	4
Those Not Confirmed Who Were Not Confirmed Later	5	6	11	3	4	29
with hearings	3	1	2	2	0	8
without hearings	2	5	9	1	4	21

Source: Adapted from Jonathan Sanford, *Senate Disposition of Ambassadorial Nominations, 1987-96* (Congressional Research Service Report No. 97-864 F, September 19, 1997).

Appointments to 33 independent regulatory and other collegial boards and commissions to which the president makes full-time appointments with the advice and consent of the Senate offer a somewhat different situation. Usually established by an act of Congress, lawmakers frequently view them more as an arm of Congress rather than the executive branch.[75] Subsequently, senators expect to play a larger role in the selection process. During the first session of the 106th Congress (1999-2001), for example, President Clinton submitted 53 nominations to the Senate, of which 30 were confirmed, two were withdrawn by the president, and 21 were carried over to the second session. On average, the Senate took 58.5 days to confirm a nomination.[76]

CONCLUSION

Both comity and conflict have marked the relationship between the Senate and the presidency throughout our history of presidential appointments. Most senators' contact with executive-branch officials is not much different from those of their House counterparts. But the Senate's special constitutional responsibilities–advising and consenting to presidential nominations and to treaties–necessitate intensified negotiations with presidents and their staff assistants.

In the 225 years that the Senate has been approving presidential nominations, the process has brought several confrontations between both ends of Pennsylvania Avenue. But different from times past, today's senators, like politicians at all levels, seem more prone to exploiting their prerogatives toward and even beyond their formal limits in order to achieve their political objectives, or even to demonstrate to the public their willingness to do so.[77] Filibusters threatened (and sometimes implemented) as well as "holds" placed upon nominations are witnessed more frequently. Similarly, recent Republican presidents have viewed nominations, particularly judgeships, as symbols and instruments of power.[78] During eight years in the Oval Office, for example, President Ronald Reagan transformed the politics of judicial appointments and changed the composition of the federal bench.[79] In short, both the White House and the Senate have allowed the appointment process to become unnecessarily lengthy, complex, and cumbersome.

Despite some high profile, highly political disputes involving ambassadorial and judicial nominees, it seems unlikely that the presidential appointment process has deteriorated significantly over time. Still, the unwillingness to move from specific cases (a single ambassadorial or judicial nominee, for example) to whole-sale disruption of Senate business is an ominous development. Major nominees may be blocked from appointment by a single senator with the strong desire to obtain a host of policy concessions from the administration. Such hostage-taking can poison inter-branch relations and stymie a president's honeymoon period with Congress and impede his ability to govern.

To avoid the untidiness of the appointment process, presidents look for ways to circumvent the Senate's role. Much to the chagrin of senators, for example, presidents increasingly make "recess appointments" during breaks in the Senate's session, thus enabling an appointee to serve until the end of the next Senate session. Another way for the administration to go around the confirmation struggle is to appoint officials on an "acting" basis.

Although the vast majority of presidential appointments are confirmed with little difficulty, the politics of the confirmation process will nonetheless always be an executive-legislative tug of war. Heightened levels of partisanship and an evenly divided Senate can force a president to moderate his nominations to high executive posts, steering clear of naming any controversial person. And, to be sure, under these current political conditions, judicial appointments will be subject to even closer Senate scrutiny. Otherwise, too much political capital will be expended early in an administration to shepherd a nomination thorough the confirmation mess–capital a president most certainly will need later on to broker important deals with Congress and its members.

NOTES

1. Rogelio Garcia, "Confirmation," in Donald C. Bacon, Roger H. Davidson, and Morton, eds., *The Encyclopedia of the United States Congress*, vol. 2 (New York: Simon & Shuster, 1995).
2. Alexander Hamilton, James Madison, and John Jay [introduction by Garry Wills], *The Federalist* (New York: Bantam Books, 1982).
3. Ibid.
4. Robert A. Katzmann, *Courts and Congress* (Washington, D.C.: Brookings Institution Press, 1997.
5. John O. McGinnis, "The President, the Senate, the Confirmation, and the Confirmation Process: A Reply to Professors Strauss and Sunstein," *Texas Law Review* 71 (1993): 633-67.
6. David A. Strauss and Cass R. Sunstein, "The Senate, the Constitution, and the Confirmation Process," *Yale Law Journal* 101 (1992): 1491; and Charles L. Black, Jr., "A Note on Senatorial Consideration of Supreme Court Nominees," *Yale Law Journal* 79 (1970): 657.
7. Louis Fisher, *Constitutional Conflicts between Congress and the President*, 3rd ed. (Lawrence, Kan.: University of Kansas Press, 1991).
8. Mark A. Peterson, "The President and Congress," in Michael Nelson, ed., *The Presidency and the Political System*, 5th ed. (Washington, D.C.: CQ Press, 1998); and Neil A. Lewis, "Clinton Has a Chance to Shape the Courts," *New York Times*, February 9, 1997, 16.
9. Raymond W. Smock, *Landmark Documents on The U.S. Congress* (Washington, D.C.: Congressional Quarterly, Inc., 1999).
10. Amy Goldstein and Helen Dewar, "Confirmation Hearings to Test Bush, Democrats," *Washington Post*, January 14, 2001, A1.
11. Susan Crabtree, "Senate Split Makes Confirmation Process Dicier," *Roll Call*, January 15, 2001, 1.
12. Harold W. Stanley and Richard G. Niemi, *Vital Statistics on American Politics*, 6th ed. (Washington, D.C.: Congressional Quarterly, Inc., 1997).
13. Charles E. Bullock, III and David W. Brady, "Party, Constituency, and Roll-Call Voting in the U.S. Senate," *Legislative Studies Quarterly* 8 (1983): 29-43; Samuel C. Patterson and Gregory A. Caldeira, "Party Voting in the United States Congress," *British Journal of Political Science* 18 (1987): 111-13; Patricia A. Hurley and Rick K. Wilson, "Partisan Voting Patterns in the U.S. Senate, 1877-1986," *Legislative Studies Quarterly* 14 (1989): 225-50; Bader 1998; and Nicol C. Rae and Colton C. Campbell, "Party Politics and Ideology in the Contemporary Senate," in Colton C. Campbell and Nicol C. Rae, eds., *The Contentious Senate: Partisanship, Ideology, and the Myth of Cool Judgement* (Lanham, Md.: Rowman & Littlefield Publishers, Inc., 2001).
14. Steven S. Smith, "Forces of Change in Senate Party Leadership and Organization," in Lawrence C. Dodd and Bruce I. Oppenheimer, eds., *Congress Reconsidered*, 5th ed. (Washington, D.C.: CQ Press, 1993); Samuel C. Patterson, "The Congressional Parties in the United States," paper presented at the annual meeting of the American Political Science Association, Chicago, Ill., 1995; and Norman J. Ornstein, Robert L. Peabody, and David W. Rohde, "The U.S. Senate: Toward the 21st Century," in Lawrence C. Dodd and Bruce I. Oppenheimer, eds., *Congress Reconsidered*, 6th ed. (Washington, D.C.: CQ Press, 1997).
15. John B. Bader, "Partisanship in the U.S. Senate, 1969-1996," University of California, typescript, 1998.
16. Alvin S. Felzenberg, *The Keys to a Successful Presidency* (Washington, D.C.: The Heritage Foundation, 2000).

17. Fisher 1991; and Rogelio Garcia, *Cabinet and Other High Level Nominations that Failed to be Confirmed, 1789-1989*, CRS Report No. 89-253 GOV, April 14, 1989, Washington, D.C.
18. Joseph P. Harris, *The Advice and Consent of the Senate: A Study of the Confirmation of Appointments by the United States Senate* (Berkeley: University of California Press, 1968).
19. Rogelio Garcia, *Presidential Appointments to Full-Time Positions on Regulatory and Other Collegial Boards and Commissions*, 106th Congress, CRS Report No. RL-30476 GOV, March 21, 2000, Washington, D.C.
20. Katzmann 1997.
21. Crabtree 2001.
22. Katzmann 1997, 19
23. Ibid.; David M. O'Brien, *Storm Center: The Supreme Court in American Politics*, 5th ed. (W.W. Norton & Company, 2000).
24. Katzmann 1997.
25. G. Calvin Mackenzie, "The Presidential Appointment Process: Historical Development, Contemporary Operations, Current Issues," in *Obstacle Course: The Report of the Twentieth Century Fund Task Force on the Presidential Appointment Process* (New York: The Twentieth Century Fund Press, 1981), 186.
26. Congressional Record, 107th Cong., 1st sess., 2001, S947
27. Ibid.
28. Goldstein and Dewar 2001.
29. Katzmann 1997, 12.
30. Glenn R. Krutz, Richard Fleisher and Jon Bond, "From Abe Fortas to Zoe Baird: Why Some Presidential Nominations Fail in the Senate," *American Political Science Review* 92 (1998): 871-81.
31. Harris 1968.
32. Karen O'Connor and Larry J. Sabato, *American Government: Continuity and Change*, 2000 ed. (New York: Longman, 2000).
33. Garcia 1995.
34. Garcia 1989.
35. Crabtree 2001.
36. Ibid.
37. Quoted in Judy Keen, "Embattled Chavez Pulls Out," *USA Today*, January 10, 2001, 1A.
38. Roger H. Davidson and Walter J. Oleszek, *Congress and Its Members*, 7th ed. (Washington, D.C., 2000), 315.
39. Dennis Thompson, *Ethics in Congress* (Washington, D.C.: Brookings Institution Press, 1995).
40. Davidson and Oleszek 2000.
41. Quoted in Helen Dewar, "Democrats Seek to Send Message With Ashcroft," *Washington Post*, February 1, 2001, A4.
42. Quoted in Helen Dewar, "A Serious Breach in Bipartisanship: Democrats Fire 'Shot Across the Bow'," *Washington Post*, February 2, 2001, A6.
43. Mackenzie 1996, 37.
44. Lori Kurtzman, "Political Appointments? No Thanks," *Washington Post*, January 15, 2000, A19.
45. Ibid.
46. Garcia 1995.
47. Garcia 2000.
48. Rogelio Garcia, *Filling Positions in Executive Departments: Average Time Required Through Confirmation*, 1981-1993, CRS Report No. 98-641 GOV, July 28, 1998, Washington, D.C.
49. Morton Rosenberg, *The New Vacancies Act: Congress Acts to Protect the Senate's Confirmation Prerogative*, CRS Report No. 98-892 A, November 2, 1998, Washington, D.C..
50. Ibid.
51. Congressional Record, 106th Cong., 1st sess., 1998, S6414

52. Quoted in Katzmann, 1997, 12.
53. Mark Silverstein, *Judicious Choices: The New Politics of Supreme Court Confirmations* (New York: W.W. Norton & Co., 1994), 4.
54. Congressional Record, 107th Cong., 1st sess., 2001, S930.
55. Constance Horn, "The Politics of Presidential Appointment: The Old and New Culture of Job Seeking in Washington," *Impressions* 4 (1993): 20-24.
56. Barbara Sinclair, Unorthodox Lawmaking: New Legislative Processes in the U.S. Congress, 2nd ed. (Washington, D.C.: CQ Press, 2000), 44.
57. O'Brien 2000.
58. Denis Steven Rutkus, *Senate Judiciary Committee Consideration of Supreme Court Nominations*, CRS Report No. 94-479 GOV, June 6, 1994, Washington, D.C.
59. Roger H. Davidson and Colton C. Campbell, "The Senate and the Executive," in Burdett A. Loomis, ed., *Esteemed Colleagues: Civility and Deliberation in the U.S. Senate* (Washington, D.C.: Brookings Institution Press, 2000).
60. Denis Steven Rutkus, *The Supreme Court Appointment Process: Should it be Reformed?* CRS Report No. 93-290 GOV, June 3, 1993, Washington, D.C.
61. Rutkus 1994.
62. Baum 2000.
63. Kurtz, Fleisher, and Bond 1998; and Rutkus 1994.
64. David M. O'Brien, "How the Republican War over 'Judicial Activism' Has Cost Congress," in Colton C. Campbell and John F. Stack, Jr., eds., *Congress Confronts the Court: The Struggle for Legitimacy and Authority in Lawmaking* (Lanham, Md.: Rowman & Littlefield Publishers, Inc., 2001); and Baum 2000.
65. Rutkus 1993.
66. Congressional Record, 102nd Cong., 2nd sess., 1992, S8866.
67. Davidson and Campbell 2000.
68. O'Brien 2001.
69. Sinclair 2000.
70. Baum 2000, 50.
71. Ibid.
72. Jonathan Sanford, *Senate Disposition of Ambassadorial Nominations*, 1987-1996, CRS Report No. 97-864 F, September 19 1997, Washington, D.C.
73. Felzenberg 2000.
74. Ibid.
75. Colton C. Campbell, "Creating an Angel: Congressional Delegation to ad hoc Commissions," *Congress & The Presidency* 25 (1998): 161-82.
76. Garcia 2000.
77. Davidson and Campbell 2000.
78. O'Brien 1998; and Sheldon Goldman, *Picking Federal Judges: Lower Court Selection from Roosevelt Through Reagan* (New Haven: Yale University Press, 1997).
79. O'Brien 2001.

Relations with Congress and Public Policy

Chapter 9

REGIME FORMATION AND MATURATION IN THE WHITE HOUSE: THE RISE OF INTERNATIONALISM DURING THE ADMINISTRATION OF THEODORE ROOSEVELT

Tom Lansford

INTRODUCTION

The end of the nineteenth century marked the beginning of a transitional period in American foreign policy. With the interior of the continental United States essentially settled, the energies and power of the emerging nation would be unleashed on the global stage. The historian Ernest May once quipped that the United States had "greatness thrust upon it," reflecting the view that the nation's rise to superpower status was the result of its unique combination of geography and natural resources and not because of specific long-range policies. However, particular decisions made during the Roosevelt administrations ultimately laid the foundation for the country's emergence as a world power. Hence the roots of the "American Century" were in the few years preceding the turn of that century.

As the United States became a more influential actor in international relations, there was a change in the diplomatic regime that included the State Department and the nation's political elites. This essay traces the development of the new political regime in foreign policy that accompanied the increased American presence on the world stage which began with the McKinley administration and became solidified during Roosevelt's tenure. The work begins with an examination of the role and influence of domestic political regimes. The essay then specifically focuses on the role of the president in regime building and the adoption of new norms and values during the period in the context of foreign policy.

REGIMES

Regimes may be defined as the "sets of implicit or explicit principles, norms, rules, and decision-making procedures around which actors' expectations converge in a given area . . ."[1] Regimes encompass the common ideologies and beliefs which link together the people, institutions and policies of government. Significantly, regimes can serve as a means to maintain common policies during a change in administration or they can expedite the implementation of new or reformist ideas and policies. For instance, during the Cold War, there developed a foreign policy regime which was embraced by both the Democratic and Republican Parties and which helped maintain a remarkable degree of continuity in American diplomacy. This regime embraced the doctrine of containment of the Soviet Union, promotion of free trade, and American involvement in world affairs.[2] In order to accomplish the goals of the regime, new institutions, including the National Security Council and the Central Intelligence Agency, were developed.

Conversely, regimes can speed the adoption of new policies by providing a common framework for incoming administrations. As such, political regimes are often influence working arrangements among institutions fashioned by new governing cadres to elaborate their particular political commitments. As regimes transform new ideas about the purposes of government into governing routines, they carry on the reformer's central contention as the political common sense of a new era, a set of base assumptions shared (or at least accepted) by all major actors in the period. In this way, political regimes come to exercise an overarching influence over the affairs of state.[3] Once accepted, regimes speed the establishment of new norms, rules, and institutions because of the cohesiveness they furnish.

Norms, Rules, and Institutions

While regimes represent ideals, norms are about behavior.[4] Norms are the "standards of behavior defined in terms of rights and obligations." Common norms include sovereignty or free trade.[5] Norms impact behavior since they are "collective beliefs that regulate the behavior and identity of actors."[6] The relationship between regimes and norms is critically important since these constructs form the basis for political identity. Thomas Risse-Kappen defines identity as predicated on:

> norms firmly embedded in the political culture of . . . states and norms shape the identity of political actors through the processes of socialization, communication, and enactment. . . . Collectively held identities not only define who "we" are, but they also delineate the boundaries against "them," the "other." Identities then prescribe norms of appropriate behavior.[7]

In regards to national security and foreign policy, norms serve several important functions. For example they have led to the acceptance of national boundaries and both established buffer zones and spheres of influence.[8] Historical examples of such norms include the 1885 Congress of Vienna, which established spheres of influence in Africa for the European states or the Root-Takahira Agreement of 1908, in which the United States and Japan recognized each other's possessions in the Pacific.[9] In addition, norms can also dissuade nations from "cheating" on global agreements by specifically detailing the conditions under which other actors are prepared to act.[10] Contemporary examples of this would include the various global treaties on nuclear, biological, and chemical weapons (NBC).[11] Norms may also codify the procedures for international transactions. This has been especially apparent in the realm of global economics. Arrangements such as the General Agreement on Tariffs and Trade (GATT) and its successor the World Trade Organization (WTO) have significantly reduced the cost of business transactions for individual nations.[12] Finally, norms promote collective action. They provide justification for states to act as a group for implementation purposes.[13]

Rules are the application of individual norms to specific circumstances. As such, they are "specific prescriptions or proscriptions for action."[14] An example of such rules would be the practices established under the WTO to outlaw certain economic practices that run counter to free trade. These rules include provisions against subsidies, product dumping, and other discriminatory economic policies. In order for rules to be effective, they must have mechanisms to enforce them and they must be accepted (either passively or under duress). As Hedley Bull wrote, "a rule, in order to be effective in society, must be obeyed to some degree, and must be reckoned as a factor in the calculations of those to whom it applies, even those who elect to violate it."[15] Bull went on to assert that the effectiveness of a rule was dependent on several factors including the manner in which the rule is communicated to the people and the enforcement potential of the rule as well as its "adaptability."[16]

Institutions are formalized versions of regimes.[17] The main difference between a regime and an institution is that regimes do not have the ability to act since they are made up of norms and principles.[18] Only institutions have enforcement capabilities. As a result, regimes rely on institutions to carry-out enforcement measures.[19] The distinction between regimes and institutions can be illustrated with the complex issue of free trade. Western Europe has developed a trade regime that encompasses tacit and explicit rules. This regime is characterized by institutions that formalize rules and employ multilateral decision making processes.[20] Hence, institutions may be defined more narrowly as "persistent and connected sets of rules and principles that prescribe behavioral roles, constrain activity, and shape expectations"[21] because of their enforcement abilities.

Political Elites

The connection between regimes and institutions is represented by the common norms and rules shared by the two. The bridge which joins these two and ensures uniformity of principles is political elites. These elites form a disproportionate share of governmental employees and policymakers and also have a disproportionate influence in the formation and development of political opinion. In regards to foreign policy, Mark Lagon found that the American people often abrogate their control over the formation of policy and instead allow elites to develop initiatives while the populace concentrates on domestic policy. Lagon contends that "elites play a surprisingly significant role in democracies, especially in the foreign policy realm, where the mass public consciously or unconsciously cedes influence to experts and self-appointed experts."[22]

In a study on the responsiveness of the mass public to political communication from elites, Richard Herrera found that elites are generally "more sophisticated politically than the average voter"and have the capability to significantly influence opinion.[23] This builds on the classic work of V.O. Key in which the noted scholar asserts that "mass opinion is not self-generating [but] a response to the cues, proposals, and the visions propagated by the political activists."[24] During regime formation, elites may even bypass the public completely until the rules and norms of a new regime are established. The elites then work to garner public support and acceptance for the regime.[25] In some case, the elites may even abrogate their responsibility to disseminate information to bureaucrats or technocrats within the government.[26] Consequently, domestic political regimes are not "synonymous" with governmental institutions, instead they may be located:

> in the linkages that elites forge between governing institutions and political commitments. These linkages are composed of political norms, public discourses, decision-making procedures, and modes of intervention into socioeconomic relations. The formative element in any given regime is . . . not its trademark institutions but the governing cadre that manages them and acts within an intellectual milieu, infusing institutions with meaning, purpose, and direction.[27]

The importance of political elites cannot be underestimated especially in regards to the acceptance and internalization of the new regime.

Jeffrey W. Legro asserts that when states change their fundamental ideas about international relations (a regime change) that change occurs in a two-step process: "First, social actors [elites] must somehow concur, explicitly or tacitly, that the old ideational structure is inadequate, thus causing its collapse. Second, actors must consolidate some new replacement set of ideas, lest they return to the old orthodoxy simply as a default mechanism."[28] Hence, political elites are responsible for not only initiating regime change, but also for securing the broad acceptance of the regime by domestic interests. Such acceptance is most likely to occur under three conditions including: "1) when events generate consequences that deviate from social expectations; 2) when the consequences are undesirable; and 3) when a socially viable replacement idea exists."[29] For instance, during the post World War II era, the end of the conflict did not produce the period of global peace that most in the United States expected. Instead the tensions generated by the initiation of the Cold War ushered in a period of global strife. However, the renewed challenge presented to U.S. interests was met with a renewed domestic commitment to global involvement centered around the drive to contain the Soviet Union.

The role of elites in American politics is heightened because of the role of the Congress, and particularly the Senate, in developing and implementing foreign policy. In many ways, the Congress serves as the mechanism to reconcile domestic and foreign policy and it is the arena in which the two are often intertwined. On an economic level, Peter Katzenstein asserts that "the main purpose of all strategies of foreign economic policy is to make domestic policy compatible with the international political economy."[30] David A. Baldwin goes further and contends that "economic statecraft" or "foreign economic policy" has begun to supplant the traditional emphasis on security-based diplomacy, as contemporary states promote their domestic economic interests.[31] Robert Putnam best summarized the connections between foreign and domestic policy as a "two-level" game:

> The politics of many international negotiations can usefully be conceived as a two level game. At the national level, domestic groups pursue their interests by pressuring the government to adopt favorable policies, and politicians seek power by constructing coalitions among those groups. At the international level, national governments seek to maximize their own ability to satisfy domestic pressures, while minimizing the adverse consequences of foreign developments. Neither of the two games can be ignored by central decision makers, so long as their countries remain interdependent, yet sovereign.[32]

In this fashion, government and elites serve as the intermediaries between domestic and international actors.

In the United States, statesmen do not formulate foreign policy in a vacuum. They are constrained in their policy options by domestic groups that can bring significant political pressures and resources to the promotion of their interests. Policymakers have also had to balance the potential costs of security policies and programs in regards to national economies and social policies.[33] This leads to actions which may appear irrational because endeavors which are rational at the international level may be "impolitic" at the domestic level, and thus may not be taken.[34] The leadership and persuasion capabilities of elites are the keys to reconciling domestic and foreign interests.

At the end of the nineteenth century, there was a small, but very powerful foreign policy elite in the United States. Members of this elite dominated the nation's diplomatic service and often moved easily between business and government service. Theodore C. Sorenson contends that the foreign policy elite at the turn of the century was "the closest thing to a governing aristocracy" in the United States.[35] This elite was "led by Protestant white male graduates of Ivy League universities with close family and business toes to each other" and existed mainly in the corridor that was made-up of Boston, New York, and Washington.[36]

Theodore Roosevelt was an ardent supporter of an internationalist foreign policy for the United States. He sought to establish a new regime in foreign policy which was based on an expanded role for the emerging superpower. The challenge for Roosevelt was not just to develop new policies, but to ensure the continuation of internationalism through regime change. In order to accomplish this, Roosevelt had to gain acceptance of his new international vision of the United States by both existing political elites, including the leadership in Congress, then by the public at large. Concurrently, Roosevelt had to actually implement the polices that corresponded with his central goal of a greater global presence for the United States.

THE OLD REGIME

Throughout the eighteenth and nineteenth centuries, American foreign policy was directed primarily toward the Western Hemisphere. The resources of the nation were concentrated in the drive to develop the interior sections of the continental United States while trade considerations dominated American global diplomacy. The westward drive to develop the interior of the nation was rooted in the belief in the superiority of the "American way." John O'Sullivan coined the phrase "Manifest Destiny" to reflect the nation's claim to the continental areas of the West. Hence new territories belonged to the United States "by right of our manifest destiny to overspread and possess the whole of the continent which

Providence has given us for the great experiment of liberative and federative self-government entrusted to us."[37] The principle of Manifest Destiny became a powerful piece of political rhetoric that was used by elites to not only justify expansion, but to garner enormous public support for the acquisition of new areas – especially as these territories were meant to be fully integrated with the rest of the nation through the application of established political and cultural norms.[38] Throughout the nineteenth century, manifest destiny formed one of the core myths of American society.[39] Political elites use the commonalities of a culture to establish national myths which incorporate the norms, rules, and principles of existent regimes.

George Washington's oft-quoted admonishment to "avoid permanent alliances" and the principles of the Monroe Doctrine acted as dual constraints on any efforts to project American influence outside of the hemisphere.[40] Michael Dunne suggests that the term most used to describe U.S. foreign policy during this period – "isolationism" – should be replaced with the more accurate phrase "hemispheric unilateralism."[41] This concept holds that Americans may have actively sought to avoid political or security entanglement with Europe, but successive administrations were able to garner public support for expansion and interaction in Central and South America.[42] The ability of elites to rally public opinion lay in the nature of American attitudes toward foreign policy. For instance, Gabriel Almond asserts that for the most part Americans are, and have traditionally been, "indifferent" to foreign affairs, but that indifference could quickly turn to "anger" with the right motivations (leading to "dangerous overreactions" on the part of the populace).[43]

This facet of the nation's foreign policy was rooted in the longstanding belief in American exceptionalism – the idea that the United States was unique among the nations of the world. This uniqueness was the combination of a variety of factors including geography, politics, and culture. The idea of American exceptionalism was expressed domestically in the doctrine of manifest destiny.[44] Joseph Lepgold and Timothy McKeown contend that the belief in this exceptionalism lay in the longstanding manner in which "Americans depreciate power politics and old-fashioned diplomacy, mistrust powerful standing armies and entangling peacetime commitments, make moralistic judgements about other people's domestic systems, and believe that liberal values transfer readily to foreign affairs."[45]

As a result of this exceptionalism, Richard Kerry asserts that successive "American presidents have been addicted to citing the absence of territorial claims as evidence of the high purpose and moral purity with which the U.S. projects power to far places. This virtue is believed by Americans to distinguish the U.S. from any other power in the world, including other democracies."[46] For those such as Theodore Roosevelt, and later Woodrow Wilson, who believed in American internationalism, exceptionalism also carried with it an implicit duty to apply uniquely American qualities such as democracy and individual rights to other nations. This belief in "democratic universalism" reflected that the political ethnocentrism at the core of most Americans' view of the world – "everyone ought to be like us."[47] Such beliefs would be used to justify intervention in Central and South America and the acquisition of territories such as the Philippines since it was incumbent upon the United States to foster democracy in these developing nations.[48] Emily Rosenberg employs the term "liberal developmentalism" to describe American efforts at economic and democratic universalism.[49] Years after Roosevelt left office, the self-declared anti-imperialist president Woodrow Wilson would justify American intervention throughout the hemisphere by claiming that the United States was deploying troops in nations such as Nicaragua in an effort to "teach them to elect good men."

This universalism became prominent within the nation's foreign policy elite toward the end of the nineteenth century. Nonetheless, hemispheric unilateralism enjoyed one final period of prominence during the second administration of Grover Cleveland (1893-1897). Cleveland and his secretaries of state Walter Q. Gresham (1893-1895) and Richard Olney (1895-1897) reversed the internationalist efforts of Benjamin Harrison's secretary of state, James G. Blaine. For instance, Cleveland withdrew the 1893 annexation treaty with Hawaii from Congress and sought to avoid entanglement in Cuba (despite increasing public domestic pressure to respond to economic losses by U.S. citizens). The administration's policies were rooted in the principle that the Western Hemisphere represented the "new" world and were open to American influence and power, while Europe, Africa and Asia were the "old" world and the U.S. should avoid commitments or involvement in these regions. Olney used the Monroe Doctrine as justification for diplomatic brinkmanship which almost led to war between the United States and Great Britain during the Venezuelan Boundary Controversy.[50]

Even as the nation acquired territory during the expansionist periods of the nineteenth century, there was not a formal regime which supported the annexation of new territory.[51] Instead, while there were often economic imperatives for the acquisition of specific areas, other underlying factors including strategic interests or domestic political reasons, were just as likely to prompt territorial expansion. The second Cleveland administration followed time-adhered policies which sought to promote American economic interests, but not necessarily advance a heightened global role for the emerging nation.

The McKinley Administration

The election of 1896 led to dramatic changes in U.S. foreign policy. The new President, William McKinley, espoused a much more assertive foreign policy than had his predecessor (including favoring the annexation of Hawaii). Concurrent with the beginning of McKinley's tenure was a series of events which would draw the United States into a more visible global role. The real turning point was the Spanish-American War of 1898. While the United States clearly had the capability to be a world power relatively early in its history, the Spanish-American War demonstrated the nation's military power and led to a recognition by the established great powers of the young democracy's nascent potential. The conflict also marked the redirection of American imperialism outside of the Western hemisphere. For instance, Michael Dunne contends that the war marked:

> an American form of imperialism, for American power (in its broadest sense) was projected abroad and imposed over unwilling subjects; and in taking American power overseas so forcefully and dramatically, the war represented both the continuity of American territorial expansion and its discontinuous passage into the Caribbean and western Pacific.[52]

For the most part, the onset of American imperialism outside of the continental United States was merely the continuation of Westward expansion. The aggressive acquisition of territory had marked the nation from its very beginning and the closing of the frontier merely prompted a redirection of American power projection outside of the continental United States.

Richard W. Van Alstyne even contended that the United States was an imperium or expanding imperial power from its very foundation.[53]

Within the United States the acquisition of new territories overseas elicited considerable domestic debate. The rise of groups such as the American Anti-Imperialist League was demonstrative of the strong sentiment which opposed American colonialism. This opposition was based on traditional isolationist sentiments as well as moral grounds. The 1899 League Platform summarized the moral objections:

> We hold that the policy known as imperialism is hostile to liberty and tends toward militarism, an evil from which it has been our glory to be free. We regret that it has become necessary in the land of Washington and Lincoln to reaffirm that all men, of whatever race or color, are entitled to life, liberty and the pursuit of happiness. We maintain that governments derive their powers from the consent of the governed. We insist that the subjugation of any people is "criminal aggression" and open disloyalty to the distinctive principles of our Government.[54]

Anti-imperialist sentiment was embraced by a number of prominent Americans including such diverse figures as Andrew Carnegie, William Graham Sumner, William Jennings Bryan, and Samuel Gompers. However, while elite opposition to imperialism remained strong throughout the Spanish-American War and afterward, elite support for the expansionist policies of the McKinley administration would initiate a regime change in the nation's foreign policy. The most prominent and public advocate for an enhanced global role for the United States was Theodore Roosevelt.

THE NEW REGIME

Long before he entered the political spotlight, Roosevelt became convinced of the need for a more assertive foreign policy. By the late 1880s, Roosevelt had gained some fame as a historian and writer (including a work on the War of 1812). After he read Alfred Thayer Mahan's *The Influence of Sea Power Upon History, 1660-1783*, Roosevelt became firmly convinced of the need for the United States to become a global naval power. In a review of Mahan's work, Roosevelt wrote that the nation needed a navy that excelled above all others:

> Our ships should be the best of their kind–this is the first desideratum. But in addition, there should be plenty of them. We need a large navy, composed not merely of cruisers, but containing also a full proportion of powerful battleships, able to meet those of any other nation.[55]

Such a navy would serve not only to protect the national interests of the United States, but it would also allow Washington to project its power anywhere around the globe.

Roosevelt, Mahan, and Massachusetts Senator Henry Cabot Lodge became the core of the elite group that advocated expansionist policies. The group was headquartered at New York's prominent Metropolitan Club. In his biography of the young Roosevelt, Edmund Morris points-out that eventually the circle of expansionists would include "Senators and Representatives, Navy and Army officers, writers, socialites, lawyers, and scientists–men linked as much by Roosevelt's motley personality as by their common political belief, namely, that Manifest Destiny called for the United States to free Cuba, annex Hawaii, and raise the American flag supreme over the Western Hemisphere."[56]

Partially through the efforts of Senator Lodge, Roosevelt was appointed Assistant Secretary of the Navy in 1897. Almost at once, Roosevelt began to agitate for war against Spain over Cuba. In his autobiography, Roosevelt wrote that "soon after I began work as Assistant Secretary of the Navy I became convinced that war would come."[57] When war broke-out in April of 1898, Roosevelt resigned his post and rode to fame at the head of the Rough Riders.[58] He parlayed his popularity into a successful campaign to be governor of the state of New York. This in turn served as a stepping stone to the vice-presidency in 1900.

Meanwhile, the Spanish-American War had resulted in an American empire. As a result of the conflict, the United States gained the territories of Puerto Rico, Guam, and the Philippines. Cuba was granted nominal independence, but remained an American protectorate through the adoption of the Platt Amendment which gave the United States the rights to two naval bases in the island and the legal right to intervene in its southern neighbor's domestic politics. The war also led to a Congressional resolution to annex Hawaii. The rapid expansion of the United States into the Pacific affirmed that the nation would be both an Atlantic and Pacific power. The new territories also permanently drew the nation into the affairs of Asia.

The United States fought a bloody and repressive war to prevent Filipino independence, and participated in the military operations against the Boxers in China during the summer of 1900. Concurrently, McKinley's second Secretary of State, John Hay, promulgated the Open Door Notes by which the United States refused to recognize the European and Japanese spheres of influence in China. The Notes marked a major turning point in the nation's diplomatic history and began the process by which the Washingtonian policy of hemispheric isolationism began to erode. Dunne provides this summation:

> These paper commitments aligned the US and British governments; but they went against German as well as Japanese and Russian interests. Hindsight shows us that, not for the last time, the US government had adopted a policy towards China which set it against two regional powers (Japan and Russia). More to the point, contemporaries appreciated that the American drive for markets, naval bases and coaling stations, and for greater political influence in the Pacific and along the shores of Asia, entailed an examination of traditional policies. As was astutely noted at the time, the very ease of American success obscured the need to reflect on the reasons and conditions for this pre-eminence and encouraged Americans to avoid a re-evaluation of their unilateralist practices.[59]

The role of the foreign policy elite in the transformation of American diplomacy was significant. Roosevelt and his circle, including judge and future president William H. Taft, were the ideological leaders of the movement which championed both the acquisition of new territories and an increased global presence. They also acted to coordinate policies and craft legislation to support a more robust foreign policy.

In his autobiography, Roosevelt asserted that one of the reasons that he accepted the vice-presidency was "the need, after 1898, of meeting in manful and straightforward fashion the extraterritorial problems arising from the Spanish War."[60] In other words, Roosevelt wanted to make sure that there was no retreat from the nation's new global prominence which was occasioned by the war with Spain.

Roosevelt's Foreign Policy

When Roosevelt became president in 1901 following the assassination of McKinley, the transformation of American foreign policy had begun and the nation had emerged onto the world stage as a major international power following its defeat of Spain and its military involvement in the Boxer Rebellion of 1900.[61] Nonetheless, in spite of the nation's increased overseas commitments, domestic opposition to internationalism remained significant in the United States. While Roosevelt's brand of internationalism (based on democratic universalism) was embraced by many within the foreign policy elite, it would only be through his efforts as President that the norms, values and ideas of internationalism became formalized. His efforts to strengthen the U.S. Navy and changes in the State Department led to the development of the institutions necessary to support a new foreign policy regime.

Once in office, Roosevelt pledged to maintain the policies of his predecessor and even asked all of the assassinated president's cabinet members to remain. During his first annual address to Congress, Roosevelt reiterated his belief in the virtue of annexing the Philippines, Hawaii, Puerto Rico, and Guam. In regards to the ongoing revolt in the Philippines, the new President also emphasized his belief in the universal mission of the nation to "help these people upward along the stony and difficult path that leads to self-government."[62] He also expressed his wish to see the current American battleship fleet increased from nine to seventeen. The President stressed the importance of the fleet as a means to enforce the Monroe Doctrine and forestall European intervention in the Western Hemisphere. Most important, Roosevelt emphasized the need for the construction of a canal across the Panamanian Isthmus. Concerning the canal, the new President claimed that "no single great material work which remains to be undertaken on this continent is of such consequence to the American people."[63]

Throughout his tenure, Roosevelt's foreign policy would be centered around these themes. He would justify the military repression used in the Philippines as necessary to instill democracy–an argument that would also be used to rationalize American military interventions in the Caribbean. For instance, Roosevelt actions in fostering a revolution in Panama were explained away through his assertions that Colombia was ruled by a dictator and that the people of the Isthmus of Panama were governed by a government "without their consent."[64] The main reason for U.S. support of the revolution was the Colombian Senate's rejection of the original canal treaty between that nation and the United States. With Panama an independent nation, Hay was free to negotiate the Hay-Bunau-Varilla Treaty which gave the United States the right to construct a canal and maintain sovereignty over a ten-mile-wide zone in exchange for $10 million and an annual payment of $250,000.

He used a similar rationale for intervention in Santo Domingo in 1904. However, the intervention in Santo Domingo was mainly the result of Roosevelt's desire to protect American bankers and business interests from German and French creditors and the possibility of domestic revolution. Roosevelt justified his actions in the Caribbean with the promulgation of the Roosevelt Corollary to the Monroe Doctrine. In the Corollary, Roosevelt declared that:

> all that this country desires to see the neighboring countries stable, orderly, and prosperous. . . . Chronic wrongdoing, or an impotence which results in the general loosening of the ties of civilized society, may . . . require intervention by some civilized

nation, and in the Western Hemisphere the adherence of the United States to the Monroe Doctrine may force the United States, however reluctantly, in flagrant cases of such wrongdoing or impotence to the exercise of an international police power. . . . We would interfere with [Latin Americans] only in the last resort.[65]

The Corollary gave the United States the right, indeed the duty, to intervene in the domestic affairs of Latin American nations when revolution or European intervention appeared imminent. The Corollary also highlighted the high degree of autonomy that American Presidents have in the realm of foreign policy. In his efforts to change the diplomatic orientation of the United States, Roosevelt extensively utilized the broad powers of the presidency, both to direct foreign policy and to oversee the military. In the Senate, Roosevelt could count on the support of his friend and mentor, Henry Cabot Lodge. Meanwhile, in the House, the President found a willing ally in Illinois Congressman Robert Hitt who was chairman of the House Foreign Affairs Committee.[66]

The Navy

In order to meet the increased commitments occasioned by his policies, Roosevelt needed to improve the capability and increase the size of the American military – mainly the Navy. Historian James R. Reckner points out that "perhaps no other President has exerted such intimate influence on the U.S. Navy as Theodore Roosevelt."[67] The importance of the Navy was underscored early in Roosevelt's Administration when in 1902 German and British warships blockaded Venezuela over that country's nonpayment of debts. Roosevelt had a fleet assemble off Puerto Rico, ostensibly for maneuvers. Roosevelt informed the German Ambassador that he intended to dispatch the fleet to Venezuela if Germany did not agree to arbitration. The threat had the desired impact and the matter was turned over to arbitration. Nonetheless, the incident underscored for the new President the potential for European intervention in the Hemisphere.

Throughout the remainder of his tenure, Roosevelt believed that Germany represented the greatest foreign threat to American interests. In April of 1901, Roosevelt wrote that "it seems to me that Germany's attitude toward us makes her the only power with which there is any reasonable likelihood or possibility of our clashing."[68] Besides potential problems in Latin America, Roosevelt also judged that Germany could cause problems for the United States elsewhere around the globe. From 1904 to 1906, tensions between France and Germany over spheres of influence in Morocco brought the two nations repeatedly to the verge of war. Roosevelt offered to mediate the crisis. The result was the 1906 Algeciras Conference which found in favor of French claims. Roosevelt's influence at the Algeciras Conference came in the wake of a 1904 incident in which a bandit leader, the Raisuli, took two Americans hostage. Roosevelt deployed the fleet off the coast and eventually pressured the Sultan of Morocco into securing the release of the hostages. In the midst of the crisis, came the 1904 Republican National Convention. Roosevelt brought the Convention to its feet when he had the chairman read a demand for either the return of the Americans or the death of the Raisuli.

In fact, Roosevelt used his foreign policy successes, including the Corollary and the Panama Canal Treaty to great success during his reelection campaign. Roosevelt appealed to the nation by stressing his activism in both domestic and foreign policies. His actions in regards to Panama and Santo Domingo were very popular with the American people as Roosevelt emphasized the nation's role in promoting democracy and protecting the Hemisphere from European intervention in his campaign speeches. When the election was over, Roosevelt won by the largest margin in the popular vote that had yet been recorded in a presidential election.[69] His victory further emboldened Roosevelt and his second term was marked by an increased assertiveness in foreign affairs.

The Far East

In 1905, Roosevelt achieved a dramatic diplomatic success when he mediated an end to the Russo-Japanese War. Roosevelt's impatience and his impetuousness worked in his favor after he became personally involved in the negotiations between the warring powers. At the peace conference in Portsmouth, New Hampshire, Roosevelt sought to maintain a balance of power between the nations. Therefore, although Japan was clearly winning the war militarily, Roosevelt wanted to ensure that Russia would not be so weakened that it could not counterbalance Japan in the future. This would continue the policy begun under McKinley of maintaining a regional balance of power in Asia.

The Portsmouth Conference and its resultant peace treaty were critically important in validating Roosevelt's heightened global role. For his role in the negotiations, Roosevelt became the first American President to win the Nobel Peace Prize. The international recognition that Roosevelt gained, and the fact that he was highly effective, legitimized the President's internationalism in the eyes of the American public and especially in regards to the nation's political elites.

When Roosevelt's first secretary of State, John Hay, died in 1905, the President asked former Secretary of War, Elihu Root to replace him. While Hay had served as a bridge between nineteenth and twentieth century diplomacy, Root emerged as a prototype of the professional secretary of state that became common in the twentieth century. Root deftly negotiated an accord with Japan, the "gentlemen's agreement," in 1906 after San Francisco passed legislation which segregated Japanese students. In the accord, Japan agreed to stop emigration to California in exchange for a repeal of discriminatory laws in California. Roosevelt had to use political pressure to enforce the agreement in California.[70] Fortunately, the governor of California, James Gillett, was a Republican and Roosevelt was able to persuade him to pressure the state senate to block additional anti-immigrant legislation. The Democrats used the anti-immigrant sentiment in the 1906 congressional elections to some success.[71]

The Gentleman's Agreement provides an example of a two-level game whereby Roosevelt and Root had to balance domestic and international issues. Roosevelt understood the domestic dangers of the agreement, but he was more concerned with the possibility of conflict with Japan. Therefore, he was willing to accept the domestic backlash and its consequences in return for the maintenance of relations with Japan.[72] Nonetheless, relations with Japan would continue to occupy a central role in Roosevelt's foreign policy throughout the remainder of his term. In May of 1907, there were anti-Japanese riots in San Francisco and tensions between the two nations surfaced again.

Manifestations of the New Regime

In the meanwhile, Roosevelt quickly overcame the minor electoral losses in the 1906 midterm elections with another major foreign policy success. On November 9, 1906, Roosevelt set sail for Panama with his wife Edith to view the progress made thus far on construction of the canal. He became the first American president to travel outside of the continental United States while in office. The trip was an overwhelming triumph. The idea of Roosevelt traveling to inspect the nation's greatest engineering feat to date had widespread public appeal.[73] By breaking the unofficial taboo on presidential voyages, Roosevelt opened the door for future presidents to travel (including his successor, William Howard Taft who also visited Panama while in office). Upon his return to the United States, Roosevelt delivered a special message to Congress on the progress of the Canal, complete with pictures and movie footage. As such, Roosevelt changed one of the central norms surrounding presidents and their ability to conduct foreign policy.

Roosevelt's concern with Japan would be chiefly responsible for his decision to dispatch an American fleet on an around-the-world voyage. He saw this as an opportunity to demonstrate to the world the capability of the United States to deploy its fleet anywhere in the world. In his autobiography Roosevelt claimed that:

> In my judgement the most important service that I rendered to peace was the voyage of the battle fleet round the world. I had become convinced that for many reasons is was essential that we should have it clearly understood, by our own people especially, but also by other peoples, that the Pacific was as much our home waters as the Atlantic, and our fleet could and would at will pass from one to the other of the great oceans.[74]

Specifically, Roosevelt saw the circumnavigation as means to demonstrate to the Japanese that the United States could deploy its forces to the Pacific quickly. The force, known as the "Great White Fleet," consisted of 16 battleships and dozens of escort vessels with a total of 18,000 sailors and marines. The fleet departed from Norfolk Naval Station in Hampton Roads, Virginia in 1907 and completed its excursion in 1909.

The Fleet's voyage was a resounding success, both strategically and in the realm of public opinion. The greatest obstacles the operation faced were domestic. Roosevelt found that Eugene Hale, the Chairman of the Senate Naval Affairs Committee, opposed the mission on grounds that it might antagonize or provoke the Japanese. Roosevelt declared that "I have almost as much trouble with our own people, like Senator Hale, who are always giving the impression to Japan that we are afraid of them, as with the other people, who insult the Japanese."[75] However, the overwhelmingly domestic public approval of the voyage easily compensated for the limited disapproval of some in Congress or members of such groups as the Anti-Imperialist League.[76]

CONCLUSION

When the Great White Fleet returned to port, Roosevelt had already left office. He was followed by his hand-picked successor, William Howard Taft. While in office, Roosevelt greatly dramatically changed the nation's foreign policy regime. He emerged as the leader of a foreign policy elite that embraced new norms and values and attempted to alter the very basis of U.S. diplomacy and engagement in the world. Roosevelt also deftly utilized this new regime to manage a series of two-level games. From his actions in initiating construction of the Panama Canal to his balancing of foreign and domestic interests in regards to Japanese immigration, the President was able to maximize the political payoffs of these situations.

By the end of his tenure in office, the public and foreign policy elites had embraced the assertive foreign policy of Roosevelt. Under his leadership, a regime developed with its requisite institutions, including an expanded Navy and other military components necessary to oversee the nation's new territories and expanded role in Asia and Latin America. In addition, as a result of his use of the "bully-pulpit," the majority of the U.S. citizenry accepted the aggressive norms and ideals of Roosevelt. Under Roosevelt, the public accepted an enhanced role for the United States as the perceived "guardian" of the Western Hemisphere. As a consequence, public support for military interventions in the Caribbean remained strong into the Wilson presidency. In addition, Roosevelt's actions at the Portsmouth Conference and the Algeciras Conference served to legitimize the status of the United States as a world power and that of the American president as the equal of the heads of state of Europe. By traveling outside of the U.S., Roosevelt also helped to elevate foreign policy to a more equal plane with domestic policy. Underlining all of these policies was Roosevelt's sense of mission – his belief in what he termed the "strenuous life." This was an extension of the general belief in democratic universalism and would form the core of Wilson's progressive idealism.

Roosevelt's accomplishments and innovations in foreign policy had a long-lasting impact on the office of the presidency. First, Roosevelt successfully established the United States as major actor on the global stage. Building upon the military success of the United States in the Spanish American War, the new President projected American power in a highly visible fashion through actions such as the construction of the Panama Canal and the circumnavigation of the Great White Fleet. Second, Roosevelt used the "bully-pulpit" to garner public support for his assertive diplomacy and lead the effort to introduce the norms, rules and principles of a new foreign policy regime. In doing so, he adroitly managed the transition to a new regime and ensured its acceptance by the nation's contemporary political elites. Roosevelt became the first president to successfully combine the trends of exceptionalism and universalism as the long-term basis for his foreign policy. Roosevelt's new regime provided the foundation for the internationalist foreign policies of Roosevelt's successors, Taft and Wilson. Third, and finally, Roosevelt's personal involvement in foreign affairs foreshadowed the later summit diplomacy whereby presidents ranging from Franklin D. Roosevelt to Ronald Reagan personally negotiated international agreements or met with their counterparts to address global issues. Roosevelt's tenure marked the decline of the strong secretary of state and the corresponding dominance of the president in foreign policy (a change that was finalized under his nephew, Franklin and his successor, Harry S. Truman, and the post-World War II division of foreign and security policy as manifested by the creation of the office of National Security Advisor).

Nonetheless, while Roosevelt's policies centered around an expanded and aggressive role for the U.S. in world affairs, Taft's foreign policy would concentrate on economic issues. Taft would term his new diplomatic outlook "dollar diplomacy" and base foreign policy on the nation's economic interests in both Asia and Latin America.[77] Still, the new president would continue to use military force to protect business and commercial interests. Conversely, it would be Wilson who took the greatest advantage of the foreign policy regime that had been established by Roosevelt. Yet, under Wilson, the nation also rejected the broad aims of democratic universalism which formed the basis of the regime and the expanded global role of the United States. The leader of the opposition to Wilson's view of a new global order based on the League of Nations was Henry Cabot Lodge who ironically helped form Roosevelt's new regime.

NOTES

[1] Stephen Krasner, "Structural Causes and Regime Consequences: Regimes as Intervening Variables," in *International Regimes*, ed. Stephen Krasner (Ithaca: Cornell University,1983), 2.

[2] John Gerard Ruggie asserted that the new foreign policy regime which developed in the post-World War II era was the nation's "third try" at implementing a broad multilateral security order (the first was Woodrow Wilson's post-World War I effort and the second was Franklin Roosevelt's endeavor to bring together the "four horsemen," the U.S., Great Britain, Russia and China, to establish a collective security regime through the United Nations); see John Gerard Ruggie, "Third Try at World Order," *Political Science Quarterly*, 109, no. 4 (Fall 1994): 553-70.

[3] Karen Orren and Stephen Skowronek, "Regimes and Regime Building in American Government," *Political Science Quarterly*, 113, no. 4 (Winter 1999), 694.

[4] Andrew Farkas, "The Evolution of International Norms," *International Studies Quarterly* 40, no. 3 (September, 1996): 362.

[5] Andrew P. Cortell and James W. Davis, Jr., "How Do International Institutions Matter? The Domestic Impact of International Rules and Norms," *International Studies Quarterly* 40, no. 4 (December 1996): 452.

[6] Robert Herman, "Identity, Norms, and National Security," in Peter J. Katzenstein, ed. *The Culture of National Security: Norms and Identity in World Politics* (New York: Columbia University, 1996), 274.

[7] Thomas Risse-Kappen, "Collective Identity in a Democratic Community," in Katzenstein, 366-67.

[8] Gregory A. Raymond, "Problems and Prospects in the Study of International Norms," *Mershon International Studies Review* 41, no. 2 (November 1997): 214.

[9] On the Root-Takahira Agreement, see Robert Bacon and James Brown Scott, *The Military and Colonial Policy of the United States, Addresses and Reports by Elihu Root* (Cambridge: Harvard, 1916).

[10] As an example, norms can determine prearranged courses of action for transgressions of international agreements: if state A violates agreement B, then the other signatories to B pledge that C course of action will result.

[11] These treaties provide mechanisms that prompt multilateral action against violators of the norms, as well as encourage compliance through incentive programs. U.S., Department of Defense, *Weapons of Mass Destruction: Reducing the Threat From the Former Soviet Union*, NSIAD-95-7 (Washington, D.C.: GAO, 1995); U.S., House of Representatives, C. Bruce Tarter, testimony, "Stemming the Proliferation of Nuclear Weapons and Other Weapons of Mass Destruction," *The Department of Energy's Budget Request for FY 1996: Hearing of the Subcommittee on Military Procurement* (Washington, D.C.: GPO, 1995), 1.

[12] As an example, the Tokyo round of the GATT negotiations in the mid-1980s, linked trade and monetary policy in such a way as encourage exports to the United States following a decision by the Reagan administration to weaken the dollar; Charles Pearson and Nils Johnson, *The*

New GATT Trade Round, FPI Case Studies, no. 2 (Washington, D.C.: Johns Hopkins, 1986), 22-23.

13. For examples of this type of behavior see Axelrod and Keohane.
14. Krasner, 2.
15. Hedley Bull, *The Anarchical Society: A Study of Order in World Politics* (New York: Columbia University, 1977), 56.
16. Ibid; 56-7.
17. Charles A. Kupchan, "The Case for Collective Security," in *Collective Security Beyond the Cold War*, ed. George W. Downs (Ann Arbor: University of Michigan, 1994), 48.
18. Andreas Hansenclever, Peter Mayer, and Volker Rittberger, "Interests, Power, Knowledge: The Study of International Regimes," *Mershon International Studies Review* 40, no. 2 (October 1996): 179.
19. Robert O. Keohane combines principles, norms and rules into a single category with his definition of international regimes: "institutions with explicit rules, agreed upon by governments, that pertain to particular sets of issues in international relations;" Robert O. Keohane, "Neoliberal Institutionalism: A Perspective on World Politics," in *International Institutions and State Power: Essays in International Relations Theory*, ed. Robert O. Keohane (Boulder: Westview, 1989), 4. However, Keohane's narrow definition has been subject to much criticism, especially over its inability to account for the relationships between the factors within a regime.
20. In addition, this regime has allowed for non-security expansion, or economic augmentation, for nation-states, which has ameliorated the security dilemma, and hence prevented security rivalries by channeling economic competition through regime norms; Randall L. Schweller, "Neorealism's Status-Quo Bias: What Security Dilemma?" *Security Studies*, Special Issue, Realism: Restatements and Renewal, 5, no. 3 (Spring 1996): 92.
21. Robert O. Keohane, Peter Haas, and Marc Levy, eds., *Institutions for the Earth: Sources of Effective International Environmental Protection* (Cambridge: MIT, 1993), 4-5.
22. Mark P. Logan, "Elite Analysis of Democracies' International Policy," *Perspectives on Political Science*, 29, no. 1 (Winter 2000), 5.
23. Richard Herrara, "Understanding the Language of Politics: A Study of Elites and Masses," *Political Science Quarterly* 111, no. 4 (Winter 1997), 620.
24. V.O. Key, *Public Opinion and American Democracy* (New York: Alfred Knopf, 1961); quoted in Herrara, 620.
25. An example of such "bypassing" occurred during the negotiations which ended Apartheid in South Africa; Jeffrey Herbst, "Prospects for Elite-Driven Democracy in South Africa," *Political Science Quarterly* 112, no. 4 (Winter 1998), 614.
26. Juan D. Lindau contends that the ruling political elite in Mexico provides an example of this trend where the distinction between the political elite and technocrats has been blurred to the point of indistinguishability; Juan D. Lindau, "Technocrats and Mexico's Political Elite," *Political Science Quarterly* 111, no. 2 (Summer 1996): 295-322.
27. Orren and Skowronek, 694.
28. Jeffrey W. Legro, "Whence American Internationalism," *International Organizations* 54, no. 2 (Spring 2000), 254.
29. Ibid.
30. See Peter J. Katzenstein, ed., *Between Power and Plenty: Foreign Economic Policy and Advanced Industrial States* (Madison: University of Wisconsin, 1978), 4.
31. David Baldwin, *Economic Statecraft* (Princeton: Princeton University, 1985), 29-50
32. Putnam, "Two-Level Games," 434.
33. Paul A. Papayoanou, "Economic Interdependence and the Balance of Power," *International Studies Quarterly* 41, no. 1 (March 1997): 117.
34. Putnam, "Two-Level Games," 436.

[35] Theodore C. Sorenson, " Foreign Policy in a Presidential Democracy," *Political Science Quarterly* 109, no. 3 (Special Issue, 1994), 521.

[36] Ibid.

[37] Quoted in Frederick Merk, *Manifest Destiny and Mission in American History: A Reinterpretation* (New York: Vintage, 1963), 31-2.

[38] This theme forms the core of Frederick Merk's seminal work, see ibid. Also see Norman Graebner, ed., *Manifest Destiny* (Indianapolis: Bobbs Merrill, 1963) or William Earl Weeks, *Building the Continental Empire: American Expansion from the Revolution to the Civil War* (Chicago: Ivan R. Dee, 1996).

[39] James Oliver Robertson underscores the importance of national myths when he states: "no human society is a rational construct. All societies depend for their continuation, for their very existence, on common assumptions, common forms of communication , common referents for thoughts and ideas, common patterns of behavior and ritual , and a common inheritance;" James Oliver Robertson, *American Myth, American Reality* (New York: Hill and Wang, 1980), 17.

[40] The quote from Washington's Farewell Address served as a constant reminder to successive administrations to shun political or military ties to foreign nations. However, bilateral and multilateral economic treaties were common during the nineteenth century. The Monroe Doctrine pledged American non-interference in European affairs in exchange for European non-interference in the Western Hemisphere (including no new colonization).

[41] Michael Dunne, "US Foreign Relations in the Twentieth Century: From World Power to Global Hegemony," *International Affairs* 76, no. 1 (January 2000), 27.

[42] Examples of public endorsement for such assertive policies in the Western Hemisphere included expansion into the Mexican territories and support for the purchase of Cuba.

[43] This indifference was the result of the tendency for Americans to became self-absorbed in their own lives and localities, leaving little time to pay attention to world events; Gabriel Almond, *The American People and Foreign Policy* (New York: Praeger, 1960), 53, 76. Conversely, reflecting traditional Marxist analyses, Richard Barnet contends that the 'manipulation" of American public opinion on foreign policy matters is the result of broad efforts by political and economic elites to ensure access to, and often control of, overseas markets; Richard Barnet, *The Roots of War* (New York: Atheneum, 1972).

[44] Robertson asserts that the basis for the notion of American exceptionalism was rooted in the broader myths that undergirded the society; see Robertson, 12-18.

[45] While the idea of American exceptionalism is a long-standing component of U.S. foreign policy, the authors conclude that there is a disconnect between the political rhetoric of elites and the actual implementation of foreign policy. In other words, elites use the idea of exceptionalism as a means to justify actions or to garner public support; Joseph Lepgold and Timothy McKeown, "Is American Foreign Policy Exceptional? An Empirical Analysis," *Political Science Quarterly*, vol. 110, 3 (Fall 1995), 369.

[46] Richard J. Kerry, *The Star-Spangled Mirror: America's Image of Itself and the World* (Savage, Maryland: Rowman & Littlefield, 1990), 3.

[47] Ibid.

[48] Following this line of reasoning, manifest destiny was rooted in the drive to spread American political and economic values throughout the continent, not in the simple drive for territory. Once the "Americanization" of the continent was fairly secure, ideological forces drove the nation to endeavor to spread these same values throughout Asia and the Caribbean; see Michael H. Hunt, *Ideology and U.S. Foreign Policy* (New Haven: Yale, 1987).

[49] Rosenberg contends that political elites in the United States used the rhetoric of peace, prosperity, and democracy as a means to satisfy domestic audiences while the nation pursued an expansionist foreign policy designed to Americanize the world. Liberal developmentalism was based on five principles: 1) the belief that other nations could copy the development patterns of the U.S.; 2) the promotion of free enterprise; 3) championing global free trade and

open markets; 4) staunch support for the free flow of information (including an open and free media); and 5) an "acceptance" of government actions to protect and promote American business interests; Emily S. Rosenberg, *Spreading the American Dream: American Economic and Cultural Expansion, 1890-1945* (New York: Hill and Wang, 1982).

50 The boundary controversy centered on a dispute between Venezuela and the British Colony of Guiana over a border area where gold had been discovered. Olney threatened to use military force against the British if they intervened in the region. British diplomatic isolation during the Great Anglo-Boer War led London to seek accommodation with the U.S. and the dispute was ultimately settled through arbitration (Great Britain was granted most of the region). The dispute also led to a general arbitration treaty between the two nations over future territorial disagreements, the Olney-Pauncefote Convention which was signed in January of 1897.

51 David M. Pletcher, *The Diplomacy of Trade and Investment: American Economic Expansion in the Hemisphere, 1865-1900* (Columbia: University of Missouri, 1998), 2-3.

52 Dunne, 26.

53 On this theme, see Richard W. Van Alstyne, *The Rising American Empire* (New York: Blackwell and Mott, 1960).

54 Anti-Imperialist League, *League Platform 1899*; reprinted in Constance Jones, Derris L. Raper, and John J. Sbrega, eds., *The American Experience: Documents and Notes*, 2nd ed., (Dubuque, Iowa : Kendall/Hunt Pub. Co., 1987), 160.

55 Theodore Roosevelt, "Review," *Atlantic Monthly* (October 1890); quoted in H. W. Brands, *TR: The Last Romantic* (New York: Basic Books, 1997), 238.

56 Edmund Morris, *The Rise of Theodore Roosevelt* (New York: Coward, McCann & Geoghegan, 1979), 568.

57 Theodore Roosevelt, *Theodore Roosevelt: An Autobiography* (New York: Scribner's, 1913); reprinted by New York: De Capo Press, 1985, 213.

58 Roosevelt's heroics during the Spanish-American War led to his promotion to colonel and the recommendation that he be awarded the Medal of Honor for his actions in the capture of San Juan Hill. He returned to the United States as one fo the most popular heroes of the conflict.

59 Dunne, 20; as an example of contemporary observations, Dunne cites John B. Henderson, Jr., *American Diplomatic Questions* (New York: Macmillan, 1901).

60 Roosevelt, 366.

61 During the summer of 1900, an anti-foreign society, the Boxers, rose-up in open revolt against the foreign powers. In response, the major international powers sent troops into China. McKinley dispatched 5,000 American soldiers. Secretary of State Hay used the presence of these forces as a bargaining tool to ensure acceptance of the second set of Open Door Notes. The deployment demonstrated the military capability of the United States and its ability to dispatch troops quickly to areas of the Pacific.

62 Theodore Roosevelt, *Annual Message to Congress*, December 3, 190; in Theodore Roosevelt, *The Works of Theodore Roosevelt*, vol. 17, Hermann Hagedorn, ed., (New York: Scribner's, 1926) 93-160.

63 Ibid.

64 Roosevelt, *Autobiography*, 533.

65 "Roosevelt Corollary" in Ruhl J. Bartlett, ed., *The Record of American Diplomacy*, 4th ed. (New York), 539.

66 Roosevelt was so pleased with Hitt's support for his policies, that he endeavored to have the Illinois Congressman placed on the ballot as vice-president in 1904. However, the nomination went to Republican insider Senator Charles Fairbanks of Indiana.

67 James R. Reckner, " TR and his Navy," *Naval History* 15, no. 1 (February 2001), 41.

68 Theodore Roosevelt to G. Meyer, April 12, 1901, quoted in Brands, 465.

69 In the election, Roosevelt received 7,628,461 popular votes and 336 electoral votes. His opponent, Democrat Alton B. Parker, received 5,084,223 popular votes and 140 electoral votes.

70 For instance, Roosevelt brought the mayor and school board of San Francisco to Washington to personally lobby them to accept the agreement.
71 In the 1906 Congressional elections, the Democrats increased their number of seats in the House from 136 to 164 while the Republican numbers decreased from 250 to 222. However, Roosevelt's Party gained 3 seats in the Senate (moving from 58 to 61 while the Democrats declined from 32 to 29 seats).
72 For a good overview of the balancing act between domestic and international concerns, see Brands, 578-83.
73 In the seminal work on the construction of the Canal, David McCullough's *The Path Between the Seas*, the author points out that even conservative newspapers such as the Washington *Star* endorsed the trip; David McCullough, *The Path Between the Seas: The Creation of the Panama Canal, 1870-1914* (New York: Simon & Schuster, 1977), 492.
74 Roosevelt, *Autobiography*, 563.
75 Theodore Roosevelt to Andrew Carnegie, July 15, 1907; quoted in Brands, 609.
76 Opposition also came from groups who were afraid that the nation would not be able to respond to a crisis if the fleet was on the other side of the world.
77 For an overview of the divergent development of Taft's foreign policy beliefs, see Ralph Eldin Minger, *William Howard Taft and United States Foreign Policy: The Apprenticeship Years, 1900-1908* (Chicago: University of Illinois Press, 1975).

Chapter 10

THE COLLAPSE OF AN INHERITED AGENDA: GEORGE BUSH AND THE REAGAN FOREIGN POLICY LEGACY

Victoria A. Farrar-Myers

INTRODUCTION

Presidents tend to be seen as entering the office of the presidency on comparatively equal footing. They all enter the White House with similar powers stemming from the Constitution that have subsequently been expanded over time. They all face a learning curve associated with the office as they try to master the policy process given their new position.[1] To the extent that differences are perceived, they are driven by contextual factors, such as electoral margins, partisan advantages in Congress, or personal characteristics.

However, newly elected presidents can and do differ from each other for structural reasons as well. By structural, I mean that presidents can take office following a model as to the type of president they are or wish to be. For example, Republican presidents of the late nineteenth century entered office following a Whiggish model of the presidency; a model to which Grover Cleveland, the only Democratic president during this time, did not adhere. As such, Cleveland was a more pro-active president than his Republican contemporaries. As another example, presidents who enter office following a major electoral realignment are in quite a different position than their counterparts who are elected during less dramatic times, both in terms of the expectations placed on them and the support they are given.

Once a presidential structure has been identified, we can analyze the behavior of the presidents who fit into that structure. This allows us to determine such things as how such a structure benefits and constrains presidents, what implications the structure holds for the institution of the presidency, and what lessons can be drawn for future presidents. In this article, I evaluate one type of presidency–the "favorite son"–and address a problem that all such presidents potentially face.

THE "FAVORITE SON" PRESIDENTIAL STRUCTURE

Presidents often are tied to the legacy of the office holders who came before them. Sometimes a president assumes the office upon the death of his predecessor and, therefore, is expected at the start of his presidency to follow the predecessor's agenda until he is able to establish his own course. History is filled with former vice presidents who were expected to further the agenda of their predecessors when they died: John Tyler; Chester Arthur; Harry Truman; and Lyndon Johnson, for example.

Other times, presidents purposely choose to follow the agenda of a predecessor. They campaign, are elected, and base their presidency on the explicit understanding that the president will continue to pursue the same policy agenda as another president who came before him. Examples include: James Madison following Jefferson; Martin Van Buren and James Polk as Jacksonian Democrats; William Taft's campaign (if not actual presidency) to follow in Theodore Roosevelt's progressivism; and, most recently, George Bush's election to carry on the Reagan Revolution.

This analysis focuses on this second set–presidents who by choice inherit a pre-established policy agenda. These "favorite sons" represent the second generation of the policy agenda developed by their predecessors. In fact, the predecessor often chooses, endorses, or otherwise supports the favorite son as the most appropriate successor to pursue the course that he has established.

A favorite son seeks this role as a means first to be elected and then to enhance his position as he assumes the presidency. Instead of developing a message for the voting public, he delivers a message that has already proven to be popular and successful.[2] Instead of having to develop an agenda to pursue, he follows the agenda laid out by his predecessor. Rather than trying to establish himself as policy leader in interacting with Congress, a favorite son seeks to continue in the same spot where his predecessor left off. In other words, a favorite son seeks to become a successful president by replicating and continuing the successes enjoyed by his predecessor.

One potential problem that these presidents face is that the tenets underlying the inherited agenda were formed at an earlier time under a different president. When the political environment alters as time moves forward, those tenets may or may not continue to be relevant to the changing world. What does a president do when the underlying tenets lose their connection to the political environment–that is, when his inherited agenda collapses? How does the president balance the expectation that he will pursue a general policy agenda with the need to address specific political circumstances?

On one hand, a president could retain the benefits of being a favorite son by having a foundation upon which he can build as he addresses new circumstances. On the other hand, the favorite son structure also could constrain the president's ability to innovate, as he may not be able to step outside of the structure. Herein lies the dilemma facing a favorite son.

When a favorite son confronts a collapsed agenda, he could tend toward one of two positions. First, he could hold steadfastly to the collapsed agenda and attempt to resolve whatever issues he faces based on its outdated tenets. Second, he could totally disregard the agenda he inherited and set forth a completely new policy agenda based on a different set of tenets. Of course, taken to extremes, both of these positions pose problems for a president. By employing the former, the favorite son would appear dogmatic, inflexible, and out of touch with the current political reality. As such, he would soon be seen as an ineffective leader. The latter position, however, could cause the president to stray too far from his previous positions and core support constituency. Further, the president could experience difficulties in effective coalition-building necessary to implement his new agenda and, as a result, also be seen as an ineffective leader.

More than likely, presidents will seek a balanced position between these two extremes; one that addresses the problems at hand without straying too far from his original policy preferences. This balanced position may or may not directly incorporate the remaining tenets from his predecessor's agenda that are still relevant, but it is likely at least to borrow from the legacy the president inherited.[3]

To address the questions raised above, this analysis considers the presidency of George Bush, specifically focusing on his choice to pursue Ronald Reagan's foreign policy agenda.[4] Certainly Bush's efforts to continue Reagan's policy agenda were not limited solely to the realm of foreign affairs. He also sought to pursue domestic policies similar to those proposed by Reagan. For the purposes of this analysis, however, I focus on foreign policy for a number of reasons. First, the tenets of Reagan's foreign policy agenda were more concisely integrated than his domestic agenda, which included an array of important themes such as reducing taxes and government spending, limiting the scope of government activity, social conservatism, etc. Second, the key international events in which Reagan and Bush were able to put his tenets into action are more discrete and more reflective of each president's respective direction. On the other hand, key domestic policy battles by necessity involved interacting with Congress, which would introduce a number of additional actors into the analysis. Finally, and most importantly as will be argued more fully below, Reagan's foreign policy agenda did collapse during the Bush administration as the world moved into a post-cold war environment. The Reagan domestic agenda did not face such a fate. Further, one could argue that it has survived well beyond the Reagan presidency itself, for example, in efforts to lower taxes (e.g., the Taxpayer Relief Act of 1997) and reduce government spending (e.g., Clinton/Gore's "Reinventing Government").

Three cases are examined in which Reagan and Bush articulated and implemented their foreign policy objectives: 1) the American military interventions in Grenada in 1983; 2) Panama in 1989; and 3) the Persian Gulf in 1990-91.[5] Cases used in case study research have been likened to experiments in which the goal is to develop analytical generalizations.[6] Applying this analogy to the analysis at hand, the Panamanian intervention will provide the "pre-test" measurements, the Persian Gulf will provide the "post-test" measurements, and Grenada shall serve as a control.[7] The treatment–that is, the phenomenon that is to be introduced between the pre-and post-test cases–is the collapse of the Reagan foreign policy legacy.[8] The behavior is evaluated of President Bush, who inherited a foreign policy agenda from Reagan, both before and after the collapse of that agenda. The Grenada intervention serves as the control because it establishes a benchmark of Reagan's behavior in implementing his foreign policy agenda with which Bush's behavior can be compared.[9]

THE REAGAN FOREIGN POLICY AGENDA

Ronald Reagan's foreign policy was predicated on the notion that it would be different from that of his predecessor, Jimmy Carter. During the 1980 campaign, Reagan utilized the perceived weaknesses and failures of Carter's foreign policy as one component of his attack against Carter's ineffectual presidency. In Reagan's words, American "foreign policy must be rooted in realism, not naivete or self-delusion."[10]

Reagan entered the presidency proclaiming "we will be seen as having greater strength throughout the world. We will again be the exemplar of freedom and a beacon of hope for those who do not now have freedom."[11] Reagan saw the tenets of his foreign policy to include strength, fairness, and balance; its goals were to restore "America's military credibility," pursue "peace at the negotiating table wherever both sides are willing to sit down in good faith," and regain "the respect of America's allies and adversaries alike."[12] In other words, as one analyst observed, the Reagan administration's "claim to leadership had three dimensions: to contain the adversary, the Soviet Union; to reinvigorate U.S. alliances and foster support for American interests and goals; and to command respect for American hegemony among the nations of the third world."[13]

The Reagan foreign policy centered on the bipolar relationship between the two superpowers in the world: the U.S. and the U.S.S.R. It continued the cold war policy of containment–limiting the Soviet Union's spread of influence over other countries. But, for Reagan, containment was about more than just gaining a strategic advantage over an opponent. He believed all that was bad and evil about the Soviet Union specifically and communism generally directly threatened all that is good about American democracy. This contrast provided both substantive and symbolic bases for the formation of specific policy efforts. As Reagan once stated when discussing the Soviet Union and comparing it to the U.S.:

> Winston Churchill, in negotiating with the Soviets, observed that they respect only strength and resolve in their dealings with other nations. That's why we've moved to reconstruct our national defenses. We intend to keep the peace. We will also keep our freedom.
> We have made pledges of a new frankness in our public statements and worldwide broadcasts. In the face of a climate of falsehood and misinformation, we've promised the world a season of truth–the truth of our great civilized ideas: individual liberty, representative government, the rule of law under God. We've never needed walls or minefields or barbed wire to keep our people in. Nor do we declare martial law to keep our people from voting for the kind of government they want.[14]

Reagan's emphasis in rebuilding America's image abroad was to overcome a perceived weakness that had its roots in two important events: the Vietnam War and the holding of American hostages in Iran. Some scholars have argued that the after-effects of the Vietnam War resulted in a "Vietnam syndrome," defined as "the reluctance on the part of the American public to support military interventions abroad."[15] For Reagan, however, a foreign policy that incorporated such a position was unacceptable. As he stated in his Inaugural Address, "Our forbearance should never be misunderstood. Our reluctance for conflict should not be misjudged as a *failure of will*."[16] Reagan's foreign policy would include using American military forces to protect and promote the nation's interests abroad. Further, when troops were committed, they would be deployed in a way to demonstrate the strength of the American military. As one scholar noted, Reagan often chided the Carter administration for "preventing the United States from 'punching its weight' in foreign policy–a failing symbolized for many by the fiasco of the Iranian hostage rescue mission in 1980–and the promise was that such humiliations would not repeat themselves in the new era. America's power would be used and would be respected."[17]

THE CONTROL CASE: THE GRENADA INVASION

Before the October 1983 intervention in Grenada, Reagan laid the foundation of why the protection of what would otherwise seem to be another small Caribbean island was such an important part of American foreign policy. In March 1983, Reagan criticized those who questioned why America should care about Communist governments in Central America and the Caribbean, specifically citing one critic who argued that "we shouldn't worry about Castro's control over the island of Grenada–their only important product is nutmeg."[18] Reagan retorted:

> People who make these arguments haven't taken a good look at a map lately or followed the extraordinary buildup of Soviet and Cuban military power in the region or read the Soviets' discussions about why the region is important to them and how they intend to use it.
> It isn't nutmeg that's at stake in the Caribbean and Central America: it is the United States national security.[19]

Reagan added later that month:

> On the small island of Grenada ... the Cubans, with Soviet financing and backing, are in the process of building an airfield with a 10,000-foot runway. Grenada doesn't even have an air force. Who is it intended for? ... The Soviet-Cuban militarization of Grenada, in short, can only be seen as power projection in the region.[20]

Clearly, Reagan's concern, even over six months prior to the actual intervention, was not the political well-being of Grenada per se, but the encroachment of the Soviet Union and Cuba further into Caribbean. The United States needed to contain such an encroachment, which would have otherwise violated or threatened its interests. As such, the intervention provided Reagan the opportunity to employ the tenets of his foreign policy more fully. It would allow him to challenge the Soviet Union, without directly doing so, as well as build up credibility for the use of the American military.

In his initial speech regarding the "rescue mission" in Grenada, President Reagan posited three justifications for the events that transpired: 1) to protect the American citizens on the island; (2) to preserve order; and (3) "assist in the restoration of conditions of law and order and of governmental institutions to the island of Grenada where a brutal group of leftist thugs violently seized power...."[21] With these three reasons, Reagan was able to promote the key tenets of his foreign policy agenda and he wasted no time doing so as he addressed the nation just a few days after the intervention.

In that speech, which addressed both the Grenada intervention and the recent bombing of U.S. Marine barracks in Beirut, Lebanon, Reagan reiterated the primary tenets of his foreign policy agenda and demonstrated how his actions reflected those tenets in action. Because American lives were perceived to be at risk, Reagan used the Grenada intervention as a means to start countering the lingering bitterness of the American hostages held in Iran. Reagan proclaimed, "I believe our government has a responsibility to go to the aid of its citizens, if their right to life and liberty is threatened. The nightmare of our hostages in Iran must never be repeated."[22] He would later strengthen this argument by citing the fact that when the Americans on the island returned to the United States, some kissed the ground in appreciation.

Reagan bolstered his efforts to use the military to promote American interests abroad by praising and demanding respect for the military and the personnel involved. He stated, "I can't say enough in praise of our military ... those who planned a brilliant campaign and those who carried it out."[23] Implicitly comparing the performance of the military in Grenada with that of the failed Iran hostage rescue attempt and even Vietnam, Reagan asserted his view that a strong, properly equipped and trained American military force should be relished and used when necessary, not shied away from or scorned. Even though Reagan acknowledged that the "operation was not without cost" in human life, probably the most significant lasting concern of the Vietnam syndrome, he proclaimed that "those who were killed, wounded, or injured in this operation, I believe, are heroes of freedom."[24] In other words, whereas one may feel that the loss of life in Vietnam was in vain, those lost in Grenada sacrificed themselves for a higher purpose. As Reagan concluded, "a few years ago it seemed that America forgot what an admirable and essential need there is for a nation to have men and women who would give their lives to protect their fellow citizens."[25]

Reagan also used the Grenada intervention to promote the key tenet of his foreign policy agenda–the containment of the "evil empire." Reagan proclaimed that Grenada was a "Soviet-Cuban colony, being readied as a major military bastion to export terror and undermine democracy."[26] He also continued the good-versus-evil analogy of his efforts to combat the Soviet Union when asked by a reporter to compare the Grenada intervention with the Soviet intervention in Afghanistan in 1979. Reagan indicated "there was no comparison between the savage invasion of Afghanistan with its slaughter of innocent men, women, and children–civilians–and the heroic rescue mission of our young Americans."[27]

Finally, Reagan used the Grenada intervention to promote American hegemony and its work with its allies. Reagan told the American people that the nation was requested to join the military operation by the members of the Organization of Eastern Caribbean States, Jamaica, and Barbados. In other words, America did not act alone, but in concert with its allies in the affected region. The United States, however, clearly was involved in Grenada to protect its international interests. In his speech to the nation on Grenada and Lebanon, Reagan stated that "Today, our national security can be threatened in faraway places. It's up to all of us to be aware of the strategic importance of such places and to be able to identify them." In addition, Reagan said elsewhere in the speech, "we're a nation with global responsibilities. We're not somewhere else in the world protecting someone else's interests; we're there protecting our own."

To summarize, Reagan clearly used the American intervention to demonstrate the effectiveness of his approach to foreign policy. In many ways, the Grenada intervention was a perfect situation for Reagan to do so. He was allowed to stress the importance of each premise upon which his policy agenda was based.

For these reasons, Grenada also represents an appropriate control case for this analysis. We are able to observe Reagan in close to "ideal" conditions to examine the implementation of his foreign policy agenda. Due to the secrecy of the mission, he faced virtually no public opposition nor any debate of his policy in Congress prior to the intervention. The intervention reflected the policy established by Reagan and his advisors. The intervention involved each component of his foreign policy; it was anti-Communist, promoted American military strength, but still allowed the United States to work closely with its allies in the region. As a result, Reagan's actions relating to Grenada provide a base set of behaviors with which one can compare the behavior of Reagan's successor, George Bush, in the implementation of his foreign policy agenda.

GEORGE BUSH AS A FAVORITE SON

The election of 1988 was touted as "likely to be less about bold initiatives than about a referendum on the status quo."[28] George Bush, Reagan's vice president, chose to pursue the Reagan agenda, predicating his own presidency on that of his predecessor. In fact, Bush's first words as President were used to honor Reagan.[29]

Bush's use of the Reagan agenda certainly extended to the realm of foreign affairs. As one analyst noted, Bush wasted no time in "presenting himself as the heir to the Reaganite foreign policy estate, and from implying that continuity of foreign policy would be one of the greatest assets he would bring to this presidency."[30] Bush emphasized the tenet of the Reagan foreign policy agenda that required American military strength, stating to the world in his Inaugural Address: "To the world, too, we offer new engagement and a renewed vow: We will stay strong to protect the peace. The 'offered hand' is a reluctant fist; but once made, strong, and can be used with great effect."[31]

The world that Bush faced when he took office in 1989 was different from the one that shaped Reagan's foreign policy agenda. The previous system was defined by a bipolar system of strength. Reagan had a clear-cut adversary, the Soviet Union and communism, by which he could define his foreign policy aims. But this system was disintegrating as the Soviet Union was collapsing from within. The world during Reagan's presidency also was one in which the United States could still use its independent military might to assert its authority and hegemony in regions of the world. For example, although the United States utilized an alliance to help gain legitimacy in the Grenada mission, the United States was the dominant partner. Another factor (not directly related to the realm of foreign military policy, but one that impacts it greatly) was changing economic relations. By the end of Reagan's second term, the United States, once an economic as well as military superpower, was seeing other nations gain and lay claim to prominence in this arena, thus, impacting the United States' ability to guide its own fate singularly.

Bush recognized the new environment he faced. Despite these changes, however, he retained a second tenet of the Reagan foreign policy, namely maintaining American leadership and prominence in world affairs. As he stated in his Inaugural Address:

> We live in a peaceful, prosperous time, but we can make it better. For a new breeze is blowing, and a world refreshed by freedom seems reborn; ... the day of the dictator is over. The totalitarian era is passing, its old ideas blown away like leaves from an ancient lifeless tree. A new breeze is blowing, and a nation refreshed by freedom stands ready to push on.[32]

Perhaps the most dramatic change between the worlds of 1981 and 1989, at least at it relates to the Reagan and Bush foreign policy agenda, was the relationship between the United States and the Soviet Union. By 1989, Bush spoke of "continuing the new closeness".[33] with the nation his predecessor referred to as "evil" a few short years earlier. Even though Reagan himself turned to negotiation with the Soviets in lieu of force, a core tenet of the Reagan foreign policy agenda as initially formulated–the adversarial relationship with the Soviet Union–was starting to lose its relevance.

One final challenge that Bush faced in implementing the Reagan foreign policy is that, as some critics have asserted, the Reagan foreign policy regime was "bankrupt." Many accused Reagan of allowing his foreign policy to be reactive and be set adrift. He often was accused of not taking the lead and giving quip cliches instead of hard policy lines. By the end of his second term, with scandal in the foreign affairs arena haunting Reagan (particularly the Iran-Contra Affair), one might argue he did not leave much of a legacy upon which to build. While Bush probably did not ascribe to these arguments himself, such critiques did help shape the environment in which he worked.

Given this, we can understand the problem that Bush faced as president in regard to foreign affairs. He inherited a certain agenda or framework that he needed to follow since Bush used that agenda to define his presidency. However, with key tenets upon which that agenda was based either changed or becoming irrelevant to the world he faced, Bush eventually could not rely solely on being able to do what Reagan did, particularly as new events unfolded–events that transpired pursuant to the new international environment.

PRE-TEST: THE PANAMANIAN INTERVENTION

The American intervention in Panama in December 1989 to remove General Manuel Noriega from his position as the nation's dictator serves as the source of pre-test measurements. Despite the fact that the changes in the world were undermining the Reagan foreign policy legacy, Bush's inherited agenda had not yet collapsed. The cold war era, while nearing its end, still was ongoing.

The Panamanian intervention is comparable to Reagan's intervention in Grenada in terms of scope and magnitude. As such, these cases allow us to assess the similarities and differences in presidential behavior. In other words, how closely did Bush in 1989 follow the model that Reagan use[34]d six years earlier in the control case of Grenada?

As Reagan did, Bush quickly spoke to the American public after the initiation of military action. He stated:

> For nearly 2 years, the United States, nations of Latin America and the Caribbean have worked together to resolve the crisis in Panama. The goals of the United States have been to safeguard the lives of Americans, to defend democracy in Panama, to combat drug trafficking, and to protect the integrity of the Panama Canal treaty.

Bush's statement reflects a continuation of the Reagan foreign policy agenda. By referencing that the United States' foreign policy toward Panama has been the same for two years (i.e., since 1987), Bush acknowledged that he has maintained the policy that was initiated under Reagan. In terms of following the model used by Reagan, Bush seemingly applied every component as well as Reagan did in Grenada.

Like the intervention in Grenada, the Panamanian intervention's primary goal was to protect Americans. Whereas in Grenada American lives were perceived to be at risk, on December 16, 1989, Panamanian Defense Forces personnel killed a Marine officer without justification. Further, a Naval officer and his wife were beaten, abused, and threatened. As Bush wrote to the leaders in Congress, "These acts of violence are directly attributable to Noriega's dictatorship, which created a climate of aggression that places American lives and interests in peril."[35] Without explicitly stating so, Bush, like Reagan before him, evoked the memory of the American hostages in Iran and was prepared to use the military to protect the 35,000 American citizens in Panama. In fact, Bush saw "no higher obligation than to safeguard the lives of American citizens."[36]

Bush continued Reagan's efforts to restore respect for the American military at both home and abroad. He praised the American military forces for "conduct[ing] themselves courageously and selflessly."[37] In the same speech, Bush discussed the efficiency of the military in achieving its objectives, concluding, "yesterday a dictator ruled Panama, and today constitutionally elected leaders govern."[38]

Bush also used the Panamanian intervention to promote certain ideals when it came to the interactions with the nation's allies. Bush expressed concern to congressional leaders over "the integrity of the [Panama] Canal Treaties... if such lawlessness [undertaken by Noriega] were allowed to continue."[39] To the American people, Bush said:

> I am committed to strengthening our relationship with the democratic nations in this hemisphere. I will continue to seek solutions to the problems of this region through dialog and multilateral diplomacy.[40]

In regard to the Panamanian intervention, Bush promoted many tenets of the Reagan foreign policy agenda. In addition, Bush implemented his/Reagan's agenda much in the same way his predecessor did in Grenada. The American adversary in Panama, however, was not the Soviet Union, nor was Noriega considered a communist.

Reagan's foreign policy centered on America's "evil" adversary, the Soviet Union. Bush adapted the "evil" component of this tenet and applied it to Noriega. Bush stated, "Many attempts have been made to resolve this crisis through diplomacy and negotiations. All were rejected by the dictator of Panama, General Manuel Noriega, an indicted drug trafficker."[41] Each of the emphasized words above connotes a sense of "evilness." Bush portrayed Noriega as a person who did not adhere to reason and dialogue, as an illegitimate ruler who abused his power, and as a direct threat to American interests through his drug activities.

For the purpose of this analysis, the Panamanian intervention provides the "pre-test" measurements. When compared to Reagan's behavior in the intervention in Grenada, Bush promoted similar policy themes as Reagan, strove to meet similar objectives, and utilized similar behavior and rhetoric in regard to the intervention. With respect to the absence of a communist threat, Bush simply adapted the Reaganite attitude toward communism and cast Noriega in a similar vein.

POST-TEST: THE PERSIAN GULF CRISIS

By January 1991, the transformation of the international environment into the post-Cold War era neared completion. The Soviet Union was splintering as a number of its former republics declared their independence. Other communist regimes that fell within the former Soviet bloc similarly were giving way to more democratic reforms.

The collapse of the Soviet Union also represented a collapse of the agenda that Bush inherited. Reagan's foreign policy legacy–premised on the containment of communism and the Soviet Union–lost its connection to the changing world. Since Bush based his presidency on the Reagan agenda, Bush faced the question of what he would do now that the tenets of the inherited agenda were no longer relevant.

Bush confronted this question as he addressed the invasion of Kuwait by Iraq. The Persian Gulf conflict provided Bush with the first major opportunity to utilize American troops in the post-cold war world. The engagement had no overtones regarding communism, nor any implications for the disintegrating bipolar international system. Thus, Bush had to take into account new issues that Reagan did not have to face during his presidency. Nothing more clearly demonstrates this than Bush's statement to a joint session of Congress in September 1990:

> I've just returned from a very productive meeting with Soviet President Gorbachev ... Clearly no longer can a dictator count on East-West confrontation to stymie concerted United Nations action against aggression. A new partnership of nations has begun.[42]

Nonetheless, Bush continued several symbolic tenets of Reagan's foreign policy agenda– use of the military as a sign of strength, respect for American military forces, and purging the "Vietnam syndrome." Throughout the conflict, Bush reminded the American people and members of Congress of the important role played by the American military forces. In his address to the nation announcing the initiation of allied military action, Bush quoted several members of the American forces, including a Marine Lieutenant General, who said: "There are things worth fighting for. A world in which brutality and lawlessness are allowed to go unchecked isn't the kind of world we're going to want to live in."[43] Bush also proclaimed early in the Persian Gulf crisis that the American military forces "are some of the finest men and women of the United States of America.... they remind us who keeps America strong: they do."[44]

Seemingly more important for Bush, however, was his concern that "there will be *no more Vietnams.*"[45] Bush sought to demonstrate to the American public, the world, and especially Saddam Hussein that America did not lack the will or the unity to engage Iraq in military battle. He pressured congressional leaders to support the resolutions approved by the United Nations Security Council.[46] He argued that the nation's "commitment to [its military forces] must be equal to their commitment to their country."[47] Bush also warned that the costs of conflict should not deter the use of the military in the Persian Gulf.[48]

One could argue that with the Persian Gulf War, Bush successfully started to remove the "Vietnam syndrome" from the nation. He demonstrated that a president could obtain a sense of unity among the American people for the use of the military as a tool of foreign policy. Bush pursued this tenet of the Reagan foreign policy agenda and implemented it more successfully than his predecessor did.

Bush was able to adapt other components of the Reagan foreign policy agenda that were premised on the bipolar, adversarial relationship with the Soviet Union. For example, as Bush did with Noriega in Panama, he portrayed Saddam Hussein as the evil enemy. Bush often cited Hussein's "ruthless, systematic rape of a peaceful neighbor"[49] and described him as a "villain."[50] Bush carried forward the tenet that the United States symbolized goodness, while its opponent violated key principles held by the nation. By adapting the "evil" component of the Reagan foreign policy, Bush maintained his connection to the past while working on the problems that he faced.

In addition, Bush, like Reagan before, proclaimed and worked toward securing a prominent place for America in the international realm. In this matter, though, Bush decided not simply to adapt the legacy left by Reagan, but instead sought to forge a new foreign policy agenda; an agenda that borrowed from Reagan, but that was distinctly Bush's own.

Whereas Reagan promoted American ideals, Bush sought to create a "new world order, where diverse nations are drawn together in common cause to achieve the universal applications of mankind–peace and security, freedom, and the rule of law."[51] Whereas Reagan focused first and foremost on American interests, Bush saw the linkages among the interests of many nations as these linkages were emerging in the post-cold war world. Compare Reagan's previous quotation: "It isn't nutmeg at stake ... it is the Unites States national security" with the following statement from Bush:

> We have seen too often in this century how quickly any threat to one becomes a threat to all. At this critical moment in history, at a time the cold war is fading into the past, we cannot fail. At stake is not simply dome distant country called Kuwait. At stake is the kind of world we will inhabit.[52]

While both Bush and Reagan argued that their respective interventions were of greater importance than simply the country at hand, Bush's concerns were more globally oriented than Reagan's. Clearly, the United States became involved in the Persian Gulf situation because of its national interests, a point Bush often made.[53] Bush, however, also attempted to make the Gulf War a defining moment in the nation's and the world's history. He sought to create his own foreign policy legacy to replace the collapsed one left by Reagan.

CONCLUSION

Before considering the substantive implications that this analysis holds for the presidency, let us first consider the limitations of the analogy made earlier to experimental research. This analogy was designed to be illustrative and to shape the nature of the inquiry, not to be an exact method of research. Thus, while several key principles of experimental research had to be relaxed in this analysis, doing so highlights several key lessons for favorite sons as they face a collapsed agenda.

For example, the distinction of pre-test and post-test and the introduction of the treatment in this analysis is not as definitive as these terms would suggest. Clearly, the cold war era in the world's history did not simply end between December 1989 (i.e., the Panamanian intervention) and August 1990 (when Iraq first invaded Kuwait). Similarly, Bush did not find himself one day facing a collapsed foreign policy agenda when the underlying tenets were still relevant the previous day. Instead, the transition to a new international environment and the collapse of the Reagan foreign policy were ongoing processes. One could argue that the Reagan foreign policy agenda started to collapse when he began to negotiate with the Soviet Union for nuclear disarmament.

The lesson to be drawn from this is that favorite sons should receive indications that their inherited agenda is collapsing well before it fully does. As such, they should be able to plan how and when they will react as the agenda collapses further. Favorite sons, however, also have a burden in that they must project forward in time as to the pace at which the tenets underlying the agenda lose their relevance. They must be careful not to jump ship too early nor go down with it (continuing the sailing metaphor from above).

Another limitation of using terminology of experimental research is that the experiment could not totally control the influence of outside variables. This fact is most prevalent in the "post-test" setting. In the Persian Gulf conflict, Bush seemingly attempted to establish a new foreign policy agenda to shape the course of American and the world's international interactions for years to come. However, Bush did not have the opportunity to develop this agenda further. After a brief period of record-level popularity, Bush and the nation's attention turned toward domestic economic problems. Bush could not put his efforts into trying to continue to craft his foreign policy agenda. The American people wanted him to address the nation's declining economic condition. In part because of his inability to respond to the economic problems in a satisfactory manner, Bush was voted out of office and his opportunity to develop his new world order was short-circuited.

Several lessons can be drawn both directly and indirectly from Bush's experience. First, a favorite son could face a collapsing agenda in one policy realm, but not others; much like Bush faced a collapsing agenda in foreign affairs, but not domestically. However, the domestic and foreign policy realms are not completely independent of each other; they are connected in that the president's successes, popularity, and ability to implement his agenda in one area (or conversely failures, unpopularity, and inability) will carry over to the other. Further, a favorite son is elected because of his promise to fulfill his predecessor's total agenda, not simply handpicked parts.

As a result, although a favorite son may have the opportunity to forge a new policy direction in the realm in which his inherited agenda has collapsed, he must remain faithful to his predecessor's total policy aims. Otherwise, the favorite son's domestic and foreign policy goals may seem disjointed. Further, he also would run the risk of alienating his core constituency.[54] Regardless of whatever changes the favorite son might encounter as president, he will continue to be linked to his predecessor, even when he wishes to establish his own agenda and identity.

We are now led back to the question: How does a president balance the expectation that he will pursue a general policy agenda with the need to address specific political circumstances? The answer rests in Bush's behavior in both of the cases examined above. In the Persian Gulf conflict, Bush started to set forth a new foreign policy agenda that was distinctly different from Reagan's, yet remained faithful to the Reagan agenda on a symbolic level. In fact, some of Bush's greatest successes were more symbolic than substantive.

For example, Bush was able to obtain political and public unity in support of the military mission and for the troops fighting in the Persian Gulf. In the wake of Vietnam, most if not all military efforts, especially one of the scope and magnitude of the Persian Gulf intervention, would be met with skepticism, concern, and opposition. Bush, however, fulfilled his pledge that the Persian Gulf would not be "another Vietnam." The unity of support that he achieved for the military operation directly counteracted the "Vietnam syndrome." This victory, one could argue, may have as much of a lasting impact on the United States as the outcome of the Persian Gulf War itself.

Another important symbolic link that Bush maintained and adapted was the analogy of good versus evil. The actors in the analogy changed, from the Soviet Union for Reagan to Manuel Noriega and Saddam Hussein for Bush. But by incorporating the analogy into his rhetoric and behavior, Bush retained a vital link to the Reagan legacy. He implicitly told the American people that if Ronald Reagan had to face the situations in Panama and the Persian Gulf, he too would view the world in the way that Bush was doing.

That message generally is the one that a favorite son needs to convey and have the American people and members of Congress believe, regardless of what he may actually be doing on a substantive policy level. By utilizing the symbolic tenets of his predecessor as Bush did, a favorite son will not be seen as abandoning his inherited agenda nor straying too far from his core supporters. As such, the favorite son can then argue that his new policy agenda is just the logical extension of the course set forth by the predecessor; it is just updated to reflect of current events. He thus would retain the favorite son structure while developing a policy agenda that bears his own stamp.

The nation will never know whether Bush's new world order would have developed. Nor we will know whether Bush could have replicated his foreign policy successes in the Persian Gulf. However, Bush at least did start successfully laying the groundwork for his transition from being Reagan's favorite son to crafting his own agenda without appearing that he was sacrificing the principles that led him to the White House in the first place.

NOTES

[1] See, for example, Paul Light, *The President's Agenda: Domestic Policy Choice from Kennedy to Reagan* (Baltimore: The Johns Hopkins University Press, 1991).

[2] Although a favorite son could try to link himself with an unpopular or unsuccessful president, such a scenario is unlikely. Instead, a favorite son will seek to capitalize on the success and goodwill of his predecessor.

[3] Other scholars have considered this theme. For example, Stephen Skowronek defines a specific type of presidential authority structure–the orthodox-innovator–who faces this challenge. See Stephen Skowronek, *The Politics Presidents Make: Leadership from John Adams to George Bush* (Cambridge, Massachusetts: The Belknap Press of Harvard University Press, 1993, specifically Chapter 3). As such, Skowronek's orthodox-innovator must address the problem of a collapsed inherited agenda. However, all presidents, not just those that fit his authority structures, potentially could face the problem of an irrelevant policy agenda if they pursue the agenda set out by their predecessor.

[4] Because this article focuses on the "favorite son" presidential structure using foreign policy as a case study, one should be aware of the scope of the analysis. This article does not address in detail substantive foreign policy issues, such as the United States' relationships with its allies and what Reagan and Bush had to do to maintain allied support for the military commitments studied herein. Nor is the article a critical evaluation of the success of the case studies, such as whether the Panamanian intervention was really as successful as it proponents purport it to be. Instead, this article is about George Bush's challenges as a favorite son president. Therefore,

5. the focus is on Bush's actions and behavior, as compared to Reagan's, in implementing the Reagan foreign policy agenda.

6. I have used these military interventions to examine Reagan's and Bush's implementation of their foreign policies for two reasons. First, because they represent fairly isolated, discrete events, they lend themselves to the experimental-style analysis discussed in the text better than, for example, ongoing relations with the Soviet Union or America's allies. Second, these cases reflect a key tenet of the Reagan foreign policy agenda, being willing and able to use the American military, in action. This is discussed elsewhere in the article.

7. Robert K. Yin, *Case Study Research: Design and Methods* (Newbury Park, California: Sage Publications, Inc., 1989).

8. For useful overviews of experimental research designs, see: Donald T. Campbell and Julian C. Stanley, *Experimental and Quasi-Experimental Designs for Research* (Dallas: Houghton Mifflin Company, 1963). See also: Thomas D. Cook and Donald T. Campbell, *Quasi-Experimentation: Design & Analysis Issues for Field Settings* (Dallas: Houghton Mifflin Company, 1979).

9. The division of pre-collapse and post-collapse is not as definitive as implied here. This issue will be discussed in more detail in the conclusion section.

10. One should note that such terms as "Reagan's foreign policy" and "Bush's behavior" are in some ways shorthand. Both Reagan and Bush relieve heavily on their advisors, who played key roles in the development of policy generally and in the resolution of the cases studied herein. But given that the focus of this article is on the "favorite son" presidency structure, I incorporated the roles that Reagan's and Bush's advisors played into the actions of the presidents themselves to simplify the analysis.

11. Ronald Reagan, "State of the Union Address," January 26, 1982. In Public Papers of the Presidents: Ronald Reagan, vol. 1 - 1982. (Washington, D.C.: U.S. Government Printing Office, 1983), p. 78.

12. Ronald Reagan First Inaugural Address, January 20, 1981. Davis Newton Lott, ed., *The Presidents Speak: The Inaugural Addresses of the American Presidents, from Washington to Clinton* (New York: Henry Holt and Company, 1994), p. 348.

13. Reagan, State of the Union, January 26, 1982, p. 77.

14. Helga Haftendorn. "Toward a Reconstruction of American Strength: A New Era in the Claim to Global Leadership," in *The Reagan Administration: A Reconstruction of American Strength?* Helga Haftendorn and Jakob Schissler, eds, (New York: Walter de Gruyter, 1988), p. 10. Haftendorn defines "hegemony" to mean, "one state is powerful enough to maintain the essential rules governing interstate relations and is willing to do so."

15. Reagan, State of the Union, January 26, 1982, p. 78.

16. Jeff McMahan, *Reagan and the World: Imperial Policy and the New Cold War* (New York: Monthly Review Press, 1985), p. 20. McMahan states that this phrase is "intended to suggest that this reluctance is a pathological condition of sorts."

17. In *The Presidents Speak*, p. 348. Emphasis added.

18. Michael Smith, "The Reagan Presidency and Foreign Policy," in Joseph Hogan, ed., *The Reagan Years: A Record in Presidential Leadership* (Manchester, England: Manchester University Press, 1990), p. 267.

19. Ronald Reagan, "Remarks on Central America and El Salvador at the Annual Meeting of the National Association of Manufactures," March 10, 1983. In Public Papers of the Presidents: Ronald Reagan, vol. 1 - 1983. (Washington, D.C.: U.S. Government Printing Office 1984), p. 373.

20. Ronald Reagan, Remarks on Central America and El Salvador at the Annual Meeting of the National Association of Manufactures, March 10, 1983, p. 373.

21. Ronald Reagan, "Address to the Nation on Defense and National Security," March 22, 1983. In Public Papers of the Presidents: Ronald Reagan, vol. 1 - 1983. (Washington, DC: U.S. Government Printing Office, 1984), p. 440.

[21] Ronald Reagan, "Remarks of the President and Prime Minister Eugenia Charles of Dominica Announcing the Deployment of United States Forces in Grenada," October 25, 1983. In Public Papers of the Presidents: Ronald Reagan, vol. 2 - 1983. (Washington, DC: U.S. Government Printing Office, 1984), p. 1505.

[22] Ronald Reagan, "Address to the Nation on Events in Lebanon and Grenada," October 27, 1983. In Public Papers of the Presidents: Ronald Reagan, vol. 2 - 1983. (Washington, DC: U.S. Government Printing Office, 1984), p. 1521. Reagan also would later state "we weren't about to wait for the Iran crisis to repeat itself, only this time, only in our own neighborhood– the Caribbean." Ronald Reagan, "Remarks to Military Personnel at Cherry Point, North Carolina, on the United States Casualties in Lebanon and Grenada," November 4, 1983. In Public Papers of the Presidents: Ronald Reagan, vol. 2 - 1983. (Washington, DC: U.S. Government Printing Office, 1984), p. 1542.

[23] Ronald Reagan, Address to the Nation on Events in Lebanon and Grenada, October 27, 1983, p. 1521.

[24] Ronald Reagan, "Remarks Announcing the Appointment of Donald Rumsfeld as the President's Personal Representative in the Middle East," November 3, 1983. In Public Papers of the Presidents: Ronald Reagan, vol. 2 - 1983. (Washington, DC: U.S. Government Printing Office, 1984), p. 533.

[25] Ronald Reagan, "Remarks at a White House Ceremony for Medical Students and United States Military Personnel from Grenada," November 7, 1983. In Public Papers of the Presidents: Ronald Reagan, vol. 2 - 1983. (Washington, DC: U.S. Government Printing Office, 1984), p. 1552.

[26] Ronald Reagan, Address to the Nation on Events in Lebanon and Grenada, October 27, 1983, p. 1521.

[27] Ronald Reagan, Remarks at a White House Ceremony for Medical Students and United States Military Personnel from Grenada, November 7, 1983, p. 1521.

[28] Bert A. Rockman, "The Leadership Style of George Bush," in Colin Campbell, S.J. and Bert A. Rockman, eds., The Bush Presidency: First Appraisals (Chatham, New Jersey: Chatham House Publishers, 1991), p. 8.

[29] Bush started his Inaugural Address by stating: "There is a man here who has earned a lasting place in our hearts and in our history. President Reagan, on behalf of our Nation, I thank you for the wonderful things that you have done for America," in The Presidents Speak, p. 358.

[30] Michael Smith, p. 267.

[31] In The Presidents Speak, p. 361.

[32] In The Presidents Speak, p. 359.

[33] In The Presidents Speak, p. 361.

[34] George Bush, "Address to the Nation Announcing United States Military Action in Panama," December 20, 1989. In Public Papers of the Presidents: George Bush, vol. 1 - 1989. (Washington, DC: U.S. Government Printing Office, 1990), p. 1722.

[35] George Bush, "Letter to the Speaker of the House of Representatives and the President Pro Tempore of the Senate on the United States Military Action in Panama," December 20, 1989. In Public Papers of the Presidents: George Bush, vol. 1 - 1989. (Washington, DC: U.S. Government Printing Office, 1990), p. 1734.

[36] George Bush, Address to the Nation Announcing United States Military Action in Panama, December 20, 1989, p. 1722.

[37] George Bush, Address to the Nation Announcing United States Military Action in Panama, December 20, 1989, p. 1723.

[38] George Bush, Address to the Nation Announcing United States Military Action in Panama, December 20, 1989, p. 1723.

[39] George Bush, Letter to the Speaker of the House of Representatives and the President Pro Tempore of the Senate on the United States Military Action in Panama, December 20, 1989, p. 1734.

40 George Bush, Address to the Nation Announcing United States Military Action in Panama, December 20, 1989, p. 1723.
41 George Bush, Address to the Nation Announcing United States Military Action in Panama, December 20, 1989, p. 1722-3. Emphasis added.
42 George Bush, "Address Before a Joint Session of the Congress on the Persian Gulf Crisis and the Federal Budget Deficit," September 11, 1990. In Public Papers of the Presidents: George Bush, vol. 2 - 1990. (Washington, DC: U.S. Government Printing Office, 1991), p. 1219.
43 Lieutenant General Walter Boomer, as quoted by George Bush, "Address to the Nation Announcing Allied Military Action in the Persian Gulf," January 16, 1991. In Public Papers of the Presidents: George Bush, vol. 1 - 1991. (Washington, DC: U.S. Government Printing Office, 1992), p. 44.
44 George Bush, Address Before a Joint Session of the Congress on the Persian Gulf Crisis and the Federal Budget Deficit, September 11, 1990, p. 1218.
45 George Bush, "Radio Address to the Nation on the Persian Gulf Crisis," January 5, 1991. In Public Papers of the Presidents: George Bush, vol. 1 - 1991. (Washington, DC: U.S. Government Printing Office, 1992), p. 10. Emphasis added. Bush added in his January 16, 1991 address to the nation: "Prior to ordering our forces to battle, I instructed our military commanders to take every necessary step to prevail as quickly as possible, and with the greatest degree of protection for American and allied service men and women. I've told the American people before that this will not be another Vietnam, and I repeat this here tonight."
46 Bush wrote to congressional leaders on January 8, 1991, stating that such congressional action "would help dispel any belief that may exist in the minds of Iraq's leaders that the United States lacks the necessary unity to act decisively in response to Iraq's continued aggression against Kuwait," George Bush, "Letter to Congressional Leaders on the Persian Gulf Crisis." January 8, 1991. In Public Papers of the Presidents: George Bush, vol. 1 - 1991. (Washington, DC: U.S. Government Printing Office, 1992), p. 13.
47 George Bush, "Address Before a Joint Session of the Congress on the State of the Union," January 29, 1991. In Public Papers of the Presidents: George Bush, vol. 1 - 1991. (Washington, DC: U.S. Government Printing Office, 1992), p., 74.
48 In a January 18, 1991 news conference, Bush stated: "It is important, however, to keep in mind two things: First, this effort will take some time. Saddam Hussein has devoted nearly all of Iraq's resources for a decade to building up this powerful military machine. We can't expect to overcome it overnight. Second, we must be realistic. There will be losses. There will be obstacles along the way. War is never cheap or easy." George Bush, "The President's News Conference on the Persian Gulf Conflict," January 18, 1991. In Public Papers of the Presidents: George Bush, vol. 1 - 1991. (Washington, DC: U.S. Government Printing Office, 1991), p. 48.
49 George Bush, Address Before a Joint Session of the Congress on the State of the Union, January 29, 1991, p. 74.
50 George Bush, "Address Before a Joint Session of the Congress on the Cessation of the Persian Gulf Conflict," March 6, 1991. In Public Papers of the Presidents: George Bush, vol. 1 - 1991. (Washington, DC: U.S. Government Printing Office, 1992), p. 219.
51 George Bush, Address Before a Joint Session of the Congress on the State of the Union, January 29, 1991, p. 74.
52 George Bush, Radio Address to the Nation on the Persian Gulf Crisis, January 5, 1991, p. 11.
53 See, for example, Bush's Letter to Congressional Leaders on the Persian Gulf Crisis dated January 8, 1991.
54 For example, despite Bush's military success in the Persian Gulf, when he reversed his campaign promise of "no new taxes," Bush lost the support of many conservatives, the original core constituency of the Reagan Revolution.

Chapter 11

DEBUNKING THE MYTH: CARTER, CONGRESS, AND THE POLITICS OF AIRLINE DEREGULATION

David B. Cohen and Chris J. Dolan[*]

INTRODUCTION

"For the first time in decades, we have deregulated a major industry. When I announced my own support of airline deregulation soon after taking office, this bill had few friends. I'm happy to say that today it appears to have few enemies."[1] With those words, President Jimmy Carter signed into law the Airline Deregulation Act of 1978, thus freeing the nation's airline industry from much of the federal oversight and protection to which it had become accustomed over four long decades. Among other things, the Act opened up the airline industry to competition from new and existing carriers, allowed automatic market entry for airlines wishing to add new routes to their system, and, as of January 1, 1985, terminated the Civil Aeronautics Board (CAB), the regulatory body that oversaw the industry.[2]

The President signed the bill after a twenty-two month struggle with Congress to enact the legislation. However, the deregulation fight did not start when Jimmy Carter entered office. Rather, the battle began in earnest after Gerald Ford ascended to the presidency and his administration assembled a domestic agenda. Carter benefitted from a process that was well underway when he was sworn in on January 20, 1977. Regulatory reform of the airline industry was ripe for an early legislative victory for the fledgling administration.[3] However, successful passage of a deregulation bill would not come for another twenty-two months.

Although it has led to some isolated difficulties, air transportation and industry experts have seen airline deregulation as having added substantial benefits to the traveling public.[4] However, analysis of the economic benefits and costs of airline deregulation will not be made

---

[*] The authors would like to thank Ed Beardsley, Betty Glad, Otis Graham, George Krause, David Welborn, and Laura Woliver for their helpful comments. Also, many thanks to the staff at the Carter Library for their assistance in gathering data for this project. Any errors or omissions, however, are the sole responsibility of the authors.

here. Rather, the intent is to examine White House strategy concerning passage of the airline deregulation bill.

THE AIRLINE INDUSTRY UNDER REGULATION

FDR Through LBJ, 1934-1969

The first major piece of legislation regulating the airline industry came in 1934 with the passage of the federal Airmail Act. The act shifted responsibility for overseeing airmail from the U.S. Army to the Post Office Department after several pilots were killed in accidents due to inexperience and faulty equipment.[5] The Post Office was also given primary responsibility over entry into the industry as well as scheduling and route assignments for the airlines.[6]

In 1936, the major airlines formed the Air Transportation Association (ATA). The ATA's original purpose was to lobby the federal government for increased aid to the industry as well as for protection from excess competition, which it contended, would eventually destroy the industry.[7] ATA lobbying helped secure passage of the Civil Aeronautics Act of 1938 that created a five-member Civil Aeronautics Board (CAB). Each member was appointed to a six-year term by the president, with one chairman, and was subject to confirmation by the Senate.

Among other things, the Civil Aeronautics Act was authorized to:

- encourage and develop an industry adapted to the present and future needs of the foreign and domestic commerce of the national defense and postal service of the US
- regulate the industry in order to foster safety, economic soundness, and coordination among the airlines
- promote adequate, economical, and efficient services at reasonable prices without the use of discriminatory or destructive practices
- promote competition to the extent necessary so as to assure sound development of the industry[8]

The framework constructed by this law was one in which power resided completely with the federal government. The CAB dominated the industry; however, most of the players within the system were content and viewed the CAB as a "benevolent dictator."[9]

Another important piece of legislation was the Federal Aviation Act of 1958, which distinguished between two main functions of airline regulation: safety and economics. The law created the Federal Aviation Administration (FAA), which was given the primary responsibility of regulating industry safety. The CAB was left with the responsibility of overseeing the economic health of the industry.[10]

Until the 1970s, life for the airlines under regulation was stable and marginally profitable. Some analysts have gone so far as to call this regulatory scheme a "brilliant success."[11] Others have not been quite so bold, but argue nevertheless that the regulated airline industry was stable and grew rapidly during this period.[12] Despite the fact that profits were small, the airlines were content under regulation as they were protected from potential new airlines that were denied access into the system.[13] The executive and legislative branches were also happy with a system that was relatively safe and problem-free.[14]

The Nixon Era

The election of Richard Nixon in 1968 marked the beginning of the end for airline regulation. During this time the CAB began to narrowly interpret its mandate and strictly enforce its regulations. An explosion in ridership occurred in the 1960s. Due to a number of discount programs offered by the airlines and a pro-competitive stance by the CAB, more people could afford to fly. However, ridership decreased at the end of the decade and Secor Browne, the CAB chairman, tightened regulatory controls as the CAB assumed an anti-competition stance.[15] When Robert Timm was appointed by Nixon to assume control of the CAB in 1973, he took an even more anti-competitive stance than his predecessor.[16]

Compounding the problem was the CAB's policy concerning domestic fares. Due to some questionable practices within the industry, the Domestic Passenger Fare Investigation began in 1969 and completely overhauled the pricing system that had guided the industry. As a result, many of the discount fares that had become so popular were abolished and the average price for a ticket increased by twenty percent.[17]

Discount fares were not the only casualties in the CAB assault. For the period 1969-1974, the CAB was guided by an unwritten policy that all applications by potential new carriers were refused consideration.[18]

These controversial moves by the CAB resulted in a swing of momentum toward those who favored reform. The Arab Oil Embargo of 1973 exacerbated the already worsening situation by increasing costs for both the airlines and consumers. Profits dropped sharply for the industry during this period.[19]

The Ford Era

The Ford era marked a turning point in the deregulation debate as a number of factors congealed which gave the regulatory reform movement cause to be optimistic. The Ford administration, as part of its anti-inflation strategy, adopted regulatory reform as a major component.[20] Chairman Timm was fired in December and replaced with the pro-reform John Robson. Though Robson did not favor complete deregulation of the industry, he was inclined toward loosening the regulatory grip. In fact, from the moment Timm was removed, the CAB began reversing its controversial anti-competitive policies.[21]

Another major factor encouraging the anti-regulatory mood was the Kennedy Hearings on CAB policy that commenced in 1975.[22] Senator Edward Kennedy (D-MA) favored radical reform of the industry and as chair of the Subcommittee on Administrative Practice and Procedures of the Senate Judiciary Committee, the hearings were constructed in such a way as to show the need for regulatory reform.[23] The Kennedy Hearings crystallized support for reform-the debate shifted from questioning whether reform was necessary to what type of reform would be optimal.

The Ford administration was very much in sync with the mood reflected at the Kennedy Hearings. In October of 1975, the administration introduced the Aviation Reform Act into the Senate.[24] Shortly following the introduction of the Ford legislation, Kennedy submitted a similar reform bill in the Senate.[25]

Both the Ford and Kennedy bills were reported to the Aviation Subcommittee of the Senate Commerce, Science, and Transportation Committee chaired by Howard Cannon

(D-NV). Cannon was an instrumental character in this drama-his subcommittee would have a great stake in determining the fate of regulatory reform. At first, Cannon was reluctant to endorse reform. Throughout his career he had favored regulation and had many friends in the industry that wanted to maintain the status quo. However, circumstances forced him to switch sides in the debate. Cannon's position as Aviation Subcommittee chairman gave him an incentive to control the reform debate and defend the committee's jurisdiction and prestige after the much-publicized Kennedy Hearings. This issue also provided an opportunity for Cannon to build up his own unremarkable legislative record. The fact that Cannon's committee staff was free-market orientated also pushed him towards reform.[26] Finally, in testimony before Cannon's subcommittee, Chairman Robson asserted that regulation was the central cause of the industry's economic woes; this pronouncement had a profound effect on Cannon and, following Robson's testimony, he endorsed reform.[27]

Gerald Ford was defeated in his quest for his own full term as president and was deprived of an opportunity to shepherd regulatory reform of the airline industry through the Congress. Jimmy Carter, an advocate of regulatory reform himself, was able to benefit from Ford's misfortune. As a staff member of Carter's CAB noted:

> Carter inherited a stage of development of deregulation in transportation where airlines were in the consciousness of government....And we walked into a CAB where the mood had already been structured for deregulation by the previous chairman, in his leadership with the board members, and in dealing with Congress.[28]

Thus, by the time Carter was sworn in as the 39th president, the momentum had swung in favor of regulatory reform.[29]

REVIEW OF THE LITERATURE: PERCEPTIONS OF CARTER'S POLITICAL LEADERSHIP OF CONGRESS

Most studies of Jimmy Carter's leadership of Congress concentrate on the failures and weaknesses associated with the President and his legislative staff. Dilemmas faced by the Carter White House are often attributed to the President's background in Georgia and his lack of Washington political experience. As one scholar put it, Carter "left a bad taste in the mouths of too many people who were personally offended by his hostility to Washington politics and his lack of sophistication about the role such politics played in fueling the policy process."[30]

Much of the literature reflects three themes concerning Carter's leadership of Congress. The first theme suggests that the President was inexperienced with the rough and tumble of Washington politics. Eric Davis claims that because Carter felt he did not "owe" anything to Washington politicians, he avoided bargaining with legislators and building coalitions.[31] Stephen Skowronek argues that Carter "exposed himself as one of the most paralyzing cases of estrangement."[32] In his discussion of Carter's decision to cut nineteen federal water projects from the budget, Skowronek contends that the "initiative was received on Capitol Hill as an ignorant, irresponsible and politically pretentious assault on the bread and butter of congressional careers."[33]

Even those who assume a more sympathetic view of Carter have argued that the President was overly apolitical. Charles Jones argues that Carter was a rationalist who believed in "doing what's right, not what's political."[34] He describes Carter as uncomfortable with political accommodation, believing those who wanted him to compromise were associated with the Washington political establishment. The public wanted him to pursue the best policies, and as their trustee, he would distinguish policy from politics.[35] Nelson Polsby contends that Carter's failure to articulate broad legislative themes led to his inability to develop working relationships with congressional leaders.[36] James Fallows, Carter's top speechwriter, even saw the President as foolishly unaware of legislative norms: he "did not know how Congressmen talked, walked, and thought, how to pressure them without being a bully or flatter them without seeming a fool."[37]

The lack of Washington political experience was not limited to the President. The second theme extends the charge to Carter's domestic policy staff, in particular the White House legislative operation. For Davis, chief legislative point man Frank Moore came to be regarded as out of touch with Washington politics because he appointed mostly inexperienced Georgians to his staff in the congressional liaison office. Also, Moore emphasized policy specialization in his organization of the office, which had been rejected by former Democratic liaison officials.[38]

The image of Carter and his staff lacking political skill was formed early in the administration. Kellerman describes the White House staff during 1977 in the following manner: "The White House congressional relations staff was ineffective for much of the year, and by October the liaison team headed by Frank Moore was under heavy fire."[39] Harold M. Barger suggests that by 1979, Carter's perception "as a bumbling chief legislator had become well established in Capitol Hill and in the nation's press."[40] Fallows argues that in his first legislative year, Carter relied much too heavily on a half dozen of his upper level advisors, who were almost all from Georgia.[41] He suggests that by ignoring those most experienced with Washington politics, Carter was unable to build an effective legislative team.[42]

The charge that Carter may have been too inexperienced in Washington politics is typically associated with his operating style, which has been perceived by some as a contributing factor in his limited accomplishments. The third theme holds that Carter's operating style was that of a self-reliant policy micro-manager. Erwin C. Hargrove sees Carter as someone who personally examined the entirety of a policy problem. Carter "sought to achieve public goods in the form of comprehensive programs through political appeals to diffuse goals rather than to specific interests and coalitions, and he developed such programs in a decision-making process that placed the highest priority on study and collegiality."[43]

Along the same line, Stephen Hess argues that Carter's goal in organizing the White House staff was establishing a rational policy process that would be open enough to produce the best policy results. "Carter trusted process to create policy and was averse to ideology, which in his view would contaminate rational selection of policy."[44] Hess also contends that Carter's preoccupation with process led him to lose control over the initiatives he introduced in Congress, which contributed to a policy environment embroiled in suffocating gridlock.[45] Jack Knott and Aaron Wildavsky claim that although Carter believed in creating a good and pure policy process that was open, honest, and comprehensive, the result was a series of unfocused legislative initiatives.[46] Similarly, Paul Quirk suggests that Carter preferred self-sufficiency and sought to construct a "self-reliant presidency as a matter of conviction."[47] His attention to the details of policy contributed to a lack of focus on legislative matters.

Taken as a whole, the prevailing literature has broad implications for the study of Jimmy Carter's political leadership of Congress. Also, some accounts have either ignored or downplayed instances in which Carter was highly successful and politically astute in his approach to legislation. These three themes may lead students of the presidency to misperceive the relationship between the Carter White House and the Congress. Unlike much of the prevailing literature, which seems to suggest that Carter had a poor reputation and strained relations with the Congress, we believe airline deregulation is case that challenges previous accounts of Carter's legislative skills.

THE CARTER ADMINISTRATION AND AIRLINE DEREGULATION: THE PLAYERS

The deregulation drama had a varied cast of characters who helped shape the battle. These included individuals in the White House, the Congress, the airline industry, and groups on both sides of the issue.

Inside the White House, the main organizational unit in charge of airline deregulation was the Domestic Policy Staff (DPS) headed by Stuart Eizenstat. Within the DPS, the responsibility for this complex and important issue was delegated to Mary Schuman under the direction of Si Lazarus, Associate Director for Government Reform. Young, (late-20s) and only a junior staff member, Schuman became the point person for aviation reform.[48] David Rubenstein, a senior member of the DPS described Schuman's role in this way:

> We had a young staff person who...had worked on the Hill. Her name was Mary Schuman and she just took this under her wing and did nothing for about a year except airline deregulation. Most people on our staff would have five or six things floating from time to time and it was a matter of juggling. She was very single minded. She said, 'I'm going to do airline deregulation, I'm going to get it through.' She did the Hill lobbying, getting Brock Adams [Secretary of Transportation] to file papers, orchestrating a memo to the President, orchestrating the interest groups, orchestrating the press. It was a real maestro performance. The result was that Carter got airline deregulation....This was a classic example of how something which was a campaign position would have died had not somebody on our staff really pushed it to the end.[49]

Stu Eizenstat also acknowledged Schuman's important role: "If it hadn't been for Mary Schuman, there wouldn't be airline deregulation because the transportation department was very lukewarm on it and it was only her pushing and the President's that led to it."[50]

Brock Adams, as head of the Department of Transportation (DOT), would normally have taken the lead on an issue such as this. However, Adams' views were not compatible with Carter's on airline deregulation, at least in the beginning. He favored a more conservative, incremental pace of reform, if any. Carter and his staff wanted a bill with more gusto than Adams cared for. Additionally, the Carter White House viewed the issue as economic and not one concerning transportation.[51] The conflict that resulted between Carter and Adams was much publicized, having occurred less than two months into the new administration.[52] The primary documents are full of instances that detail the rift between the White House and

DOT. For example, Si Lazarus wrote to Stu Eizenstat concerning a telephone call from Brock Adams to Eizenstat three days earlier:

> As background, Stu, you should know that, by going over Mary's [Schuman] head to get you to modify her directions, Adams is in effect trying to undermine her capacity to coordinate the Administration's approach to the airline issue. Even if, after consulting with her, you disagree with her, you have got to lean over backwards to support her in what you decide to do, and most importantly, in how your decision is presented to Adams. Consult with her before agreeing to anything nd usually let her communicate the response, if you feel her position needs to be modified. Otherwise, we lose our ability to see that the President's policies are not undermined by DOT's day-to-day behavior.[53]

Nonetheless, Adams did partake in the later stages of the deregulation struggle.

By virtue of his position as head of the White House congressional liaison office, Frank Moore was an important player. Much of the communication between the administration and Congress went through Moore's office. Moore supported regulatory reform and was a willing participant in the process.

Another key figure for the administration was Alfred Kahn who was appointed by Carter to succeed Robson as head of the CAB. Kahn was a noted economist and had written extensively on the subject of regulation.[54] He was also an avid reformer and free-marketeer. Kahn's appointment was crucial because after he assumed control of the CAB, the Board initiated a series of moves, which began to deregulate the industry long before any bill was passed. Kahn's CAB moved at a pace much faster, and his reforms went much further, than Robson's had. Kahn described their differences:

> The main difference between the preceding chairman and me was not on the general efficacy of deregulation, he had in fact come out in favor of it,- but in his attitude toward moving before a bill. Now in that he was extraordinarily conservative...."[55]

In order to ensure that the CAB moved in a pro-competition direction, Kahn also brought in a number of his own people who were similarly free-market advocates.[56]

Finally, the President himself must be considered an important player. Carter put economic deregulation of the transportation industries near the top of his agenda when he moved into the Oval Office. Though he shied away from much of the day-to-day lobbying of Congress and important interest groups, he did resort to public and private persuasion when the time called for it.[57]

Other players outside of the administration were instrumental in the deregulation battle. The White House went to great pains to organize various pro-reform interest groups to put pressure on Congress. The Ad Hoc Committee for Airline Regulatory Reform was a baffling patchwork of organizations that would normally not have worked together.[58] Included in this committee were Ralph Nader's Aviation Consumer Action Project, the American Conservative Union, the National Association of Manufacturers, the National Association of State Aviation Officials, the American Farm Bureau Federation, the National Federation of Independent Business, and Common Cause.[59] Some groups within the industry also pushed for reform. They included most of the commuter, charter (e.g., Trans International Airlines, World Airways, and Evergreen International) and all-cargo airlines (e.g., Federal Express and

Flying Tiger Line) and some of the intrastate carriers (e.g., Pacific Southwest). Eventually, some of the major carriers (e.g., Continental and United) and smaller airlines (e.g., Hughes Airwest) joined the coalition.[60]

There were key people within Congress who were advocates for reform and played important roles. Both Howard Cannon and Edward Kennedy were very influential by virtue of their respective positions as chairs of important Senate subcommittees. It is the Cannon-Kennedy bill (S. 689) that became the foundation for the deregulation bill (S. 2493) eventually enacted. Kennedy later emerged as a bitter rival and critic of Carter, challenging him for the Democratic nomination in 1980; however, on the issue of airline deregulation, they worked well together. By virtue of his position as chair of the Senate Commerce Committee, Warren G. Magnuson (D-WA) was also important to the White House. Although he generally deferred to Cannon on aviation matters, the administration made sure to maintain his support.[61]

James B. Pearson (R-KS) was also an important player in the Senate on aviation reform. As the ranking minority member on the Commerce Committee, it was crucial for the administration to gain his favor if they wanted support from the other Republicans on the committee. In fact, Pearson and Howard Baker (R-TN) submitted their own, more "conservative" version of an aviation bill (S. 292) which was eventually merged into the Cannon-Kennedy legislation that was signed by Carter.[62]

Over on the House side, two California Democrats, Harold T. (Bizz) Johnson and Glenn M. Anderson, were key figures. Anderson chaired the House Subcommittee on Aviation of the Committee on Public Works and Transportation. It was here that the airline bill stalled in the later stages of the process and Anderson became a key actor in the drama. Johnson, as chair of the Public Works Committee, was instrumental in quickly reporting the bill out of his Committee to the Conference Committee. His actions allowed a vote to occur before the 95th Congress recessed.

Finally, academics, especially economists, played a role in the debate. Had it not been for a number of articles and books that attacked airline regulation, it is doubtful that regulatory reform would have been placed so high on the agenda by the Ford and Carter administrations.[63] Also, most research favored total economic deregulation of the industry, not gradual change, which encouraged the Carter administration eventually to favor a complete overhaul of the industry.[64]

The deregulators were opposed by a number of powerful groups. First and foremost were the airlines and their executives. Most of the major airlines (e.g., American, Delta, and Trans World) and local carriers (e.g., Allegheny, Ozark, Piedmont, and Southern) initially opposed any type of regulatory reform.[65] Though not entirely happy with life as they knew it under the strict control of the CAB, it was better than the potential disaster that could befall the airlines in an unregulated environment. Delta Air Lines, based in Atlanta, was especially vehement in its opposition. W.T. Beebe, Chairman of the Board and Chief Executive Officer of Delta wrote to President Carter:

> Because you and I have had a long relationship in Georgia, I particularly want you to know what we are doing in the way of opposing this bill so that there will not be any secrets involved....It is my intention for Delta to expend whatever energy and resources we have available to us to fight deregulation in its present form. I am extremely sorry that we apparently are on opposite sides of this issue, but we expect to make our fight on the

basis of issue and to avoid any personality involvements. I notice with interest that you have Mary Schuman canvassing the country trying to sell deregulation in its present form, and we shall try to counteract effectively her mission and any and all such future efforts which we conceive as being very misguided.[66]

The Air Transportation Association and the Association of Local Transport Airlines opposed deregulation from the beginning. The ATA, however, was an unwieldy and disorganized organization and proved to be a weak guardian of the industry.[67]

Most every union within the industry lined up against deregulation.[68] These included the Air Line Pilots Association (ALPA), the International Brotherhood of Teamsters, the Transport Workers Union of America, the Association of Machinists and Aerospace Workers, the Brotherhood of Railway and Airline Clerks, and the Flight Engineers International Association. Fearing that wages would fall and jobs would dry up in a deregulated airline industry, the unions fought hard against reform.[69] Typical of the union stance on deregulation, John J. O'Donnell, ALPA head, noted the following:

[W]e firmly believe that prudent government regulation of the privately owned and operated air transportation system is in the public interest, and that efforts to get the Federal Government out of the airline business in the name of free enterprise and more competition is contrary to the best interests of consumers, airlines, and employees. Historically, public transportation systems have been regulated by government to insure regular, reliable, and reasonably priced service to the traveling and shipping public that depend on them. We believe that such regulation is as vital today as it was in the early days of aviation to maintain and develop a stable and integrated network of air transport services.[70]

Other entities such as commercial banks and insurance groups with a large stake in the industry were likewise concerned about reform.[71] A deregulated environment brought uncertainty, something banks and insurance companies do not look kindly upon. Some state and local organizations representing airports and small communities, especially those in rural areas, similarly opposed legislation. It was thought that deregulation would encourage major carriers to pull up their stakes and abandon unprofitable routes in the "hinterland," leaving small cities and the airports that serviced them with inferior and inconvenient service.[72]

Finally, some notable figures in Congress were vehemently opposed to deregulation. Among others, Senate Aviation Subcommittee members Barry Goldwater (R-AZ), Daniel K. Inouye (D-HI), and John Melcher (D-MT) were vocal in their opposition. Like the rural states they represented, Senators such as Melcher had a real fear that service from the big carriers might dry up.[73]

WHITE HOUSE STRATEGY

With all of the various interests lined up for and against airline reform, the Carter administration fashioned a multi-faceted strategy to help push the legislation through the Congress: 1) administrative (relaxation of aviation regulation through the Civil Aeronautics Board); 2) public (public speeches and a media blitz to effect public opinion); 3) persuasion (a Beltway tactic aimed at pressuring key members of Congress); 4) and divide and conquer (organization of interests sympathetic to deregulation; and 5) cooptation of key members of the opposition to weaken those opposed).

The Administrative Strategy

The first area of focus targeted the executive branch. Alfred Kahn's nomination as CAB chair was the initial step in the process. Under his leadership, the CAB embraced price and service competition as the main policy objective of the agency.[74] In so doing, Kahn and the CAB were able to accomplish by administrative fiat much of what the Airline Deregulation Act legitimized. In a January 1978 interview, Kahn remarked that:

> [W]e have done a lot already and will do more in the next few months to liberalize what we do and to remove a great deal of the dead hand of CAB....Within the last month or two, for the first time in history I think, two carriers applied for a route-Washington to Cincinnati-and we told them they might both go in if they choose. In one swoop, we undermined the traditional character of certification, which is its exclusivity and its correspondingly mandatory character....We will be making more strides within a couple of months to undermine the essential character of cartel-like restrictions on entry....All this, of course, is counter to a competitive system. Our moving against exclusivity and requiring that the carrier has to serve the route strikes at the heart of the process.[75]

The economic results that poured in after significant regulatory liberalization by the CAB in 1977 were positive, enabling the deregulationists to capture the momentum away from the anti-reform opposition.[76] The administrative strategy, although very successful, would not suffice. Stu Eizenstat and Mary Schuman explained the necessity of reform legislation to the President:

> Although Chairman Kahn has made extraordinary progress in making the industry more competitive, he is perhaps the most forceful advocate of strong legislation. First, a future Board could easily reverse his reforms. Second, the CAB is taking substantial risks by interpreting current law as liberally as it is. Kahn states privately that there is a substantial risk that many decisions will be overturned. The CAB is taking these risks because they are counting on strong legislation to back them up. Third, the CAB can improve regulation, but it cannot make fundamental changes that will gradually reduce it.[77]

Going Public

The administrative strategy was just part of the overall Oval Office scheme. Carter and his team frequently "went public" to usher support.[78] In a number of speeches, Carter discussed the benefits of airline deregulation for both consumers and the industry alike. He began addressing the topic in March 1977, after he had sent a letter to Congress urging passage of a reform bill. At a "town meeting" in Clinton, Massachusetts, Carter stressed the need for deregulation of the major transportation industries:

My staff has begun to assess the need for deregulation of the transportation industry as much as possible. The first step in that process has now been completed [Air-Cargo Deregulation]. And I've already sent to the Congress a message which supports Senator Kennedy's bill and Senator Cannon's bill to deregulate to a major degree the airline industry. The next one on the list will be the surface transportation industry, which would certainly have the trucking industry as a major factor.[79]

Until deregulation was finally passed in October 1978, Carter kept a steady pace of public pronouncements on the subject. In June 1977, Carter held a public briefing for industry representatives, interest groups, influential Congresspersons, and the press, outlining the argument for deregulation and White House support of it. Among other things, Carter argued that the benefits included flexibility for changing markets, lower fares which would give more Americans the opportunity to fly, and greater entry into new, untapped markets. He also pledged that the bill would include guarantees in the form of subsidies to small communities to make sure that these areas did not lose their service.[80]

Due to a lengthy and complicated legislative process, the administration failed to pass an airline bill in 1977 and 1978 became a crucial year for airline deregulation. In his State of the Union Address, Carter noted:

This year, I will continue to work for passage of the airline regulatory reform bill for passengers. That bill will allow air carriers to compete through lower fares, new services, and new markets, without excessive government interference or disruption of service to small communities.[81]

Following that address, Carter began to put overt pressure on Congress to pass a deregulation bill. In a speech to newspaper editors concerning the administration's war on inflation, Carter asserted that airline deregulation was a major tenet of his anti-inflation policy and held that legislation "...must be enacted this year."[82] The link with inflation was made a week later in a statement by Carter congratulating the Senate for voting in favor of a deregulation bill on April 19.[83]

In a series of speeches in the summer and fall of 1978, Carter continued to address the deregulation issue. In front of Missouri farmers, Carter argued again that deregulation of the airlines was an important step if inflation was to be brought under control. He also noted that deregulation was necessary to bring fares down via competition.[84] In front of steelworkers in September, Carter highlighted similar themes.[85] Later that day, he reiterated that message at a Democratic fund-raiser.[86] In fact, the last month prior to the passage of the deregulation bill, Carter made six speeches or statements in which he endorsed deregulation.[87]

Carter was not the only one taking the deregulation issue to the public. Mary Schuman spent an inordinate amount of time canvassing the country for the administration. For instance, in August 1977 alone, Schuman visited 14 cities, meeting with press, consumer, and transportation groups including the *Atlanta Constitution*, *Chicago Sun-Times*, *Flint Journal*, WQUA radio in Moline, Illinois, and Penjer Del Corporation in Philadelphia. DOT Secretary Brock Adams also made a number of speeches on behalf of deregulation.[88]

Public opinion appears to provide a favorable political environment for airline deregulation to gain support. Throughout most of 1977, the public's general approval of the way Carter was handling his job as president averaged 65 percent and peaked at 75 percent in

March 1977. Public support for Carter dropped steadily through the first half of 1978, averaging 48 percent between January and July 1978. However, riding the crest of his successful conclusion of the Camp David talks between Israel and Egypt, in September and October, Carter's public approval jumped to an average of 53 percent.[89]

Persuasion

Another tactic used by the administration was one of persuasion.[90] Though much of the conventional wisdom regarding the Carter presidency holds that Carter and his staff were ineffective in their dealings with Congress, the case of airline deregulation demonstrates that this was not always true. Carter and his staff, at least in regards to this issue, effectively utilized persuasion. The President was not reluctant to flatter, and at times, prod and harangue Congress into enacting a bill. The targets of this Beltway strategy were usually the membership of those committees and subcommittees that were crucial to passage of aviation reform.

The most basic way that the Washington strategy was accomplished was to "thank" respective members for all their hard work on airline reform. Even during the transition, plans were made to initiate this persuasion strategy. Stu Eizenstat recommended to the President-elect that he "call to compliment [the chairmen and ranking minority members of the relevant Senate committees on] their efforts and to encourage them to have their staff work with our staff in developing a sound, effective bill for early enactment."[91]

Once in office, this "complimentary" tack was continued as evidenced, for example, by the suggestion to Carter from Eizenstat and Schuman that he "may wish to commend Senators Cannon, Kennedy and Representative Anderson for their leadership on this issue." Eizenstat and Schuman later reminded the President that Cannon had requested a picture be taken of the two of them at an upcoming meeting on aviation reform.[92] Similarly, after a suggestion from Senator Kennedy, Eizenstat urged Carter to call Cannon:

> I recommend that you call Senator Cannon to congratulate him for his leadership and for his three weeks of hearings. I would re-emphasize your commitment to legislation, pledge our assistance in working out a small communities provision, and let him know that he will have the active support of the Administration as he "hangs tough" in the months ahead.[93]

Though these seem like petty details, such minor displays of etiquette and courtesy are very important inside the Washington Beltway.[94]

Another way persuasion was accomplished was through formal correspondence by the President. In fact, Carter's first communication to Congress on the subject was in the form of a letter: "As a first step toward our shared goal of a more efficient less burdensome Federal government, I urge the Congress to reduce Federal regulation of the domestic commercial airline industry." Carter then asked the Congress to act "without delay" and pass a reform bill.[95] In a July 1978 letter to Howard Cannon, Carter used both flattery and cajolery. He wrote that:

Reducing regulation of the airline industry is the first major opportunity to meet our shared goal of eliminating outdated and excessive government regulation. Sound regulatory reform is a top priority of my Administration. I commend you for the progress you and your colleagues have made in working toward that goal. I urge you to speed the pace of your deliberations so that a bill can be acted upon by the Senate this year. You have already made significant decisions on many parts of the bill. But the most important decisions still lie ahead. [96]

Carter then described four provisions that the White House wanted as part of the legislation: automatic route entry, presumption in favor of entry, unused route authority, and pricing flexibility.

Besides these innocuous forms of persuasion, the White House utilized more involved tactics such as direct lobbying of Congress. From the administration's point of view, canvassing the Hill was necessary to counteract lobbying by the airline industry. In April of 1977, Mary Schuman observed: "Industry pressure on Capitol Hill is intense, and unless we get up there to rebut the misinformation that the industry is claiming (massive unemployment, breakdown of the system, etc.) we are going to lose the bill."[97] Thus proceeded a visible administration presence within the halls and corridors of the Capitol. Mary Schuman and Les Francis documented administration efforts that summer:

> *Meeting with Senators.* Bob Thomson, Linda Kamm (General Counsel - DOT), Mark Aron (DOT), Bob Francis (Cong. Relations - DOT) and Mary Schuman have divided ourselves [sic] into two groups and met with every Senator who would see us, and with the staff many times.
> *Meetings with the Industry and Public Interest Groups.* DOT and Mary Schuman met continuously (and to the point of exasperation) with outside groups to listen to the changes they want in the bill, and to try to build their support.
> *Media.* The White House Media Liaison Office has prepared a summary of our position. It is being sent to all editorial boards, and all transportation, consumer and financial writers. Mary has participated in the semi-weekly White House briefing for 30 out-of-town editors.
> *Other Administration Lobbying.* We have recommended that OMB, Justice and Esther Peterson write to the Committee this week to point out the reorganization/reform and consumer aspects of the legislation, and to urge speedy Committee action. Secretary Adams wrote a letter to all governors urging support of reform; Mary has suggested that we send a copy to each member of the Committee. Alfred Kahn, CAB Chairman, has begun to lobby individual Senators, and we expect him to write a letter to all members urging speedy action.[98]

Even Vice President Walter Mondale was not immune from such actions as evidenced by this memo sent to him from Congressional Liaison Frank Moore:

> The Senate is expected to begin consideration on Wednesday of S. 2493, the Cannon/Kennedy airline deregulation bill. The bill was reported by the Senate Commerce Committee 13-3. We expect the vote to be favorable, but many Senators are still in the

undecided column, including, as far as we know, Senators Humphrey and Anderson. We suggest that you give them a phone call to urge them to support the bill.[99]

At other times, the administration utilized a number of different allies outside the White House to put pressure on those lawmakers that were wavering. In a strategy memo sent to her superiors at DPS, Mary Schuman broke down the prospective votes by Senator on the Cannon-Kennedy bill in the Aviation Subcommittee. Those categorized as undecided were: Russell Long (D-LA), Daniel Inouye (D-HA); those noted as voting against were: John Melcher (D-MT) and Barry Goldwater (R-AZ). For each of these Senators, a carefully crafted strategy was enacted in an attempt to pressure them to vote in favor of the administration-supported bill:

> *Long*: Bud Thar of the National Governor's Conference, is getting the Louisiana Governor to work on Long. Bob Thomson, Secretary Adams, and Charles Schultze have spoken with him. Any ideas? VP?
> *Inouye*: Congressman Mineta and Dan Tate are working on him. I will follow up on Mike Masaoka. Any Ideas? VP?
> *Melcher*: Montana is served by Frontier and Hughes Air West, both of whom now support reform. Al Feldman and Russ Stephenson, their presidents, are working on him. DOT has provided the most extensive analysis known to woman on how the legislation would directly benefit Montana.
> *Goldwater*: Bud Thar of the Governors Conference, the American Association of Retired Persons, the American Conservative Union, and the American Enterprise Institute are working on him.[100]

Finally, quid pro quos and veiled threats were utilized in an attempt to persuade. Glenn Anderson, Aviation Subcommittee chair in the House, was treated in such a manner. For a good part of 1978, Anderson had stalled consideration of the deregulation bill as he wanted to pass an aircraft noise bill that was supported by the airline industry. The noise bill would have funneled federal dollars to the airlines so that they could comply with noise regulations. In the summer of 1977, Mary Schuman recognized that Anderson was going to be a problem for the administration:

> In the House, we must convince Rep. Anderson that he needs our support to get a noise bill passed and that we will help him only if (1) he makes necessary revisions in the noise bill and (2) introduces and begins acting on a reform bill....Since Anderson has shown no inclination to introduce or act upon a reform bill until the noise bill is reported, a bill may not be introduced until next year. Before his noise testimony, Secretary Adams told Rep. Anderson that the president would veto any noise bill that was not accompanied by a reform bill.[101]

In a memo sent to the President to prepare him for a meeting with Anderson, Frank Moore advised Carter to make clear to Anderson that the deregulation bill was of much higher priority than a noise bill. He described the situation this way:

The problem is that Rep. Anderson and the industry are beginning to feel that they can get a noise bill without an airline deregulation bill. We must impress upon Rep. Anderson before he goes to the markup that the Administration's number one priority is the airline regulatory reform bill....Emphasize to Rep. Anderson that the airline regulatory reform bill is the centerpiece of your campaign commitment to have less government regulation in private business. Encourage Rep. Anderson to markup an airline regulatory reform bill that will not be weaker than the consensus reform bill that has been introduced. Impress upon Rep. Anderson that the regulatory reform bill is of higher priority at the White House than the aircraft noise bill, and imply that the chances of an aircraft noise bill being signed into law are improved with the passage of a strong airline regulatory reform bill. [Emphasis added]. [102]

Divide & Conquer

A final strategy used by the administration was one targeted at organizing the efforts of supporters and dividing the opposition. The Ad Hoc Committee for Airline Regulatory Reform was an effort to organize the plethora of diverse interests sympathetic to reform. The Committee was instrumental in facilitating communication among its members as well as organizing speakers for the many Congressional hearings held on the topic.

Concerning the opposition, the administration utilized two different tactics. First, and most importantly, the White House sought to drive a wedge between the various airlines. The airlines were poorly organized and neither the administration, nor the Congress, feared them.[103] Derthick and Quirk labeled this strategy one of "divide and conquer" and the Carter White House was successful in using it. The airline resistance was weak to begin with, especially after United and some of the smaller carriers endorsed deregulation. Smelling blood, the White House went in for the kill. In one incident, Derthick and Quirk assert that the administration made an overt attempt to buy support from Frontier Airlines by amending White House proposals for a small community service program in a way that only affected Frontier. There were also allegations that the administration used future route assignments as an incentive for support. The change was worth a few million dollars to the airline and Frontier jumped at the chance. The "Frontier Amendment" was important as Frontier was the first small airline to support reform.[104]

In an attempt to appease labor and small community interests, the White House sought to include labor protection and small community subsidy provisions in the bill. Guarantees of service for small and rural communities were included in White House proposals from the start, as evidenced by Carter's early public pronouncements, with labor protection provisions adopted later. For the administration, a labor protection clause was a no-lose proposition. One of the assumptions of deregulation was that it would improve the economic situation of the industry- there was little worry about jobs being lost because it was thought that market competition would benefit the industry and maintain, if not create jobs. A memo sent to the President late in the deregulation fight illustrated this thinking:

We also recommend that you state your strong preference for the Senate labor protection provision, which permits the payment of benefits only if there are serious dislocations in the industry directly resulting from airline deregulation. Recent events show that airline employees benefit from airline competition, so the prospects for having to invoke this provision are not great.[105]

By including these provisions, groups representing labor and small communities reluctantly supported a bill that seemed destined to pass anyway.[106]

The Carter administration's multi-faceted strategy was a success. After a 22 month struggle, the measure was signed by Carter on October 24, 1978. Among other things, the Airline Deregulation Act of 1978:

- instructed the CAB to focus on competition in its regulation of the industry, to prevent anti-competitive practices, and to preserve service to small and rural communities
- provided for an automatic market entry program
- permitted carriers to lower rates 50% below or 5% above the standard industry fare (based on fares as of 7/1/77) without prior approval
- exempted commuter aircraft, weighing less than 18,000 pounds and carrying fewer than 56 passengers from most CAB regulation
- required the CAB to impose rules and requirements on charter airlines that were no more rigid than those it imposed on other types of carriers
- provided that the CAB would be abolished January 1, 1985 unless Congress voted otherwise
- provided compensation for industry employees who could prove they lost their job or had their wages decreased as a result of the deregulation bill

The CAB was abolished in 1985 and its responsibilities were shifted to DOT.

CONCLUSION

In the end, the Carter administration's multi-faceted strategy was triumphant. By using such a strategy, the White House was attacking all fronts on all sides. The administrative strategy was propitious as Kahn and the CAB received favorable reviews from CAB liberalization of regulations. This administrative strategy significantly increased the momentum of regulatory reform.

The White House strategy to organize interests sympathetic to deregulation, and to divide and conquer those who opposed, was also a success. The airline opposition was weak to begin with. The conversion of major trunk carriers such as Continental and United and smaller airlines such as Hughes Airwest and Frontier, drove a wedge through the airlines and neutralized the ATA as an opposition force. The cooptation of labor and small community interests also hastened the opposition's demise. The administration's ability to organize such a mixed-bag of interest groups in support of regulatory reform is admirable. This included Ralph Nader working effectively with the National Association of Manufacturers and the American Conservative Union with Common Cause.

Finally, at least regarding airline deregulation, the Carter administration worked effectively with the Congress. Although Carter and his staff have often been criticized for failing to deal productively with the legislative branch, airline deregulation demonstrates that this was not always the case. In fact, the Carter administration's Washington strategy helped shepherd an airline bill through a Congress not altogether amenable to such legislation. Much of the credit for this achievement must go to Mary Schuman and the rest of the Domestic Policy Staff whose concerted and persistent efforts on behalf of aviation reform made the Airline Deregulation Act of 1978 a reality. It is highly questionable whether airline deregulation would have been achieved absent the intense and effective White House lobbying effort.

We argue that the case of airline deregulation be viewed as a case that questions a prevailing myth of Jimmy Carter's ineffectiveness in regards to his relationship with Congress as well as his penchant for micro-managing the White House. This study finds that, at least in regards to airline deregulation, Carter was neither a micro-manager nor ineffective in his dealings with Congress. Rather, Carter delegated a great deal of responsibility to his White House staff and effectively participated in a multi-faceted strategy geared towards passage of the legislation. The case of airline deregulation aids in debunking the myth that suggests the Carter White House was politically ineffective in its relationship with Congress. However, it is stressed here that the single case of airline deregulation cannot be seen as one that refutes an entire body of literature that appears to suggest that the Carter White House was ineffective in attaining its legislative goals. Rather, it is a case that provides evidence that perhaps the conventional wisdom surrounding Carter's management of the White House and legislative branch has exaggerated his failings.

The case of airline deregulation is also important because it demonstrates that presidents have different tools at their disposal that can be utilized in their quest for legislative success. Though the strategy used by the Carter team to pass the deregulation bill cannot be considered a one-size-fits-all solution for presidents and other chief executives seeking legislative success, it can be utilized by social scientists and policy makers alike as a learning tool.

NOTES

1. "Airline Deregulation Act of 1978: Remarks of Signing S. 2493 Into Law. October 24, 1978," *Public Papers of the Presidents of the United States: Jimmy Carter, 1978*, Book II. (Washington, DC: USGPO), 1837.
2. For an excellent summary of the Airline Deregulation Act of 1978 as well as a brief legislative history see "Congress Clears Airline Deregulation Bill," *Congressional Quarterly Almanac*, (1978), 496 - 504.
3. "Transportation and Commerce: Regulatory Reform," *Congressional Quarterly Almanac*, (1977), 527.
4. For a general assessment of the benefits attained by consumers of air transportation services from 1978 to 1998, see Carol B. Hallett (Air Transport Association), "Airfares Are a Bargain," *USA Today*, February 27, 1998. She argues that competition within the industry has led to a doubling of consumers who traveled on the major airlines- from 275 million in 1978 to 600 million in 1997. Hallett also points to evidence showing an increase in the number of competing airlines- from 39 to 95 over those 20 years. Furthermore, she states that airline deregulation has led to substantially lower airfares, which are 37% cheaper today than they were in 1978. Also, see Steven A. Morrison and Clifford Winston, *The Economics Effects of Airline Deregulation* (Washington, DC: The Brookings Institute, 1986); Ivan R.

Pitt, and J.R. Norsrothy, *Economics of the U.S. Commercial Airline Industry: Productivity, Technology, and Deregulation* (Kluwer Academic Publishers, 1999); and, John Robert Meyer, Clinton V. Oster, Benjamin Berman, *Airline Deregulation: The Early Experience* (Greenwood: Greenwood Publishing Inc., 1981).

5. Larry N. Gerston, Cynthia Fraleigh, and Robert Schwab, *The Deregulated Society* (Pacific Grove, CA: Brooks/Cole Publishing, 1988), 86.
6. Ibid., 87.
7. Ibid.
8. Melvin A, Brenner, James O. Left, and Elihu Schott, *Airline Deregulation* (Westport, CT: ENO Foundation for Transportation, 1985), 3.
9. Gerston, Fraleigh, and Schwab, 87.
10. For a summary of the Federal Aviation Act of 1958 see "Legislative History of the Airline Deregulation Act of 1978," Committee on Public Works and Transportation, US House of Representatives. 96th Congress., 1st Session.
11. Brenner, Left, and Schott, 15.
12. Gerston, Fraleigh, and Schwab, 87; Elizabeth E. Bailey, David R. Graham, and Daniel P. Kaplan, *Deregulating the Airlines* (Cambridge, MA: The MIT Press, 1985), 23.
13. Gerston, Fraleigh, and Schwab, 88. In fact, the CAB had not allowed any new trunk (large commercial) airline to enter the industry during the 40 years of regulation- 230 applications were filed and the CAB did not allow hearings on 95% of them after 1950.
14. Ibid., 87.
15. Anthony E. Brown, *The Politics of Airline Deregulation* (Knoxville, TN: University of Tennessee Press, 1987), 99.
16. Martha Derthick and Paul J. Quirk, *The Politics of Deregulation* (Washington, DC: The Brookings Institution, 1985), 58.
17. Bailey, Graham, and Kaplan, 20; Brown, 100.
18. "Amending the Federal Aviation Act of 1958: Report to Accompany S. 2493," Committee on Commerce, Science, and Transportation, US Senate. 95th Congress, 2nd Session. (Washington, DC: USGPO), February 6, 1978, 2.
19. Brenner, Left, Schott, 19.
20. Brown, 106.
21. Ibid., 112.
22. See "Oversight of Civil Aeronautics Board Practices and Procedures: Hearings," Subcommittee on Administrative Practice and Procedures of the Senate Judiciary Committee. 94th Congress, 1st Session. (Washington, DC: USGPO, 1975).
23. Brown, 107.
24. The title is important as it demonstrates that the political environment had not shifted to one of total deregulation. Rather, regulatory reform was the goal sought after.
25. Ibid., 112.
26. Derthick and Quirk, 108 - 109.
27. Brown, 113 - 114.
28. "Alfred Kahn Session, December 10 - 11, 1981," Jimmy Carter Oral History Project. (University of Virginia, White Burkett Miller Center), 93.
29. Though the focus of this paper is primarily on White House strategy, one of the more interesting stories of airline deregulation is how a number of factors congealed thus making the political environment receptive to such legislation. Carter, no doubt, inherited a situation that was ripe for change. One could argue that because of this, airline deregulation is not a good case to make the argument that Carter was more skilled at legislative politics than

previously thought. The authors disagree, however. History if full of examples when presidents squandered opportunities to change the status quo even though the political environment had changed in a favorable direction. President Clinton and health care is an obvious example. President Carter's airline deregulation legislation did benefit from a change in the prevailing political conditions; however, passage of the legislation was not ensured by any means. The Carter administration's skill in attaining passage made the difference. For an excellent description of the underlying environment that existed at this time as well as a more general theoretical argument describing the fusion of policy streams which makes "radical" legislation like the Airline Deregulation Act of 1978 possible, see John Kingdon, *Agendas, Alternatives, and Public Policies*, 2nd ed. (New York: Harper Collins, 1995.)

30. Barbara Kellerman, *The Political Presidency: Practice of Leadership from Kennedy through Reagan* (New York: Oxford University Press, 1984), 210.
31. Eric L. Davis, "Congressional Liaison: The People and the Institutions," In Anthony King, Ed. *Both Ends of the Avenue* (Washington DC: American Enterprise Institute, 1983).
32. Stephen Skowronek, "Presidential Leadership in Political Time." In Michael Nelson, Ed. *The Presidency and the Political System* (Washington DC: Congressional Quarterly, 1998), 163. See also, Stephen Skowronek, *The Politics Presidents Make: Leadership from John Adams to George Bush* (Cambridge, MA: Belknap Press, 1993). Skowronek's study is an anecdotal account that relies mostly on biographies, periods of historical study, and administration chronicles. A limited number of primary materials, derived mainly from the Public Papers Of The Presidents of the United States, are used to supplement secondary sources.
33. Ibid.
34. Charles O. Jones, *The Trusteeship Presidency: Jimmy Carter and the United States Congress* (Louisiana State University Press, 1988), 6. Jones's work is based on a series of interviews conducted with President Carter and certain members of his senior staff at the Miller Center at the University of Virginia. Although Jones provides firm evidence to the contrary, the authors of this study rely on documentary materials at the Carter Library to argue that Carter was able to establish close working relations with key members of the so-called Washington political establishment. Airline deregulation provides a compelling case study that Carter was not always averse to working with members of Congress and interest groups to attain his legislative objectives.
35. Ibid.
36. Nelson Polsby, *The Consequences of Party Reform* (New York: Oxford University Press, 1983), 108 - 109.
37. James Fallows, "The Passionless Presidency," *Atlantic Monthly*. (May 1979), 33 - 48.
38. Eric L. Davis, "Legislative Liaison in the Carter Administration," *Political Science Quarterly* 95 (Summer 1979), 287 - 302.
39. Kellerman, 216. Kellerman's work is a theoretical examination of the political leadership skills of six US presidents. Her case study of President Carter focuses mainly on his energy proposals.
40. Harold M. Barger, *The Impossible Presidency* (Glenview, IL: Scott Foresman, 1984), 107.
41. James Fallows, 33 - 48.
42. Ibid.
43. Erwin C. Hargrove, *Jimmy Carter as President: Leadership and the Politics of the Public Good* (Baton Rouge: Louisiana State University Press, 1988), 162. Hargrove's account of the Carter presidency is based on interviews with the former president and several aides and

is focused on the internal mechanics of policymaking. The authors contend that documentary material at the Carter Library in Atlanta provide firm and compelling evidence that suggests Carter was not always bogged down in studying, evaluating, or even micro-managing the policymaking process.

44. Stephen Hess, *Organizing the Presidency* (Washington DC: Brookings, 1988), 167. Although he makes relative use of the Public Papers Of The Presidents of the United States and lists annotated memos of the Carter Transition of 1976/1977, Hess's study relies mainly on secondary accounts of the Carter Administration's legislative objectives. Although secondary sources are perfectly reasonable considering the fact that the book was published less than ten years after Carter left office, we believe that the documentary evidence provided in this case is very compelling.
45. Ibid.
46. Jack Knott and Aaron Wildavsky, "Jimmy Carter's Theory of Governing," *Wilson Quarterly*. (Winter 1977), 49 - 65.
47. Paul J. Quirk, "Presidential Competence." In Michael Nelson, Ed. *The Presidency and the Political System* (Washington DC: Congressional Quarterly, 1998), 173.
48. Ironically, the president who was often accused of overzealous micro-management may not have been sure of Schuman's identity. In response to an inquiry from Carter, Eizenstat explained in a memo sent to the President who Schuman was and some of the roles she was playing in the deregulation battle: "Mary Schuman is the member of the Domestic Policy Staff principally concerned with the Airline Deregulation Bill. At the request of the White House press office, DOT Public Affairs Office, and Frank Moore's office [Congressional Liaison], she has taken speaking engagements before Chambers of Commerce and similar groups to discuss airline deregulation. A need for activity along these lines by our staff was seen because of the lack of similar efforts by the Department of Transportation." Memo, Stu Eizenstat to President Carter, 6/9/78 (filed), ôCA,ö Box CA-1, WHCF-Subject File, Jimmy Carter Library.
49. "Carp and Rubenstein Session, March 6, 1982," Jimmy Carter Oral History Project, 41.
50. "Stuart Eizenstat Session, January 29 - 30, 1982," Jimmy Carter Oral History Project, 55.
51. Richard E. Cohen, "Airline Deregulation is Not Cleared for Take-Off," *National Journal* (July 30, 1977), 1195.
52. For a summary of the Carter - Adams conflict over airline deregulation see Richard E. Cohen, "Carter Shows Who's the Boss When It Comes to Airline Deregulation," *National Journal* (March 5, 1977), 352 - 53; see also Carole Shifrin, "Adams Voices Doubts on Airline Industry Deregulation," Washington Post (March 3, 1977), D13, D17.
53. Memo, Si Lazarus to Stu Eizenstat, 3/21/77, "Aviation - Airline Regulatory Reform (2) [O/A 6232] [3]," Box 148, Domestic Policy Staff, Eizenstat, Jimmy Carter Library.
54. For examples of his writings see Alfred Kahn, *The Economics of Regulation: Principles and Institutions* Vols. 1 and 2. (New York: Wiley, 1970 & 1971), and Alfred Kahn, "Applications of Economics to an Imperfect World," *American Economic Review*, Vol. 69 (May 1979), 1 - 13.
55. "Alfred Kahn Session," Jimmy Carter Oral History Project, 93.
56. Derthick and Quirk, 78.
57. Brown, 103.
58. "Airline Deregulation," *Congressional Quarterly Almanac*, (1977), 555.
59. Brown, 103; Gerston, Fraleigh, and Schwab, 90; Memo, Mary Schuman to Stu Eizenstat, 3/31/77, "Aviation - Airline Regulatory Reform (1) [O/A 6232]," Box 148, Domestic Policy Staff, Eizenstat, Jimmy Carter Library. For a complete list of the members of the Ad Hoc

Committee, see "Hearings on Aviation Regulatory Reform," Committee on Public Works and Transportation, US House of Representatives. 95th Congress, 2nd Session. (Washington, DC: USGPO, March 6 and 7, 1978), 202 - 203.

60. "Airline Deregulation," 555; Brown, 104; Memo, Mary Schuman to Stu Eizenstat, 3/31/77, "Aviation - Airline Regulatory Reform (1) [O/A 6232]," Box 148, Domestic Policy Staff, Eizenstat, Jimmy Carter Library.
61. Memo, Mary Schuman to Stu Eizenstat, 3/1/77, "Aviation - Airline Regulatory Reform [O/A 6232] [3]," Box 148, Domestic Policy Staff, Eizenstat, Jimmy Carter Library.
62. For an excellent summary of the views of key members on the Commerce Committee, see Latter, Senator Edward M. Kennedy to Stuart E. Eizenstat, 4/18/77, "Aviation - Airline Regulatory Reform (2) [O/A 6232] [3]," Box 148, Domestic Policy Staff, Eizenstat, Jimmy Carter Library.
63. For a review of some of the more important economics literature on the subject see Bailey, Graham, and Kaplan (introduction).
64. Initially, however, the administration and Carter favored reform, not complete deregulation of the industry. In a memo to Stu Eizenstat, Mary Schuman cautioned Eizenstat to "avoid talking about "deregulation," a code word that some take to mean totally free entry and the abolition of the CAB. Talk about "reform". Secretary Adams has always taken the position that total deregulation is not in the customer's interests. President Carter agrees with this position and does not support the elimination of the Civil Aeronautics Board, but instead supports a measured, phased transition to a system which relies more on competition and less on regulation." Memo, Mary Schuman to Stu Eizenstat, 3/1/77, "Aviation - Airline Regulatory Reform [O/A 6232] [3]," Box 148, Domestic Policy Staff, Eizenstat, Jimmy Carter Library. See also George Williams, The Airline Industry and the Impact of Deregulation. (Cambridge, UK: Ashgate, 1993), 10 - 11.
65. Bailey, Graham, and Kaplan, 32.
66. Letter, WT Beebe to President Carter, 8/8/77, "Aviation - Airline Regulatory Reform (2) [O/A 6232] [2]," Box 148, Domestic Policy Staff, Eizenstat, Jimmy Carter Library.
67. Derthick and Quirk, 152 - 153, 155 - 156; Brown, 104.
68. Gerston, Fraleigh, and Schwab, 91.
69. Brown, 104.
70. "Hearings on Aviation Regulatory Reform," Committee on Public Works and Transportation, US House of Representatives. 95th Congress, 2nd Session. (Washington, DC: USGPO, March 6 and 7, 1978), 186.
71. Bailey, Graham, and Kaplan, Deregulating the Airlines, 32 - 33; Brenner, Left, and Schott, Airline Deregulation, 10.
72. Brown, 105.
73. For example, in a dissenting opinion expressed in the report accompanying the Cannon-Kennedy bill, Melcher stated that "There are many reasons for my concerns; the Automatic Entry provision contains too many serious, unanswered risks to justify an experiment of the magnitude proposed that could well lead to excessive competition, reduce service to more marginal markets and small communities, increase industry competition, serious [sic] adverse impact on the smaller carriers and the weaker of the larger trunk lines, pressures for fare increases, and reduced opportunity for new entrants. Neither the hearings nor the Committee mark-up sessions adequately disposed of these risks, and there is substantial evidence that these are real risks." (Amending the Federal Aviation Act of 1958: Report to Accompany S. 2493, 223.)

74. For a summary of Kahn's reign at CAB, see Paul Stephen Dempsey and Andrew R. Goetz, *Airline Deregulation and Laissez-Faire Mythology* (Westport, CT: Quorum Books, 1992), chapter 16.
75. Richard E. Cohen, "The CAB's Kahn on Aggravations of Airline Deregulation," National Journal (January 14, 1978), 50.
76. Brown, 98 - 99.
77. Memo, Stu Eizenstat and Mary Schuman to President Carter, 5/12/78, "Aviation - Airline Regulatory Reform (2) [O/A 6232] [1]," Box 148, Domestic Policy Staff, Eizenstat, Jimmy Carter Library.
78. For a general description and analysis of the power of the president to exercise public leadership, see Samuel Kernell, *Going Public: New Strategies for Presidential Leadership*, 2nd ed. (Washington, DC: Congressional Quarterly Press, 1993). He defines "going public" as a "strategy whereby a president promotes himself and his policies in Washington by appealing to the American public for support." (p. 2). By so doing, it is hoped that public support of the president will force compliance by the Congress.
79. "Clinton, Massachusetts: Remarks and a Question-and-Answer Session at the Clinton Town Meeting. March 16, 1977," Public Papers Of The Presidents of the United States: Jimmy Carter, 1977, Book I, p.389. The primary documents provide supporting evidence that the administration viewed airline deregulation as one of the first steps to deregulating other industries. For example, Charles Schultze, head of the Council of Economic Advisers, noted, "The air reform bill will have far-reaching precedental value. Our efforts to reform other inefficient regulatory programs via legislation will be more readily accepted by the Congress and the public if we can point to the success of the air transport industry under comprehensive reform legislation." Memo, Charlie Schultze to President Carter, 5/1/78, "Aviation-Airline Regulatory Reform (2) [O/A 6232] [1]," Box 148, Domestic Policy Staff, Eizenstat, Jimmy Carter Library. Similarly, Stu Eizenstat asserted, "If airline deregulation fails, there is little realistic hope of realizing your aim of eliminating anti-competitive regulation in other sectors." Memo, Stu Eizenstat to President Carter, 3/3/77, "Aviation-Airline Regulatory Reform (2) [O/A 6232] [3]," Box 148, Domestic Policy Staff, Eizenstat, Jimmy Carter Library.
80. "Airline Industry Reform Legislation: Remarks at a Briefing for Representative of the Airline Industry and Public Interest Groups. June 20, 1877," Public Papers of the Presidents of the United States: Jimmy Carter, 1977, Book I, 1834.
81. "The State of the Union: Annual Message to the Congress. January 19, 1978," Public Papers Of The Presidents of the United States: Jimmy Carter, 1978, Book I, p.109.
82. "Anti-Inflation Policy: Remarks to Members of the American Society of Newspaper Editors Announcing the Administration's Policy. April 11, 1978," Public Papers Of The Presidents of the United States: Jimmy Carter, 1978, Book I, p.724. This link with inflation is observed early on in the White House documents as deregulation of the nation's transportation industries was viewed as part of the administration's "war on inflation"; e.g., see Memo, Si Lazarus to Stu Eizenstat & Mary Schuman, "Aviation-Airline Regulatory Reform (2) [O/A 6232] [3]," Box 148, Domestic Policy Staff, Eizenstat, Jimmy Carter Library, and Memo, Stu Eizenstat to The President, 3/3/77, "Aviation-Airline Regulatory Reform (2) [O/A 6232] [3]," Box 148, Domestic Policy Staff, Eizenstat, Jimmy Carter Library.
83. "Airline Deregulation Legislation: Statement by the President. April 19, 1978," Public Papers Of The Presidents of the United States: Jimmy Carter, 1978, Book I, p.762. The Carter administration was very concerned with inflation and with good reason. At the time, the country was experiencing double-digit inflation and skyrocketing interest rates. Gallup

Poll data showed the American public to be extremely nervous about the high cost of living as inflation consistently was ranked as the most important problem facing the nation. For example, in a Gallup Poll dated April 10, 1977, 58% of respondents held that inflation was the most important problem facing the country. A little over a year later (May 14, 1978), that figure remained steady at 54%. In July, that figure rose to 60%. Finally, in August 1978 as his approval rating tumbled to 39% from 67% a year earlier, only 22% of the country approved of the way President Carter was addressing the inflation problem. Clearly, inflation was becoming an albatross around the President's neck and deregulation was viewed as a way to reverse the trend as well as demonstrate that the administration had an active plan for combating the situation. Gallup Data was drawn from The Gallup Poll: Public Opinion 1972-1977; 1978 (Wilmington, DE: Scholarly Resources Inc.).

84. "Columbia, Missouri: Remarks to Members of the Midcontinent Farmers Association. August 14, 1978," Public Papers Of The Presidents of the United States: Jimmy Carter, 1978, Book II, p.1424.

85. "Atlantic City, New Jersey: Remarks at the United Steelworkers of America Convention. September 20, 1978," Public Papers Of The Presidents of the United States: Jimmy Carter, 1978, Book II, p.1549.

86. "Atlantic City, New Jersey: Remarks at a Democratic Party Campaign Luncheon. September 20, 1978," Public Papers Of The Presidents of the United States: Jimmy Carter, 1978, Book II, p.1553.

87. These include the two Atlantic City speeches already mentioned as well as a statement the next day congratulating the House for passing their version of the bill, a speech to the Democratic National Committee in which he noted that subsequent passage of an airline deregulation bill proves that Democrats believe in free market principles, and remarks at two different Democratic fund-raisers three days prior to his signing the bill. For the complete texts of these speeches see "Atlantic City, New Jersey: Remarks at the United Steelworkers of America Convention. September 20, 1978," "Atlantic City, New Jersey: Remarks at a Democratic Party Campaign Luncheon. September 20, 1978," "Airline Deregulation Legislation: Statement on House of Representatives Action Approving the Legislation. September 21, 1978," "Democratic National Committee: Remarks at a Fundraising Dinner. September 27, 1978," "Wichita, Kansas: Remarks at a Rally for Bill Roy and John Carlin. October 21, 1978," "Minneapolis, Minnesota: Remarks at a Democratic-Farmer-Labor Party Victory Rally. October 21, 1978," all in Public Papers Of The Presidents of the United States: Jimmy Carter, 1978, Book II.

88. Memo, Mary Schuman & Les Francis to Frank Moore & Stu Eizenstat, 7/18/77, "Aviation-Airline Regulatory Reform (2) [O/A 6232] [2]," Box 148, Domestic Policy Staff, Eizenstat, Jimmy Carter Library.

89. See The Gallup Poll: Public Opinion 1972-1977; 1978 (Wilmington, DE: Scholarly Resources Inc.). We believe rising presidential approval added to the momentum of Carter's ability to push deregulation over the top in Congress.

90. For an assessment of the president's power to persuade elites inside the Beltway, see Richard E. Neustadt, Presidential Power. (New York: John Wiley & Sons, 1964 [1960]). In his classic statement of executive power, Neustadt informs readers that "presidential power is the power to persuade" and that "the power to persuade is the power to bargain." (pp. 23 and 45). From Neustadt's vantage point, presidents must bargain–schmooze, coax, cajole, convince, etc.–if they are to be successful in accomplishing their goals. Since power is shared in the American political system, the executive branch cannot afford to ignore the legislature; to do so is to risk failure. Therefore, presidents must pursue a strategy of "going

Washington" if they are to achieve their legislative goals. Richard Rose utilized the term "going Washington" as a way to compare Neustadt's bargaining strategy with Kernell's public strategy; see Rose, *The Postmodern President: George Bush Meets the World*, 2nd ed. (Chatham, NJ: Chatham House Publishers, 1991).

91. Memo, Stu Eizenstat to The President-elect, 1/10/77, "Aviation-Airline Regulatory Reform (1) [O/A 6232] [2]," Box 148, Domestic Policy Staff, Eizenstat, Jimmy Carter Library.
92. Memo, Stu Eizenstat & Mary Schuman to President Carter, 6/18/77, "CA," Box CA-1, WHCF-Subject File, Jimmy Carter Library.
93. Memo, Stu Eizenstat to The President, 4/12/77, "Aviation-Airline Regulatory Reform (2) [O/A 6232] [2]," Box 148, Domestic Policy Staff, Eizenstat, Jimmy Carter Library.
94. For a discussion of the "folkways" of Congress (unwritten rules, traditions, and norms), see for example Donald Matthews, *U.S. Senators and Their World* (Chapel Hill, NC: University of North Carolina Press, 1960), chap.5 and Hedrick Smith, *The Power Game: How Washington Really Works* (New York: Ballantine Books, 1988), chap.6.
95. "Airline Industry Regulation: Message to the Congress. March 4, 1977," Public Papers Of The Presidents of the United States: Jimmy Carter, 1977, Book I, 277-278.
96. Letter, President Carter to Howard Cannon, 7/28/77, "CA," Box CA-1, WHCF-Subject File, Jimmy Carter Library.
97. Memo, Mary Schuman to Stu Eizenstat, 4/11/77, "Aviation-Airline Regulatory Reform (2) [O/A 6232] [2]," Box 148, Domestic Policy Staff, Eizenstat, Jimmy Carter Library.
98. Memo, Mary Schuman & Les Francis to Frank Moore & Stu Eizenstat, 6/18/77, "Aviation-Airline Regulatory Reform (2) [O/A 6232] [2]," Box 148, Domestic Policy Staff, Eizenstat, Jimmy Carter Library.
99. Memo, Frank Moore to Vice President Mondale, 4/19/78 (filed), "CA," Box CA-1, WHCF-Subject File, Jimmy Carter Library.
100. Memo, Mary Schuman to Bert Carp & Les Francis, 10/7/77, "CA," Box CA-1, WHCF-Subject File, Jimmy Carter Library; In the end, these particular tactics were unsuccessful as Inouye, Melcher, and Goldwater voted against reporting the bill out of the Commerce Committee and Long was absent for the vote.
101. Memo, Mary Schuman & Les Francis to Frank Moore & Stu Eizenstat, 6/18/77, "Aviation-Airline Regulatory Reform (2) [O/A 6232] [2]," Box 148, Domestic Policy Staff, Eizenstat, Jimmy Carter Library.
102. Memo, Frank Moore to President Carter, 3/7/78, "CA," Box CA-1, WHCF-Subject File, Jimmy Carter Library.
103. Derthick and Quirk, 152.
104. Ibid., 60; There is documentary evidence, however, that the Frontier Amendment was neither an administration ploy nor was it supported by the White House. Mary Schuman addressed the issue: "The 'Frontier amendment' is a backroom deal never discussed at markup that gives windfall profits to local service carriers while the current subsidy system is being phased out. Carriers who don't benefit from this provision are claiming that the bill has become 'special interest' legislation. We support eliminating it. The problem is that Senator Cannon supports it to help defuse opposition to the bill by local carriers." Memo, Mary Schuman to Stu Eizenstat, 2/21/78, "Aviation-Airline Regulatory Reform (2) [O/A 6232] [1]," Box 148, Domestic Policy Staff, Eizenstat, Jimmy Carter Library.
105. Memo, Frank Moore & Stu Eizenstat to The President, 9/27/78, "Aviation-Airline Regulatory Reform (2) [O/A 6232] [1]," Box 148, Domestic Policy Staff, Eizenstat, Jimmy Carter Library.

106. Brenner, Left, and Schott, Airline Deregulation, 28 - 30; Fraleigh, and Schwab, The Deregulated Society, 95 - 96.

Chapter 12

CLINTON'S GREATEST LEGISLATIVE ACHIEVEMENT? THE SUCCESS OF THE 1993 BUDGET RECONCILIATION BILL

Patrick Fisher

THE PRESIDENT'S ROLE IN THE MODERN BUDGET PROCESS

Congress and the presidency are designed not to get along. The Founding Fathers, in order to insure that one branch of the government did not become too powerful, designed a system of government where the legislative and executive branches would be rivals. Due to the fact that Congress is a decentralized body of 535 members, Congress often appears weak compared to the executive branch, which is more likely to speak with one voice. Since the New Deal era, the presidency has gradually taken on increasing budgetary power while Congress has often seemed unable to gain control over its own diverse institutional self-interests. Today, there seems to be little doubt that the executive branch has become a more powerful player in the budget process than Congress, despite the intentions of the Founding Fathers. The nature of the presidency, combined with the tremendous rise in scope of the federal government, has made the president the major player in the budget process in the twentieth century. This does not mean, however, that Congress has become irrelevant – far from it. In order for presidential budgetary proposals to become law, after all, they must be passed by Congress.

The modern presidency began with the Budget and Accounting Act of 1921, in which Congress delegated its traditional powers over compiling the preliminary draft of the budget to the president. The law required the president to develop and submit a budget to Congress and established the Bureau of the Budget (later the Office of Management and Budget). Congress gave the president more power in the budget process because it found itself unable to cope with the rising demands of government and the dogma of public administration in the Progressive Era placed great faith in the nonpolitical executive which would be brought into strengthened executive offices. The result is that the president has become the dominant force in developing budget policies and procedures. Even though the president's proposed budget is not necessarily an accurate guide to congressional action, it has been transformed into an opening bargaining maneuver.[1]

Given the importance of the presidential role in the budget process, it is fair to conclude that the White House plays an important role in determining whether or not the federal government produces a budgetary deficit or surplus, though certainly many factors (the state of the economy, congressional priorities) are beyond the control of the presidency. At the same time, the size of the deficit or surplus that the federal government produces can be expected to have an important effect on what the president can propose to do.

PRESIDENT CLINTON AND THE 1993 BUDGET RECONCILIATION BILL

Bill Clinton, unlike most other recent presidents, demonstrated that he would immerse himself in the details of the budget. Despite the fact that it was not an issue that he emphasized while running for the presidency in 1992, Clinton demonstrated a willingness early in his presidency to reduce the deficit. It was widely held that if Clinton was to get a handle on the deficit as he promised, he must do so in the first year of his presidency, when his political capital was at its peak.[2]

One month into his presidency, Clinton proposed a budget that included spending cuts, but which relied overwhelmingly on tax increases to bring the deficit downward. At the same time, Clinton proposed to quickly boost short-term job creation by pumping billions of dollars into new spending programs. Clinton's deficit-cutting plan was the largest in history, proposing to save nearly $500 billion over four years. Of that amount, roughly two-thirds would go to reduce the deficit, while another third would be used to pay for increased job creation and long-term investment spending, making net deficit reduction at the end of the four years of the plan about $325 billion.[3]

The deficit-reduction package proposed a cut of $493 billion over four years, $247 of it coming from spending cuts and $246 billion from tax increases, almost exactly a 1-to-1 ratio. The ratio of tax increases to spending cuts quickly emerged as the major conflict point in congressional reaction to the plan. Republicans and conservative Democrats were upset that the ratio of cuts to taxes was much less than the 2-to-1 ratio that Clinton advisor, Leon Panetta, had advocated during his confirmation hearings. Though the deficit-reduction plan made notable spending cuts, its heavy reliance on tax increases highlights the difficulties the Clinton economic team had coming up with acceptable spending cuts.

Clinton's call for a tax increase was a direct repudiation of the economic philosophies of his two Republican predecessors. By aiming the taxes primarily at corporations and the well-off, Clinton suggested that the programs of Ronald Reagan and George Bush, which were designed to stimulate economic growth through tax cuts, came at the price of high deficits. Clinton believed that he could convince the American public – and a majority in Congress – that the economic expansion of the 1980s held negative consequences in the long run. Clinton proposed to raise most of the new revenue with an array of higher taxes on upper-income Americans and corporations, including $126.3 billion over six years mainly through a new top income tax bracket of 36 percent and a surtax on income over $250,000. Overall, more than half of the new taxes were projected to fall on families making more than $200,000 a year.[4] Table 1 shows the distribution of tax burden by income group.

Table 1: Effect Clinton's Tax Proposals Would Have on Income Groups

Family Income Group	Tax Burden (1993)		Clinton Proposals		Change	
	Total Paid By Group	As % of Pretax Income	Total Paid By Group	As % of Pretax Income	Total Paid By Group	As % of Pretax Income
$0-10,000	$6.7	7.8	$6.5	7.6	-.2	-.2
10-20,000	26.9	9.8	26.9	9.8	0	0
20-30,000	55.7	14.0	56.0	14.1	.4	.1
30-50,000	152.1	17.3	156.5	17.8	4.4	.5
50-75,000	203.1	19.0	210.7	19.7	7.6	.7
75-100,000	174.3	20.4	180.2	21.1	5.9	.7
100-200,000	242.6	21.2	250.6	21.8	8.0	.7
200,000+	247.5	20.9	281.8	23.8	34.3	2.9

Tax Amounts are in billions of $.
Source: *Congressional Quarterly Weekly* (February 20, 1993), p. 364 and Treasury Dept.

President Clinton's proposed budget faced its biggest obstacle in Congress with the vote on the budget reconciliation bill. The budget resolution only locked in the broad deficit-reduction numbers, but left virtually all of the specifics to the reconciliation process. The reconciliation bill was designed to reconcile tax and spending policy with deficit-reduction goals outlined in the budget resolution. The measure was the heart of Clinton's plan to reshape the nation's economic policy.

In the end, Clinton's economic plan emerged victorious, though just barely. The Omnibus Budget Reconciliation Act was approved in August 1993 without a single vote to spare in either chamber: it passed 218-217 in the House and 51-50 in the Senate (with Vice-President Al Gore making the tie-breaking vote). The measure passed without any Republican votes, the first time in postwar congressional history and possibly the first time ever that the majority party has passed major legislation with absolutely no support from the opposition.[5]

With Republicans unwilling to compromise and unable to drive the process themselves, the struggle to get the anti-deficit package through Congress was exclusively one of rounding up enough Democrats. This was the case even though the proposal had something to offend almost every Democrat; conservatives were uncomfortable with the entire range of tax increases, and liberals were uncomfortable with some of the $87 billion in cuts over five years in entitlement spending programs such as Medicare and Medicaid as well as the $102 billion in cuts over five years in appropriated spending.[6] Liberals and the Congressional Black Caucus, however, endorsed the bill early on, making moderates and conservatives the critical swing votes. Overall, the Clinton economic plan was expected to shrink, but not eliminate the deficit. Annual deficits under the law were expected to be around $200 billion and since nearly $500 billion in deficits was to be eliminated over five years, the national debt was expected to rise by "only" $1.1 trillion.[7] The plan not only marked a major step away from the low-tax and high-deficit policies of his Republican predecessors, but also from the spending-oriented policies of Democratic Congresses. By embracing the plan, if only barely, congressional Democrats gambled on their political futures, betting that deficit reduction would improve the economy in the long-run and improve their reelection prospects.

CONGRESSIONAL SUPPORT OF THE 1993 BUDGET RECONCILIATION BILL: AN ANALYSIS

The president has been viewed as having relatively little influence to wield over Congress.[8] Yet, when it comes to budgeting, it is clear that the president's position on budgetary priorities greatly affects congressional actions on the budget. At the same time, presidential policy success depends in part upon contextual factors that are beyond his control.[9] As a result, a president needs to devote a great deal of attention to congressional relations in order to get a budget through Congress.

This section will analyze who supported the Clinton-supported 1993 Budget Reconciliation Bill. Tables 2 and 3 compare representatives who supported the 1993 Budget with those who voted against it. The variables analyzed in Tables 2 and 3 include demographic and political characteristics of their districts. Both tables demonstrate just how vast the differences were between those who supported the tax increases of the 1993 Budget and those who opposed them.

The partisan and ideological nature of the debate surrounding the bill, as well as the fact that no Republicans voted in support of the bill, indicate that party and ideology were strongly correlated with the vote for the budget proposals. This is consistent with the findings of John Kingdon, who found that members of the president's party are much more open to his influence than are members of the opposing party.[10] Similarly, George Edwards found that members of the president's party in Congress consistently gave him strong support compared to members in the opposing party.[11] The shared party affiliation of the president and some members of Congress serves as a source of influence for him. The president's party affiliation seems to be a source of influence in Congress, although a limited one. In domestic matters, Edwards found that party affiliation plays its greatest role when the president's policies are contrary to the normal stances of his party and when constituency pressures are lax enough to allow members of the president's party in Congress to respond to the pull of a member of their party in the White House.[12] To measure the importance of ideology in the vote on the 1993 Budget, a member's floor vote history was analyzed to study the degree by which the vote on the 1993 Budget was consistent with other votes the member made during the 103rd Congress. The Ideology variable is the representative's ideological score according to the *National Journal* (with 0 being most conservative and 100 most liberal) and was chosen as a means of determining how ideological the division over the Clinton budget was.

Three district demographic characteristics were chosen as factors to determine if district demographic characteristics (including urbanization characteristics, racial characteristics, and per capita income) offered any predictive value of the actions of representatives and senators on budgetary issues; previous studies have found that constituency factors predict a good share of the variation in policy positions.[13] "Rural" denotes the percentage of the representative's district that is classified as rural, "White" is the percentage of the population of representative's district that is classified as white, and "Income" is the per capita income of the representative's district (in thousands of dollars).

District political characteristics were also chosen as a means of analyzing whether or not the district's vote in presidential elections (a rough, tough imperfect, indicator of the district's political leanings) were correlated with congressional budgetary actions. "Pres92" is the percentage of the vote that Clinton received in the district in 1992, "Pres88" is the percentage of the vote that Dukakis received in 1988, and "Perot" is the percentage of the vote that Perot received in the district in 1992. It would be expected that those districts that gave Democrats Clinton and Dukakis a higher percentage of the vote would more likely elect representatives who would support the Clinton budget. Districts that gave Perot a higher percentage of the 1992 presidential vote, on the other hand, may be the home of representatives who either tended to dislike the Clinton proposal because it did not cut spending enough. It is possible, however, that those coming from a district with a higher Perot vote may have tended to support the proposal because it reduced the deficit--as a candidate Perot advocated both massive spending cuts and tax increases to reduce the deficit.

Finally, four factors representing characteristics of individual members were chosen as possible determinants of budgetary action. The "Genvote" variable is the percentage of the vote that the representative received in their last general election. This variable was chosen to determine if previous electoral success meant that one would be more likely to support a potentially unpopular tax-raising measure, as George Edwards found.[14] "Terms" is the number of terms the representative has served in the House (for the Senate models the variable used is Years, which is the number of years the senator has served in the Senate); since those with more seniority tend to come from politically "safer" districts and have more of a stake in appeasing the political leadership of the party, it may be that those with more years in their respective bodies are more likely to follow the lead of their party. This was the finding of studies done by Barbara Sinclair and Steven Smith.[15] "Unity" is the representative's party unity scores for the 103rd Congress – the percentage of the time the representative voted for a majority of their party against a majority of the other party. This factor was chosen with the belief that those who tended to support their party more often in general were also the most likely to support the position of their party on the Clinton budget. Finally, the "Support" variable was chosen as a factor in order to determine if the vote on the Clinton budget was typical in terms of support within the Democratic and Republican parties.

Table 2 shows means tests for eleven factors for those who supported and opposed the 1993 Budget. This analysis displays the vast differences between those representatives, and the districts they represent, who supported the 1993 Budget Reconciliation Bill and those who opposed it.

The strength of these predictors can be seen by the fact that all of the t-ratios in Table 2 were statistically significant for the House with the exceptions of the "Genvote" and "Terms" variables. For the Senate, the variables based on district characteristics proved to be poor predictors: the "Rural," "White," and "Income" variables are not statistically significant in either the analysis, as Table 2 displays. However, the "Ideology," "Pres92," "Pres88," and "Support" variables were statistically significant. Overall, therefore, the partisan leanings of a senator's state and the partisan and ideological attributes of a senator were the best predictors of the vote on Clinton's budget proposals in the Senate.

These findings should not come as much of a surprise because of the extreme partisan conflict over Clinton's proposal. Republicans saw the Clinton budget as a means of raising taxes and undoing the Reagan legacy that they revere. Democrats, though they were not enamored with the tax increases, felt that it was important to support the first Democratic president in twelve years. The result was a divide over the proposal that was along partisan and ideological lines, as was demonstrated by the statistical significance of the "Ideology" variable.

The degree to which partisanship explains the support for the presidential budget in 1993 leads to another question – namely, what were the factors among congressional Democrats (since Republicans in Congress unanimously opposed the Clinton plan) that led them to support or oppose the plan of a president of their own party? Since partisanship was so dominant on the vote of the bill, this may be a more consequential consideration. Table 3 shows the means for eleven factors for those Democrats who voted for the Clinton-supported 1993 reconciliation bill and those who voted against it, where the variables are the same as in Table 2.

Table 2: District Characteristics and Vote on 1993 Budget Reconciliation Bill

House:	Voted For Clinton Budget	Voted Against Clinton Budget	t
Ideology	73.64	26.91	34.06***
Rural	21.70	27.96	-3.01**
White	68.40	83.08	-7.28***
Income	13.83	15.04	-2.97**
Pres92	51.00	36.48	15.01***
Pres88	53.69	38.73	15.83***
Perot	16.77	20.19	-6.03***
Genvote	64.43	62.37	1.85
Terms	5.75	4.81	1.55
Unity	91.78	84.77	7.16***
Support	80.49	49.84	26.98***
Senate:	**Voted For Clinton Budget**	**Voted Against Clinton Budget**	**t**
Ideology	72.84	27.42	15.16***
Rural	30.16	33.52	-1.15
White	82.84	84.68	-.78
Income	13.98	13.30	1.44
Pres92	43.30	39.10	3.70***
Pres88	46.16	42.36	3.54**
Perot	18.86	20.86	-1.89
Genvote	59.82	60.90	-.51
Years	10.78	11.66	-.51
Unity	86.74	84.42	.97
Support	89.72	42.64	16.55***

*$p < .05$; **$p < .01$; ***$p < .001$

Explanation of Table 2 Variables: IDEOLOGY = member's ideological score as measured by the *National Journal*, with 100 being most liberal and 0 most conservative; RURAL = % of district living in rural areas; WHITE = % of district that is white; INCOME = district's per capita income (in thousands); PRES92 = % of the vote Bill Clinton received in the district in 1992 presidential election; PRES88 = % of the vote that Michael Dukakis received in the district in the 1988 presidential election; PEROT = % of the vote Ross Perot received in the district in the 1992 presidential election; GENVOTE = % of the vote the member received in the 1992 congressional elections; TERMS = number of years the representative has served in the House; Years = number of years Senator has served in the Senate; UNITY = member's party unity score (% of the time the member voted with a majority of his/her party against a majority of the other party); SUPPORT = member's presidential support score (% of the time that the member supported the Clinton administration's position on a bill).

Table 3: Democrats and the 1993 Budget Reconciliation Bill

House:	Voted For Clinton Budget	Voted Against Clinton Budget	t
Ideology	73.63	49.73	13.10**
Rural	21.78	32.10	-2.96**
White	68.57	79.00	-4.03**
Income	13.85	12.32	3.20**
Pres92	51.01	38.98	8.85**
Pres88	53.68	41.78	8.95**
Perot	16.77	19.20	-2.34*
Genvote	64.27	63.27	.58
Terms	5.70	3.83	3.29**
Unity	91.76	73.56	8.45**
Support	80.49	72.17	5.25**
Senate:	**Voted For Clinton Budget**	**Voted Against Clinton Budget**	**t**
Ideology	72.84	52.33	3.85**
Rural	30.16	27.33	.42
White	82.84	76.17	1.19
Income	13.98	13.67	.28
Pres92	43.30	40.67	1.11
Pres88	46.16	40.67	2.64*
Perot	18.86	16.83	.93
Genvote	59.82	70.83	-2.47*
Years	10.78	12.50	-.45
Unity	86.74	75.83	2.35*
Support	89.72	80.83	3.19**

*p < .05; **p < .01

Explanation of Table 3 Variables: IDEOLOGY = member's ideological score as measured by the *National Journal*, with 100 being most liberal and 0 most conservative; RURAL = % of district living in rural areas; WHITE = % of district that is white; INCOME = district's per capita income (in thousands); PRES92 = % of the vote Bill Clinton received in the district in 1992 presidential election; PRES88 = % of the vote that Michael Dukakis received in the district in the 1988 presidential election; PEROT = % of the vote Ross Perot received in the district in the 1992 presidential election; GENVOTE = % of the vote the member received in the 1992 congressional elections; TERMS = number of years the representative has served in the House; Years = number of years Senator has served in the Senate; UNITY = member's party unity score (% of the time the member voted with a majority of his/her party against a majority of the other party); SUPPORT = member's presidential support score (% of the time that the member supported the Clinton administration's position on a bill).

For House Democrats, the difference between the means for those who voted for and against the budget were statistically significant for all variables except "Genvote," the percentage of the vote the representative received in 1992 – those who voted for the 1993 budget received approximately the same share of the vote in the 1992 elections as did those who voted against it. For Senate Democrats, the smaller number (56 total, 6 of whom opposed the Clinton budget) made for a less consistent pattern of differences between the two groups, but there were still statistically significant differences between the two groups on "Ideology," "Pres88," "Genvote," "Unity," and "Support."

In the House, Democrats who voted for Clinton's proposed budget tended to be more liberal, to have served more terms, to be more supportive of the party and Clinton in general, and were elected from districts that more were more urban, had a higher proportion of minorities, were wealthier, gave the Democratic presidential candidates a higher proportion of the vote in 1988 and 1992, and gave Perot a lower share of the vote in 1992. In the Senate, Democrats who voted for the Clinton budget tended to be more liberal, more supportive of a majority of the party, more supportive of Clinton's positions, came from states that gave the Democratic presidential candidate of 1988 a higher share of the vote, and received a lower percentage of the vote in their last election. Thus, there were considerable differences between those districts that elected those Democrats who supported Clinton's budget proposal and those who voted against it. The vote of the district was related to the member's vote on key budget votes during the 103rd Congress. Those representatives that supported the reconciliation bill tended to come from districts that gave Clinton and Dukakis relatively large percentages of the vote in 1992 and 1988 respectively. They also tended to come from districts that gave Perot a lower percentage of the vote in 1992.

Thus, not only was the vote on the 1993 Budget consistent with the partisan and ideological traits of individual members of Congress, but at the same time a member's vote on the budget was heavily influenced by the political beliefs of their district, as measured by presidential vote, as well as the demographics of the district. The characteristics of one's district therefore played an instrumental role in determining whether or not one would support the 1993 Budget Reconciliation Bill.

POLITICAL CONSEQUENCES OF THE 1993 BUDGET RECONCILIATION BILL

The difficulty of the passage of the 1993 Budget Reconciliation Bill demonstrates the degree that Members of Congress fear the electoral retribution for raising taxes. The anticipation of retrospective voting helps to focus legislative attention on the possible electoral consequences of voting to raise taxes even when they hear little from their constituents in advance of congressional action. Even though there was little evidence that members of Congress incurred significant electoral risks for approving new taxes prior to 1993, policymakers fear the potential consequences of voting for increased taxes.[16]

As a result, Congress plans very carefully for tax increases. They plan the timing, devise and use processes that insulate them from interest groups, strategize to minimize the pain to voters, and build coalitions of support.[17] Congress's aversion of risk extends to the type of taxes members of Congress are willing to raise when revenue must be increased. As experiences at the state level have shown, it is much more difficult to impose new taxes than to raise existing ones.[18] This means that Congress tends to refuse to repeal established taxes because of the fear of losing revenue, and at the same time it does not want to introduce new taxes because a new tax can potentially have an unfavorable impact upon the electorate. By making few changes, members of Congress keep past laws in effect as the best means of minimizing the political costs of taxation while maximizing tax revenue.[19] By treating tax policy as a "nondecision" rather than as a matter of legislative choice, informal rules and behavioral patterns assure that a policy already in place will continue in effect without new explicit decisions being made.[20]

The fact that not a single Republican in either chamber voted in support of the 1993 Budget indicates the degree of by which partisanship and ideology dominated the vote on the bill.[21] Republicans saw the Clinton budget as a means of raising taxes and undoing the Reagan legacy that they revere. Democrats, though they were not enamored with the tax increases, felt that it was important to support the first Democratic president in twelve years. The result was a divide over the proposal that was along partisan and ideological lines. By embracing the plan, if only barely, congressional Democrats gambled on their political futures, betting that deficit reduction would improve the economy in the long-run and improve their reelection prospects. Since they passed the budget package without a single Republican vote, Democrats hoped that they would get sole credit for future success of the bill.

Democrats were buoyed by polls suggesting public support for deficit reduction, even at the cost of higher taxes. It was hoped by congressional Democrats that citizens may have come to realize that real deficit reduction would necessitate more taxes. After the Clinton budget was passed by Congress in August 1993, citizens were asked about the budget deal. Despite the bitter controversy over rising taxes, Americans were surprisingly willing to pay for the new levies called for in the budget plan. According to a Gallup Poll taken after the budget plan was implemented, 52 percent of the respondents said that they did not object to new taxes, and only 47 percent said that they objected. Of those who also claimed that the American public was partly to blame for the deficit, 60 percent said that they did not object to the tax increases (see Table 4).

Democratic optimism that the 1993 Budget would not be a political hindrance, however, evaporated as the 1994 congressional elections approached. As the 1994 elections proved, the Democrats' support of tax increases did not help them politically.[22] Despite a relatively healthy economy in November 1994, Democrats who supported the Clinton economic plan did poorly in the midterm elections. Of the 228 House Democrats that sought reelection, 34 lost, including 28 who voted for the 1993 Budget Reconciliation Bill. More tellingly, not a single Republican incumbent lost a reelection bid for Congress in 1994. Even in an environment wherein voters were calling for deficit reduction, voting to raise taxes or cut programs proved to be a politically hazardous move for members of Congress.

Table 4: Willingness to Pay New Taxes

Question: Do you object to paying the new taxes, or not?

		Yes	No	No Opinion
	Total	47	52	1
Sex				
	Male	45	54	1
	Female	48	51	1
Education				
	College post-grad	33	67	0
	College graduate	41	59	0
	College inc.	77	20	3
	No college	46	53	1
Politics				
	Republicans	66	33	1
	Democrats	26	74	0
	Independents	49	50	1
Ideology				
	Liberal	32	68	0
	Moderate	39	61	0
	Conservative	59	40	1
Income				
	$50,000 and over	46	54	0
	$30,000-49,999	47	52	1
	$20,000-29,999	41	59	0
	Under $20,000	49	50	1

Source: Gallup Poll (August 8-10, 1993; Survey GO 422004, Q.19). Based on national survey of 799 interviews. Poll number 335 of 1993.

THE SUCCESS OF THE 1993 BUDGET RECONCILIATION BILL: THE ADVENT OF BUDGET SURPLUSES

Overall, the 1993 Budget Reconciliation Bill was expected to shrink, but not eliminate, the deficit. Annual deficits, however, have shrunk dramatically since the measure was enacted–indeed they have shrunk much more than anyone, including the Clinton administration, predicted. Every year during the Clinton administration the federal government has produced a budget with a lower deficit or higher surplus. In a development that would have been thought impossible just a few years ago, there were budget surpluses from 1998-2000, the first years since 1969 that the federal government has not run in the red. In 2000, the federal government had a surplus of a staggering $236 billion, the eight consecutive year with a declining deficit or increased surplus, a postwar record (see Table 5). As Allen Schick states, "liquidating the deficit ranks as one of the supreme budgetary accomplishments in American history."[23] The elimination of the deficit has completely changed the dynamics of the federal budget process; the deficit-reducing conventions of the 1990s are being replaced by a new set of ideas for fiscal policy.[24] Though other factors, such as strong economic growth (which started at the end of the Bush administration) and the Fed's monetary policies under the direction of Alan Greenspan, undoubtably aided the cause of deficit reduction, the 1993 Budget Reconciliation Bill without question has been remarkably successful in its goal of reducing the federal budget deficit.

Table 5: The Federal Deficit and the National Debt during the Clinton Administration

Year	Federal Deficit or Surplus (+)	Total Public Debt	Debt as % of GNP
1992	290	3,000	48.2
1993	255	2,249	49.5
1994	203	3,433	49.4
1995	164	3,605	49.2
1996	108	3,735	49.9
1997	22	3,773	47.3
1998	+69	3,722	44.3
1999	+124	3,633	39.9
2000	+236	3,410	34.9

Deficit/Debt totals are in billions of $.
Source: Congressional Budget Office

Despite the unprecedented reduction of the federal budget deficit throughout his presidency, however, Clinton has seemingly garnered few political rewards for this achievement. The elimination of a federal budget deficit may be Clinton's greatest accomplishment as president. Every year that Clinton was president, the economy flourished and the federal budget picture improved. The Clinton administration, however, has been unable to sell the achievements of his budgetary blueprint. According to one poll, 32 percent said that Clinton deserved no credit at all for balancing the budget. When asked who deserved more credit for reducing the deficit, the number who said Clinton was virtually even with the number who claimed Republicans in Congress.[25]

For most of his presidency, Clinton did not necessarily pursue a budgetary strategy consistent with produces budget surpluses. He did not commit to the concept of a balanced budget until 1995, and that was for budgets in the future, when he would be no longer be occupying the White House. Surpluses, however, arrived earlier because the strong economy produced an unexpected surge in revenues.[26] Once the surplus did arrive, it dramatically changed the nature of the debate over the budget.

Once the reality of long-term surplus projections set in, the White House and congressional Republicans quickly laid claim to the revenues to finance their competing agendas. For Clinton, that included new spending on domestic programs and a new Medicare prescription drug benefit. Republicans, on the other hand, rallied behind tax cuts. Lawmakers, however, were nowhere near a consensus on how the extra revenues should be distributed.

The surplus allowed Clinton to pursue many of the goals that his administration had previously abandoned and put on hold. In health care and other social programs, Clinton at the end of his administration began to pursue the same goals as he sought at the beginning of this presidency in 1993, though usually by different means. For example, in 1993 Clinton proposed an expansion of the food stamp program and a Democratic Congress approved much of his proposal. The 1996 welfare law cut food stamp spending, but Clinton won restoration of some of the cuts in 1998 and in 2000 asked Congress to restore even more.[27] Essentially, the surpluses of the end of his presidency allowed Clinton to successfully adopt a more incremental approach in support of his policy goals.

Many Republicans, however, continued to believe that Congress should force the White House to bend to its will and supported a political strategy of avoiding surpluses. For example, Tom DeLay, the House majority whip, claimed that draining the surplus was a deliberate strategy designed to force President Clinton to submit to congressional Republicans' political will. The plan, DeLay said, was for Republicans to drain all of the surplus out of next year's budget and force President Clinton to pay for any of his additional spending requests out of the Social Security surplus, which both parties have pledged to protect. It was hoped that this strategy would force Clinton to sign the Republican spending bills or break his pledge to keep his hands off Social Security funds. From a public opinion perspective, however, it seemed as though President Clinton may have had the upper hand. As Tables 6 displays, the Republicans call for tax cuts did not resonate with the American public. When asked budget priorities, Americans appeared to desire increasing spending on domestic programs and reducing the national debt more than they are clamoring for tax cuts.

Table 6: Public Opinion on the Surplus
How should the budget surplus be used?

Increase Government Spending	43%
Pay Down National Debt	30%
Reduce Income Taxes	22%

Source: Gallup August 17-18, 1999

Although there were trillions of dollars in projected future surpluses, Congress and the White House cold not agree on what to do with the windfall of new projected revenues. There was no large tax cut nor an expansion in spending programs. Gridlock, however, had important policy consequences. It meant that the surplus was left intact. The result was that running a surplus automatically went to paying down the debt the nation ran up the previous three decades. Should the federal government continue on this course, it could eliminate the national debt in 10 to 15 years. While this approach was never put to a vote or debated fully debated in Congress, it resulted in an outcome that most economists consider very positive for the economy over the long run. As economist Robert Samuelson argued, the nation is "at one of those times when doing nothing–or, at any rate, doing very little, is preferable to doing something".[28]

Since voting has been so closely divided between the two major parties in recent congressional elections, neither party has been willing to compromise for fear that doing anything that might give the other side even the tiniest advantage.[29] Debt reduction was a fallback position. It was embraced by President Clinton blocked the Republican effort to cut taxes and Republicans refused to go along with Democrats calls for more government spending.

CONCLUSION

Congress has looked toward the President to lead the process of forming the national budget ever since the Budget and Accounting Act of 1921 made the president responsible for submitting a budget proposal to Congress. Yet, for the most part, presidents have tended to focus on other priorities. After he was elected president, Clinton proved to be an exception to this trend. Clinton proposed a politically risky budgetary blueprint that relied heavily on increased taxes–what was to become the 1993 Budget Reconciliation Bill. An analysis of the congressional vote on the 1993 Budget Reconciliation Bill displays the extreme partisan conflict over the proposal. Party and ideology were the primary factors determining one's vote on the budget. Furthermore, the significant differences between the districts among those who supported the 1993 Budget Reconciliation Bill and those who opposed it, both demographically and politically, demonstrates the potential effects of the constituency and representation on the budget process. Without a vote to spare, Clinton was able to get Congressional approval of his budget blueprint in an extremely partisan environment.

With the help of a strong economy, the 1993 Budget Reconciliation Bill has been extraordinary successful in what it set out to do: reduce the federal budget deficit. The elimination of nearly 30 years of federal budget deficits is undoubtably a remarkable achievement. The creation of a federal budget surplus has totally changed the dynamics of political debate over budget priorities. To illustrate how much the budgetary picture has changed, in 1993 the Congressional Budget Office projected a fiscal 1998 deficit of $357 billion; the actual 1998 fiscal budget had a surplus of $63 billion.[30] Americans who have been so accustomed to political discourse over how to reduce the deficit now encounter presidential candidates debating how to spend a projected budget surplus. Interestingly, Americans facing a possible budget surplus for the first time in nearly 30 years appear to be only lukewarm to the idea of tax cuts; more people were found to back paying down the federal debt than were found to back tax cuts.[31] Following public opinion on this matter would be consistent with the General Accounting Office's position that "until the fiscal path for a period of budget surpluses is fully and clearly articulated there is a risk of losing the opportunity to enhance our long-term economic well-being."[32] The projected surpluses are a rare window of opportunity for tackling the largest fiscal challenges facing the country today.[33]

President Bush faced a much rosier budget picture than that inherited by Clinton when he was elected president, in spite of predictions of an economic turndown. As a result, Bush initially had more flexibility to act than Clinton (until the terrorist attacks on September 11, 2001). When Clinton assumed the presidency, the budget deficit was a central fact of life which limited what the federal government could do. New spending projects were taboo. With the deficit eliminated, it was possible to once again have a debate over whether the federal government should do more or cut taxes.[34]

NOTES

1. Schick, Allen. 1990. *The Capacity to Budget*. Washington, D.C.: The Urban Institute.
2. Hager, George and David Cloud. 1993. "Clinton Team's Similar Lines Focus on Deficit Reduction." *Congressional Quarterly* (January 16), pp. 120-123.
3. Hager, George. 1993. "President Throws Down Gauntlet." *Congressional Quarterly* (February 20), p. 356.
4. Cloud, David. 1993. "Package of Tax Increases Reverses GOP Approach." *Congressional Quarterly* (February 20), p. 361.
5. Hager, George and David Cloud. 1993b. "Democrats Tie Their Fate To Clinton's Budget Bill." *Congressional Quarterly* (August 7), p. 2122.
6. Hager, George and David Cloud. 1993c. "Democrats Pull off Squeaker in Approving Clinton Plan." In *Congressional Quarterly* (May 29), p. 1341.
7. Lee, Robert and Ronald Johnson. 1994. *Public Budgeting Systems*, 5th ed. Gaithersburg, MD: Aspen Publishers.
8. Edwards, George. 1980. *Presidential Influence in Congress*. San Francisco: W.H. Freeman and Company.
9. Mezey, Michael. 1989. *Congress, the President, and Public Policy*. Boulder: Westview Press.
10. Kingdon, John. 1989. *Congressmen's Voting Decisions*, 3rd ed. Ann Arbor: University of Michigan Press.
11. Edwards, George. 1980. *Presidential Influence in Congress*. San Francisco: W.H. Freeman and Company.
12. Ibid.
13. Alder, E. Scott. 2000. "Constituency Characteristics and the 'Guardian' Model of Appropriations Subcommittees 1959-1998." *American Journal of Political Science* 44 (1): 104-114; Page, Benjamin, Robert Y. Shapiro, Paul W. Gronke, and Robert M. Rosenberg. 1984. "Constituency, Party, and Representation in Congress." *Public Opinion Quarterly* 48: 741-756; Clausen, Aage. 1973. *How Congressmen Decide: A Policy Focus*. New York: St. Martin's Press; Shannon, W. Wayne. 1968. *Party, Constituency and Congressional Voting*. Baton Rouge: LSU Press.
14. Edwards, George. 1980. *Presidential Influence in Congress*. San Francisco: W.H. Freeman and Company, pp. 108-110.
15. Sinclair, Barbara. 1993. "House Majority Party Leadership in an Era of Divided Control." *Congress Reconsidered*, 5th ed., Lawrence Dodd and Bruce Oppenheimer eds., pp. 237-258. Washington, D.C.: CQ Press; Smith, Steven. 1993. "Forces of Change in Senate Party Leadership and Organization." *Congress Reconsidered*, 5th ed., Lawrence Dodd and Bruce Oppenheimer eds., pp. 259-290. Washington, D.C.: CQ Press.
16. Arnold, R. Douglas. 1990. *The Logic of Congressional Action*. New Haven: Yale University Press.
17. Rubin, Irene. 1990. *The Politics of Public Budgeting*. Chatham, NJ: Chatham House.
18. Hansen, Susan. 1983. "Extraction: The Politics of State Taxation." *Politics in the American States*, Virginia Gray, Herbert Jacob, and Kenneth Vines, eds., pp. 335-358. Glenview, IL: Scott, Foresman and Company.
19. Rose, Richard. 1986. "Maximizing Tax Revenue While Minimizing Political Costs." *Journal of Public Policy* 5: 289-320.
20. Schick, Allen. 1990. *The Capacity to Budget*. Washington, D.C.: The Urban Institute.
21. Fisher, Patrick. 1999. "The Prominence of Partisanship in the Congressional Budget Process." *Party Politics* 5(2): 225-236.
22. Killian, Linda. 1998. *The Freshman*. Boulder, CO: Westview.
23. Schick, Allen. 2000. "A Surplus, If We Can Keep It." *The Brookings Review* 18(1): 36-39.

24. Lemieux, Jeff. 1999. "Federal Budgeting in an Era of Surpluses." *Georgetown Public Policy Review* 5(1).
25. Page, Susan and William M. Welch. 1998. "Poll: Don't Use Surplus to Cut Taxes." *USA Today* (January 16), pp. 1A and 6A.
26. Samuelson, Robert J. 2000a. "Who Governs? Maybe Nobody." *Newsweek* (February 21), p. 33.
27. Pear, Robert. 2000. "One Step at a Time, Clinton Seeks More Help for Poor and Elderly." *New York Times* (February 7), p. A1.
28. Samuelson, Robert J. 2000b. "Let Them Be Lame Ducks." *Newsweek* (February 7), p. 30.
29. Dionne, E.J. 2000. "Why Americans Hate Politics: A Reprise." *The Brookings Review* 18 (1): 8-11.
30. Schick, Allen. 2000. "A Surplus, If We Can Keep It." *The Brookings Review* 18(1): 36-39.
31. Page, Susan and William M. Welch. 1998. "Poll: Don't Use Surplus to Cut Taxes." *USA Today* (January 16), pp. 1A and 6A.
32. General Accounting Office. 2000. *Budget Surpluses: Experiences of Other Nations and Implications for the United States*. Washington, DC: GAO Press.
33. Lemieux, Jeff. 1999. "Federal Budgeting in an Era of Surpluses." *Georgetown Public Policy Review* 5(1).
34. Dionne, E.J. 2000. "Why Americans Hate Politics: A Reprise." *The Brookings Review* 18 (1): 8-11.

RESEARCHING AND EVALUATING THE PRESIDENCY

Chapter 13

RANKING AND EVALUATING PRESIDENTS: THE CASE OF THEODORE ROOSEVELT

Max J. Skidmore

RANKING THE PRESIDENTS

Presidential rankings are part of the great American preoccupation with lists. The enterprise began in 1948 when Arthur Schlesinger, Sr. reported in *Life Magazine* the results of his queries to fifty-five experts on the presidency.[1] He repeated his study in 1962, publishing the results of his new survey, this time of seventy-five experts, in *The New York Times Magazine*.[2] Each of his lists consisted of five sections, those presidents who were "Great," "Near Great," "Average," "Below Average," and those at the bottom, who fell into the category of "Failure." Although Thomas Bailey and others have criticized the enthusiasm for rankings[3], many scholars including Bailey himself have followed Schlesinger's lead.

Bailey, who "regarded the Schlesinger polls as a Harvard-eastern elitist-Democratic plot," came up with a scheme involving no fewer than forty-three separate measures.[4] Sometimes these studies have grown to large proportions. Ridings and McIver, for example, "polled seven hundred and nineteen historians and political scientists for their 1997 book *Rating the Presidents*."[5]

Undoubtedly, as critics charge, there is a bias in favor of activist presidents. One might say, "well, of course." After all, the purpose of the ranking effort is to determine which presidents are the most effective, which is to say the ones who accomplished the most in a positive sense. In no walk of life does greatness come to those who consistently defer to others, who merely conduct "business as usual," or who set about to diminish their own authority or that of the enterprise in which they function. To discard ratings as reflecting an activist bias would be similar to rejecting a rating of deserts because it is biased toward the flavorful.

One may, however, share a general suspicion of such lists as being superficial when noting that fairly often (not including the Schlesinger studies) they will rank James A. Garfield, who was assassinated after only six months in office. Even if it were possible to make a case for including Garfield, it would seem impossible to justify ranking William Henry Harrison, who had the shortest presidency on record: he died a month following his inauguration. Nevertheless, some listings rank even his evanescent presidency. In the year 2000, a C-SPAN study of "90 presidential experts rating ten qualities of presidential leadership," rated the unfortunate Harrison fifth from the bottom, ahead only of Harding, Pierce, Andrew Johnson, and Buchanan in that order.[6]

Arthur Schlesinger, Jr. followed his father in 1996 by conducting another study rating presidents for The New York Times Magazine. After publishing it there, he expanded it for the Political Science Quarterly.[7] He included an additional category: "High Average."

There is considerable consistency, especially at the top and bottom, throughout these numerous lists compiled by a wide variety of scholars. Lincoln virtually always heads them, and Franklin D. Roosevelt and George Washington come in second or third. The "near great" tier generally includes Thomas Jefferson, Andrew Jackson, Theodore Roosevelt, Woodrow Wilson, Harry Truman, and often James K. Polk. At the bottom (sometimes rated as "failures") tend to be James Buchanan, Andrew Johnson, Ulysses S. Grant, Warren Harding, Richard Nixon, and often Franklin Pierce.

There is variation, of course. "The choice of best and worst presidents has remained relatively stable through the years," but in between the extremes there is much more fluctuation. "Some presidents – particularly J. Q. Adams, Buchanan, Andrew Johnson, and Cleveland – have declined in the later polls."[8]

Presidential ratings will probably always attract attention, but it is doubtful that they will ever be able to provide more than the crudest of measures. The extremes are usually rather obvious, while relative rankings for the remainder likely will remain so imprecise as to strip them of any true meaning other than to reflect the views of those providing the ratings. The entire enterprise, in fact, is vulnerable to the criticism that it is to oversimplified to be worthwhile.

Consider the difficulty that Schlesinger, Jr. faced. He noted that he had been "stumped" in making judgments about several of the presidents since Eisenhower. Kennedy and Ford, for instance, were in office too briefly, and LBJ, Nixon, and George Bush presented special challenges "because their foreign and domestic records are so discordant." He said that scholars might be inclined "to rate Johnson higher in domestic than in foreign affairs and do the reverse for Nixon and Bush." Moreover, "the most recent presidents always seem more controversial and harder to classify." He quoted Walter Dean Burnham as discussing "dichotomous or schizoid profiles. On some very important dimensions," Burnham said, "both Wilson and L.B. Johnson were outright failures in my view; while on others they rank very high indeed. Similarly with Nixon." Along the same lines "Alan Brinkley said: 'There are presidents who could be considered *both* failures *and* great or near great (for example, Wilson, Johnson, Nixon).' James MacGregor Burns observed of Nixon, 'How can one evaluate such an idiosyncratic president, so brilliant and so morally lacking?'"[9]

EVALUATING PRESIDENTS

Evaluations of individual presidents on their own merits – rather than narrowly comparing one with all the others – are more likely to offer genuine insights, although as always, these evaluations, too, are subjective. Sometimes there have been sharp changes in individual reputation. During much of his time in office, Abraham Lincoln – the president now most often honored above all others – was highly unpopular and at one time even assumed that he could not be re-elected. Those old enough to remember Harry Truman's presidency will recall how unpopular he was in office, despite his unanticipated victory in 1948. William McKinley was very popular in office but is little remembered today. This may result more from the overwhelming nature of his successor's presidency than from any failing on McKinley's part, but no doubt also reflects a generally sparse awareness of the details of American history.

Dwight Eisenhower ranked rather poorly in the 1962 ratings, but Ike's reputation has since risen after Fred Greenstein discovered his "hidden-hand presidency."[10] Even Grant, who uniformly has ranked at or near the bottom, may be on the verge of a rise in the rankings as historians reconsider the Civil War and dispel the arguments of the Southern vindicators and the revisionists who dismissed slavery as the War's basic cause.[11]

Reevaluation has gone so far as to affect the memory of the only president forces from office, Richard Nixon. No less solid a figure than Forrest McDonald wrote in 1994 that "it is my personal belief, that some day he will be reckoned among the 'great' or 'near great' presidents..."[12]

THE RISE, FALL, AND RISE OF THEODORE ROOSEVELT

The process by which presidential reputations ebb and flow is not always clear. Nevertheless, those reputations themselves are relatively easy to discern, and they are arguably as influential in the shaping of the presidency as are the concrete actions of presidents, court decisions, and legislative enactments. Thus, this paper will examine the course of the reactions toward one of the most significant of America's chief executives.

That president, Theodore Roosevelt, was the first to serve entirely in the twentieth century, and the youngest person ever to hold the office. He was the first to be called affectionately by his initials, and he characterized an age and captured the imagination of his country in a way that only Washington, Jefferson, Jackson, Lincoln, his distant cousin Franklin, and perhaps to a lesser extent Wilson could rival. He also was the most vigorous. His energetic approach to the executive set the tone for his successors, and laid much of the groundwork for the modern presidency.

Thomas A. Bailey, certainly not among TR's admirers, has illustrated how difficult it is not to give the Colonel at least grudging respect. He concedes that Roosevelt used his "dynamic leadership" to strengthen the presidency, but qualifies this by sniffing that it was "often a bulldozing kind of leadership," and that it might even have "overbalanced" the office. Still, TR was "the first of the Modern Presidents," and he was "undeniably a strong Executive." He had "considerable success" with an often hostile – although Republican – Congress, and he:

> permitted few dull moments. Whether a radical conservative or a conservative radical, he acted as a kind of lightning rod to deflect or absorb radical movements, and may have headed off socialism with a noisy if overrated dose of reformism. Seeking s Square Deal for the forgotten man, he marshaled, moulded, and muddied public opinion.[13]

On the whole, though, Bailey reflected the views of TR's more hostile critics – even though he was compelled to say that "Roosevelt was a great personality, a great activist, a great preacher of the moralities, a great controversialist, a great showman. He dominated his era as he dominated conversations." And "the masses loved him; he proved to be a great popular idol and a great vote getter."[14]

Theodore Roosevelt so clearly dominated the country during his time in the White Houe (the name he officially bestowed upon the Executive Mansion) and for some years thereafter, that his contemporaries could have been forgiven if they had assumed that his reputation would continue to overwhelm all others. In actuality, it was enormous when he left office, dropped, and then rose during the latter years of Wilson's administration, declined then for decades, and once again began a steady rise. Today's assessments tend to place him at least on the threshold of greatness.

This is all the more impressive when one recognizes that he is the only such figure who served at a time when there was no great national crisis or other upheaval. Wilfred Binkley has written that great presidents have served "when certain historic ideas in the life of the nation had to be clarified," and that outstanding leadership generally could come forth only in times of crisis.[15] "A man cannot possibly be judged a great President unless he holds office in great times," Clinton Rossiter remarked. Moreover, "to be a great President a man must think like a great President; he must follow Theodore Roosevelt and choose to be a 'Jackson-Lincoln,' a man of strength and independence, rather than a 'Buchanan,' a deferential Whig.[16] Even without war, TR's foreign policy catapulted the United States into the ranks of the major powers – and he provided enormous benefits to the world by securing the Panama Canal, however questionable his tactics.

It was unfortunate for the Colonel, Rossiter noted (although he said it was probably fortunate for the country), that there was no real crisis during TR's time in office. Nevertheless, there had been enough opportunity to exercise authority that TR had been able "to state the famed 'Stewardship Theory,' which is still the most adroit literary justification of the strenuous Presidency." That theory, as Roosevelt described it, is that the president has not only the right, but the "duty to do anything that the needs of the Nation demanded unless such action was forbidden by the Constitution or the laws."[17] Even Bailey admits that TR would rank higher if a major war had occurred during his presidency – assuming, of course, that he won it."[18]

Roosevelt's enthusiasm for the presidency and for the country generated enormous enthusiasm for him as well. When "captains of industry" sought to deal with him as an equal, he set them in their place and let them know that no industrialist was the equal of the President of the United States. the people loved it. He sought to restore railroad competition in the Northwest by successfully suing to dissolve the Northern Securities Company, he secured the passage of the Pure Food and Drug and the Mean Inspection Acts, he moved against trusts in the beef, oil, and tobacco industries, he made the first use of governmental power in labor disputes on behalf of workers rather than owners, and he became America's greatest conservationist, setting aside more than 150 million acres of public forest land and preventing its sale to private interests.

In addition, this most boisterous man astonished many of his fellow citizens – certainly not limited to his critics – by demonstrating skill and subtlety in diplomacy, and even more astonishing by becoming a force for international peace. His adroit efforts to negotiate an end to the Russo-Japanese War brought him the Nobel Prize for Peace, the first American to be so honored. Only one other American president has received the Peace Prize, TR's nemesis, Woodrow Wilson.

Roosevelt was the first vice president to fill an unexpired term (in his case, it was nearly a full term, three and one-half years) and then to be elected in his own right. When he won a resounding victory in 1904, he promised not to run in 1908. He held to his promise, even though he loved being president, and even though it was apparent that he could have won easily. When he attempted a comeback in 1912, the increasingly progressive TR won the bulk of the presidential primaries, but could not unseat the incumbent, William Howard Taft, who had the support of the conservative political machinery that controlled most state Republican parties.

TR than conducted his historic campaign as a "Bull Moose Progressive." He lost to Wilson, but came in far ahead of Taft in both popular and electoral vote. Taft carried only Utah and Vermont.

Although his actions had antagonized many Republicans, TR remained the idol of the Bull Moose Progressives. The Progressive Party nominated him again in 1916, but he declined to run that year; the Republicans nominate Charles Evans Hughes who eventually received Roosevelt's support. In 1918, he declined to be nominated as the Republican candidate for governor of New York.

His "strenuous life" continued to boost his colorful reputation, but it had taken its toll. His health had declined. Among other things, he suffered recurring bouts of fever from his near-death experiences exploring the Brazilian jungle in 1914. No doubt he also was the victim of lead poisoning from the bullet that had remained lodged near his heart since an attempt on his life in 1912.

Despite his ailments, he remained vigorously active as President Wilson's major opponent. His popularity began to resurge, even among Republicans. "By 1918," wrote his biographer, William Harbaugh, "Roosevelt's booming exhortations had made him the loyal opposition's uncrowned leader and the Republican party's foremost candidate for the presidency in 1920."[19]

John Gable, arguably the foremost expert on Theodore Roosevelt, has affirmed the likelihood of a TR candidacy in 1920 had fate not intervened. "By 1918 Roosevelt was again the most prominent leader of the Republican Party and the odds-on favorite for the nomination in 1920," he has written. "The Colonel made plans for 1920, chose a campaign manager, and began drawing up a new progressive program. The dream of a reconstructed, progressive G.O.P., however, was not to be. Roosevelt died on January 6, 1919..."[20]

Shortly after his death, memorials sprang up around the country honoring the great reform president. A group of civic leaders met in Duluth, Minnesota in February 1919 to plan the most extensive memorial of all, the Theodore Roosevelt International Highway. Now largely forgotten, the 4,060-mile road soon spanned the continent from Portland, Maine to Portland, Oregon, and became the northernmost of nine named transcontinental highways in the 1920s.[21] In those days before the numbering system, naming highways was common. TR's name also designated the current U.S. 6, and many other routes.

During the 1920s, the energy that had driven the huge reform impulse in the century's first two decades had dissipated. The war diverted much of it, as wars generally do, and the public had wearied of reform and became cynical. Moreover, the understandable anti-war sentiment that had developed generated a wariness regarding the Rough Rider. When Henry F. Pringle produced an engaging biography of TR in 1931, asserting that Roosevelt was not much of a reformer anyway – that he produced more noise than results – he won a Pulitzer Prize. Pringle seems to have attempted (but with little success) to be fair to a subject whom he obviously disliked. One word that he used over and over to refer to Roosevelt was "adolescent."[22]

Pringle in the 1920s had "specialized in deflationary sketches of prominent figures," according to his friend Arthur Schlesinger, who said that Pringle's TR biography was "a brilliant, witty, skeptical account based on thorough and careful research." it "set the tone of commentary on TR for a generation or two," Schlesinger noted, demonstrating how influential the written word can be. He quotes Ernest May's 1998 comment that Pringle's biography "suffered from not taking Roosevelt seriously... For Pringle, almost every episode in Roosevelt's life played as *opera bouffe*." According to Schlesinger, Pringle's 1939 biography of William Howard Taft was "less mischievous," and although "we have come to think better of the first Roosevelt... Pringle's disenchanted portrait remains to be reckoned with."[23]

The Pringle interpretation tended to hold sway until 1954, when John Morton Blum published his much more balanced and equally influential study, *The Republican Roosevelt*. Blum gracefully assessed the Bull Moose: "Roosevelt wrote the poet Robinson,"he said, "there is not one among us, in whom a devil does not dwell." Before TR's "devil mastered him," Blum wrote, "he left the record of his Presidency – in spite of all its failings, a splendid record." Along with his shortcomings, he "left a model of how to govern, a chart – not accurate, but suggestive – of modern social order, and a vibrant lesson in how to live."[24]

Among the huge volume of literature on Theodore Roosevelt, several works stand out. Considering only those that deal with his full life and career, the best remains William H. Harbough's *The Life and Times of Theodore Roosevelt*.[25] In 1992, Nathan Miller published another splendid biography, the first full biography in over three decades, and one that took into account a vast store of newly-discovered information.[26]

For example, TR had claimed that he had forced the Germans to accept jurisdiction of the Permanent Court of International Justice at the Hague to settle the Venezuelan crisis of 1902 and 1903, when Americans suspected them of seeking Venezuelan territory.[27] Miller wrote that "hostile writers pointed out there was no documentary evidence to support [the story] and claimed Roosevelt had fabricated the account under the influence of his anti-German fervor prior to the American entry into World War I." Such attacks, Miller said, helped "create a picture of the ex-president as boastful and somewhat of a fraud," and "all this contributed to the precipitate decline of his historical reputation during the 1930s." When researchers after the Second World War studied TR's enormous volume of correspondence, however, "at least fifteen instances were discovered prior to World War I – dating back to 1905 – in which he had privately imparted to friends partial details of the incident."[28]

In contrast to Pringle's work, Miller's is thoughtful and balanced. Like Pringle's, it is well written. There is another full biography, more recent than Miller's. *TR: The Last Romantic*, by H. W. Brands, is even more voluminous, but less balanced or perceptive.[29] It also is less comprehensive, despite its bulk, than Miller's.

As John Gable ably put it in his review, some readers will probably view the work "as a balanced biography. Others will find it an essentially negative biography that neglects important aspects of Roosevelt's public life and presents a picture of TR's character and personality that seems at odds with the views of those who knew him best." He points out that the coverage of the Roosevelt presidency is "highly selective and lacks depth. The meat inspection law is discussed but not the more important Pure Food and Drug Act, though TR signed both measures on the same day, June 30, 1906. Brands devotes approximately three pages to TR's amusing and futile fight for simplified spelling, but finds no space for TR's long and successful battle for employers' liability legislation. The coverage of TR's work with natural resources is lacking in specifics and is wrong-headed."[30]

Other reviews of *The Last Romantic* have tended to be favorable. Even Gable makes it clear that the book is well written, and that Brands evidently displays "an affection for the old Rough Rider, and he clearly admires Roosevelt." He thinks it destined to be "a classic TR biography." Perhaps. It may be, though, that many readers will prefer Miller, or possibly the forthcoming volume by Edmund Morris that will compliment his Pulitzer Prize-winning treatment of TR's pre-presidential years.[31]

REVISITING THE LEGACY

The public may have lost the sense of just what Theodore Roosevelt was, frequently seeing him (if at all) in caricature – all flashing teeth with shouts of "bully," and "charge." This is a part of the picture, but only a part. Serious students of the office now are more inclined to accept a portrait of the Bull Moose as a complicated figure who contributed considerably to the presidency, and to American life. He was, for example, an honored historian, an internationally-accepted expert on song birds and big game animals, and a prolific author.

The picture that John Milton Cooper, Jr. presents, in his fascinating comparison of TR with his opponent Woodrow Wilson, is certainly closer to the truth than the snide dismissals of a Pringle. Cooper points out that TR exploited the "varied dimensions of his office to a dgree that has never since been fully matched. His redecoration and renaming of the White House foreshadowed an interest in government promotion of the arts that had not existed since the 1920s." TR himself boasted that he gave the country the "most beautiful coinage since the days of Hellenistic Greece," he successfully sought funds for scientific research and cultural projects, he "cared deeply about the public impact of art and literature, and he pursued the Renaissance political ideal of "the state as a work of art."[32] No one, including Jefferson, presented a broader vision.

Roositer's view of TR as one who "contributed a great deal to the office," as "a brilliant molder and interpreter of public opinion," who gloried in the White House as a bully pulpit, and who "scored several genuine triumphs as leader of Congress," is closer to today's opinion than was the negativism of earlier decades. "Who can say that he did not act grandly," Rossiter asked, "when he started the fleet off around the world and left it up to Congress to buy enough coal to bring it back?"[33] Or, one might add, how could a critic such as Brands fail to recognize the grandeur of TR's brilliant action of behalf of the environment when he preserved more than 17,000,000 acres of public land for the future by setting it aside – thus keeping it free from development – just prior to signing legislation stripping him of the power to do so?[34]

Brands looked askance at what he called the "midnight acres." Although he admitted that Roosevelt was sincere in his desire to foster conservation, and although he conceded both that resources were "fast being lost to the public" and that Congress failed "to overturn his coup," he nonetheless wrote that TR had "fooled no one. It was patent," Brands said, "that, Congress having outmaneuvered him, he was fighting a spirited rearguard action."[35]

Blum, in the 1950s, identified some of the discomfort with Roosevelt that critics such as Pringle had encouraged. "Today's insouciant critics," he noted, "censure as quixotic adolescence or dangerous diversion the intensity of act and feeling they no longer share." But, "as his motion was forceful, so his standards were high. In that combination Roosevelt had faith. By positive government he sought to promote national strength and to assure to each individual unfettered opportunity for realizing the dignity and the satisfactions of honest work. Whatever his shortcomings, his habit of action had enduring value. He made a virtue of dutiful vitality applied in an age of vigor and confidence. In a more troubled time the world learns painfully again the need for deciding firmly what is right and laboring assiduously to achieve it."

The shifts in attitude toward Theodore Roosevelt through the years to some extent have come full circle, reflecting Blum much more than Pringle. They reflect the process by which the public and scholars evaluate presidents. That process not only mirrors the trends in the thought of the day, but clearly can be susceptible to well-crafted arguments, however ill-founded.

The lesson is clear. Critical interpretation is crucial. It is vital to evaluate the actual record, rather than to rely solely – or even primarily – upon secondary interpretations of that record. There is more at stake than the reputation of any given president. At stake is the future direction of the presidency itself, which will be influenced – inevitably and indelibly – by interpretations of the performance of those who have come before.

NOTES

[1] *Life* XXV (1 November 1948), pp. 65-66.
[2] *New York Times Magazine* (29 July 1962).
[3] See Thomas A. Bailey, *Presidential Greatness* (New York: Appleton-Century, 1966).
[4] Arthur M. Schlesinger, Jr., "Rating the Presidents: Washington to Clinton," *Political Science Quarterly* 12:2 (1997), pp. 179-190; quotation on p. 181.
[5] Ibid., p. 185.
[6] Reported in "How Historians Rank the Presidents Now," in *The Washingtonian* (April 2000), p. 55.
[7] Schlesinger, Jr., pp. 179-190.
[8] Ibid., p. 182.
[9] Ibid, p. 183.
[10] See Fred I. Greenstein, *The Hidden-Hand Presidency: Eisenhower as Leader* (New York: Basic Books, 1982); among other relevant studies see Robert Murray and Tim Blessing, *Greatness in the White House: Rating the Presidents from George Washington through Ronald Reagan*, 2nd ed (University Park: Pennsylvania State University press, 1994).
[11] See, e.g., Brooks D. Simpson, "Continuous Hammering and Mere Attrition: Lost Cause Critics and the Military Reputation of Ulysses S. Grant," in Carl Gallagher and Alan T. Nolan, eds. *The Myth of the Lost Reconstruction Presidents* (Lawrence: University Press of Kansas, 1998), and his biography of Grant, *Ulysses S. Grant: Triumph Over Adversity, 1822-1865* (Boston: Houghton-Mifflin, 2000). See also Geoffrey Perret, *Ulysses S. Grant: Soldier and President* (New York: Random House, 1997).

12. Forrest McDonald, *The American Presidency: An Intellectual History* (Lawrence: University Press of Kansas, 1994), p. 468.
13. Bailey, pp. 306-307.
14. Ibid, p. 308.
15. Wilfred Binkley, *The Power of the Presidency* (Garden City, NY: Doubleday, Doran, 1937), p. 267.
16. Clinton Rossiter, *The American Presidency*, rev. ed. (New York: Harcourt, Brace and World, 1960), pp. 143-144.
17. Ibid, pp. 103-104.
18. Bailey, p. 308.
19. William H. Harbaugh, *The Life and Times of Theodore Roosevelt* (New York: Oxford University Press, 1975), p. 428.
20. John A. Gable, *The Bull Moose Years: Theodore Roosevelt and the Progressive Party* (Port Washington, NY: Kennikat Press, 1978), p. 250.
21. See Max J. Skidmore, "The Theodore Roosevelt International Highway," *Theodore Roosevelt Association Journal* XXII: 1 & 2 (Fall 1997), pp. 15-19 and "Portland to Portland: The Theodore Roosevelt International Highway," SCA Journal 17: 1 (Spring 1999), pp. 14-21; see also Max J. Skidmore, "Remembering TR: North Dakota and the Theodore Roosevelt International Highway," *North Dakota History* 67: 1 (Spring 2000), pp. 23-25.
22. See Pringle, Theodore Roosevelt.
23. Arthur M. Schlesinger, Jr., *A Life in the Twentieth Century* (New York: Houghton-Mifflin, 2000), p. 264.
24. John Morton Blum, *The Republican Roosevelt* (New York: Antheneum, 1973), p. 161.
25. Harbough.
26. Miller, *Theodore Roosevelt: A Life* (New York: William Morrow, 1992).
27. Ibid., p. 391.
28. Ibid., pp. 392-393.
29. Brands.
30. John Allen Gable, "The Last Romantic," review in *Theodore Roosevelt Association Journal* XXII: 3 (1998), p. 18.
31. Edmund Morris, *the Rise of Theodore Roosevelt* (New York: Ballantine Books, 1979).
32. John Milton Cooper, Jr., *The Warrior and the Priest* (Cambridge, MA: Belknap Press, 1983), pp. 86-87.
33. Rossiter, pp. 102-103.
34. In 1907, responding to their own hostility to TR as well as to lobbying from timber, mining, and utility companies, some Western members of his own party attached a rider to a Department of Agriculture appropriation bill that removed Roosevelt's power in six states to create new forest reserves or to extend existing ones without the express approval of Congress; vetoing the act would have destroying the administration's timber program.
35. Brands, pp. 623-624.

Chapter 14

THE EMERGING SCHOLARLY CONSENSUS ON PRESIDENTIAL LEADERSHIP: A NEW REALISM, AN OLD IDEALISM

Raymond Tatalovich and Thomas S. Engeman

AN EMERGING CONSENSUS

The original Federalist conception of the presidential office provoked fears in the anti-Federalists that ultimately yielded a Whig philosophy of executive restraint. Yet that simple political divide does not do justice to the various philosophical permutations that have characterized the executive-legislative relationship over the course of American history. There have been at least six shifts in intellectual opinion about the role of the president in the political order.[1] In our memory, the most lasting imprints have been characterized as the heroic or "idealized" president as well as the "textbook" presidency, given its prominence in academic textbooks.[2] Spanning the 1930s to the 1960s, an early propagandist was British political scientist, Harold Laski, a left-wing Labourite who viewed FDR as an historic figure in American class politics. But Roosevelt's style and policies also influenced such home-grown liberals as the historian Arthur M. Schlesinger, Jr., James MacGregor Burns, and especially Richard E. Neustadt.[3] They favored activist presidents who championed liberal domestic programs, who would tame a Congress viewed as a bastion of localism and conservatism, and who possessed the requisite political skills to engage the policy process, given the inadequacy of constitutionally-based powers. In sum, the president must be central to our political universe.[4]

It has been over 40 years since Neustadt penned his Machiavellian study of presidential power and, though most of us still pay homage to his classic statement, many of the leading presidential scholars are abandoning the tenets of Neustadtian orthodoxy. The myth of the "heroic" presidency has given way to an emerging consensus which blends a new realism with an old idealism. The new realism is that the president is no master of Congress, but rather one, albeit important, political actor in the legislative process. The old idealism is a renewed appreciation for the Framers' keen sense for why the separation of powers was essential both for liberty and good government. Arguably the most holistic statement of this emerging consensus was the 1985 award-winning *The Personal President* by Theodore J. Lowi, but no one scholar can produce a working consensus.[5] Lowi was assisted by many presidency scholars who represent a variety of traditions and approaches: some normative, others historicist, many empiricist and behavioral. We identify four inter-related themes that characterize this emerging consensus: (1) expectations gap and the dangers of plebiscitory leadership, (2) divided government and policy-making, (3) the ennobled Congress, and (4) presidential constraints.

Expectations Gap

Most fundamental, we believe, is the belief that an "expectations gap" exists between presidential power and presidential performance. Waterman and his associates claim that this thesis "has been a mainstay of the presidency literature for more than thirty years."[6] White House commentators long suspected that his official responsibilities are more than a match for one man, going back to Laski and two decades later to Herman Finer[7], but that truism was no rallying point to raise normative objections against heroic leadership. A contemporary example will suffice. Two decades ago, Thomas E. Cronin diagnosed this "paradox" of the presidency, that we "ask our presidents to raise hopes, to educate, to inspire" though "few presidents in recent times have been able to keep their promises and fulfill their intentions," but that pretty much ended his commentary.[8] Like Cronin, therefore, previous authors did not even hint that the expectations gap held dire implications for the regime.

It was Lowi who dramatized the dangers to republicanism from the mismatch between presidential promises and performance. Some academics embraced Neustadt, he says, for "the selfish reason" of justifying John F. Kennedy but many also "sincerely accepted the redefinition of democratic theory with the presidency at its core."[9] By redefinition, Lowi means our collective abandoning of representation as the basis for governmental legitimacy in favor of a "new social contract" based on service delivery. "They [the people] have invested fully in it [the presidency], they have witnessed the vesting of the 'capacity to govern' in the office, they have approved, and they now look for delivery on all the promises as their measure of democracy and legitimacy." Beware, however, that "[t]here are built-in barriers to president's delivering on their promises, and the unlikely occasion of one doing so would only engender another round of new policies, with new responsibilities and new demands for help."[10] Worse yet are its effects on the incumbent. "The desperate search is not longer for the good life but for the most effective presentation of appearances. This is a pathology because it escalates the rhetoric at home, ratcheting expectations upward notch by notch, and fuels adventurism abroad, in a world where the cost of failure can be annihilation."[11]

What Lowi did was take to its logical conclusion what Jeffrey Tulis identified as the "rhetorical presidency" and why its workings are at odds with original intent. In his highly celebrated work[12], Tulis distinguishes three eras in American history: the "old" way of the Founding, the "middle" way personified by Theodore J. Roosevelt, and the "new" way of Woodrow Wilson. Of utmost concern to the Framers was majority tyranny from below and demagoguery from above. The proscription against policy speeches aimed at the populace was never breached until President Andrew Jackson, who nearly paid the ultimate political price of impeachment. Roosevelt's moderation was put asunder by Wilson who "[b]y justifying Roosevelt's practice with a new theory that would make popular rhetoric routine, Wilson would transform the bully pulpit and Roosevelt's America."[13] Wilson was the first "modern" president, and surely the country is the worse because of it. Because separated powers are "the central defect" of our regime, Wilson's solution was the president as "leader-interpreter" who receives "his authority independently through a mandate from the people."[14] The downside of rhetorical leadership was illustrated by Wilson's ill-fated popular campaign for the League of Nations and the 1960s War on Poverty because Johnson "not only produced a hastily packaged program, his clear victory ensured that he and not Congress would be blamed if the program failed. And fail it did." For Tulis, such leadership "is more deleterious than beneficial to American politics" because rhetorical leadership involves routine appeals to public opinion.[15]

Others cite the specter of an expectations gap as a drag on presidential credibility. Bond and Fleisher argue that one result of rising public expectations is "often the perception of a failed presidency,"[16] while Charles O. Jones offers these humbling words: "The American presidency carries a burden of lofty expectations that are simply not warranted by the political or constitutional basis of the office."[17] Those concerns are given added weight by Samuel Kernell as well as Paul Brace and Barbara Hinckley. Kernell coined the phrase "going public" to describe "new strategies of presidential leadership" that involve "appealing to the American public" to support his incumbency and his policies.[18] Kernell is troubled about "the deleterious side effects of public activity on bargaining" though a "more damaging" consequence is that "public discussion tends to harden negotiating positions as both sides posture as much to rally support as to impress the other side."[19]

Modeling presidential popularity has become a fetish (usually devoid of normative issues), but Paul Brace and Barbara Hinckley give serious thought to values.[20] Where once presidents disregarded public opinion to do what was right (Truman), today "[a]t best, there is an uneasy balance between popularity and the tasks Americans expect a president to do" and "[a]t worse, the popular basis of government has slipped somehow, and democracy has been turned on its head" because presidents "govern in the name of the public, using poll reports and other devices as substitutes for more basic opinions and beliefs." Elections no longer bestow legitimacy given that the "electoral mandate is continually updated" as a "monthly [polling] referendum" on the president's performance. Which brings them back to the expectations gap: "We thus find an idealized portrait of the office that contrasts sharply with real-world events. This contrast supplies both power and limits to individuals in office: power insofar as they inherit the unrealistic expectations, limits when these expectations cannot be fulfilled."[21] Is there escape from the dire implications of Brace and Hinckley? One palliative is to achieve "a new realism" in our expectations regarding popular support, and hopefully "increased consciousness on the part of the presidents, the news media, and the public" would help foster this new realism.[22]

If a bit myopic, a more sure-footed resolution is offered by Jeffrey E. Cohen, who also confronts the dilemma over whether presidents can lead but also follow public opinion.[23] Studying this dynamic through the problem identification and position taking, policy formulation, and policy legitimation stages of the policy process, he concludes that "[p]residents will be symbolically responsive to the public when doing so does not constrain substantive choices about policies; however, responsiveness to the public declines as decisions become more substantive."[24] The presidency, Cohen believes, is "arguably the most democratic" yet "the least policy responsive" branch of government, and this "logic of responsiveness" – the gap between symbol and substance – "may be one cause of the high degree of public cynicism toward government during the past three decades." Which returns us to the expectations gap thesis: "One implication may be the alienation and cynicism of the public from the political process because its expectations are not met in reality."[25]

Divided Government

For most of the early twentieth century the norm of "unified" party government deeply influenced major party theorists, like V.O. Key, Pendleton Herring, and E.E. Schattschneider, and led to a love affair between political science and the British-type responsible party doctrine.[26] How ever, since 1968 the normal state of affairs has been "divided government," most typically a Democratic Congress facing a Republican president, and this new reality spawned a cottage industry among congressional researchers seeking to understand its causes and consequences. No behavioralist would suggest that divided government was a "rational" response by the electorate, that is, until Morris Fiorina dared a "purposeful" explanation that voters acted strategically to balance a conservative Republican executive against a liberal Democratic legislature to assure moderate policy outcomes. In doing so, Fiorina answered the normative indictment against our separated regime by James L. Sundquist. So emotionally charged was this debate, wrote Fiorina, that "divided government has the potential to become the new organizing principle of American politics research in the 1990s."[27] More germane for us is how this debate was joined by David R. Mayhew and Charles O. Jones.

Mayhew's *Divided We Govern* was honored as a singular contribution to presidency studies.[28] In it, he challenged Sundquist-styled critics who attributed political deadlock and policy stalemate to divided government, saying that "one of political science's best-known axioms" is that political party is "'the indispensable instrument that [brings] cohesion and unity, and hence effectiveness, to the government as a whole by linking the executive and legislative branches in a bond of common interest.'" This conventional wisdom Mayhew demonstrates "wrong, or at least mostly or probably wrong," based on his analysis during 1947-1990 of 31 high-profile congressional investigations and 267 pieces of major legislation. To the question of whether more oversight and lawmaking activity occurs during periods of unified or divided government, the results indicated "'very little difference'" though the normative implications stretched far beyond that simple conclusion. Especially telling was that "notable American laws tend to pass by broad majorities, regardless of conditions of party control," meaning they pass with two-thirds and bipartisan support. Mayhew also attacked orthodoxy by arguing that unified party rule "can foster a pathological enactment logic all its own" and, like Tulis, showed this disfunctionalism with LBJ's Great Society as being "a 'politics of haste' in which 'solutions were often devised and rushed into law before the problems were understood.'"[29]

Since Mayhew was preoccupied with debunking the party theorists, it was left to Charles O. Jones to focus specifically on the presidential role.[30] Jones grounded his analysis in an issue as old as presidency studies – which branch had the more decisive role in shaping major legislation? Though Mayhew barely touched on this question, what he said puts him and Jones on the same page. While the Fair Deal, New Frontier, Great Society, and Reaganomics may sound more impressive than the domestic agendas of Eisenhower, Nixon, Ford, Carter, and Bush, Mayhew reminds us that Truman "largely failed," Kennedy "did little better," and Johnson "of course succeeded" but "so did Reagan," whereupon he favorably quotes from a previous work of Charles Jones: "'Very few Presidents can claim legislative triumphs that are truly turning points in domestic policy.'"[31] To proceed with Jones, the first lines of his 1994 volume set the tone: "The President is not the presidency. The presidency is not the government. Ours is not a presidential system." Jones deliberately begins "with these starkly negative themes as partial correctives to the more popular interpretations of the United States government as presidency-centered,"[32] but his rebuttal is grounded in 28 legislative enactments (from Mayhew's data) – 16 under divided and 12 under unified party control. For each, Jones details step-by-step the lawmaking process and finds that there are both instances of "presidential preponderance" (N=6) and "congressional preponderance" (N=7) were fewer than cases of "joint presidential-congressional influence" (N=15) to indicate "that presidency-centered analysis of lawmaking is misleading if it conveys the impression of presidential dominance, either as an empirical fact or as a normative conclusion growing out of the principles upon which the system is built." Jones came away "quite in awe" of the American regime and, though not perfect, believing that ours is "the most intricate lawmaking system in the world. It will not be made better through simplification. Preponderance of one branch over the other should be a cause for concern, not celebration."[33]

Ennobled Congress

To denigrate the presidency-centered model is to elevate the political significance of Congress. Some years ago Michael Mezey observed that congressional and presidential scholars hold very different views of executive-legislative relations.[34] Presidential scholars assume the White House can make demands on Congress. Congress scholars know that Representatives and Senators are subjected to many political forces. This bit of wisdom has been affirmed in empirical analysis by Edwards, Bond and Fleisher, and Peterson.

At the Margins updated an earlier work by Edwards, with similar conclusions that all three presidential resources (party, popularity, skills) operate "at the margins" of legislative leadership.[35] Party, says Edwards, "is unlikely to provide the basis for the direction of major change" and, even worse, "[p]ublic support is not a dependable resource for the president, and it is not one that he can easily create when he needs it to influence Congress."[36] Based on his subjective assessment of legislative skills, Edwards tried but "failed to reveal systematic evidence of their impact on presidential support" so "[i]t seems reasonable to assert that legislative skills are not at the core of presidential leadership of Congress...[since] [t]heir utility is at the margins, in exploiting rather than creating opportunities for change." Edwards' grand conclusion was that since presidents "must largely play with the hands" dealt them by voters' electoral decisions and citizens evaluations of his performance, "[t]hey are rarely in a position to augment substantially their resources. They operate at the margins as facilitators rather than as directors of change."[37] Edwards' formulation of the president as "facilitator" of the legislative process has gained wide currency among his peers, including Bond and Fleisher.[38]

Bond and Fleisher incorporated presidential variables (skill and popularity) within a "Congress-centered" model of voting behavior. Like Edwards, they ask under what conditions do presidents succeed on floor votes in Congress.[39] Where the "prevailing perspective" is to emphasize presidential variables (skill and popularity) "as the key to understanding presidential-congressional relations," they believe that "none of the[se] linkage agents are exceptionally strongly" and, again, the hidden-hand of electoral forces is at work. Their central thesis "is that congressional support for the president is mainly a function of members' [of Congress] partisan and ideological predispositions operating within constraints imposed by the institutional structure of Congress. Between elections, the basic parameters of presidential-congressional relations set by these political and institutional forces in Congress are relatively fixed. Although presidential variables...may influence success at the margins, there is little that the president can do to move members of Congress very far from their basic political predispositions."[40]

After verifying that the "party linkage...is relatively weak," Bond and Fleisher proceed to assess other variables. Here the findings "are consistent and clear: the effects of the president's public approval on success in Congress are limited" because "the president does not consistently win more votes nor does he consistently receive higher levels of support from the party factions when he is popular than when he is unpopular." In judging legislative skills, they are forced to conclude that "the evidence...provides little support for the theory that the president's perceived leadership skills are associated with success on roll call votes in Congress.[41] At base, although "presidency-centered explanations have dominated much of the literature," analyses "of presidential success on roll call votes...tend to support the Congress-centered thesis rather than the one emphasizing presidential variables." They chide Neustadt who correctly disparaged the ability of parties to fuse the separated powers but who oversold the impact of presidential leadership or popularity. "In fact, the forces that Neustadt stressed as the antidote for weak parties are even less successful in linking the president and Congress than are weak parties."[42]

Another influential study by Mark Peterson also confronts the "presidency-centered perspective," which he calls "the most pervasive interpretation of...executive-legislative relations," in favor of a "tandem-institutions perspective" that offers "a more realistic prescriptive and descriptive appraisal of the symbiotic relationship" between the president and Congress.[43] In looking at the level of congressional-presidential conflict over legislative enactments, Peterson like Edwards plus Bond and Fleisher argues that the political hand a president plays is largely dealt to him by "pure" (institutional) and "malleable" (political and economic) contexts. Any presidential influence over the legislative process is a function of the "policy" context–agenda-setting–though hardly the decisive factor. "Knowing something about the condition of major political institutions, the political position of the president and the opposition, the state of the economy, and the nature of the president's programs, we can say quite a bit about why Congress responded to the president by affirmation or condemnation, or by something in between."[44]

Presidential Constraints

This theme in presidency studies is not exactly novel. It was a mainstay of "histories" written by JFK staffers, including a well-know monograph by speech-writer Theodore C. Sorensen.[45] Unlike the arguments of those JFK apologists, the catalogue of presidential constraints today are more defined by the forces of history and globalism than the dynamics of White House decision-making. We proceed from micro- to macro-level constraints.

One inherent constraint is personality. Neustadt wrote his classic to rebut Edward Corwin's legalistic view of executive power, but one especially prophetic insight from Corwin was that truly gifted presidents were few and far between. That thought was rejected wholesale by Neustadt who countered that presidents should be professional politicians with a keen political antennae for maximizing their power options. The White House was no place for amateurs (namely Eisenhower, whom Corwin admired), and presumably we would have no difficulty recruiting talented individuals for the highest office.

It took a scholar with the prestige of Fred Greenstein to challenge those stereotypes about Dwight D. Eisenhower[46], and to single-handedly inaugurate a revisionist scholarship that has come to pervade the presidency studies.[47] Ideology played no small part in how Ike was portrayed, says Greenstein, since "most writers on the presidency viewed him through the lens of his 1950s liberal critics as an aging hero who reigned more than he ruled and lacked the energy, motivation, and political know-how to have a significant impact on events." In short, to those commentators Eisenhower exemplified "how *not* to conduct the presidency."[48] The key to understanding Eisenhower, Greenstein asserts, was his unique style of "hidden-hand" leadership, which he doubted "many other presidents capable of adopting the full Eisenhower style," though one element – his organizational sense (see below) – may be worthy of emulation.[49]

A sympathetic critique of Neustadt was penned by Barbara Kellerman. Seeking to understand the "practice of leadership" using case studies of decision-making, Kellerman agrees with Neustadt's presumption that presidential power is political, not prerogative, though her focus was limited to understanding the "skill" of incumbents.[50] Since leadership is conceptualized as a transactional (two-way) process, Kellerman inquiries about the modes of influence used by the leader to solicit cooperation and, in turn, what motivates followers to accept his lead? Yes, personality matters but too few have the requisite personality and, unlike the heroic school, Kellerman dissents from any JFK hero-worship by declaring "the best politicians, and the most effective directive leaders, were Lyndon Johnson and Ronald Reagan. Both were other-directed in the behavior and inner-directed in their rather fierce determination to see a very particular policy become law."[51]

If Franklin D. Roosevelt was the ideal-type heroic president, most commentators now doubt that we will see his analogue anytime soon. A celebrated study of presidential "character" by James David Barber affirmed, apart from the fact that maladjusted "active-negative" types do get elected, that no one-to-one relationship exists between personality type and presidential leadership.[52] For example, a well-received psychological study of William Jefferson Clinton argues that, despite considerable politically gifts, Clinton nonetheless suffers from serious character flaws.[53]

Another constraint is time. It is accepted wisdom that the secular decline in presidential popularity coupled with the mid-term congressional losses by his party implies that any legislative victories must come shortly after the inauguration. While advocates of the heroic presidency have elevated this hypothesis into holy grail, through repeated references to FDR's One Hundred Days, only recently has empirical analysis showed what common sense implied: the "crisis" of the Great Depression caused an outpouring of legislation unmatched by any administration since.[54] Time is an "internal" as opposed to "external" constraint on presidential leadership, according to Paul Light.[55] Best known is Light's hypothesis that the ebb and flow of these variables create two distinct cycles: "The *cycle of decreasing influence* appears as time, energy, and congressional support drop. The *cycle of increasing effectiveness* enters as information and expertise grow."[56] In other words, to the plain speaking advice – move it or lose it – Light would argue that things are not so simple. In fact Light contrasted the "No Win Presidency" of the 1980s as decidedly weaker than the presidency of the 1960s, mainly because newly elected presidents are ill-equipped to define and promote a policy agenda when their political capital is greatest whereas later in their term, when presidents more fully understand the governing process, it is now too late to promote decisive domestic initiatives.

Thus, counsels Light, the "structure of incentives" must be changed to reward presidents "for patience, not haste; for planning, not short-term success" and, therefore, unless "Congress, the public, the media, even political scientists are willing to wait for careful policy, the President must respond to our impatience."[57] Shades of the expectations gap, with his calls for re-education to permit our presidents to act with rational deliberation, not forced dispatch, when defining a policy agenda.

A third constraint is organization. When the Brownlow Committee proclaimed that the president "needs help," its advice that six presidential assistants be installed in a new Executive Office of the President (EOP) commenced the institutionalized presidency. Long before EOP there were attempts by presidents (since Taft) to improve their bureaucratic "span of control" through reorganization plans[58] most notably Nixon's failed effort to consolidate agencies into four super-departments, but scholars also have come to recognize the additional dimension of EOP expansion and the perplexing problem of coordinating White House-Cabinet relationships. The "swelling" of the White House mini-bureaucracy under the Nixon was not such a departure in what has been styled the "presidential branch" of government.[59] Now most pundits take for granted that the EOP has become a managerial problem in its own right. Early observations that Democrats pursued a different managerial strategy (spokes of the wheel) than Republicans (hierarchical) have yielded more detailed and nuanced portraits of White House staffing.[60]

According to Greenstein, Eisenhower's ultimate legacy was his "keenness as an organizer of the advice he received" because "[r]igorous staff work and systematic institutional back-up for policy making is persistently lacking in modern presidencies, as is the teamwork that is an informal offshoot of this procedure."[61] Eisenhower was omitted from Warshaw's analysis of White-House-Cabinet relations but, in the years since, only Ronald Reagan was successful at creating true "power-sharing," which she argues is the only appropriate remedy to deep-seated structural conflicts between presidential staffers and departmental secretaries.[62] Reagan is known for his ideological screening of judicial appointees, but the most prevalent ("criteria-driven") approach to recruiting Supreme Court nominees was first employed by Eisenhower, and his appointees "may rank historically as among the finest group ever to be appointed by one president."[63]

Eisenhower also gets high marks from the most comprehensive study of the White House since Leonard White chronicled the administrative Founding.[64] Contrary to the Neustadtian stereotype, Charles Walcott and Karen Hult claim that "by the time Lyndon Johnson left office, much of what Eisenhower had introduced to the White House Office remained – and persists today." As to impact, they "repeatedly observed" that "the Eisenhower system was far more diverse and flexible than the charicatured 'military model' its detractors envisioned. Indeed, given his governance duties, [chief of staff Sherman] Adams could scarcely have afforded to be simply the rigid martinet he was sometimes portrayed as being."[65]

Walcott and Hult merge the previously dominant paradigms, based on structural attributes or (presidential) personality needs, into a more inclusive "problem-contingency" analysis borrowed from organizational theory. They proceed "from the premise that staff structures emerge primarily from strategic responses by presidents to environmental demands" and then "add an organizational dimension. Once organizational structures are in place, even in such volatile settings as the ones the White House faces, structures can exercise an independent effect on the subsequent recognition and definition of problems that impinge from the external environment." In sum, "as the White House becomes more organizationally complex, that complexity itself shapes perceptions of and responses to the environment, and often *constrains* presidential choices" (italics added).[66] Their multifaceted analysis identified no fewer than seven distinctive "governance structures" within the Executive Office of the President from Hoover to Johnson. "It is crucial to underscore at the outset that hierarchy [power flowing from top to down] is by no means the only structural form that has characterized the White House. Of course, the White House Office as a whole must be viewed as a hierarchy, with the president at its apex. Within that hierarchical skeleton, however, a diverse array of subordinate structures has emerged."[67]

Other macro-constraints on presidential leadership are the forces of history and globalization. Both Schlesingers had argued that "cycles" of American history alternate between periods of liberalism and conservatism[68], but their crude formulations have been refined in more current scholarship[69], with the most ambitious historicist interpretation authored by Steven Skowronek.[70] Skowronek draws the line with scholars who magnify the importance of the contemporary presidency, notably Neustadt whose "periodization of presidential history – his distinction between modern and premodern contexts for the exercise of power – introduced a sense of coherence...[into leadership studies, but] "[t]he notion of a prior age when presidents did not *have* to be leaders...is nothing more than a conceit of modern times." What impressed Skowronek was that presidents "widely celebrated for their mastery of American politics" (e.g., Lincoln and Roosevelt) were immediately preceded by others "judged politically incompetent" (e.g., Buchanan and Hoover).[71] To bring rationality to this discontinuity, Skowronek differentiates between political time (when an ideological regime exists) and secular (or chronological) time.

The key analytical questions are whether an incumbent *accommodates* or *opposes* the prevailing regime and whether that regime is politically *robust* or *vulnerable*. But there is a further complication due to the passing of secular time, which bears on "the progressive development of the institutional resources and governing responsibilities of the executive office and thus to the repertoire of powers the presidents of a particular period have at their disposal to realize their preferences in action." Thus, secular time poses obstacles to fundamental reforms since the "repertoire of [presidential] powers" may be inadequate to the institutional "thickening" that allows "other actors to mount more formidable resistance to their [presidents'] will."[72]

Though Skowronek was impressed by the Reagan Revolution, nonetheless our "[f]aith in the transformative capacities of the presidency seemed to be giving rise to ever greater expectations and ever more profound frustrations" absent any serious effort to understand "those capacities in a systematic way." Even Reagan could not fully impact the political regime at an optimal moment in political time, when the presidency was launching an ideological assault on a "vulnerable" (liberal) regime.[73] Looking ahead, it is not too extravagant to suggest that Clinton and both Bushes were trapped in political time. One reason for the institutional "thickening" of which Skowronek speaks is the decline of political party, the subject of Sidney Milkis' work.[74]

At the electoral level, the evidence seems clear: growing ranks of independents, weakened loyalty of partisans, greater split-ticket voting, and the rise of insurgent third-party candidates. Yet there is also an organizational side to the atrophy of parties and, on this score, if parties are in decline, then Milkis places the blame on Franklin D. Roosevelt (and today's liberal Democrats). Milkis describes our party system in "transformation" and hints that the New Deal was the realignment to end realignments because FDR conceived of welfarism in "rights" terms. His reforms were dedicated to liberating the president from the constraints of partisan politics but, in so doing, also weakened the president's institutional base of support. Thus, presidents now subjected to the programmatic demands of the post-New Deal era "have been encouraged to rely on plebiscitary politics and unilateral executive action to circumvent the regular procedures of constitutional government, as well as formal partisan channels."[75]

Milkis' insight was that "the New Deal did not simply replace constitutional government with an administrative state; rather, the programmatic rights of the New Deal constituted the beginning of an administrative constitution, which was shielded from the uncertainties of public opinion, political parties, and elections." Of course the coming of the administrative state will affect the quality of democratic life, which troubles Milkis for many reasons, one being that weakened parties and executive hegemony will exalt "the *personal* responsibility of the president, thus making *collective* partisan appeals less meaningful in the eyes of the voters."[76]

We close with British political scientist Richard Rose, who directly raises the question of governing capacity.[77] Rose argued that traditional presidents "had little to do" while the moderns "had a lot to do at home and abroad" but today's "postmodern" presidents "may have too much expected" of them. The difference now is that presidents "can no longer dominate the international system" since "[i]nterdependence characterizes an international system in which no nation is the hegemonic power. The President is the leader of a very influential nation, but other nations are influential too." The mega-constraint arising from globalization is fairly obvious: "A postmodern President must start from the assumption: *To govern is to cooperate*. A President has always needed to cooperate with Congress in order to succeed in a constitutional system that separates powers. What is novel is that a postmodern President must cooperate with foreign governments to achieve major economic and national security goals. Cooperation requires a mutuality of interests between nations."[78]

The problem is magnified because U.S. presidents are not especially trained in diplomacy, as Rose underscores that "[w]hat it takes to become President has nothing to do with what it takes to be President" and, even more troubling, "[w]hat it takes to become President actually makes it more difficult to be a successful postmodern President."[79] Any prospect for success involves facing three imperatives: going public, going Washington, and going international. Any president "would like to take charge" but that is easier said than done, because post-modern presidents cannot calibrate foreign opinion or, for that matter, the views of the American people or official Washington, nor can presidents control events that happen worldwide and, worst yet, actions taken to appease one audience, like domestic constituencies, may anger international elites. Is there any solution to Rose's "responsibility gap" between these global challenges and the limitations of the Oval office? Minimally Rose hopes that postmodern presidents can avoid the pitfalls of the "biggest illusion," namely "the belief that we can turn the clock back to the era when Franklin D. Roosevelt created the modern Presidency, and Dwight D. Eisenhower could rely on American wealth and military force to sustain a global *Pax Americana*."[80]

A New Consensus

This corpus of contemporary presidency literature embodies four themes: expectations gap, divided government, ennobled Congress, and presidential constraints. The first and second themes are of recent vintage, reflecting new trends in political life. Yet what is telegraphed by all four themes is that mainstream scholars now explicitly repudiate the myopic teachings of the heroic presidency advocates. The Neustadtian paradigm has been challenged because his idealized view was largely shaped by Franklin D. Roosevelt, but FDR is disconnected from today's political reality because of his unique "crisis" presidency. The age-old adage that presidents propose and Congresses dispose would not be accepted by the Framers, but at least we contemporaries have come to terms with the fact that sometimes presidents propose, other times Congress proposes, but that at all times Congress must acquiesce. Inter-branch agreement would seem virtually impossible given the prognoses of deadlock, gridlock, and stalemate that critics argue is a necessary byproduct of divided government. Yet things appear to get done, and curiously it fell to those empiricists among us to confirm the rightful place of Congress in the legislative process, even as the normatively inclined were bemoaning the separated system.

The president is a mortal with all the failings and potentialities–writ large–of any person. Personality is a frail quality, and there is no ready political recipe for recruiting the right person at the opportune time in history. Besides, we are humbled in our knowledge that even a presidential tour de force must cope with the inexorable march of time, his lonely status within a huge bureaucracy coupled with a weakened if not dysfunctional party system, and caught in the grips of political time, for better or worse. Beyond our shores lies an ever interconnected, global political and economic system that has replaced the neat dichotomy between international and domestic issues with today's "intermestic" policies like trade, immigration, multi-national corporatism, and global environmentalism.

In all these cross-currents of presidential theory, there is one more theme–so apparent though unstated. Barely has a generation passed without some prominent intellectual–Lord Bryce, Woodrow Wilson, Harold Laski, Herman Finer, James Sundquist, Richard Rose–praising parliamentary government and executive-legislative hegemony as a superior political regime. With the current body of graduate students reading the treatises explored in this essay, we are hopeful that the next generation of presidency scholars will abandon that political mythology to uphold the benefits of a separated system.

Notes

[1] See Scott E. Yenor, Travis S. Cook, and Raymond Tatalovich, "The Normative Study of the Presidency," in Ryan J. Barilleaux, ed., *Presidential Frontiers: Underexplored Issues in White House Politics* (Westport, CT: Praeger, 1998), pp. 3-21. The six intellectual shifts began with the "intended" presidency (Founding), then the "imperiled" (Progressive critique),

"idealized" (FDR), "imperial" (LBJ and Nixon), "impotent" (Ford and Carter), and "inflated" (since Reagan, as we elaborate here).

2   See Thomas E. Cronin, *The State of the Presidency* (Boston: Little, Brown, 1980), 88-90 Cronin developed his thesis of the "textbook" presidency as early as 1970 in a paper delivered to the American Political Science Association.

3   Harold J. Laski, *The American President, An Interpretation* (New York: Harper & Brothers, 1940; one book in The Age of Roosevelt series by Arthur M. Schlesinger, Jr. was *The Coming of the New Deal* (Boston: Houghton Mifflin, 1958); James MacGregor Burns, *Roosevelt: The Lion and the Fox* (New York: Harcourt, Brace and World, 1956); James MacGregor Burns, *Presidential Government* (Boston: Houghton Mifflin, 1965); Richard Neustadt, *Presidential Power* (New York: New American Library, 1960).

4   It is argued that 1940s-1960s liberals disparaged Congress just as 1970s-1980s conservatives did to advance a policy agenda embodied in the executive branch. See Robert J. Spitzer, *President and Congress: Executive Hegemony at the Crossroads of American Government* (Philadelphia: Temple University Press, 1993), pp. 248-249.

5   The problem is to define the boundaries of this contemporary literature, apart from solely our judgment. One noteworthy criteria is that several won the Neustadt Award as the best book on the presidency, awarded yearly by the Presidency Research Section of the American Political Science Association. Of the sixteen books so distinguished through 1985-2000, nine are cited or discussed in this essay. This distinction will be noted alongside each reference.

6   Richard W. Waterman, Robert Wright, and Gilbert St. Clair, *The Image-Is-Everything Presidency* (Boulder, CO: Westview, 1999), p. 4. They cite (p. 8) a "classic article" which attributed the downward spiral of presidential popularity to unrealistic expectations by segments of the electorate. See James A. Stimson, "Public Support for American Presidents: A Cyclical Model," *Public Opinion Quarterly* 40 (Spring 1976): 1-21. A previously Waterman anthology was based explicitly on the expectations gap thesis: Richard W. Waterman, ed., *The Presidency Reconsidered* (Itasca, IL: F.E. Peacock, 1993).

7   Both wanted a degree of collective responsibility, with Laski advocating a secretariat to assist the president and Finer recommending a team of eleven vice presidents. See Laski, *The American President, An Interpretation*, p. 262; Herman Finer, *The Presidency: Crisis and Regeneration* (Chicago: University of Chicago Press, 1960), pp. 303-306.

8   Thomas E. Cronin, *The State of the Presidency*, 2nd ed. (Boston: Little, Brown, 1980), pp. 9-10. A recent volume detailing nine paradoxes argues that "[w]hen Americans realize that the presidency is incapable of dealing with everything well and that democratic politics, in general, is not suited to provide quick answers to every social and economic malaise, then we will be more responsible in the way we judge presidents." Thomas E. Cronin and Michael A. Genovese, *The Paradoxes of the American Presidency* (New York: Oxford University Press, 1998), p. 28.

9   Theodore J. Lowi, *The Personal President: Power Invested, Promise Unfulfilled* (Ithaca, NY: Cornell University Press, 1985), p. 8. His subtitle proclaims the centrality of the expectations gap thesis. Lowi won the Neustadt Award in 1986.

10 Ibid.

11 Ibid.

12 Jeffrey K. Tulis, *The Rhetorical Presidency* (Princeton, NJ: Princeton University Press, 1987).

13 Ibid., p. 116.

14 Ibid., pp. 119-120, 128.

15 Ibid., pp. 158, 172, 181.

16 Jon R. Bond and Richard Fleisher, *The President in the Legislative Arena* (Chicago: University of Chicago Press, 1990), p. 220.

17 Charles O. Jones, *The Presidency in a Separated System* (Washington, DC: The Brookings Institution, 1994), p. 281.

18. Samuel Kernell, *Going Public: New Strategies of Presidential Leadership* (Washington, DC: CQ Press, 1986), p. 1.
19. Ibid., p. 218
20. Paul Brace and Barbara Hinckley, *Follow the Leader: Opinion Polls and the Modern Presidency* (New York: Basic Books, 1992). They won the Neustadt Award in 1993.
21. Ibid., pp. 7, 18-19, 23.
22. Ibid., pp. 176, 178.
23. Jeffrey E. Cohen, *Presidential Responsiveness and Public Policy-Making: The Public and the Policies That Presidents Choose* (Ann Arbor, MI: University of Michigan Press, 1999). Cohen won the Neustadt Award in 1999.
24. Ibid., p. 27.
25. Ibid., pp. 240, 242, 244.
26. Recall how political science once endorsed responsible parties: Committee on Responsible Parties, American Political Science Association, *Toward a More Responsible Two-Party System* (New York: Rinehart, 1950).
27. Morris Fiorina, *Divided Government* (New York: Macmillan, 1992), p. 3. Arguing that Fiorina assumes a too highly sophisticated voter, Gary C. Jacobson counters that divided government results because voters have different reasons for electing Democratic legislators, who cater to their local interests, but Republican executives who safeguard the national well-being. See Gary C. Jacobson, *The Electoral Origins of Divided Government* (Boulder, CO: Westview Press, 1990), p. 106. The indictment of separation of powers that Fiorina and others (see Mayhew and Jones) sought to refute was James L. Sundquist, "Needed: A Political Theory for the New Era of Coalition Government in the United States," *Political Science Quarterly* 103 (1988): 613-635.
28. David R. Mayhew, *Divided We Govern: Party Control, Lawmaking, and Investigations 1946-1990* (New Haven, CT: Yale University Press, 1991). Mayhew won the Neustadt Award in 1992.
29. Ibid., pp. 1, 3, 100, 119, 181.
30. Charles O. Jones, *The Presidency in a Separated System* (Washington, DC: The Brookings Institution, 1994). Jones won the Neustadt Award in 1995
31. Mayhew, *Divided We Govern*, p. 92. Jones' quote was taken from Charles O. Jones, "Ronald Reagan and the U.S. Congress: Visible-Hand Politics," in Charles O. Jones, ed., *The Reagan Legacy: Promise and Performance* (Chatham House, NJ: Chatham House, 1988), p. 37.
32. Jones, *The President in a Separated System*, p. 1.
33. Ibid., pp. 209, 273, 297.
34. Michael L Mezey, "The Legislature, the Executive and Public Policy: The Future Quest for Congressional Power," *Congress & The Presidency* 13 (Spring 1986): 1-20. This article won an award for the Best Paper Published in the First Ten Years of *Congress & The Presidency*.
35. George C. Edwards, III, *At the Margins: Presidential Leadership of Congress* (New Haven, CT: Yale University Press, 1989). His previous work was George C. Edwards, III, *Presidential Influence in Congress* (San Francisco: W.H. Freeman, 1980).
36. Ibid., pp. 100, 143.
37. Ibid., pp. 185, 221, 223-224.
38. This concept was referenced in the last sentence of a new study of landmark enactments that ranked contemporary presidents according to legislative effectiveness: "Presidents can fulfill crucial roles in this process as they exercise their leadership skills and make their strategic choices, but–like Roosevelt–as facilitators rather than directors of policy change." See William W. Lammers and Michael A. Genovese, *The Presidency and Domestic Policy* (Washington, DC: CQ Press, 2000), p. 356-357.
39. Jon R. Bond and Richard Fleisher, *The President in the Legislative Arena* (Chicago: University of Chicago Press, 1990).
40. Ibid., pp. 40-41.

41 Ibid., pp. 120, 194, 218.
42 Ibid., pp. 222-223.
43 Mark A. Peterson, *Legislating Together: The White House and Capitol Hill From Eisenhower to Reagan* (Cambridge, MA: Harvard University Press, 1990), p. 2.
44 Ibid., p. 196.
45 This 1960s perspective was heavily colored by the experience of John F. Kennedy "whose rhetoric proclaimed vast responsibilities for his office" and which led to "inevitably an inclination for those who served in his administration to blame his frustrations, disappointments, and failures on the constraints surrounding the presidency and the President's lack of power to overcome them." See David L. Paletz, "Perspectives on the Presidency," in Norman C. Thomas and Hans W. Baade, eds., "The Institutionalized Presidency," *Law and Contemporary Problems* 35 (Summer 1970), p. 435. The Theodore C. Sorenson monograph was based on his Gino Speranza Lectures at Columbia University: *Decision-Making in the White House: The Olive Brance or The Arrows* (New York: Columbia University Press, 1963). The heart of Sorenson's defense was that "too often a President finds that events or the decisions of others have limited his freedom of maneuver–that, as he makes choices, that door closes behind him" (p. 21). Later he lists these limitations on presidential decision-making: permissibility, available resources, available time, previous commitments, and available information (p. 23).
46 Fred I. Greenstein, *The Hidden-Hand Presidency: Eisenhower as Leader* (New York: Basic Books, 1982).
47 Examples of revisionism that cast doubt on Neustadt's interpretation are: Phillip G. Henderson, *Managing the Presidency: The Eisenhower Legacy–From Kennedy to Reagan* (Boulder, CO: Westview Press, 1988); John W. Sloan, *Eisenhower and the Management of Prosperity* (Lawrence, KS: University Press of Kansas, 1991); Meena Bose, *Shaping and Signaling Presidential Policy: The National Security Decision Making of Eisenhower and Kennedy* (College Station, TX: Texas A&M University Press, 1998).
48 Ibid., pp. 5-6.
49 Ibid., p. 233.
50 Barbara Kellerman, *The Political Presidency: Practice of Leadership from Kennedy Through Reagan* (New York: Oxford University Press, 1984), pp. xi-xii.
51 Ibid., pp. 53, 256.
52 James David Barber, *The Presidential Character: Predicting Performance in the White House* (Englewood Cliffs, NY: Prentice-Hall, 1972). Barber's timely forecast that Nixon would self-destruct earned him instant scholarly fame, although his psycho-biographical portraits better predicted stylistic attributes, than performance. His so-called healthy "active-positives" included those identified by the heroic school (FDR, Truman, Kennedy) but also every president from Ford through Clinton (except Reagan). Scholarly accounts of policy performance would not categorize Ford, Carter, the senior Bush, or Clinton--even Kennedy– alongside Roosevelt or Truman.
53 Stanley A. Renshon, *High Hopes: The Clinton Presidency and the Politics of Ambition* (New York: Routledge, 1998). First published in cloth in 1996, Renshon won the Neustadt Award in 1997.
54 See John Frendreis, Raymond Tatalovich, and Jon Schaff, "Predicting Legislative Output in The First One-Hundred Days, 1897-1995," *Political Research Quarterly* (Forthcoming, 2001). Not only were most of FDR's enactments Depression-specific laws (many of which did not survive the 1930s) but statistical analysis verifies that presidential success is linked to structural variables, like economic conditions and electoral outcomes. An earlier version of this paper won the Best Paper Award from the Presidency Research Group of the APSA in 1999.
55 Paul C. Light, *The President's Agenda: Domestic Policy Choice from Kennedy to Carter* (Baltimore: Johns Hopkins University Press, 1983). The hardback was published in 1982.

56 Ibid., p. 10.
57 Ibid., p. 233.
58 Peri E. Arnold, *Making the Managerial Presidency: Comprehensive Reorganization Planning, 1905-1980* (Princeton, NJ: Princeton University Press, 1986). Arnold won the Brownlow (best book) Award from the American Academy of Public Administration in 1986.
59 Perhaps the first scholar to target Nixon's excessive use of staff was Thomas Cronin, "The Swelling of the Presidency: Can Anyone Reverse the Tide?," in Peter Woll, ed., *American Government: Readings and Cases*, 8th ed. (Boston: Little, Brown, 1984). Also see John Hart, *The Presidential Branch* (Chatham, NJ: Chatham House Press, 1987).
60 One of the few studies of White House organization (which Jimmy Carter purportedly for his guidance) was Stephen Hess, *Organizing the Presidency* (Washington, DC: The Brookings Institution, 1976).
61 Greenstein, *The Hidden-Hand Presidency*, p. 247.
62 Shirley Anne Warshaw, *Powersharing: White House-Cabinet Relations in The Modern Presidency* (Albany, NY: State University of New York Press, 1996).
63 David Alistair Yalof, *Pursuit of Justices: Presidential Politics and the Selection of Supreme Court Nominees* (Chicago: University of Chicago Press, 1999), pp. 68, 177. Yalof won the Neustadt Award in 2000.
64 Charles E. Walcott and Karen M. Hult, *Governing the White House: From Hoover Through LBJ* (Lawrence, KS: University Press of Kansas, 1995). Best known of the four classic volumes by Leonard D. White was his *The Federalists: A Study in Administrative History* (New York: Macmillan, 1948). Walcott and Hult won the Neustadt Award in 1996.
65 Ibid., pp. 8, 245.
66 Ibid., pp. 3, 5.
67 Ibid., p. 14.
68 Arthur M. Schlesinger, "Tides of American Politics," *Yale Review* 29 (December 1939); Arthur M. Schlesinger, Jr., *The Cycles of American History* (Boston: Houghton Mifflin, 1986).
69 Another more sophisticated model views presidential leadership relative to the three cycles of preparation, then achievement, and finally consolidation. See Erwin C. Hargrove and Michael Nelson, *Presidents, Politics, and Policy* (New York: Alfred A. Knopf, 1984), pp. 66-83.
70 Stephen Skowronek, *The Politics Presidents Make: Leadership from John Adams to George Bush* (Cambridge, MA: Harvard University Press, 1993). Skowronek won the Neustadt Award in 1994.
71 Ibid., pp. 5, 8.
72 Ibid., pp. 30-31.
73 Ibid., p. vii.
74 Sidney M. Milkis, *The President and the Parties: The Transformation of the American Party System since the New Deal* (New York: Oxford University Press, 1993).
75 Ibid., p. 10.
76 Ibid., pp. 145, 262-263, 301.
77 Richard Rose, *The Postmodern President: The White House Meets the World* (Chatham, NJ: Chatham House Publishers, 1988).
78 Ibid., pp. 2-4.
79 Ibid., p. 6.
80 Ibid., pp. 44, 73, 304.

Chapter 15

RESEARCH ON THE PRESIDENCY: THE USUAL PROBLEM OF BIOGRAPHICAL ACCOUNTS

William Cunion[*]

INTRODUCTION

Given the vast attention that the presidency continues to receive from scholars in a number of fields, it is ironic that one of the key problems plaguing presidency research is a lack of reliable data. While countless books and articles provide mountains of materials for scholars, the abundance can occasionally become an obstacle to developing good theories to explain presidential behavior. Specifically, theories that focus on psychology to explain presidential decision-making often depend on information about a president's private life – information that is frequently unreliable. Because such information rarely meets the usual standards of social science, it should be treated more cautiously than "ordinary" data. James David Barber's treatment of John Kennedy illustrates the point well. The many accounts of Kennedy's youth provide substantial evidence for Barber to identify him as a psychologically healthy person able to make good decisions in the White House. However, many other accounts support a portrait of a very troubled childhood, one riddled with severe health problems, an insatiably demanding father, and a frustrating sibling rivalry. As researchers, we should pause to ask: How much do we *really* know about John Kennedy's youth? This reexamination should not only stimulate Kennedy scholars, but should serve as a reminder to all scholars to tread lightly with biographical data. Theory should not guide the selection of evidence.

---

[*] The author would like to thank Kathryn Cunion and two anonymous reviewers for a number of thoughtful comments and excellent suggestions that substantially improved this paper.

EXPLAINING THE PRESIDENTS WITH PSYCHOLOGY

Scholars of the presidency have long been interested in examining the psychology of chief executives. Sigmund Freud himself co-authored a psychobiography of Woodrow Wilson, in which a variety of mental neuroses are alleged to have caused pathological behaviors. For example, Freud argued that Wilson never overcame the boyhood passivity toward his father, an unresolved tension that played out on the international stage: "After the loss of his father, [Wilson] began…to hate with unreasonable intensity distinguished men who disagreed with him."[1] Regardless of one's views toward Freudian psychology or this particular biography, it seems obvious that some character traits might facilitate good decision making while others may inhibit it. A host of political scientists and historians have attempted to determine what moral, intellectual, and emotional qualities would best serve a president. Although most, like Freud, employ psychological theories to explain particular presidents,[2] others have sought to use psychology as the basis for understanding presidential behavior more generally,[3] or at the very least have incorporated individual character traits as part of an explanation of presidential actions.[4] While some scholars have argued for completely omitting all personal factors from theories of the presidency,[5] the unparalleled popularity of the subject outside of academia will probably continue to attract researchers.

It is safe to assume that no book in political science has been more widely read than James David Barber's *The Presidential Character*. In the first edition, in 1972, Barber boldly predicted the tragic downfall of Richard Nixon:

> As the election approaches, Nixon's Presidential fate will clarify itself. If the uncertainties fade in the light of the polls, and the probability of defeat for Nixon rises sharply, this President will be sorely tempted to do what he feels he must do before it is too late. The loss of power to forces beyond his control would constitute a severe threat. That would be a time to go down, if go down one must, in flames.[6]

As the events known as Watergate began to unfold publicly in the two years following, Barber's warnings proved to be so accurate that he revisited his argument every four years – usually in *Time* magazine – to assess the new slate of candidates. And with considerable success: his cautious optimism regarding Jimmy Carter was more correct than most of critics have given him credit for (though one does cringe when reading the prediction that Carter would "turn out to be a pleasured President"); he also forecast that Ronald Reagan would "have disaster thrust upon him"; and warned of the danger of war under George H.W. Bush.[7]

Because the book is so well known, my description will be especially brief.[8] Barber evaluates presidents along two dimensions, active/passive and positive/negative. The first measures the level of effort a president puts into the job, and the second the amount of pleasure he receives from it. Some character types, the theory posits, are better prepared psychologically to handle the challenges of being president. Because he has high self-esteem and is able to adapt and grow while in office, the Active-Positive is best suited for the presidency. In contrast, the Active-Negative views life as a "hard struggle" that may cause him to be defensive or aggressive; the real danger associated with this character type is that he will become so personally attached to a failing policy that he will insist upon continuing it at all costs.[9] Beyond explaining the reasons behind notable presidential successes and failures, Barber's goal is to provide voters with a means to evaluate which candidates can be trusted with the awesome authority of the office, and which ones may have pathological problems that should keep them out. After all, the subtitle of the book is *Predicting Performance in the White House*. In some respects, the simplicity of the thesis masks the complexity of the task, and it would be an understatement to say that the academic community has been skeptical that the goal has been met.

Barber's Many Critics

Despite the popularity of *The Presidential Character*, and some of its notable successes, Barber's work has been mercilessly criticized. In his broad review of literature on the presidency, Paul Quirk contends that Barber probably *set back* research on the psychology of the presidency, noting that others have steered clear of the subject "as if to avoid guilt by association."[10] Criticisms of Barber's work tend to fall into three camps. The first argues that Barber's categories are inappropriate. Michael Nelson, for example, rightly questions Barber's claim that the two dimensions lead into "four basic character patterns long familiar in psychological research," suggesting tersely that they are not, and that Barber vastly oversimplifies the complexities of personality theory.[11] In an early and extensive review of Barber's book, Alexander George concedes that the general approach has some merit, but challenges the components of the categories themselves, suggesting that Barber's theory would be enriched by developing links with findings from cognitive psychology, for example.[12] Whether the categories are poorly derived, or are just too simple, this first criticism reveals the inherent problem with a theory that groups Jimmy Carter in with Bill Clinton.[13]

The second line of criticism takes the categories at face value, but asks whether they are of any use. Jeffrey Tulis provides an insightful critique of Barber in demonstrating that Abraham Lincoln exhibited the same pattern of inflexibility as Woodrow Wilson and Lyndon Johnson. Add Lincoln's melancholy, self-doubts, and sense of painful duty, and Tulis's description of Lincoln as "an incessant worker who didn't enjoy his work, but doggedly unwavering in pursuit of objectives he considered to be 'right,'" and his conclusion that Lincoln best fits the dreaded Active-Negative category is convincing.[14] While it would be far too demanding to expect Barber's theory to produce accurate predictions without fail, it is certainly troubling that our most widely revered president fares so poorly under this scheme. In questioning the value of the approach itself, this line of criticism asks whether the categories can actually predict presidential performance.

The critique here represents a third line of criticism, which accepts both the categories and their utility, but questions the process of placing individuals in the "correct" categories. To be sure, others have made this point (including Tulis and George); Simonton actually attempted to use judges to classify the many presidents that Barber did not, but determined that a reliable consensus could not be obtained.[15] Generally, this problem is thought to be methodological, though Barber has provided substantial description of the instructions he originally gave to his students.[16] As I see it, the primary problem is not one of adequate methods, but one of adequate data.

Character Development: The Importance of Childhood

According to Barber, "The solution to predicting a President's character...is in knowing where to look."[17] Too many commentators, he notes, assess presidents and candidates by looking at their recent successes or failures. While this seems logical – surely we learned much about President George W. Bush by looking closely at how he handled the job of governor of Texas – Barber suggests that this is the period one is least likely to find reliable indicators of character. In the years prior to running for president, one's true character is often obscured, as "the man on the way to the Presidency (deliberately or not) operates in a context of upward political mobility – he is on the make."[18] Signs of character during this period can thus be very misleading.

Barber argues that clearer clues are evident during a person's childhood, when one's enduring character undergoes its main development. During these early years:

> Life is experimental; ... a person tries out various ways of defining and maintaining and raising self-esteem. He looks to his environment for clues as to who he is and how well he is doing. These lessons of life slowly sink in ... Slowly the child defines an orientation toward experience; once established, that tends to last despite much subsequent contradiction.[19]

Though a future president continues to grow and change as he matures and experiences new situations, the fundamental elements of his personality that he formed as a child will persist. If we can obtain insight into a president's character by examining his childhood, sufficient data *should* be easy to collect; after all, every president is the subject of numerous biographies – even relatively obscure executives like James Garfield continue to attract biographers.[20] Ironically, the sheer volume of biographical accounts is the source of the problem with obtaining reliable data, particularly for presidents who are popular biographical subjects. There are well over a hundred accounts of the life of President John F. Kennedy (a more exact count is inhibited by the fact that so many books about him are primarily concerned with his assassination), which is precisely what makes an assessment of his childhood so difficult.

Before discussing Kennedy, however, I briefly review Barber's analyses of the early years of two other Active-Positives, Franklin Roosevelt and Harry Truman, and two Active-Negatives, Woodrow Wilson and Richard Nixon. This quick look will show why childhood is important to the theory, and why capturing the essence of a president's youth is critically important.

FUTURE PRESIDENTS

Despite the extreme difference in their upbringings, Franklin Roosevelt and Harry Truman both learned valuable lessons in their early lives that they carried with them into the Oval Office. Roosevelt's childhood seems to have been completely without great drama – "no scenes of terror, no fantasies of glory, no poignant confessions of the inevitable doubts and confusion a growing boy experiences." Barber quotes one biographer's observation that compared to the other presidents, "one searches in vain for the story of a childhood more serene and secure." Regardless of the serenity and security, though, FDR was not a coddled child. His parents consistently both challenged and encouraged young Franklin, but gave him considerable space to grow on his own. Their conscious decision to establish a framework within which he could develop his own abilities demonstrated to Franklin that "in human relations one can be caring without being anxious." This lesson of restrained commitment would carry Roosevelt through the Great Depression.[21]

To an outside observer, Harry Truman's childhood could not have been more different from Franklin Roosevelt's. There were few luxuries and certainly no thought of private academies. But underneath these outward appearances, Truman's upbringing seems to have been remarkably healthy; Barber states flatly, "Truman's early life sounds warm and happy." From his youngest days, Truman learned that "effort and pleasure were not opposites," and developed a fascination for history by reading avidly. Among the figures he particularly admired were Cincinnatus, Hannibal, and George Washington, who "fought for what they thought was right and for their countries." Attila, Genghis Khan, and Napoleon, on the other hand, met with Truman's disdain, "because while they were great leaders of men, they fought for conquest and personal glory." Of course, liking Washington and disliking Napoleon is not especially profound, but Truman deeply internalized the lessons of these leaders, and in his own life, he exhibited the same kind of selflessness he found so admirable. A financial disaster forced him to find work to help his family, dashing his hopes for college. Always the optimist, Truman did not despair at this turn of events; he had learned that "life was something of a gamble, and that it paid to wait out adversity with an easy mind." Like Roosevelt, Truman's peaceful and productive childhood provided the framework for his entire life.[22]

In contrast, the early years of Woodrow Wilson and Richard Nixon clearly contain the seeds of their later problems with self-esteem and unhealthy perfectionism. Like Roosevelt, Woodrow Wilson (known as Tommy as a child) was born into a family already well established financially and culturally. His grandfather had been a college president, and his father was a minister of a large church who later taught college himself. Although Tommy was generally well loved by his family, he did not perform well in school and exhibited no intellectual gifts as a child; Barber claims that Wilson was considered a "retarded" child. His father, Joseph Wilson, set out to correct Tommy's shortcomings, lecturing him endlessly on various academic subjects, and requiring written compositions to demonstrate understanding. Barber describes young Wilson's incessant desire to please his father and the extreme difficulty in doing so. The picture that emerges of Wilson's father is very clear: a highly demanding taskmaster who was never quite satisfied. Though one could hardly question the results – Wilson is still the only U.S. president to have earned a doctorate – the severe methods seem to have had a lasting effect on Wilson's orientation toward life. "Genius," Wilson wrote during his college days, "is divine *perseverance*." The idea that life is a constant struggle, and that inconvenient emotions must be controlled became a major theme for Wilson: "It is only by working with an energy which is almost superhuman and which looks to uninterested spectators like insanity that we can accomplish anything worth the achievement." His intransigence during the fight with the Senate over League of Nations is not as surprising or incomprehensible in this light.[23]

Although his childhood did not resemble Wilson's in the slightest, Richard Nixon also exhibited psychologically troubling traits as an adult that seem to stem directly from his early days. The various health problems that occasionally threatened his life were probably the least traumatic events of Nixon's youth. The unexpected deaths of two of his brothers, the resulting financial and emotional burden the family faced as a result, the long absences of his mother, and the explosive and unpredictable temper of his father surely shaped Nixon in obvious and unfortunate ways. Though Barber probably overanalyzes certain events in Nixon's youth,[24] his conclusions about the effects of the future president's childhood are hard to dispute:

> Out of his childhood Nixon brought a persistent bent toward life as painful, difficult, and – perhaps as significant – uncertain.... Severe as the deprivations were, they were not crippling, did not leave him disabled for political life. The family hung together – at considerable psychic cost....He would be able to grow, but there would always be that expectation of trouble ahead, that concentration on challenge and suffering.[25]

If Barber's descriptions are accurate, he seems to have identified a valuable source of information for clues about a president's enduring character. Common sense would dictate this as well – the claim that individuals develop much of their broad orientation toward life during their childhood is hardly controversial.[26] But much depends on the accuracy of the biographical account, and here we confront the problem of acquiring reliable data. Even if we accept the whole of Barber's theory and methods, the challenge of presenting a "true" picture of a president's childhood is a daunting task.[27] In the following section, I discuss John Kennedy, whose early years are particularly difficult to assess, due to the numerous books about his life, many of which seem to point to a childhood that more closely resembles Woodrow Wilson's than Franklin Roosevelt's. Rather than trying to prove that Barber's description of Kennedy is incorrect (though I believe that it is), my fundamental point is only that the biographical data on JFK permit a starkly different interpretation, one that would not predict an Active-Positive character. The methodological warning extends well beyond James David Barber, and is an important reminder to scholars, particularly those interested in developing theories of the presidency that require biographical analysis.

GROWING UP KENNEDY

The Youth of an Active-Positive?

Because John Kennedy exhibited the primary qualities of an Active-Positive while he was president – high self-esteem and a willingness to adapt – Barber places him firmly in that elite group. In his extended look at Kennedy's youth, Barber identifies many clues that suggest the formation of a psychologically healthy character. He emphasizes the advantages that a wealthy upbringing allows, including elite schooling, world travel, and the sophisticated dinner conversations regarding current events and international politics. Under his father's strong influence, the young Kennedy learned "to adapt by focusing energy and attention on doing interesting things joyfully, with an expectation of growth, in a framework of discipline."[28]

To be sure, Barber's assessment of Kennedy's childhood is not entirely a one-sided idyllic picture of love and happiness. John's well-known competitiveness with older brother Joe is discussed at some length, including some disturbing stories of physical violence between the two. There are also clear indications that Joe Sr. was extremely hard to please: he "pressed his children hard to compete, never to be satisfied with anything but first place. The point was not just to try; the point was to win."[29] But on balance, much less is made than one might expect of the agonizing pressures of the intense sibling rivalry, and of growing up under a demanding, authoritarian father. With some justification, one Kennedy biographer accuses Barber of basing his analysis "almost exclusively on books highly favorable to the late president."[30] It is easy to "predict" Active-Positive behavior if one focuses primarily on those aspects that lead to that conclusion. Other biographical accounts permit a much different view of Kennedy's childhood, one that would surely point toward another conclusion.

In one of the first biographies of JFK, James MacGregor Burns wrote, "Looking back today, Kennedy cannot remember any unhappy times during his childhood. It was an easy prosperous life, supervised by maids and nurses."[31] Kennedy may have said this, but such an account of his early life is rather selective memory. Kennedy no doubt favored this image that his biographers projected, but his formative years probably did not resemble the peaceful and psychologically healthy ones of FDR and Truman. Like Richard Nixon, John Kennedy endured a youth filled with emotional trauma and severe physical illness; and like Woodrow Wilson, lived in loving fear of a father who taught his children never to be satisfied with anything less than perfection.

Maintaining an Image

During John Kennedy's bid for the presidency in 1960, one campaign worker astutely acknowledged, "Nobody knows the Kennedys good. They don't let you know them good. That's one thing about them."[32] The object of American obsession, it is likely that more has been written about the Kennedys than any other family in the history of the world. But behind the scenes, the Kennedys have actively covered up any negative images of their family, and particularly of John. In the years immediately following her husband's death, Jacqueline Kennedy pressured John's friend Red Fay into cutting about two thousand words from his memoir *The Pleasure of His Company*. She convinced Random House not to publish Jim Bishop's *The Day Kennedy was Shot*. She went to court demanding substantial deletions in William Manchester's family-authorized *Death of a President*, and with the aid of Senator Robert Kennedy successfully persuaded *Look* magazine to drop portions of a serialization of the book. After the ordeal, Manchester "likened his persecution by the Kennedys and their attorneys and private detectives to an encounter with Nazis."[33] Through the years, the Kennedys have continued to pressure authors and publishers into suppressing unflattering details of their family, and even today only "approved" historians and journalists are granted interviews with most family members.

Health Problems

Of course, their desire for privacy does not necessarily mean that the Kennedys are hiding anything. But recent discoveries about John's medical troubles as a child indicate otherwise. Besides his heroic war injury, a chronic bad back,[34] John Kennedy's public image as a presidential candidate was a model of good health. To be sure, Burns mentioned a number of maladies in the first biography, but primarily to dismiss rumors (or to emphasize the severity of the war injury, for the purposes of adding to the Kennedy mystique). During the primary campaign, Lyndon Johnson supporters raised questions about Kennedy's health. Robert Kennedy explained that the Burns biography had settled doubts about his brother's health, responding angrily that such charges were "outrageous and irresponsible."[35] But the truth about his brother's health warranted such concerns. By age three, Jack had had whooping cough, measles, chicken pox, and a particularly virulent form of scarlet fever (from which he very nearly died in 1920). By eleven, he had developed asthma, contracted German measles, suffered from bronchitis, and had his appendix removed. Throughout his youth, Kennedy was chronically underweight and frequently confined to bed. Poor health continued to plague him into adulthood; at various times, he fought jaundice, hepatitis, malaria, and acute gastroenteritis. At age 30, Kennedy was diagnosed with Addison's Disease, a failure of the adrenal glands that was often fatal. In fairness to Burns and others, these facts were either unavailable to early Kennedy biographers, or they were misinformed by members of the Kennedy family and even their doctors.[36] Rorabaugh calls Kennedy's chronic poor health "a carefully guarded secret," an assessment supported by the fact that most of his medical records mysteriously remain sealed.[37]

"Dominion over his Children's Youthful Souls"

By itself, of course, JFK's health problems surely would not have determined his enduring character (they certainly did not account for Nixon's). And in the larger picture of his difficult childhood, illness is little more than a footnote. To fully grasp the impossible challenges of John Kennedy's early years, one must understand the expectations and influence of his father, Joe Sr. From their youngest days, the children of Joe Kennedy would do almost anything to please their father, and they rarely did anything without considering what his reaction might be. Joe Kennedy recognized early on his children's extraordinary potential, which he tirelessly – and sometimes ruthlessly – sought to develop. His tight control over his children extended into their adulthoods and political careers. Thomas Reeves calls Joe Kennedy "the major figure in an account of the life of John F. Kennedy" and claims that "his teachings and example were assimilated by all the youngsters, forming their essential core values."[38] Herbert Parmet notes that John "could no more insulate himself from his father's thinking than escape his genes."[39] Even family friend Doris Kearns Goodwin, in one of the most favorable biographies of the family, makes this point very clearly: "Joe Kennedy, having achieved an almost primitive dominion over his children's youthful souls, would rule his boys and girls for the rest of their lives."[40]

Joe Kennedy probably had his own political aspirations. Both his father and his father-in-law were well-known and highly respected public officials, and he valued greatly the idea of public service (so much so that he generally refrained from calling it "politics"). He held top-level appointments, including the prestigious post of Ambassador to England, and was named the first chairman of the Securities and Exchange Commission in 1934 (where he set out to abolish many of the same questionable practices that had made him rich). Franklin Roosevelt briefly (and reluctantly) considered him as a running mate in 1940, and there was even some talk of Kennedy replacing Roosevelt at the top of the Democratic ticket.[41] Whether Joe

Kennedy might have succeeded in politics is a matter of speculation, because his energies and aspirations were focused on his sons.

Joe instilled in his children from their earliest ages the value and importance of power, and they learned early that acquiring political power required winning. To this end, the young Kennedys knew that they were never to settle for second place in any endeavor. Even as very small children, the Kennedys were enrolled in competitive sports, such as swimming and sailing – and apparently not for the healthiest of purposes. Years later, Eunice Kennedy recalled, "Daddy was always very competitive. The thing he always kept telling us was that coming in second was just no good. The important thing was to win, don't come in second or third, that doesn't count – but win, win, win."[42] This was a particularly important message to convey to his sons, in whom Joe saw the possibilities of greatness. And no one ever achieved greatness, he believed, by coming in second; certainly no one ever became president by doing so. Echoing his father, John Kennedy told a columnist during his 1960 campaign for the presidency, "For the Kennedys, it's either the outhouse or the castle, nothing in between."[43]

Joe's emphasis on winning has taken on legendary qualities, so much so that it is actually very difficult to separate fact from fiction. Perhaps more importantly, it becomes difficult to avoid exaggerating the importance of very trivial events. How much does it reveal, for example, that as a baseball player in college, Joe once pocketed the game ball, rather than giving it to the winning pitcher, as tradition warranted? One biographer asserts that the incident was typical of "an approach that would mark Kennedy's life."[44] Such vignettes may sometimes be useful, but scholars relying on such data always risk selection bias. More convincing and more instructive is Goodwin's observation:

> Taken as a whole, [Joe's] letters to his children represent a guidance in manners, not morals. Not once in more than two hundred letters did he put forward any ultimate moral principles for his children to contemplate. On the contrary, he stressed to his children the importance of winning at any cost and the pleasures of coming in first. As his own heroes were not poets or artists but men of action, he took it for granted that his children too wanted public success, and he confined himself to advising them how they could get it.[45]

Even exercising appropriate caution, one can hardly escape making a conclusion that Joe Kennedy continually emphasized these Machiavellian values. Biographers of all stripes have discussed occasions in which Joe would order one or more of his children from the dinner table for doing poorly in some contest, or treat one of his children with silence for losing a race. But even here it is easy to formulate pre-conceived conclusions. More critical biographers, for example, have sometimes ignored the fact that his punishments were generally not for losing per se, but because the child had failed to pay attention or maintain his or her focus during the event. It is true that he occasionally prevented anyone from breaking up fistfights between his boys (especially Joe Jr. and Jack), but mainly because he believed that it was important that they learn to stand on their own. Though his tactics may sometimes have been questionable, his concern for the long-term well-being of his children is easy to overlook.

Some scholars have suggested that Joe Kennedy was a tyrannical father, and his children's "respect" for him would be more properly characterized as fear. One biographer (in a very insightful study) actually contends that "Jack was among at least several of the Kennedys who suffered emotional damage in their youth," and suggests that Kennedy was incapable of being close to anyone in a psychologically healthy manner.[46] Naturally, the surviving children provide a much different interpretation of their upbringing. Ted Kennedy recently described his father to journalist Adam Clymer: "His standards were the highest for each of his sons, but they were different standards for each one….Often, he compared us to each other, but only in a way which raised each of our expectations for what we hoped to accomplish."[47] Some biographers largely share this assessment of Joe Kennedy: Koskoff calls him "a good father in every way" and says that beneath the façade, he had "a deeply humble view of himself."[48] Another biographer quotes a friend of John's as saying, "Mr. Kennedy had as much love for his children as any man could have. They were his real interest in life."[49]

Others take an even different view, suggesting that his influence on their childhoods has been exaggerated, as he was away much of the time, leaving the primary childrearing tasks to their mother.[50] Although he was often absent (so was Rose, for that matter), it seems very unlikely that Joe Kennedy would ever voluntarily surrender his influence. The sizable trusts he established for his children (and their restrictive terms) may have reflected this desire to maintain control.[51] But the most troubling indication of Joe's need to be in total command was his fateful decision in 1941 to have his daughter Rosemary lobotomized. The decision itself can be defended – Rosemary (who was either born mildly retarded, or had developed a mental illness) had been exhibiting very dangerous and unpredictable behavior, and a frontal lobotomy was an uncommon but widely accepted procedure to correct such problems. What cannot be as easily defended is the fact that Joe made the decision unilaterally, without so much as informing his wife, or discussing it with any members of his family. Moreover, when it became obvious that the procedure had not succeeded, Joe actively sought to cover up his mistake, and simply informed everyone that the time had come to place Rosemary in an institution. Goodwin reports that Rose Kennedy did not learn the truth about what had happened to her daughter for twenty years.[52] Even if we accept a more benign view of Joe Kennedy, it is extremely difficult to believe that he would have allowed others to develop the character and values of his children.

Regardless of whether Joe's parenting was "appropriate," or whether his children respected him out of love or out of fear, it is indisputable that he was the dominant figure of his entire family. His unmatched influence on his children is not surprising, but it is noteworthy that even his nieces and nephews were drawn to him. Mary Lou McCarthy, daughter of Joe's sister Loretta, told one biographer, "Everything was figured by how Uncle Joe would react to it. He was the yardstick by which we were all measured, whether it was sports, our schoolwork, or our knowledge. 'Would Uncle Joe be proud of us?'"[53] Even sympathetic biographers lend insight into the awe the children felt towards their charismatic father. Heeding Joe's well-understood rule that "Kennedy's don't cry," eight-year-old Robert once concealed a broken toe for hours after dropping a large cast-iron radiator on it.[54] Even the adulatory James McGregor Burns contributes to the picture: "'Every single kid,' a close friend of the family told a reporter, 'was raised to think, First, what shall I do about this problem? Second, what will Dad say about my solution of it?'"[55] What is less certain, though, is how we are to assess the effects of this influence. Specifically, did the Kennedy children integrate Joe's lessons about winning into a psychologically healthy framework, or did the warnings about the perils of losing severely damage their self-esteem? Did it motivate them to succeed, or did it contribute to reckless behavior? Answers to such questions are not at all obvious, and scholars ought to maintain balance when the evidence is unclear. Scholars must avoid the temptation (intentional or not) to simply fit their conclusions to their argument, as contradictory data will allow.

Sibling Rivalry

Consider the possible conclusions that one could draw from the rivalry between the two oldest Kennedy children, Joe Jr. and John. Unarguably, Joe Jr. was his father's favorite, and in a variety of respects, his responsibilities were immense. With his parents away much of the time, he became something of a surrogate father to his siblings (especially the youngest ones), a position he took very seriously. One family friend claimed, "It wasn't the father they were afraid of, it was Joe, Jr. The real reason they didn't sneak a smoke here and there was that they were afraid he would find out and beat the hell out of them."[56] Joe Jr. was also expected to be a role model to his brothers and sisters. His father once explained, "I think a lot depends on the oldest one, and how he turns out. The younger ones follow his example....If the oldest one tries to set a good example, the other ones try to live up to it."[57] Joe Jr. was also clearly expected to fulfill the political aspirations of his father, who believed that his oldest son would someday be president. An incredibly talented and ambitious individual, Joe Jr. seemed headed for greatness, and probably exceeded his father's expectations. Biographers seem to agree that of all the Kennedy children, Joe Jr. was the one who was most like his father. Barber describes the father-son relationship as "deep and intense."[58] Koskoff goes even further, calling Joe Jr. "not a son but an alter ego."[59]

The rivalry between the two oldest boys seems to have been a significant piece of John Kennedy's childhood, though once again, we confront the difficulty of identifying the effects on his character development. On the facts, the biographical accounts are virtually identical. Much of Jack's young life was spent trying to leave up to the high standards set by his older brother. He followed Joe to boarding school at Choate in 1931, where his older brother was already a star football player who would soon become the editor of the school paper, and would receive the highly coveted Harvard Trophy for best combined scholarship and sportsmanship. Much smaller in stature and much less mature academically, Jack was simply unable to compete on this level. Following graduation, he chose not to attend Harvard with Joe, opting for Princeton instead. But a bout with jaundice during his first weeks there forced him to return home, and he enrolled at Harvard the next fall. By then Joe was a popular junior, who excelled on the football field, in the classroom, and in student government. Again, Jack found it impossible to live up to his brother's record. After two years, he had attained only a "C" average in his course work, taken severe punishment on the football team before finally quitting, and failed to qualify even for the run-offs for class council. Economist John Kenneth Galbraith (who would later serve as personal adviser to President Kennedy), knew both boys as Harvard students; he described Joe as "every faculty's favorite," and Jack as "irreverent" and "far from diligent."[60] It was not until after his brother graduated that Jack showed real signs of improvement. By the time of his own graduation, the younger Kennedy had clearly become more devoted to his studies; his senior thesis, *Why England Slept*, was published to favorable reviews and exceptional sales. What is the upshot of the rivalry? On the one hand, it seems to have forced Jack to focus his energies and improve himself. But on the other, he was still clearly within his brother's shadow – in second place in a family that only accepted first.

Thrust into Politics?

In 1944, everything changed suddenly for the Kennedys – 29-year-old Joe Jr. was killed when his plane exploded over England on a mission so dangerous that Goodwin claims that successful completion "would have been one of the two or three greatest feats in the war."[61] His father was devastated; for the rest of his life he rarely spoke of his favorite son without losing control of his emotions. For Jack, his older brother's death meant that he would now be expected to live out his father's dreams of the presidency. In 1957, Joe Sr. bragged one journalist, "I was the one who got Jack into politics. I was the one. I told him Joe was dead and therefore it was his responsibility to run for Congress. He didn't want to...but I told him he had to."[62] Biographers have described Joe's influence in similarly forceful terms: "Joe gave Jack his orders: He was to take Joe Jr.'s place and enter politics";[63] "Once Joe determined that Jack 'had the goods,' the pressure on Jack was fierce."[64] Kennedy himself intimated that that his entry into politics was "understood" as the oldest surviving son, and once said that his father "*demanded*" it.[65] He even suggested that prior to his brother's death, he had little interest in a political career: "I don't know what I would have done if my brother had lived. I never gave much thought to politics then. I don't even remember writing letters to the editor of any newspaper. I suppose if he had not been killed, I would have gone to law school."[66]

However, a number of authors suggest that this view is inaccurate. Parmet argues that "the much-discussed question of Jack Kennedy having been virtually drafted to fulfill his brother's career objectives has been oversimplified. Jack, in fact, was deeply interested in public affairs long before Joe's death."[67] Hamilton quotes a family friend who dismisses the notion that Joe forced Jack to enter politics because of Joe Jr.'s death: "Nothing could have kept Jack out of politics: I think this is what he had in him, and it would have just come out, no matter what."[68] Likewise, Koskoff suggests that Joe's "imprudent boasts" and Jack's "self-effacing parallel comments...were all no doubt overstated. There was much more to John Kennedy's entrance into politics than merely Papa's bald insistence."[69]

Throughout John Kennedy's political career, the nature of his father's involvement and influence would always remain something of a question mark. To be sure, Kennedy himself tended to dismiss charges that he was not his "own man." He once firmly reminded a Jewish audience that *he* was running for the Senate, not his father (who had often expressed anti-Semitic views).[70] Scholars, however, have been more divided on the matter of Joe's influence. Some call Joe Sr. the "mastermind" of his son's entire political career, and even allege that he *ordered* John to appoint Robert to the post of Attorney General.[71] Others suggest that Joe played a much more limited role, providing advice and helping his son whenever possible, but respectfully deferring to him as well.[72] Once again, we find substantial evidence of competing accounts that point in starkly different directions.

CONCLUDING THOUGHTS

Of John Kennedy, Barber concludes, "The inner confidence he had acquired as a youth freed him to grow as president, through one crisis after another to grasp the full potentialities of the office."[73] Given the vast amount of contradictory data, one wonders about the certainty of this conclusion. A broader look at the biographical accounts of Kennedy's childhood and early political career clearly invite a number of plausible assessments of the effects on his psychological health. Although I would hesitate to draw strong conclusions about the nature of Kennedy's formative years, I think it is safe to say that Barber's portrait is far too rosy. Though he did not exhibit many of the same unhealthy traits as an adult, Kennedy's youth was similar to Wilson's in many important respects. It is worth noting that Barber himself is aware of the similarities, and makes a point of pausing to mention that, despite appearances, the Kennedy household "was *not* a Wilsonian home."[74]

Regardless of the nature of his early years, Kennedy operated in the White House like a true Active-Positive. Like Truman, JFK grew during his presidency, and at the very least, he certainly conveyed the image of an Active-Positive; Ted Sorenson, one of JFK's closest advisors, collected some snippets from press conferences and interviews that attest to Kennedy's Active-Positive character: "This job is interesting....It represents a chance to exercise your judgment on matters of importance....I find the work rewarding....You have an opportunity to do something about all problems....This is a damned good job."[75] Apparently, Barber places Kennedy in the correct category (though one biographer has explicitly compared his personality traits with Active-Negatives Lyndon Johnson and Richard Nixon[76]). Ironically, the Kennedy family façade probably predicted JFK's presidential performance better than a more balanced view would have.

That Kennedy's childhood may not have predicted this Active-Positive behavior is not a fatal blow to Barber's theory. Social science is not physics; every theory will have exceptions. A critique that identifies Kennedy as an anomaly is not intended to rise to the level of those that impugn the theoretical foundations. Still, scholars interested in work that involves the personal lives of presidents must deal with the fact that presidents are among the least accessible people in the world, and we need to guard carefully against "fitting" contradictory or ambiguous data to a theory. Intentionally or not, Barber's selection of data provides comfortable evidence to support his claims. Suppose Kennedy had lived, that he had been trapped by the quagmire of Vietnam, and ultimately exhibited Active-Negative behavior. Would the story of his childhood be one of a sickly boy in a losing competition for a demanding father's approval?

One might be tempted to conclude that the problem highlighted in this paper is an intractable one, as every president will be the subject of dramatically differing biographical accounts. My point is not to abandon research on individual presidents, nor even to suggest that we cannot develop theories that incorporate their psychological characteristics. Rather, I am arguing that we must apply the same rigorous standards to biographical data as we do to other types of data,[77] and especially to be more cautious to guard against selecting evidence to fit a theory. And where conclusions remain uncertain, scholars should concede that point. Historical hindsight is twenty-twenty, and the selection of evidence is an inevitable fact of research. But if political scientists are going to continue to try to develop theories about presidential behavior, normal rules must apply.

NOTES

[1] Sigmund Freud and William C. Bullitt, *Thomas Woodrow Wilson: A Psychological Study* (Boston: Houghton Mifflin Company, 1967), pp. 112-13. Incidentally, Barber considers this

to be the worst book written about Woodrow Wilson (James David Barber, *The Presidential Character*, 4th ed. (Englewood Cliffs, NJ: Prentice Hall, 1992), p. 13). Although I have not examined numerous Wilson biographies, the approach of the book and its excessively critical tone would lead me to agree presumptively with Barber.

[2] For example: Alexander L. George and Juliette L. George, *Woodrow Wilson and Colonel House: A Personality Study* (New York: John Day, 1956); Stanley A. Renshon, *High Hopes: The Clinton Presidency and the Politics of Ambition* (New York: NYU Press, 1996).

[3] For example: Dean Keith Simonton. *Why Presidents Succeed: A Political Psychology of Leadership* (New Haven, CT: Yale University Press, 1987); Susan T. Fiske, "Cognitive Theory and the Presidency," in George C. Edwards III, John H. Kessel, and Bert Rockman (eds), *Researching the Presidency: Vital Questions, New Approaches* (Pittsburgh: University of Pittsburgh Press, 1993).

[4] For example: Fred I. Greenstein, *The Presidential Difference: Leadership Style from FDR to Clinton* (New York: Martin Kessler Books, 2000); Erwin Hargrove, "Presidential Personality and Leadership Style," in George C. Edwards III, John H. Kessel, and Bert Rockman (eds), *Researching the Presidency: Vital Questions, New Approaches* (Pittsburgh: University of Pittsburgh Press, 1993).

[5] Terry M. Moe, "Presidents, Institutions, and Theory" in George C. Edwards III, John H. Kessel, and Bert Rockman (eds), *Researching the Presidency: Vital Questions, New Approaches* (Pittsburgh: University of Pittsburgh Press, 1993).

[6] Barber, *The Presidential Character*. Barber is (justifiably) proud of this prediction, and he casually points out in a footnote that this section appears verbatim from the 1972 edition (see p. 496).

[7] Barber, *The Presidential Character*, pp. 431, 227, 460.

[8] For a more thorough examination, see William David Pederson (ed) *The "Barberian" Presidency: Theoretical and Empirical Readings* (New York: Peter Lang, 1989).

[9] Barber, *The Presidential Character*, pp. 9, 46-47.

[10] Paul J. Quirk, "What Do We Know and How Do We Know It? Research on the Presidency," in William J. Crotty and Alan D. Monroe (eds), *Political Science: Looking to the Future*, vol. 4 (Evanston, IL: Northwestern University Press, 1991): 52.

[11] Michael Nelson, "The Psychological Presidency," in Michael Nelson (ed), *The Presidency and the Political System*, 6th ed. (Washington, DC: CQ Press, 2001): 208. Barber, *The Presidential Character*, p. 9.

[12] Alexander L. George, "Assessing Presidential Character," *World Politics* 26, no. 2 (January 1974): 245.

[13] I should point out that Barber himself has from the beginning been very forthright in his position that no individual *perfectly* fits any one category, which, he acerbically notes, "has not stopped some critics from beating the dead horse of an absolutism they imagine I propose." James David Barber, "Strategies for Understanding Politicians," *American Journal of Political Science* 18, no. 2 (May 1974): 453.

[14] Jeffrey Tulis, "On Presidential Character," in Joseph M. Bessette and Jeffrey Tulis (eds), *The Presidency in the Constitutional Order* (Baton Rouge: Louisiana State University Press, 1981): 301.

[15] Simonton, p. 208.

[16] Tulis; Barber, "Strategies for Understanding Politicians."

[17] Barber, *The Presidential Character*, p. 84.

[18] Barber, *The Presidential Character*, p. 84.

[19] Barber, *The Presidential Character*, p. 7.

[20] See Allan Peskin, *Garfield: A Biography* (Kent, OH: Kent State University Press, [1978] 1998).

[21] Barber, *The Presidential Character*, pp. 268, 271, 272.

22. Barber, *The Presidential Character*, pp. 305, 306, 308, 310.
23. Barber, *The Presidential Character*, pp. 86, 90 (emphasis in original).
24. The examination of the symbolism in ten-year-old Richard's letter to his mother is especially dubious. See Barber, *The Presidential Character*, p. 128.
25. Barber, *The Presidential Character*, pp. 128-29.
26. George and George trace Woodrow Wilson's ego-defensive rigidity to his difficult childhood relationship with his authoritarian father. Also see Hargrove, p. 90.
27. Incidentally, I leave aside the much more formidable challenge of acquiring reliable information about the childhood of a presidential *candidate*. Though Barber is primarily interested in identifying the character of these individuals, their biographical histories are rarely anything other than "puff" pieces, and more than anything validate Barber's caution about politicians being "on the make."
28. Barber, *The Presidential Character*, p. 347.
29. Barber, *The Presidential Character*, pp. 348, 345.
30. Thomas C. Reeves, *A Question of Character: A Life of John F. Kennedy* (New York: Free Press, 1991), p. 15.
31. James MacGregor Burns, *John Kennedy: A Political Profile* (New York: Harcourt, Brace and Company, 1959), p. 23.
32. Quoted in Ralph G. Martin, *A Hero for Our Time: An Intimate Story of the Kennedy Years* (New York: MacMillan Publishing Company, 1983), pp. 21-22.
33. Thomas C. Reeves, p. 5.
34. Some biographers contend that the war merely exacerbated what was already a bad back (e.g., Thomas C. Reeves, p. 38). At any rate, Kennedy underwent surgery in 1954 to relieve the pain, and was so near death that last rites were pronounced.
35. Victor Lasky, *J.F.K.: The Man and the Myth* (New York: The MacMillan Company, 1963), p. 376.
36. Thomas C. Reeves, pp. 38-39; Donald Kessler, *Sins of the Father: Joseph P. Kennedy and the Dynasty He Founded* (New York: Warner Books, 1996), p. 247. Doris Kearns Goodwin, *The Fitzgeralds and the Kennedys* (New York: Simon and Schuster, 1987), p. 734-35, 745. Rorabaugh reports that Kennedy's doctor, Janet Travell, admitted years later that she lied when she denied during the 1960 campaign that Kennedy had had Addison's Disease. W.J. Rorabaugh, "Moral Character, Policy Effectiveness, and the Presidency: The Case of JFK," *Journal of Policy History* 10, no. 4 (1998): 453.
37. Rorabaugh, p. 452; Thomas C. Reeves, p. 38.
38. Thomas C. Reeves, p. 413.
39. Herbert S. Parmet, *Jack: The Struggles of John F. Kennedy* (New York: The Dial Press, 1980), p. 157.
40. Goodwin, p. 351.
41. Kessler, p. 168; Goodwin, pp. 533-34; Martin, p. 41; David E. Koskoff, *Joseph Kennedy: A Life and Times* (Englewood Cliffs, NJ: Prentice Hall, 1974), p. 234.
42. Quoted in Jack Newfield, *Robert Kennedy: A Memoir* (New York: E. P. Dutton and Company, 1969), pp. 45-46. Also Lasky, p. 68.
43. Quoted in Newfield, p. 45.
44. Kessler, p. 23.
45. Goodwin, p. 351.
46. Thomas C. Reeves, pp. 40, 57, 87-88. Reeves suggests that Kennedy was so emotionally distant that he actually proposed to Jackie via telegram (p. 111).
47. Adam Clymer, *Edward M. Kennedy: A Biography* (New York: William Morrow and Company, 1999), p. 62.
48. Koskoff, p. 400.
49. Nigel Hamilton, *J.F.K.: Reckless Youth* (New York: Random House, 1992), p. 217.

50. See James MacGregor Burns, *Edward Kennedy and the Camelot Legacy* (New York: W. W. Norton and Company, 1976), p. 26.
51. Kessler, pp. 48-50; see also Goodwin, p. 602.
52. Goodwin, p. 643.
53. Kessler, p. 41.
54. Lester David and Irene David. *Bobby Kennedy: The Making of a Folk Hero* (New York: Dodd, Mead and Company, 1986), p. 15.
55. Burns, *John Kennedy*, p. 20.
56. Quoted in Thomas C. Reeves, p. 38; also see Goodwin, p. 352.
57. Quoted in Richard J. Whalen, *Founding Father: The Story of Joseph P. Kennedy* (New York: New American Library, 1964), p. 359.
58. Barber, *The Presidential Character*, p. 347.
59. Koskoff, p. 238.
60. Quoted in Martin, p. 36.
61. Goodwin, p. 687. Many authors have speculated that Joe Jr. volunteered for such a risky mission to please his father, to make up for his father's reputation for cowardice, or at the very least, as a result of a "lifetime of pressure" to be the very best at everything. See Kessler, p. 285; Koskoff, p. 334; Goodwin, p. 687; Thomas C. Reeves, p. 71.
62. Eleanor Harris, "The Senator is in a Hurry," *McCall's* (August 1957): 123.
63. Kessler, p. 287.
64. Goodwin, p. 705.
65. Quoted in Kessler, p. 287.
66. Quoted in Martin, p. 46.
67. Parmet, p. 125.
68. Lem Billings, John Kennedy's lifelong friend, quoted in Hamilton 1992, p. 673.
69. Koskoff, p. 405.
70. Goodwin, p. 763.
71. Kessler, pp. 369, 389; Thomas C. Reeves, p. 76; Richard Reeves, *President Kennedy: Profile of Power* (New York: Simon and Schuster, 1993), p. 29.
72. Parmet, p. 138; Burns, *John Kennedy*, pp. 68-69.
73. Barber, *The Presidential Character*, p. 384.
74. Barber, *The Presidential Character*, p. 345 (emphasis added).
75. Theodore C. Sorenson, *Kennedy* (New York: Harper and Row, 1965), p. 367. See Barber, *The Presidential Character*, p. 364.
76. Thomas C. Reeves, p. 420.
77. On this point more broadly, see Gary King, Robert O. Keohane, and Sidney Verba, *Designing Social Inquiry: Scientific Inference in Qualitative Research* (Princeton, NJ: Princeton University Press, 1994). See especially pp. 27-28.

Chapter 16

PRESIDENTS AFTER THE WHITE HOUSE: A PRELIMINARY STUDY

Max J. Skidmore

INTRODUCTION

Bill Clinton left the White House in January of 2001 at the age of only 54, a vigorous and youthful man whose most stunning achievements — two terms as President of the United States, however controversial — were behind him. At his inauguration he was 46, which made Clinton the third youngest person to hold the office. Only Theodore Roosevelt at 42 and John Kennedy at 43 were younger. Grant, like Clinton, was 46 at his inauguration but he turned 47 the following month, while Clinton was in office approximately seven months before reaching that age.

Few presidents, then, were younger than Clinton when they left the presidency even though he had served a full eight years. Those who were younger include James K. Polk and Millard Fillmore who left office at 53, Franklin Pierce at 52, Grover Cleveland at 51 – each having served only one term or, in Fillmore's case, less – and Theodore Roosevelt at 50 after almost two full terms. John Tyler and Ulysses S. Grant each also became a former president at the age of 54, but each was almost 55; Grant's birthday was the following month and Tyler's came within a few days. Clinton's birthday, as indicated, was not for seven months.

TR remained active and influential, but died slightly before the passage of a decade. Both he and Fillmore – who lived after leaving office for more than two decades – came back to became presidential candidates another time and ran on third-party tickets. No doubt their relative youth was a factor. Had Roosevelt lived, as will be made clear below, there is every indication not only that he would once more have been the Republican nominee, but that he would overwhelmingly have been elected President for a third term in 1920.

Clinton has no such prospect. The Twenty-Second Amendment now forbids it. Although his age is no guarantee of a lengthy post-presidential career – witness Polk, who despite his relative youth died barely more than three months after he left office – Clinton is a vibrant man, and the odds are good that he will remain an influential force in American politics for years to come. It would be highly unlikely that the president who became America's most potent political presence at the century's end – causing great tearing of hair and gnashing of teeth among his enemies – would simply fade away.

Note that the current incumbent, George W. Bush, was 54 when he assumed office. He therefore, despite his youthful demeanor, is considerably older than the youngest presidents. Thus even if he serves only one term he will not be especially young for a former president; nevertheless, he will be sufficiently young that he might have a lengthy career thereafter.

What contributions are these men likely to make during their post-presidential lives? Even though each post-presidential experience is of course as individual as each presidency, the experiences of former presidents may offer insights. Except for specific biographers, few writers have paid much attention to the lives of former presidents. Fewer still have considered post-presidential influence upon American political development. Thomas A. Bailey did provide a lively but very brief chapter dealing with former presidents in his 1966 *Presidential Greatness*, but he concentrated upon their reputations rather than their influence.[1] Yet four of Clinton's predecessors even returned to become presidential candidates again – one, in fact actually was successful.

This preliminary study reveals, as one would expect, that presidents who leave office at an early age are more likely to remain active and influential than those who are older. Other less obvious factors might appear also to be relevant in predicting how active a former president is likely to be. Was his administration highly active? Did he leave office with a reputation of success? None of these appears to offer much in the way of a reliable guide, however. In fact, not even age is completely reliable. Franklin Pierce, for example, despite his youth gave the country no more reason to remember him fondly in retirement than he had as president. John Quincy Adams, on the other hand, left office at sixty-one and then entered upon another distinguished political career.

The other factors appear even less reliable as guides than age. Carter, Hoover, and Taft for example left office without an aura of success but each continued to provide substantial service. Fillmore's later candidacy for the office came despite a rather lackluster performance when he had held it. Others deemed more successful in varying degrees — Jackson, Eisenhower, and Reagan come to mind — were considerably less active after than during their presidencies; they were, however, the three oldest former presidents (Reagan was older by far than any other). Nixon and Lyndon Johnson were among our most active presidents, but were less active in retirement, while TR was enormously active both during and following his presidency.

More research is in order. American presidents may be so varied as to offer little, if anything, that would be predictive. On the other hand, further study might be able to discern some elements that could serve as guides with respect to the kinds of influence former presidents would be likely to wield.

It is common for those who leave the presidency to continue to influence public affairs in several different ways. Four broad categories seem apparent, (although, of course some fit into more than one): those who have sought to regain the presidency and thus have exercised political influence; those who have exercised influence by securing other political office; those who have made contributions to education and to public understanding, and those who have become active in humanitarian causes. Additional miscellaneous activities are also frequent apart from these major groupings, and can constitute a fifth category.

FORMER PRESIDENTS AS PRESIDENTIAL CANDIDATES

Martin Van Buren went down to defeat in 1840 when he ran for re-election. In 1844, he was again a major contender for the Democratic nomination, and actually received more than half the ballots cast in the convention.[2] Because of opposition from Southern delegates, however, he was unable to achieve the two-thirds majority that the Democrats had begun requiring in 1836 (a requirement that remained in place for a century). He therefore lost the nomination to James K. Polk.

As president, Van Buren had treated slavery largely as a state issue. He even flirted to no avail with the slave-holding South when he attempted to win re-election in 1840. By the time he was out of office for eight years, though, he had moved so far from his initial position and toward opposition to slavery that the vigorously anti-slavery Free Soil Party in 1848 named him its candidate for president. Van Buren's vice-presidential running mate was Charles Francis Adams, the son of President John Quincy Adams (who, in his own post-presidential career became the scourge of slavery's defenders).

Van Buren as a former president came to take a vital part in defeating the Democrat Lewis Cass and electing the Whig, Zachary Taylor, thus changing the course of American political history. His third-party candidacy "played a decisive role in the election. Van Buren registered an impressive showing, polling 10 percent of the national vote. Although he won no states outright, he placed second behind Taylor in Massachusetts, Vermont, and his native New York. By forcing Cass into third place in those states, Van Buren helped to deny the Democrats a victory."[3]

Millard Fillmore won election to the vice presidency in 1848, and succeeded to the highest office upon the death of President Taylor. After leaving the presidency, Fillmore like Van Buren came back to become a presidential candidate. He had been the final Whig president, one of only three (or four, if Tyler is counted as a Whig), none of whom served a full term. Fillmore failed to receive the Whig nomination in 1852 despite Southern support. The party chose General Winfield Scott instead. The Democrats jabbed the General (and by implication Fillmore as well), with the slogan: "We Polked you in '44; we shall Pierce you in '52" – and so they did.

Fillmore did his reputation no good by accepting nomination in 1856 as the candidate of the American, or "Know Nothing," Party – a bitter nativist, anti-immigrant, and anti-Catholic group – but he was a substantial force. "He received 21 percent of the vote, a record for a third-party candidate until 1912."[4] His effort may have been impressive, but it was not enough to affect the election's outcome. The Whigs were badly divided, largely over the question of slavery, while the Democrats were unified and well-organized. Fillmore did, however, carry one state, Maryland. Its eight electoral votes were the first ever won by a third-party candidate.[5] Then, in Bailey's words, Fillmore continued to "hurt himself. Favoring conciliation rather than coercion, he criticized Lincoln's conduct of the war and in 1864 supported the Democratic candidate, General McClellan. Branded a Copperhead, Fillmore antagonized his neighbors in Buffalo. At the time of Lincoln's assassination he was so busy at the sickbed of his wife that he was unaware of the request to drape private houses. He awoke one morning to find his home smeared with ink."[6]

Ex-President	Year attempted	Candidate of	Outcome	Result
Martin Van Buren (Democrat, 1837-1841)	1848	Free Soil Party	Lost	Affected outcome; took 10% of vote
Millard Fillmore (Whig, 1850-1853)	1856	American (Know Nothing) Party	Lost	Carried one state; did not change outcome
Grover Cleveland (Democrat, 1885-1889)	1892	Democratic Party	Won	Became the only president to serve non-consecutive terms
Theodore Roosevelt (Republican, 1901-1909)	1912	Progressive (Bull Moose) Party	Came in second in both popular and electoral (88) votes	Affected outcome

Grover Cleveland, elected as a Democrat in 1884, lost the 1888 election to Benjamin Harrison. Like George W. Bush in the year 2000, Harrison narrowly won the electoral vote while receiving fewer votes than his Democratic opponent. Former President Cleveland again became the Democratic nominee in 1892, and this time he defeated Harrison. His successful race made him the only president in American history to serve non-consecutive terms, and the only former president to achieve the nomination of a major party.

The fourth and thus far last former president to enter another presidential race was Theodore Roosevelt. He had become president in 1901 upon the assassination of President McKinley, and in 1904 was the first vice president who had filled a presidential vacancy to go on and win election in his own right. When he did so, he promised not to run again in 1908. It was a promise he came to regret, because he delighted in being president and could easily have been re-nominated and elected.

Dissatisfaction with his hand-picked successor, William Howard Taft, led him to attempt to secure the Republican nomination once more in 1912. When the convention re-nominated Taft, despite TR's victories in the primaries that existed then and despite his popularity among the rank and file, he ran his famous "Bull Moose" campaign on the Progressive Party ticket.[7] The bitter race split the dominant Republicans, and enabled the Democrat, Woodrow Wilson, to win. Roosevelt lost, but he came in far ahead of Taft in the popular vote and in the electoral college where he won 88 votes. Taft carried only Utah and Vermont. TR's Bull Moose race marked the only time a third-party candidate has come in ahead of one of the two major parties in either popular or electoral vote.

These four form the only instances in which former presidents actually have run again. There were, however, two more instances — historical footnotes — in which a former president almost became a major-party candidate.

The first was in 1880, when Grant came near to being nominated for a third, and non-consecutive, term. After being out of office for nearly four years, he was the major contender at that year's Republican Convention. He did come close, but was never quite able to gain a majority over his major opponent, James G. Blaine. The eventual winner, James A. Garfield, came from behind to defeat Grant on the 36th ballot.[8] Grant supported Garfield in the general election.

The second instance involved Theodore Roosevelt. In 1916, the Bull Moose Progressives whom TR had led in 1912 nominated him once again, but he rejected the nomination. He also declined to run for governor of New York in 1918. By that year he again had become, as William Harbaugh noted, the Republican Party's "foremost candidate for the presidency."[9] In the words of John A. Gable: "by 1918 Roosevelt was again the most prominent leader of the Republican Party and the odds-on favorite for the nomination." Gable pointed out that TR had, in fact, planned for 1920 by drawing up a new progressive platform and choosing a campaign manager.[10] Harbaugh is the author of one of the best biographies of TR ever written. Gable, arguably the foremost expert on the details of Roosevelt's life, is a TR scholar and Executive Director of the Theodore Roosevelt Association.

Despite the conclusions of two such outstanding scholars, there may be objections to such a sweeping statement regarding TR's chances for election in 1920. What seemed obvious nearly a century ago may seem questionable today, especially to Americans who often have a weak understanding of their own history. Did not TR go down to defeat in 1912? He did, to be sure. In that year, however, he was the candidate of a minor party and therefore faced opposition not only from Democrats, but from Republicans as well. Were not the Republican leaders who denied him the nomination still powerful? Yes, they were, but many had changed their minds and had come to his support.

As a contemporary observer (TR's most enthusiastic and uncritical biographer, Hermann Hagedorn) indicated in 1919:

> The leaders of the Republican Party who had robbed him of the nomination in 1912 and rejected him in 1916, came to him by the middle of 1918, hat in hand, to make amends and tell him that the Republican Presidential nomination in 1920 would be his for the taking.[11]

Such a view among his contemporaries was not limited to TR's supporters. In 1931, his most *un*enthusiastic and most critical biographer, Henry Pringle, wrote that "had he lived, he might have been elected President in 1920 and then there would have been, in all probability, no era of shame and scandal at Washington."[12]

As for Republican Party leaders, the newly-appointed Chairman of the Republican National Committee, Will Hays, made at least his understanding of the party's position clear:

> One of the first things Hays did in his new capacity was to announce that the nomination of Roosevelt for the presidency in 1920 was a virtual certainty. Even William Barnes, Jr., the Republican boss who'd dragged Roosevelt into court for libel in 1915, was now a supporter. When another politician told Barnes that Roosevelt would likely be nominated in 1920 by acclamation, Barnes answered, "Acclamation, hell! We're going to nominate him by assault![13]

His "political star was rising rapidly," John Milton Cooper, Jr., wrote:

By early 1918 many of his once implacable Republican foes, including Taft, Root, and Penrose, were turning to him for counsel and leadership. As the year wore on, Old Guardsmen, insurgents, and ex-Progressives alike touted his presidential candidacy in 1920, and he looked like the odds-on favorite for the Republican nomination.[14]

Cooper went so far as to speculate regarding TR's effect on the Republican Party had he lived and been elected again. There is the "intriguing possibility," he said that Roosevelt "might have chastened the Republicans' love affair with business and material prosperity." Despite the Party's rightward inclination, TR's popularity rested partly "on the acceptability of his domestic reform views." He noted that by the time of his death, "Roosevelt and the Republicans had found mutually acceptable grounds for reconciliation," and he could hardly have been prevented from "winning the nomination and the presidency." As president in the 1920s, "he could at least have dampened the rampant materialism of the decade and leavened his party's pro-business ardor with a different brand of conservatism." They might have become "champions of governmental action after the manner of the Tory party in Britain during the next three generations," he surmised.[15]

Most of Roosevelt biographers agree – along with those mentioned above – that TR by the time of his death had become the leading candidate for the nomination in 1920. Edmund Morris, whose massive and excellent biography has yet to proceed beyond the Roosevelt presidency, has not yet dealt with that period. Among the others John Morton Blum is the least assertive. He wrote that, "working with Republican leaders, Roosevelt had begun to build for 1920. Some of them and some of his old friends hoped that he might then bear the party's standard. He sensed that he could not, but he surely would have liked to."[16]

Others tend to be more definite. Nathan Miller, who wrote the best of the recent single-volume studies, said of TR that, "by 1918 he was regarded as the front runner for the Republican presidential nomination in 1920." Miller, too, quoted the comment from "Boss Barnes" about nominating Roosevelt "by assault."[17] Peter Collier in his more gossipy study wrote regarding the defeat of the Democrats in the congressional elections of 1918, "When the voters repudiated the administration, most political observers agreed that it was to some degree a Roosevelt victory and that TR, the only candidate for the Republicans in 1920, was likely to be President again."[18] Wilson Sullivan noted that TR died "while Republicans were hatching plans to run him again for president in 1920."[19] Finally, in the most recent single-volume biography on TR, H. W. Brands, while expressing doubts that even Theodore Roosevelt could have stemmed the tide of reaction that followed the war, conceded nevertheless that he "might well have won the election of 1920."[20]

History, of course, is full of "could have beens," and "might have beens," many of which are highly doubtful. One that seems as close to a sure thing as any, though, is that had TR lived, he would have been nominated, and elected by a landslide. The Republican Party in 1920 had no dominant candidate, and ultimately chose the obscure Ohio Senator, Warren G. Harding. Harding won by the greatest popular-vote landslide yet to occur in American politics. If Harding won so overwhelmingly under the circumstances, it is highly likely that TR — the figure who was wildly popular and who had dominated much of the century's politics — would have become America's first three-term president, and by an even greater majority than Harding's. It was not to be, but in a twist of irony America's first (and only) president to achieve a third term was another Roosevelt, a distant cousin who had patterned much of his career upon that of his illustrious relative, and who then went on to overshadow even the great Bull Moose.

Also among historical footnotes, Gerald Ford provided a strange if obscure entry during the election of 1980. Ford, like Grant and Roosevelt, had been out of office for one term that year when the Republican Party nominated Ronald Reagan as its standard bearer. In what can only be described as one of the most bizarre episodes in presidential history, a former president actually considered running again — but not for president.

Ford had decided not to enter the 1980 presidential race, but after Reagan's nomination:

> excitement at the GOP national convention reached a climax when word was leaked from Reagan headquarters that Ford would join the ticket as candidate for the vice presidency. Ford confirmed in TV interviews that he was available for the nomination. Some newspapers went to press announcing the Reagan-Ford ticket as an accomplished fact. But at the last minute the two leaders were unable to agree on a mutually acceptable plan to share the powers of the presidency.[21]

To describe the disagreement as merely an inability to arrive at an acceptable plan of sharing power appears to be a considerable understatement. "In 1980 there was an effort to put Ford on the Reagan ticket as Vice President, but Ford insisted on a virtual 'co-presidency' in which he would share presidential powers," and the Reagan camp aborted the effort.[22]

FORMER PRESIDENTS AS OFFICERS OF THE GOVERNMENT

Clinton can never run again for president, of course, but he already has demonstrated that he will remain active politically. Until the events of 11 September directed the attention of Americans to the threat of political violence, Clinton continued to command more headlines than President George W. Bush. He has been enormously effective as a fund-raiser for the Democrats, and he likely will continue to work for the party. In addition to other activities that he may undertake directly – and whether they may bring him another office – he is unique among former presidents in having a vicarious political future. Hillary Clinton is the only presidential spouse ever to run for office – let alone to be elected – so the family quickly achieved a first. Her efforts brought her a seat in the United States Senate, making her the only member of Congress who had ever been First Lady. As a matter of fact, she took her seat a few days before the end of her husband's presidency, so she was in the Senate briefly while still the wife of a sitting President.

Two former Presidents themselves served in Congress, John Quincy Adams and Andrew Johnson. After his presidency Adams had a long and distinguished career in the U. S. House of Representatives, where he is noted for his lengthy and ultimately successful battle against the "gag rule" that the House had adopted to forbid receipt of petitions against slavery. Bailey said that he was "a savage anti-slavery battler for seventeen years on the floor of Congress."[23] Similarly, Andrew Johnson became a United States senator, although without such distinction as Adams. Johnson died a few months after taking office.

John Tyler, too, presents a unique case. He was the first vice president to succeed to the office upon the death of a president, "His Accidency" serving all but one month of William Henry Harrison's term. Having antagonized both parties as his time in office progressed, he had no prospect of receiving a nomination in 1844, and thus did not run again. He left Washington for his Virginia home in March of 1845. There, with his new young wife, he began a second family that grew to include seven children.

Although he had run on the Whig ticket with Harrison, the Whigs soon rejected him. After leaving the presidency Tyler returned to the Democratic Party and supported the Compromise of 1850 and the Kansas-Nebraska Act. Initially, he opposed secession. Seeking to avert it, he sponsored and presided over the "Richmond Convention" that sought to achieve some accommodation. When that failed, this former president of the United States not only worked to take Virginia out of the Union that he had headed[24], but became a member of the Provisional Congress of the Confederacy. He subsequently won election to the Confederate House of Representatives, but died in January of 1862 before that body convened. "With the taint of treason clinging to his name, invading Union soldiers ravaged his beautiful Virginia estate and home, Sherwood Forest. Fifty years after his death Congress voted a modest monument to his memory in Richmond."[25]

William Howard Taft had one of the most significant of all post-presidential careers (Bailey described him as having lived on "usefully for decades").[26] He had left the presidency in March of 1913. In contrast to the sentiments of his wife, Nellie, Taft had always expressed more interest in being a justice of the U. S. Supreme Court than in being president.[27] He achieved his life's goal in June of 1921 when he accepted appointment from Warren G. Harding as Chief Justice.

Taft served on the Court for nearly nine years and wrote an unusual number of opinions before retiring in February of 1930. He is the only person to have served both as president and as member of the Supreme Court, although Associate Justice Charles Evans Hughes did resign from the Court to become the Republican candidate against Woodrow Wilson in 1916. Hughes lost, but by only 23 electoral votes. In 1930, President Hoover appointed him Chief Justice to replace Taft[28], so Hughes was twice a member of the Court and once a presidential candidate, but never a president.

OTHER PUBLIC AND EDUCATIONAL ACTIVITIES OF PRESIDENTS

Many former presidents continued to participate actively in public affairs. Washington had wanted only a peaceful retirement, but world events intervened. In 1798, tension with France increased, and President Adams prevailed upon him to accept a renewed commission at the newly-created rank of Lt. General to raise and command a restored Army of the United States. For several months he fulfilled his new and unwanted duties.[29] Of all his "many public services, this one was the least happy. Controversies over the appointment of officers were bitter," but at least he was able to remain at his beloved Mount Vernon except for one trip to Philadelphia to confer with President Adams.[30] Also fortunately, the threat subsided, and Washington soon entered genuine retirement without having to lead troops. Nevertheless, he is the only president to have commanded the American military after having left office. Congress did, however, in those days long before presidential pensions, restore his general's rank and salary to former President U. S. Grant shortly before his death.

John Adams came out of retirement briefly in 1820 to become a presidential elector, casting his vote for James Monroe. That year he also accepted election as a delegate to the Massachusetts Constitutional Convention. In 1829 former Presidents James Madison and

James Monroe both served on the Virginia Constitutional Convention, with Monroe as its Chair. Former President Martin Van Buren also served as an elector, twice. In 1852 he cast a vote for Pierce, and in 1856 for Buchanan.

Forrest McDonald has given us a touching description of Thomas Jefferson as he left office. "He remained in Washington about a week, packing his belongings, before quitting the place forever," McDonald wrote. "Then the sixty-five-year-old Father of American Liberty mounted a horse, to ride through snow and storm for three days and nights until he regained the sanctuary of his home at Monticello. In the seventeen years that remained of his life, he never again left the foothills of the Blue Ridge Mountains."[31] Of course Jefferson did not – could not – become idle. Among his activities was the founding of the University of Virginia. He designed the buildings at Charlottesville, supervised their construction, chose the faculty, and constructed the curriculum. The University opened to students in 1825, and Jefferson became its rector.[32] When he died in 1826, another former president, Madison, succeeded him in that position. Yet a third former president, James Monroe, also served on its board.

After their presidencies John Tyler served as Chancellor of the College of William and Mary, James Buchanan became a member of the Board of Trustees of Franklin and Marshall College, and Rutherford B. Hayes became a member of the Board of Trustees of Ohio State University along with other educational institutions. Former President Grover Cleveland became the Henry Stafford Little Lecturer in Public Affairs at Princeton University, served on the University's Board of Trustees, and became its chairman (where he quarreled with University President and future President of the United States, Woodrow Wilson).

Former President Benjamin Harrison lectured on constitutional law at Stanford University. As the nineteenth century drew to a close, he served as counsel for Venezuela at an international commission in Paris regarding its boundary dispute with Great Britain over British Guiana. Although he did not prevail, he provided able and vigorous representation.

Former President Taft became Kent Professor of Law at Yale. During the First World War he served as co-chair of the National War Labor Board. Former President Herbert Hoover devoted his prodigious energy to public service. During World War Two, drawing upon his experience from the First World War, he directed relief for Poland, Finland, and Belgium with little success. "After the war he served as coordinator of the European Food Program, advised the U.S. government on occupation policies in Germany and Austria, and chaired two Commissions on the Organization of the Executive Branch of Government." He remained an adviser to conservative Republicans, until his death at age 90; John Adams was the only President who lived longer"[33] while retaining his mental capacity (note that in December of 2001 former President Reagan, who was born 6 February 1911, became older than Adams had been when he died; Reagan, however, a victim of Alzheimer's disease, had long since ceased to function mentally).

Former Presidents Ford and Nixon joined President Carter as official American representatives to Anwar Sadat's funeral in 1980, and former President Carter served several times as an official or unofficial observer of elections during troubled times in various countries. Lyndon Johnson spent his retirement tending to his ranch and writing, but he maintained ties with the University of Texas and with the LBJ Library where he spoke to a seminar on civil rights shortly before his death. He and Richard Nixon gave extensive interviews for television, LBJ to Walter Cronkite, and Nixon to David Frost. Both Gerald Ford and Jimmy Carter have participated in seminars on the presidency, and Carter has lectured at Emory University. In what no doubt was a unique activity for a former president,

Nixon in 1985 mediated a dispute in professional baseball between the league and the umpires.

NOTABLE HUMANITARIAN ACTIVITIES BY FORMER PRESIDENTS

One frequently hears people referring to Jimmy Carter not as a great president, but as a great former president. This stems from his varied humanitarian activities, most notably his dedication to Habitat for Humanity. Carter donates his services periodically, and actually helps construct houses for low-income people.

Rutherford B. Hayes, similarly, in retirement worked diligently to support the vote for women, and became the director of the George Peabody Educational Fund and the John F. Slater Fund, each of which promoted education for black citizens. Hayes is reputed personally to have provided a scholarship to the young W. E. B. DuBois. He also became president of the National Prison Association, an organization that advocated prison reform and rehabilitation.[34]

ADDITIONAL INFLUENTIAL CONTRIBUTIONS OF FORMER PRESIDENTS

Among the more subtle, but nonetheless influential contributions to America's political development were the numerous letters that the second and third presidents (and the first and second vice presidents) exchanged during their retirements. The former antagonists, John Adams and Thomas Jefferson, had reconciled and had become faithful correspondents until the day of their deaths – each died on the 4th of July, 1826. They carried on voluminous correspondence with others as well, and their letters have become classics of American political thought. Legend has it that on his deathbed Adams said, "Jefferson survives," (or "Jefferson lives") not knowing that it was Jefferson's day of death also.

Among Jefferson's letters after he left the presidency were his original ideas regarding "ward republics" as safeguards for the people's rights and for the preservation of a republic. He seems to have developed his ideas after leaving the presidency, and appears to have mentioned them first in a letter to John Tyler in 1810. He described them also to John Adams in 1813, and in several other letters at various times to others. Few writers have dealt with the implication of these ideas and their potential – Hannah Arendt and Richard K. Matthews are exceptions – but they remain a major contribution, and may yet be developed.[35]

Another of Jefferson's contributions was the nucleus for the second Library of Congress, his collection of books that many writers have described as "magnificent." The British had burned the original Library during their attack on Washington during the War of 1812. Afterward Jefferson, who suffered chronically from severe financial difficulty, sold his personal 6500-volume library to the government. Unfortunately, much of that collection also fell victim to another fire in 1851.

James Madison lived to the age of 85. Among his contributions following his presidency one stands out. He pulled together his notes on the Constitutional Convention of 1787, and arranged for publication of the only journal of the Convention's activities.

John Quincy Adams is well-known for his opposition to slavery when the former president served in the House of Representatives, but his blows against slavery were not limited to his duties as a representative. He successfully argued the case before the Supreme Court in defense of the African crew charged with having committed mutiny aboard the slave ship *Amistad*, and he won their freedom. Nor were his official concerns limited to slavery. He strongly supported scientific endeavors, and helped secure approval for acceptance of the grant from James Smithson that established the Smithsonian Institution.

Martin Van Buren as a former president, and his son John as a member of the U. S. House of Representatives, spoke out increasingly against slavery in the decades following Van Buren's defeat in 1840. Van Buren probably should be given credit for his staunch support of the party system before, during, and following his presidency. As much as any single person, he was responsible for moving the country away from the romantic notion that a republic should be free from parties, and toward practical acceptance of parties as necessary to secure a free society against both a powerful government and irresponsible leaders.

James Buchanan attempted to justify his failed administration and its policies of appeasement toward the slavery interests by producing his memoirs. He published *Mr. Buchanan's Administration on the Eve of Rebellion* in 1866. Buchanan seemed to assume that historians would judge him well. He was unconvincing, and they have not. Although he had "surrounded himself with a narrow set of advisers, shut out dissenting viewpoints, adopted policies that were excessively pro-Southern, was insensitive to Northern public opinion, failed to assess accurately the political consequences of his actions, and evidenced no ability to shape or mobilize public opinion"[36] – an incredibly damning indictment – to his credit he did oppose secession, and did support Lincoln and the Union during the War.

In stark contrast to Buchanan, former President U. S. Grant produced in his own memoirs a literary masterpiece. Grant was suffering from extreme financial distress, but even so he rejected an offer of the then enormous sum of $100,000 from the impresario P. T. Barnum to display his trophies from the Civil War. He wrote magazine articles about the War, and Mark Twain offered him a book contract. As he began work on his book, he discovered that he had terminal cancer of the esophagus. Desperate to complete the work and provide for his wife, Julia, he rushed to complete it, and did so in only ten months.

Grant biographer William McFeely wrote that in an astonishingly short time, Grant had "completed a great book. No other presidential memoir can match it in literary quality; critics as diverse as Gertrude Stein and Edmund Wilson have hailed it. The *Personal Memoirs of U. S. Grant*," said McFeely, "is a classic account of the Civil War."[37] Two weeks after putting the final touches on the manuscript, Grant died. He had won his race with death, as he had won the contest with General Lee. Julia Grant received record royalties, and American literature became richer as a result.

Other former presidents who have provided memoirs – all worthwhile – include Harry Truman, Dwight Eisenhower, Lyndon Johnson, Richard Nixon, and Jimmy Carter. Theodore Roosevelt brought out a complete autobiography in 1913. This excellent work was one of a huge number of books on a wide variety of subjects that he wrote both before and after his presidency. He, Grover Cleveland, Benjamin Harrison, Calvin Coolidge, and FDR's wife Eleanor produced regular articles. Eleanor Roosevelt's column was the widely syndicated, "My Day." Coolidge's syndicated columns perhaps had more zest in their title: "Thinking Things Over with Calvin Coolidge."

Former President Gerald Ford accepted high pay for corporate board memberships, but he engaged in civic and educational activities as well. Not only did he participate in lecture series and seminars, he became concerned about the political influence of the religious right. He therefore accepted the co-chairmanship of People for the American Way, Norman Lear's organization created to counter influence from Jerry Falwell's Moral Majority.

If the *New York Times* is correct, former President George H. W. Bush has played a major role in foreign policy. The elder Bush shares with John Adams the distinction of being the only presidents to have offspring who followed in their footsteps (Benjamin Harrison was William Henry Harrison's grandson), but Bush had an advantage. After John Adams left the presidency, twenty-four years passed before the inauguration of his son; the elder Adams was nearly 90 at the time. Bush had to wait only for eight years, and remains vigorous in his 70s.

His son, George W. Bush, had taken a hard line as president on relations with North Korea. Numerous Korean experts were alarmed, and considered such an approach to be counter-productive at best, and dangerous at worst. They approached the elder Bush, who, according to the *Times*, sent his son a memo "forcefully arguing the need to reopen negotiations with North Korea, according to people who have seen the document. The advice in the memo appears to have been largely incorporated into the decision" that the new administration announced indicating that it would open discussions with North Korean leaders on a wide range of topics.[38]

It is impossible to ascertain the extent to which former President Bush influences his son. Numerous press reports indicate that the current administration initially made a conscious effort to avoid any appearance of influence in order to assert the president's independence and maturity. In the aftermath of 11 September, however, the new administration appeared to develop more confidence. In November of 2001, George W. Bush dispatched his father to London as his personal representative to a memorial service for British subjects who were killed in the attack on the World Trade Center. As his experience increases, it is possible that the current President Bush will make increased use of his father's experience.

A NOTE ON FORMER VICE PRESIDENTS

There have been 45 former vice presidents, from John Adams to Albert Gore. Of these, 14 – some 31 percent or nearly one-third of the total – went on to become president. Others, such as Hubert Humphrey, Walter Mondale, and Al Gore in recent years, were presidential candidates. The office has always had more potential than its detractors conceded, but in recent years it has become clear that vice presidents can now play major roles as the examples of Walter Mondale, Al Gore, and Richard Cheney (and to a lesser extent George H. W. Bush) so forcefully demonstrate. One should not overlook an office that since the middle half of the twentieth century has attracted such figures of quality as Richard Nixon, Lyndon Johnson, Hubert Humphrey, Gerald Ford, Nelson Rockefeller, Walter Mondale, George Bush, Al Gore, and Richard Cheney.

Conclusion

So there is life after the White House – at least for most Presidents. For a substantial minority, however, there was none at all. Nine of Clinton's predecessors – more than one fifth of the total – failed to complete their terms, and eight of these died in office.

Many of those who survived continued to exercise considerable influence on American political history; as indicated, some exercised dramatic influence. There is no way to tell whether Clinton will remain a potent political force, but examples from history suggest that he may — especially in view of his unusual youth, energy, and talent.

William Henry Harrison (Whig)	Died 1841
Zachary Taylor (Whig)	Died 1850
Abraham Lincoln (Republican)	Died 1865*
James Abram Garfield (Republican)	Died 1881*
William McKinley (Republican)	Died 1901*
Warren Gamaliel Harding (Republican)	Died 1923
Franklin Delano Roosevelt (Democrat)	Died 1945
John Fitzgerald Kennedy (Democrat)	Died 1963*
Richard Milhous Nixon (Republican)	Resigned 1974

* Assassinated

Notes

[1] Thomas A. Bailey, "The Post-Presidential Glow," in *Presidential Greatness*, New York: Appleton Century, 1966, pp. 112-114.
[2] John J. Patrick, Richard M. Pious, and Donald A. Ritchie, *The Oxford Guide to the United States Government*, New York: Oxford University Press, 2001, p. 670.
[3] Yanek Mieczkowski, *The Routledge Historical Atlas of Presidential Elections*, New York: Routledge, 2001, p. 46.
[4] Patrick, et al., p. 242.
[5] Mieczkowski, p. 51.
[6] Bailey, p. 119.
[7] The best book on the Progressive campaign is John A. Gable, *The Bull Moose Years*, Port Washington, NY: Kennikat, 1978; for an examination of TR's post-White House years, see Joseph Gardner's *Departing Glory*, New York: Scribner's, 1973.
[8] See Brooks D. Simpson, *The Reconstruction Presidents*, Lawrence: University Press of Kansas, 1998, p. 226.
[9] Harbaugh, p. 428.
[10] Gable, p. 250.
[11] Hermann Hagedorn, "Theodore Roosevelt: A Biographical Sketch," in H. Hagedorn and Sidney Wallach, eds., *A Theodore Roosevelt Round-Up*, New York: The Theodore Roosevelt Association, 1958, p. 51.
[12] Henry Pringle, *Theodore Roosevelt*, Norwalk, Conn: The Easton Press, 1988, p. 603.
[13] Edward J. Renehan, Jr., *The Lion's Pride: Theodore Roosevelt and His Family in Peace and War*, New York: Oxford University Press, 1998, p. 174.

[14] John Milton Cooper, Jr., *The Warrior and the Priest: Woodrow Wilson and Theodore Roosevelt*, Cambridge: Belknap Press of Harvard University, 1983, p. 259.
[15] Ibid., p. 260.
[16] John Morton Blum, *The Republican Roosevelt*, New York: Antheneum, 1973, p. 159.
[17] Nathan Miller, *Theodore Roosevelt: A Life*, New York: William Morrow, 1993, pp. 558-559.
[18] Peter Collier, *The Roosevelts: An American Saga*, New York: Simon and Schuster, 1994, p. 239.
[19] Wilson Sullivan, "Theodore Roosevelt," in Michael Bechloss, ed., *American Heritage Illustrated History of the Presidents*, New York: Crown Publishers, 2000, p. 327.
[20] H. W. Brands, *TR: The Last Romantic*, New York: Basic Books, 1997, pp. 811-812.
[21] David C. Whitney, *The American Presidents: Biographies of the Chief Executives from George Washington to George W. Bush*, 9th ed., Garden City, NY: Guild America Books, 2001, p. 381.
[22] Patrick, Pious, and Ritchie, p. 249.
[23] Bailey, p. 116.
[24] Patrick, Pious, and Ritchie, p. 654.
[25] Bailey, p. 119.
[26] Ibid., p. 116.
[27] See, e.g., Gardner, p. 89.
[28] See Patrick, Pious, and Ritchie, p. 303.
[29] David Witney, *The American Presidents*, Garden City, NY: Doubleday, 1969, p. 16.
[30] Herbert Sloan, "George Washington," in *The Reader's Guide to the American Presidency*, Alan Brinkley and Davis Dyer, eds., Boston: Houghton Mifflin, 2000, p. 21.
[31] Forrest McDonald, *The Presidency of Thomas Jefferson*, Lawrence: University Press of Kansas, 1976, p. 159.
[32] See Merrill D. Peterson, *Thomas Jefferson and the New Nation*, New York: Oxford University Press, 1970, p. 975.
[33] See Patrick, Pious, and Ritchie, p. 300.
[34] James A. Rawley, "Rutherford B. Hayes," in *To the Best of My Ability: The American Presidents*, James M. McPherson, ed., New York: Society of American Historians, 2000, p. 114.
[35] See Hannah Arendt, *On Revolution*, New York: Viking, 1965, pp. 252-259 and 323-324.
[36] William E. Gienapp, "James Buchanan," in Brinkley, p. 185.
[37] William McFreely, "Ulysses S. Grant," ibid., p. 227.
[38] Jane Perlez, "Fatherly Nudge May Have Shaped a Shift on North Korea," *New York Times* (10 June 2001), p. 8Y.

APPENDIX A. THE PRESIDENTS

President	Term	Party*	Birth	Death	State**
1. George Washington	1789-1797	Fed	Feb 2, 1732	Dec 14, 1799	Virginia
2. John Adams	1797-1801	Fed	Oct 30, 1735	Jul 4, 1826	Massachusetts
3. Thomas Jefferson	1801-1809	D-R	Apr 13, 1743	Jul 4, 1826	Virginia
4. James Madison	1809-1817	D-R	Mar 16, 1751	Jun 28, 1836	Virginia
5. James Monroe	1817-1825	D-R	Apr 28, 1758	Jul 4, 1831	Virginia
6. John Quincy Adams	1825-1829	D-R	Jul 11, 1767	Feb. 23, 1848	Massachusetts
7. Andrew Jackson	1829-1837	Dem	Mar 15, 1767	Jun 8, 1845	Tennessee
8. Martin Van Buren	1837-1841	Dem	Dec 5, 1782	Jul 24, 1862	New York
9. William Henry Harrison	1841	Whig	Feb 9 1773	Apr 4, 1841	Virginia
10. John Tyler	1841-1845	Whig	Mar 29, 1790	Jan 18, 1862	Virginia
11. James K. Polk	1845-1849	Dem	Nov 2, 1795	Jun 15, 1849	N. Carolina
12. Zachary Taylor	1849-1850	Whig	Nov 24, 1784	Jul 9, 1850	Virginia
13. Millard Fillmore	1850-1853	Whig	Jan 7, 1800	Mar 8, 1874	New York
14. Franklin Pierce	1853-1857	Dem	Nov 23, 1804	Oct 8, 1869	New Hamp.
15. James Buchanan	1857-1861	Dem	Apr 23, 1791	Jun 1, 1868	Pennsylvania
16. Abraham Lincoln	1861-1865	Rep	Feb 12, 1809	Apr 15, 1865	Kentucky
17. Andrew Johnson	1865-1869	Rep	Dec 29, 1808	Jul 31, 1875	N. Carolina
18. Ulysses S. Grant	1869-1877	Rep	Apr 27, 1822	Jul 23, 1885	New York
19. Rutherford B. Hayes	1877-1881	Rep	Oct 4, 1822	Jan 17, 1893	Ohio
20. James A. Garfield	1881	Rep	Nov 19, 1831	Sep 19, 1881	Ohio
21. Chester A. Arthur	1881-1885	Rep	Oct 5, 1829	Nov 18, 1886	New York
22. Grover Cleveland	1885-1889	Dem	Mar 18, 1837	Jun 24, 1908	New Jersey
23. Benjamin Harrison	1889-1893	Rep	Aug 20, 1833	Mar 13, 1901	Ohio
24. Grover Cleveland	1893-1897	Dem	Mar 18, 1837	Jun 24, 1908	New Jersey
25. William McKinley	1897-1901	Rep	Jan 29, 1843	Sep 14, 1901	Ohio
26. Theodore Roosevelt	1901-1909	Rep	Oct 27, 1858	Jan 6, 1919	New York
27. William Howard Taft	1909-1913	Rep	Sep 15, 1857	Mar 8, 1930	Ohio
28. Woodrow Wilson	1913-1921	Dem	Dec 28, 1856	Feb 3, 1924	Virginia
29. Warren G. Harding	1921-1923	Rep	Nov 2, 1865	Aug 2, 1923	Ohio
30. Calvin Coolidge	1923-1929	Rep	Jul 4, 1872	Jan 5, 1933	Vermont
31. Herbert Hoover	1929-1933	Rep	Aug 10, 1874	Oct 20, 1964	Iowa
32. Franklin D. Roosevelt	1933-1945	Dem	Jan 30, 1882	Apr 12, 1945	New York
33. Harry S Truman	1945-1953	Dem	May 8, 1884	Dec 26, 1972	Missouri
34. Dwight D. Eisenhower	1953-1961	Rep	Oct 14, 1890	Mar 28, 1969	Texas
35. John F. Kennedy	1961-1963	Dem	May 29, 1917	Nov 22, 1963	Massachusetts
36. Lyndon B. Johnson	1963-1969	Dem	Aug 27, 1908	Jan 22, 1973	Texas
37. Richard M. Nixon	1969-1974	Rep	Jan 9, 1913	Apr 22, 1994	California

President	Term	Party*	Birth	Death	State**
38. Gerald R. Ford	1974-1977	Rep	Jul 14, 1913	-	Nebraska
39. Jimmy Carter	1977-1981	Dem	Oct 1, 1924	-	Georgia
40. Ronald Reagan	1981-1989	Rep	Feb 6, 1911	-	Illinois
41. George Bush	1989-1993	Rep	Jun 12, 1924	-	Massachusetts
42. Bill Clinton	1993-2001	Dem	Aug 19, 1946	-	Arkansas
43. George W. Bush	2001-	Rep	July 6, 1946		Connecticut

KEY:

* Political Party Dem (Democrat), Rep (Republican), Fed (Federalist), D-R (Democrat-Republican) John Quincy Adams was a National Republican, a splinter of the Democrat-Republican Party. George Washington was not a member of a political party but aligned with the Federalists.
** Birth The president's state of birth is listed.

APPENDIX B. ARTICLE II OF THE CONSTITUTION

ARTICLE II

Section 1.

The executive Power shall be vested in a President of the United States of America. He shall hold his Office during the Term of four Years, and, together with the Vice President, chosen for the same Term, be elected, as follows:

Each State shall appoint, in such Manner as the Legislature thereof may direct, a Number of Electors, equal to the whole Number of Senators and Representatives to which the State may be entitled in the Congress: but no Senator or Representative, or Person holding an Office of Trust or Profit under the United States, shall be appointed an Elector.

The Electors shall meet in their respective States, and vote by Ballot for two Persons, of whom one at least shall not be an Inhabitant of the same State with themselves. And they shall make a List of all the Persons voted for, and of the Number of Votes for each; which List they shall sign and certify, and transmit sealed to the Seat of the Government of the United Stateds, directed to the President of the Senate. The President of the Senate shall, in the Presence of the Senate and House of Representatives, open all the Certificates, and the votes shall then be counted. The Person having the greatest Number of Votes shall be the President, if such Number be a Majority of the whole Number of Electors appointed; and if there be more than one who have such Majority, and have an equal Number of Votes, then the House of Representatives shall immediately chuse by Ballot one of them for President; and if no Person have a Majority, then from the five highest on the List the said House shall in like manner chuse the President. But in chusing the President, the Votes shall be taken by States, the Representation from each State having one Vote; A quorum for this Purpose shall consist of a Member or Members from two thirds of the States, and a Majority of all the States shall be necessary to a Choice. In every Case, after the Choice of the President, the Person having the greatest Number of Votes of the Electors shall be the Vice President. But if there should remain two or more who have equal Votes, the Senate shall chuse from them by Ballot the Vice President.

The Congress may determine the Time of chusing the Electors, and the Day on which they shall give their Votes; which Day shall be the same throughout the United States.

No Person except a natural born Citizen, or a Citizen of the United States, at the time of the Adoption of this Constitution, shall be eligible to the Office of the President; neither shall any person be eligible to that Office who shall not have attained to the Age of thirty five Years, and been fourteen Years a Resident within the United States.

In Case of the Removal of the President from Office, or of his Death, Resignation, or Inability to discharge the Powers and Duties of the said Office, the Same shall devolve on the Vice President, and the Congress may by Law provide for the Case of Removal, Death, Resignation or Inability, both of the President and Vice President, declaring what Officer shall then act as President, and such Officer shall act accordingly, until the Disability be removed, or a President shall be elected.

The President shall, at stated Times, receive for his Services, a Compensation, which shall neither be increased nor diminished during the Period for which he shall have been elected, and he shall not receive within that Period any other Emolument from the United States, or any of them.

Before he enter the Execution of his Office, he shall take the following Oath or Affirmation: – "I do solemnly swear (or affirm) that I will faithfully execute the Office of President of the United States, and will to the best of my Ability, preserve, protect and defend the Constitution of the United States."

Section 2.

The President shall be Commander in Chief of the Army and Navy of the United States, and of the Militia of the several States, when called into the actual Service of the United States; he may require the Opinion, in writing, of the principal Officer in each of the executive Departments, upon any Subject relating to the Duties of their respective Offices, and he shall have Power to grant Reprieves and Pardons for Offenses against the United States, except in Cases of Impeachment.

He shall have Power, by and with the Advice and Consent of the Senate, to make Treaties, provided two thirds of the Senators present concur; and he shall nominate, and by and with the Advice and Consent of the Senate, shall appoint Ambassadors, other public Ministers and Consuls, Judges of the Supreme Court, and all other Officers of the United States, whose Appointments are not herein otherwise provided for, and which shall be established by Law: but the Congress may be Law vest the Appointment of such inferior Officers, as they think proper, in the President alone, in the Courts of Law, or in the Heads of the Departments.

The President shall have Power to fill up all Vacancies that may happen during the Recess of the Senate, by granting Commissions which shall expire at the End of their next Session.

Section 3.

He shall from time to time give to the Congress Information of the State of the Union, and recommend to their Consideration such Measures as he shall judge necessary and expedient; he may, on extraordinary Occasions, convene both Houses, or either of them, and in Case of Disagreement between them, with Respect to the Time of Adjournment, he may adjourn them to such Time as he shall think proper; he shall receive Ambassadors and other public Ministers he shall take Care that the Laws be faithfully executed, and shall Commission all the Officers of the United States.

Section 4.

The President, Vice President and all civil Officers of the United States, shall be removed from Office on Impeachment for, and Conviction of, Treason, Bribery, or other high Crimes and Misdemeanors.

APPENDIX C. CONSTITUTIONAL AMENDMENTS PERTAINING TO THE PRESIDENCY

AMENDMENT XII [RATIFIED JUNE 1804]

The Electors shall meet in their respective states, and vote by ballot for President and Vice President, one of whom, at least, shall not be an inhabitant of the same state with themselves; they shall name in their ballots the person voted for as President, and in distinct ballots the person voted for as Vice-President, and they shall make distinct lists of all persons voted for as President, and of all persons voted for as Vice-President, and of the number of votes for each, which lists they shall sign and certify, and transmit sealed to the seat of the government of the United States, directed to the President of the Senate; – The President of the Senate shall, in the presence of the Senate and House of Representatives, open all the certificates and the votes shall then be counted; – The person having the greatest number of votes for President, shall be the President, if such number be a majority of the whole number of Electors appointed; and if no person have such majority, then from the persons having the highest numbers not exceeding three on the list of those voted for as President, the House of Representatives shall choose immediately, by ballot, the President. But in choosing the President, the votes shall be taken by states, the representatives from each state having one vote; a quorum for this purpose shall consist of a member or members from two-thirds of the states, and a majority of all the states shall be necessary to a choice. And if the House of Representatives shall not choose a President whenever the right of choice shall devolve upon them, before the fourth day of March next following, then the Vice-President shall act as President, as in the case of the death or other constitutional disability of the President. – The person having the greatest number of votes as Vice-President, shall be the Vice-President, if such number be a majority of the whole number of Electors appointed, and if no person have a majority, then from the two highest numbers on the list, the Senate shall choose the Vice-President; a quorum for the purpose shall consist of two-thirds of the whole number of Senators, and a majority of the whole number shall be necessary to a choice. But no person constitutionally ineligible to the office of President shall be eligible to that of Vice-President of the United States

AMENDMENT XV [RATIFIED FEBRUARY 1870]

SECTION 1. The right of citizens of the United States to vote shall not be denied or abridged by the United States or by any State on account of race, color, or previous condition of servitude.

SECTION 2. The Congress shall have power to enforce this article by appropriate legislation.

AMENDMENT XIX [RATIFIED AUGUST 1920]

The right of the citizens of the United States to vote shall not be denied or abridged by the United States or by any State on account of sex.

Congress shall have power to enforce this article by appropriate legislation.

AMENDMENT XX [RATIFIED JANUARY 1933]

SECTION 1. The terms of the President and Vice President shall end at noon on the 20th day of January, and the terms of Senators and Representatives at non on the 3d day of January, of the years in which such terms would have ended if this article had not been ratified; and the terms of their successors shall then begin.

SECTION 2. The Congress shall assemble at least once in every year, and such meeting shall begin at noon on the 3d day of January, unless they shall by law appoint a different day.

SECTION 3. If, at the time fixed for the beginning of the term of the President, the President elect shall have died, the Vice President elect shall become President. If a President shall not have been chosen before the time fixed for the beginning of his term, or if the President elect shall have failed to qualify, then the Vice President elect shall act as President until a President shall have qualified; and the Congress may by law provide for the case wherein neither a President elect nor a Vice President elect shall have qualified, declaring who shall then act as President, or the manner in which one who is to act shall be selected, and such person shall act accordingly until a President or Vice President shall have qualified.

SECTION 4. The Congress may by law provide for the case of the death of any of the persons from whom the House of Representatives may choose a President whenever the right of choice shall have devolved upon them, and for the case of the death of any of the persons from whom the Senate may choose a Vice President whenever the right of choice shall have devolved upon them.

SECTION 5. Sections 1 and 2 shall take effect on the 15th day of October following the ratification of this article.

SECTION 6. This article shall be inoperative unless it shall have been ratified as an amendment to the Constitution by the legislatures of three-fourths of the several States within seven years from the date of its submission.

AMENDMENT XXII [RATIFIED FEBRUARY 1951]

SECTION 1. No person shall be elected to the office of the President more than twice, and no person who has held the office of President, or acted as President, for more than two years of a term to which some other person was elected President shall be elected to the office of the President more than once. But this Article shall not apply to any person holding the office of President when this Article was proposed by the Congress, and shall not prevent any person who may be holding the office of President, or acting as President, during the term within which this Article becomes operative from holding the office of President or acting as President during the remainder of such term.

SECTION 2. This article shall be inoperative unless it shall have been ratified as an amendment to the Constitution by the legislatures of three-fourths of the several States within seven years from the date of its submission to the States by Congress.

AMENDMENT XXIII [RATIFIED MARCH 1961]

SECTION 1. The District constituting the seat of Government of the United States shall appoint in such manner as the Congress may direct:

A number of electors of President and Vice President equal to the whole number of Senators and Representatives in Congress to which the District would be entitled if it were a State, but in no event more than the least populous State; they shall be in addition to those appointed by the States, but they shall be considered, for the purposes of the election of President and Vice President, to be electors appointed by a State; and they shall meet in the District and perform such duties as provided by the twelfth article of amendment.

SECTION 2. The Congress shall have power to enforce this article by appropriate legislation.

AMENDMENT XXIV [RATIFIED JANUARY 1964]

SECTION 1. The right of citizens of the United States to vote in any primary or other election for President or Vice President, for electors for President or Vice President, or for Senator or Representatives in Congress, shall not be denied or abridged by the United States or any State by reason of failure to pay any poll tax or other tax.

SECTION 2. The Congress shall have power to enforce this article by appropriate legislation.

AMENDMENT XXV [RATIFIED FEBRUARY 1967]

SECTION 1. In case of the removal of the President from office or of his death or resignation, the Vice President shall become President.

SECTION 2. Whenever there is a vacancy in the office of the Vice President, the President shall nominate a Vice President who shall take office upon confirmation by a majority vote of both House of Congress.

SECTION 3. Whenever the President transmits to the President pro tempore of the Senate and the Speaker of the House of Representatives his written declaration that he is unable to discharge the powers and duties of his office, and until he transmits to them a written declaration to the contrary, such powers and duties shall be discharged by the Vice President as Acting President.

SECTION 4. Whenever the Vice President and a majority of either the principal officers of the executive departments or of such other body as Congress may by law provide, transmit to the President pro tempore of the Senate and the Speaker of the House of Representatives their written declaration that the President is unable to discharge the powers and duties of his office, the Vice President shall immediately assume the powers and duties of the office as Acting President.

Thereafter, when the President transmits to the President pro tempore of the Senate and the Speaker of the House of Representatives his written declaration that no inability exists, he shall resume the powers and duties of his office unless the Vice president and a majority of either the principal officers of the executive department or of such other body as Congress may by law provide, transmit within four days to the President pro tempore of the Senate and the Speaker of the House of Representatives their written declaration that the President is unable to discharge the powers and duties of his office. Thereupon Congress shall decide the issue, assembling within forty-eight hours for that purpose if not in session. If the Congress, within twenty-one days after receipt of the latter written declaration, or, if Congress is not in session, within twenty-one days after Congress is required to assemble, determines by two-thirds vote of both Houses that the President is unable to discharge the powers and duties of his office, the Vice President shall continue to discharge the same as Acting President; otherwise, the President shall resume the powers and duties of his office.

AMENDMENT XXVI [RATIFIED JULY 1971]

SECTION 1. The right of citizens of the United States, who are eighteen years of age or older, to vote shall not be denied or abridged by the United States or by any State on account of age.

SECTION 2. The Congress shall have power to enforce this article by appropriate legislation.

APPENDIX D. LAW OF PRESIDENTIAL SUCCESSION

[The Law of Presidential Succession was first passed on July 18, 1947 and was subsequently amended in 1965, 1966, 1977, and 1979.]

If by reason of death, resignation, removal from office, inability, or failure to qualify there is neither a president nor a vice president to discharge the powers and duties of the office of president, then the speaker of the House of Representatives shall upon his resignation as speaker and as representative, act as president. The same rule shall apply in the case of the death, resignation, removal from office, or inability of an individual acting as president.

If at the time when a speaker is to begin the discharge of the powers and duties of the office of president there is no speaker, or the speaker fails to qualify as acting president, then the president pro tempore of the Senate, upon his resignation as president pro tempore and as senator, shall act as president.

An individual acting as president shall continue to act until the expiration of the then current presidential term, except that (1) if his discharge of the powers and duties of the office is founded in whole or in part in the failure of both the president-elect and the vice president-elect to qualify, then he shall act only until a president qualifies, and (2) is his discharge of the powers and duties of the office is founded in whole or in part on the inability of the president or vice president, then he shall act only until the removal of the disability of one of such individuals.

If, by reason of death, resignation, removal from office, or failure to qualify, there is no president pro tempore to act as president, then the officer of the United States who is highest on the following list, and who is not under any disability to discharge the powers and duties of president shall act as president; the secretaries of state, treasury, defense, attorney general, secretaries of interior, agriculture, commerce, labor, health and human services, housing and urban development, transportation, energy, education, veterans affairs.

APPENDIX E. SOURCES FOR STUDYING THE PRESIDENCY

SITES ON THE WEB

- PBS: The American President
  Web: www.pbs.org/wnet/amerpres/
- C-SPAN: American Presidents - Life Portraits
  Web: www.americanpresidents.org
- The White House: History of the Presidents
  Web: www.whitehouse.gov/history/presidents/

JOURNALS/PERIODICALS

- *Congress and the Presidency*
  School of Public Affairs
  American University
  4400 Massachusetts Ave., NW
  Washington, DC 20016-8130
  Web: www.american.edu/academic.depts/spa/ccps/
- *Presidential Studies Quarterly*
  Center for the Study of the Presidency
  1020 Nineteenth St., NW, Suite 250
  Washington, DC 20036
  Web: www.cspresidency.org
- *White House Studies*
  P.O. Box 756
  Boca Raton, Florida 33429-0756
  Web: www.whitehousestudies.com

LIBRARIES

- Rutherford B. Hayes Presidential Center and Library
  1337 Hayes Avenue
  Fremont, Ohio 43420
  Web: www.rbhayes.org
- Herbert Hoover Presidential Library
  P.O. Box 488
  West Branch, Iowa 52358
  Web: www.hoover.nara.gov
- Franklin D. Roosevelt Library and Museum
  511 Albany Post Road
  Hyde Park, New York 12538
  Web: www.academic.marist.edu/fdr/
- Truman Presidential Museum and Library
  500 U.S. Highway 24
  Independence, Missouri 64050
  Web: www.trumanlibrary.org
- Dwight D. Eisenhower Library
  Abilene, Kansas 67410
  Web: www.redbud.lbjlib.utexas.edu/eisenhower/ddehp.htm
- John Fitzgerald Kennedy Library
  Columbia Point
  Boston, Massachusetts 02125
  Web: www.cs.umb.edu/jfklibrary
- Lyndon Baines Johnson Library
  2313 Red River Street
  Austin, Texas 78705
  Web: www.lbjlib.utexas.edu
- Richard Nixon Library and Birthplace
  18001 Yorba Linda Blvd.
  Yorba Linda, California 92686
  Web: www.nixonfoundation.org
- Gerald R. Ford Library
  1000 Beal Avenue
  Ann Arbor, Michigan 48109-2114
  Web: www.ford.utexas.edu
- Jimmy Carter Library and Carter Presidential Center
  One Copen Hill Avenue
  Atlanta, Georgia 30307
  Web: www.carterlibrary.galileo.peachnet.edu/
- Ronald Reagan Library
  40 Presidential Drive
  Simi Valley, California 93065
  Web: www.reagan.utexas.edu

- George Bush Presidential Library
  1000 George Bush Drive West
  College Station, Texas 77845
  Web: csdl.tamu.edu/bushlib
- William J. Clinton Presidential Materials Project
  1000 LaHarpe Blvd.
  Little Rock, Arkansas 72201
  Web: www.clinton.archives.gov
- National First Ladies' Library
  Saxton-McKinley House
  331 South Market Avenue
  Canton, Ohio 44702
  Web: www.firstladies.org

CENTERS/ASSOCIATIONS

- Center for Congressional and Presidential Studies
  School of Public Affairs
  American University
  4400 Massachusetts Avenue, NW
  Washington, DC 20036
  Web: www.american.edu/academic.depts/spa/ccps/
- Center for the Study of the Presidency
  1020 Nineteenth Street, NW, Suite 250
  Washington, DC 20036
  Web: www.cspresidency.org
- Center for Presidential Studies
  Texas A&M University
  College Station, Texas 77843-4349
  Web: www-bushschool.tamu.edu
- Miller Center for Public Affairs
  2201 Old Ivy Road
  Charlottesville, Virginia 22904-4406
  Web: millercenter.virginia.edu
- White House Historical Association
  740 Jackson Place, NW
  Washington, DC 20503
  Web: www.whitehousehistory.org
- Presidency Research Group
  American Political Science Association
  1527 New Hampshire Avenue, NW
  Washington, DC 20036-1206
  Web: www.apsanet.net or sunsite.unc.edu/lia/prgnet

BOOKS

Presidency

- Edward S. Corwin, *The Presidential Office and Powers*
- Thomas E. Cronin, *Inventing the American Presidency*
- Thomas E. Cronin & Michael A. Genovese, *The Paradoxes of the American Presidency*
- George C. Edwards & Stephen J. Wayne, *Presidential Leadership*
- Richard F. Fenno, *The President's Cabinet*
- Louis Fisher, *The Politics of Shared Power: Congress and the Executive*
- Michael A. Genovese, *Power and the American Presidency*
- Fred I. Greenstein, *The Presidential Difference: Leadership Style from FDR to Clinton*
- Lauren L. Henry, *Presidential Transitions*
- Stephen Hess, *Organizing the Presidency*
- Charles O. Jones, *The Presidency is a Separated System*
- Richard Neustadt, *Presidential Power*
- Bradley H. Patterson, Jr., *The White House Staff: Inside the West Wing and Beyond*
- James Pfiffner, *The Strategic Presidency: Hitting the Ground Running*
- Robert J. Spitzer, *The Presidential Veto*
- Clinton Rossiter, *The American Presidency*
- Mark Rozell, *Executive Privilege: The Dilemma of Secrecy and Democratic Accountability*

Reference Works on the Presidency

- Leonard W. Levy and Louis Fisher, *Encyclopedia of the American Presidency* [encyclopedia]
- Tracy Irons-Georges, *The American Presidents* [encyclopedia]
- Michael Nelson, *The Presidency*

First Ladies

- Carl Sferrazza Anthony, *First Ladies: The Saga of the Presidents' Wives and Their Power*
- Betty Boyd Caroli, *First Ladies*
- Myra Gutin, *The President's Partner: The First Lady in the Twentieth Century*
- Gil Troy, *Mr. and Mrs. President*
- Robert P. Watson, *The Presidents' Wives: Reassessing the Office of First Lady*
- Robert P. Watson & Anthony J. Eksterowicz, *The Presidential Companion*

Reference Works on the First Ladies

- Lewis L. Gould, *American First Ladies: Their Lives and Their Legacy*
- Robert P. Watson, *American First Ladies [encyclopedia]*
- Robert P. Watson, *First Ladies of the United States*

The White House and First Families

- Carl Sferrazza Anthony, *America's First Families*
- William Seale, *The President's House*
- Robert P. Watson, *Life in the White House*
- John Whitcomb & Claire Whitcomb, *Real Life at the White House*

ABOUT THE CONTRIBUTORS

Colton C. Campbell, Ph.D. is Assistant Professor of Political Science at Florida International University and has served as Visiting Assistant Professor of Political Science at American University and an APSA Congressional Fellow from 1998 to 1999 in the office of U.S. Senator Bob Graham. Campbell is the author or co-editor of numerous books including *New Majority or Old Minority? The Impact of Republicans on Congress*, *The Contentious Senate: Partisanship, Ideology, and the Myth of Cool Judgment*, and *Congress Confronts the Court: The Struggle for Legitimacy and Authority in Lawmaking*.

David B. Cohen, Ph.D. is Assistant Professor of Political Science at the University of Akron. His research on executive politics has been published in *American Politics Quarterly*, *Congress & the Presidency*, *Presidential Studies Quarterly*, and *Southeastern Political Review*. His primary areas of interest are executive politics, Congress, and U.S. foreign policy making. His Ph.D. is from the University of South Carolina.

Richard S. Conley, Ph.D. is Assistant Professor of Political Science at the University of Florida. His research on presidential-congressional relations has appeared in *American Politics Research*, *Political Research Quarterly*, *Polity*, and *Presidential Studies Quarterly*. He is the author of *The Presidency, Congress, and Divided Government: A Post-War Assessment*.

William Cunion is Visiting Assistant Professor of Political Science at Ohio University, where he teaches a variety of courses on American government. He is presently completing his dissertation from the University of Illinois at Urbana-Champaign, which focuses on presidential rhetoric.

Christopher J. Deering, Ph.D. is Professor of Political Science at George Washington University. His research interests are primarily in American national institutions with a special interest in congressional committees. He is co-author of *Committees in Congress*.

Chris J. Dolan, Ph.D. received his doctorate from the University of South Carolina and is Assistant Professor of Political Science at the University of Central Florida. His teaching and research interests include presidential politics and history, Congress, and U.S. foreign policymaking.

Thomas S. Engeman, Ph.D. is Professor of Political Science at Loyola University Chicago and is the author, co-author, or editor of three books: *Concordance of the Federalist Papers*, *Amoral America*, and *Thomas Jefferson and the Politics of Nature*. His research has also been published in numerous journals, including the *Journal of Politics* and *The Review of Politics*.

Victoria A. Farrar-Myers, Ph.D. is Associate Professor of Political Science at the University of Texas-Arlington. She is the author of several publications on such topics as American politics, campaign finance reform, electoral politics, and the presidency and has received awards for her research and teaching.

Patrick Fisher, Ph.D. is Assistant Professor of Political Science at Monmouth University. His research interests include the congressional budget process, public policy, and political culture. Articles published by Dr. Fisher include those in *The Social Science Journal* and *Party Politics*.

Douglas Steven Gallagher is a Ph.D. candidate in history at the University of Florida. His primary research interests center around intellectual movements in post-World War II America, particularly the liberal anti-Communism of the American for Democratic Action (ADA) and the Congress for Cultural Freedom (CCF).

Karen M. Hult, Ph.D. is Professor of Political Science and an adjunct faculty member at the Center for Public Administration at Virginia Polytechnic Institute and State University (Virginia Tech). Her primary research interests are in the U.S. executive, organization theory and institutional design, and social science methodologies. She is the author of *Agency Merger and Bureaucratic Redesign*, co-author, with Charles E. Walcott, of *Governing the White House: From Hoover Through LBJ*, and *Governing Public Organizations*. Her articles have appeared in *Administration & Society*, *American Journal of Political Science*, *Polity*, and other scholarly journals.

Tom Lansford, Ph.D. is Assistant Professor of Political Science at the University of Southern Mississippi-Gulf Coast and a Fellow of the Frank Marie Center for International Politics and Ethics. Lansford is the author or co-author of several books including *Theodore Roosevelt*, *Evolution and Devolution: The Dynamics of Sovereignty and Security in Post-Cold War Europe*, *Teaching Old Dogs New Tricks: International Organizations in the Twenty-First Century*, and *Untying the Gordian Knot: Great Power Interests in the Persian Gulf*. He has previously published articles in journal such as *Defense Analysis*, *The Journal of Conflict Resolution*, *European Security*, *The International Journal of Political Studies*, *International Studies*, and *Strategic Studies*.

James P. Pfiffner, Ph.D. Is Professor of Public Policy at George Mason University and the author or editor of ten books on the presidency and American government, including *The Strategic Presidency: Hitting the Ground Running* and *The Modern Presidency*. He has worked at the U.S. Office of Personnel Management and been a member of the faculty at the University of California, Riverside and California State University, Fullerton. He is a member of the National Academy of Public Administration and worked on the staff of the National

Commission on the Public Service (the Volker Commission). In 1970, he received the Army Commendation Medal for Valor in Vietnam and Cambodia.

Jennifer L. Saunders is a Ph.D. candidate in Political Science at George Washington University. Her current research focuses on the politics of ballot initiatives.

Jon Schaff, Ph.D. recently completed his dissertation entitled The Domestic Lincoln: Presidential Leadership, Realignment and Public Policy and is Assistant Professor of Political Science at Northern State University in Aberdeen, South Dakota.

Lee Sigelman, Ph.D. is Professor of Political Science at George Washington University. He has written numerous books and articles on a broad array of topics in American politics and is the editor of the *American Political Science Review*.

Max J. Skidmore, Ph.D. is University of Missouri Curators' Professor at the University of Missouri-Kansas City, where he teaches political science. He has been Distinguished Fulbright Lecturer in American Studies in India, Senior Fulbright Scholar at the University of Hong Kong, and held a Fulbright for administrators in Germany. Skidmore is the author of numerous books and scores of articles and chapters on politics, political thought, popular culture, American studies, and the presidency. His most recent books are *Social Security and Its Enemies*, *Legacy to the World: A Study of America's Political Ideas*, and *Hong Kong and China: Pursuing a New Destiny*, and his books include translations in Arabic, Armenian, Chinese, French, Hungarian, Russian, and Spanish. Skidmore is currently completing a book for St. Martin's Press titled *Former Presidents as Private Citizens*. His Ph.D. is from the University of Minnesota.

Raymond Tatalovich, Ph.D. is Professor of Political Science at Loyola University Chicago, where his teaching and research interests include American government, the presidency and executive branch, policy analysis, and Congress. He has published several books, including *The Modern Presidency and Economic Policy* and *To Govern a Nation: Presidential Power and Politics*, and over 50 chapters, monographs, and scholarly articles, which have appeared in such journals as the *Journal of Politics*, *Political Research Quarterly*, *Social Science Quarterly*, *Polity*, *American Politics Quarterly*, *Women & Politics*, and *Presidential Studies Quarterly*. He is a member of the governing board of the Presidency Research Group.

Michael J. C. Taylor, Ph.D. is Assistant Professor of History at Dickinson State University in North Dakota. His research and publications focus on the Civil War, Antebellum history, and Franklin Pierce's presidency. He is currently completing a biography of Pierce.

Charles Walcott, Ph.D. is Professor of Political Science at Virginia Polytechnic Institute and State University (Virginia Tech). His primary research interest is the U.S. presidency, especially as it can be understood through organizational theory. He is the author or co-author of four books, including *Governing the White House: From Hoover Through LBJ*, with Karen

M. Hult. His articles have appeared in *Polity*, *American Journal of Political Science*, *Policy Studies Journal*, and other scholarly journals.

Robert P. Watson, Ph.D. is Editor of the journal *White House Studies* and has authored or edited 12 books and published over 100 scholarly articles, essays, and reviews. Watson has been interviewed by CNN, MSNBC, *USA Today*, and dozens of media outlets, appeared on C-SPAN's *Book TV* program, was a guest for CNN.com's coverage of the 2001 presidential inaugural, and directed the first-ever "Report to the First Lady," which was presented to Laura Bush and Lynne Cheney after the 2001 inauguration. He has taught at several universities including, most recently, the University of Hawaii, Hilo and is currently with Florida Atlantic University.

INDEX

#

11 September attacks, 51
1993 Budget Reconciliation Bill, vi, 189, 190, 192, 193, 195-198, 201

A

abolitionists, 7, 15, 16
Adams, John Quincy, 76, 250, 251, 255, 259, 263, 264
Adams, John, 6, 11, 12, 76, 159, 181, 231, 256-258, 260, 263
advice and consent, 47, 109-112, 116-118, 120
Afghanistan, 51, 152
Air Transportation Association (ATA), 164, 171, 178
Airline Deregulation Act, 163, 172, 178-181
airline deregulation, 163, 168, 170, 172-175, 177-180, 182, 184, 185
airline industry, 163, 164, 166, 168, 171, 173-176
Algeciras Conference, 137, 140
American intervention, 132, 152, 154
American military interventions, 136, 149
American political system, 23, 37, 48, 49, 185
appointment process, 110, 111, 115, 116, 118, 121
Arthur, Chester, 148
Ashcroft, Attorney General John, 49
assassination, 136, 236, 251, 252

B

balance of power, 138
bin Laden, Osama, 51
biographical data, 233, 238, 245
Bleeding Kansas, 13, 17, 22
Bork, Robert, 118
Boxer Rebellion, 136
Brown, John, 18
Brzezinski, Zbigniew, 64, 70
Buchanan, James, 19, 25, 26, 58, 208, 210, 225, 257, 259, 262, 263
budget surplus, 200, 201
budget(ary) proposals, 189, 192, 193
Bush v. Gore, 51, 54
Bush, Barbara, ix
Bush, George H.W., 234
Bush, George W., x, xiv, 39, 48-50, 52, 110, 112, 113, 236, 250, 252, 255, 260, 262, 264

C

Cabinet, 35, 39, 40, 44-46, 110, 112, 113, 120, 123, 224, 231, 278
Camp David, 174
capitalist economy, xi
Carter, Jimmy, vi, x, 7, 57, 58, 62-68, 70, 71, 75, 82, 95, 107, 111, 149, 150, 163, 166-186, 220, 228, 230, 231, 234, 235, 250, 257-259, 264, 276
Central Intelligence Agency, 128
Chase, Salmon, 27
Chase, Secretary, 30, 32
checks and balances, xi, xiii, 88
Cheney, 61, 62, 260, 284
Cheney, Richard, 61, 70, 260
Civil Aeronautics Board (CAB), 163-166, 169, 170, 172, 175, 178, 180, 183, 184
civil rights, 9, 42, 43, 114, 257
civil service, 14, 40, 46-49, 120
Civil War, v, 18, 21, 23, 34, 37, 41-43, 45, 143, 209, 259, 283
class politics, 217

Cleveland, Grover, 23, 39, 43, 133, 147, 249, 252, 257, 259, 263
Clinton budget, 192, 193, 196, 197
Clinton, Bill President, x, xii, xiv, 9, 76, 79, 86, 91, 104, 106, 111, 114, 116, 118, 120, 181, 190, 191, 194, 195, 200, 235, 249, 264
Clinton, Chelsea, ix
Clinton, Hillary, 255
Clinton's deficit-cutting plan, 190
Cold War, 128, 130, 142, 156, 160, 282
colonization, 6, 143
commander-in-chief, 34
communism, 150, 153, 155, 156
confirmation hearings, 110, 111, 118, 190
confirmation process, 109, 110, 112, 114, 118, 121
congressional debates, 78
congressional elections, 138, 195, 197, 200, 254
congressional opposition, 119
congressional support, 93, 94, 96, 98, 100, 103, 222, 223
conservatism, 149, 217, 225, 254
constitutional authority, 21, 103, 117
Constitutional Convention, 5, 6, 8, 256, 258
constitutional system, xiii, 226
constitutionality, 28, 76, 78, 80, 82, 86, 88
containment, 128, 150, 152, 156
Continental Army, 4
Coolidge, Calvin, 23, 82, 110, 259, 263
corruption, 40, 47, 110
Cuba, 133, 135, 143, 151
Custis, Martha Dandridge, 4

D

Daschle, Thomas A., 114
de Lafayette, Marquis, 5
deficit reduction, 14, 190, 191, 197, 199
Democratic platform, 26
Department of Labor, 97, 102, 105
Department of Transportation (DOT), 168, 169, 173, 175, 176, 178, 182
deregulation, 163, 165, 166, 168-173, 176-185
divided government, x, 76, 79, 83-85, 94, 104, 218, 220, 227, 229
domestic legislation, 32
domestic policy, 46, 62, 64, 86, 95, 96, 106, 129, 130, 140, 149, 167, 221
Douglas, Senator, 15, 18, 19
Dred Scott decision, 51

E

economic growth, 190, 199
economic recession, 49
Eisenhower, Dwight D., 58, 68, 69, 75, 84, 106, 208, 209, 214, 220, 223, 224, 227, 230, 250, 259, 263, 276
electoral majority, 39
electoral margins, 147
electoral support, 101
electoral votes, 48, 52, 144, 251, 256
executive branch, 24, 25, 110, 112, 118, 120, 172, 185, 189, 228, 283
executive restraint, 217
expansionist policies, 134
expectations gap, 218-220, 224, 227, 228

F

Fair Deal, 220
favorite son(s), 14, 147, 148, 157-160, 244
FDR, x, 23, 94, 106, 164, 217, 223, 226-228, 230, 237, 239, 246, 259, 278
Federal Aviation Administration (FAA), 164
federal budget, 95, 199, 201
federal government, ix, x, 16, 20, 26, 27, 95, 164, 189, 190, 198, 200, 201
federal oversight, 163
Fillmore, Millard, 249-252, 263
Ford, Gerald, ix, x, 57-64, 66-70, 75, 83, 91, 96, 107, 163, 165, 166, 170, 208, 220, 228, 230, 255, 257, 260, 264, 276
foreign policy, x, 86, 97, 112, 127-141, 143, 145, 149-160, 210, 260, 281
former presidents, 250, 252, 255, 256, 259
framers of the Constitution, 109
Franklin, Benjamin, 7, 11
Freud, Sigmund, 234, 245

G

Garfield, James A., 207, 253, 263
Garrison, William Lloyd, 18, 22
General Agreement on Tariffs and Trade (GATT), 129, 141
Germany, 47, 137, 257, 283
Goldwater, Barry, 171, 176
Gore, Al, 38, 48, 51, 54, 149, 191, 260
Grant, President U. S., 256, 259
Great Britain, 31, 37, 133, 141, 144, 257
Great Depression, x, 223, 237
Great Society, 220
Great White Fleet, 139, 140

Grenada intervention, 149, 151, 152
Gulf War, 104, 108, 156, 157, 159

H

Hamilton, Alexander, 33, 78, 109, 122
Harding, Warren, 80, 208, 254, 256, 261, 263
Harrison, Benjamin, 37, 38, 43, 45, 49-51, 53, 133, 252, 257, 259, 260, 263
Harrison, President, 37-39, 43-50, 52-54, 208, 252, 255, 256, 260, 261, 263
Hayes, President Rutherford B., 37-44, 49-54, 257, 258, 262, 263, 276
Henry, Patrick, 7
homeland security, x
Homestead Act, 24-27, 32
Hoover, Herbert, 74, 257, 263, 276
House of Representatives, 7, 13, 31, 52, 73, 93-95, 97, 99, 101, 106, 141, 161, 180, 183, 185, 255, 256, 259, 265, 269, 270, 272, 273
Hughes, Charles Evans, 211, 256

I

ideological conflict, 98, 99
ideology, 20, 75, 98, 111, 167, 192, 197, 201
impeachment, x, 74, 79, 89, 219
imperialism, 133, 134
inaugural address, 14, 21, 39, 40, 45, 46, 79, 82, 83, 91
income tax, 24, 32, 190
incumbent president, 48
inflation, 30, 31, 88, 165, 173, 184
institutional presidency, xiv, 75, 86
interest groups, xi, xiv, 49, 114, 168, 169, 173, 178, 181, 196
Interior Department, 25, 40
international relations, 127, 130, 142
internationalism, 131, 132, 136, 138
Iran-Contra, x, 154
isolationism, 132, 135

J

Jackson, Andrew, 16, 22, 38, 52, 73, 74, 76, 86, 89, 91, 208, 218, 263
Japan, 98, 101, 103, 105, 108, 128, 135, 138, 139
Jefferson, Thomas, 7, 9, 10, 11, 76, 89, 148, 208, 209, 213, 257, 258, 262, 263, 282
Johnson, Andrew, 40, 89, 91, 208, 255, 263
Johnson, Lyndon, xiv, 57, 79, 148, 223, 224, 235, 240, 245, 250, 257, 259, 260
judicial nominees, 118, 119, 121

K

Kansas-Nebraska Act, 14, 15, 20, 256
Kennedy, Edward, 165, 170, 248
Kennedy, Joe, 240, 241, 242
Kennedy, John F. (JFK), 218, 222, 223, 230, 233, 236, 238-241, 243-245, 247-249, 263
Kennedy, Robert, 239, 240, 247

L

legislative branch, xiii, 24, 78, 178, 179
legislative presidency, 93, 94, 104
legislative process, 27, 32, 74, 173, 217, 221, 222, 227
legislative success, 94, 96, 104, 179
legislative veto, xiii
legitimacy, 40, 51, 153, 218, 219
Lewinsky scandal, x
liberalism, 225
Lieberman, Senator Joseph, 112
Lincoln, President Abraham, 23-25, 27, 29, 30-35, 134, 208-210, 225, 235, 251, 259, 261, 263, 283
line-item veto, xiii

M

Madison, James, 7, 11, 22, 74, 76, 78, 82, 85, 86, 89-91, 109, 122, 142, 148, 256-258, 263
manifest destiny, 131, 132, 135, 143
Mason, George, 6, 9, 51, 282
McKinley, William, 48, 90, 127, 133-136, 138, 144, 209, 252, 261, 263, 277
military repression, 136
minority presidents, 38, 39, 49, 50
Mitchell, George, 102
modern presidency, x, 23, 24, 33, 34, 57, 68, 94, 189, 209
Mondale, Vice President Walter, 175
Monroe Doctrine, 132, 133, 136, 137, 143
Monroe, James, 76, 86, 256, 257, 263
Mount Vernon, 4, 5, 8, 9, 256

N

NAACP, 61
national bank system, 27, 30, 32
national debt, 191, 200
National Security Council, 128
national security, 64, 128, 151, 152, 157, 226
national unity, 79
New Deal, 24, 189, 226, 228, 231

new realism, 217, 219
news media, 44, 219
Nixon, Richard, xiii, xiv, 58-62, 64, 66-70, 83, 95, 165, 208, 209, 220, 224, 228, 230, 231, 234, 236-240, 245, 250, 257, 259-261, 263, 276
Noriega, 154, 155, 157, 159

O

Oglethorpe, James, 6
omissions, 7
Omnibus Budget Reconciliation Act, 191
opposition party, 78, 94, 98, 99
override attempts, 97, 101

P

Pacific Railroad, 24, 26, 27, 32
Panama Canal, 137, 140, 145, 154, 210
Panamanian intervention, 149, 154, 155, 157, 159
partisan advantages, 147
partisan language, 79, 82, 85, 86
partisan politics, 226
partisanship, 20, 79, 80, 83, 84, 86-88, 98, 99, 101, 102, 121, 194, 197
party factions, 94, 120, 222
Penn, William, 6
Pentagon, 51
Persian Gulf conflict, 156, 158
personality theory, 235
Pierce, Franklin, 13-22, 208, 249, 250, 257, 263, 283
polarization, 110
policy agenda, xi, 100, 148, 149, 152-154, 156, 158-160, 224, 228
policy goals, 58, 200
political advantage, 19, 103
political agenda, xii
political appointees, 109, 120
political culture, xi, 13, 128, 282
political debate, 78, 201
political disputes, 121
political elites, 127, 129-131, 138, 140, 143
political leadership, 168, 181, 193
political parties, xi, 14, 20, 37, 226
political regimes, 127, 128, 130
political rights, 6
political skills, xii, xiv, 217
political strategy, xiv, 57, 58, 200
political tactics, 13, 65
Polk, James, 14, 21, 23, 148, 208, 249, 251, 263
polling, xiii, 25, 219, 251

popular support, 219
Powell, Colin L., 112
power politics, 132
presidency research, 233
President's character, 236
presidential behavior, xii, xiv, 154, 233, 234, 245
presidential constraints, 218, 222, 227
presidential election, 27, 49, 51, 113, 138, 194, 195
presidential elections, 192
presidential history, 225, 255
presidential leadership, xi, 24, 57, 208, 219, 221-223, 225, 231
presidential nomination(s), 109, 110, 113, 121, 254
presidential popularity, 98, 219, 223, 228
presidential power, x, xii, xiii, 33, 96, 185, 217, 218, 223
presidential psychology, xiv
presidential reputations, 209
presidential rhetoric, 58, 74-77, 82, 86, 281
presidential transitions, 39
presidential veto(es), 73, 76
press corps, ix, x, 60
psychology, 233, 234, 235
public opinion, x, xiii, 42, 102, 132, 139, 143, 171, 200, 201, 209, 213, 219, 226, 259
public presidency, 75, 86
Puerto Rico, 135, 136, 137

R

Reagan, Ronald, vi, ix, x, 52, 66, 68, 75, 93-95, 97, 102, 107, 111, 115, 116, 118, 121, 124, 140, 141, 147-162, 181, 190, 193, 197, 214, 221, 223-225, 228-230, 234, 250, 255, 257, 264, 276
Reagan's foreign policy, 149, 150, 153, 155, 156, 160
recess appointees, 109
reconstruction, 42, 43, 49, 52, 160, 214, 261
regime building, 127
regulatory reform, 165, 166, 169, 170, 173, 175, 177, 178, 180
Reno, Attorney General Janet, 116
Republican National Committee, 59, 253
Republican platform, 25, 26
retirement, 250, 256, 257, 258
Revolutionary War, 4, 9
roll-call votes, 96
Roosevelt Corollary, 136, 144

Roosevelt, Franklin D., x, 23, 24, 25, 41, 140, 141, 208, 223, 226, 227, 236-238, 240, 263, 276
Roosevelt, Theodore, vi, x, 23, 41, 76, 86, 127, 131, 132, 134, 137, 144, 145, 148, 207-215, 249, 252-254, 259, 261-263, 282
Rumsfeld, Donald, 59, 69, 161

S

Scott, Winfield, 14, 251
sectionalism, 8, 41
Senate confirmation, 115, 116, 117
Senate Judiciary Committee, 111, 114, 118, 124, 165, 180
Senate, 18, 21, 25-27, 30-32, 40, 44, 46, 47, 48, 73, 89, 90, 102, 103, 108-113, 115-123, 130, 137, 139, 145, 161, 164, 165, 170, 173, 175, 177, 180, 191, 193, 195, 196, 237, 244, 255, 265, 266, 269, 270, 272, 273
senatorial courtesy, 113, 119
separation of powers, 37, 88, 218, 229
Seward, William, 15, 18
Shays' Rebellion, 20
slave labor, 5
slavery, 3-11, 14-21, 33, 209, 251, 255, 259
social policy, 95
Social Security, 114, 200, 283
sovereignty, 14, 15, 16, 20, 88, 128, 136
Soviet Union, 64, 128, 130, 141, 150-160
Spanish-American War, 133-135, 144
speechwriters, 57, 58, 61, 68, 69, 77
speechwriting, 58, 59, 61, 63, 64, 66-68
spending cuts, 190, 193
spheres of influence, 128, 135, 137
spin control, xii
State Department, 26, 44, 127, 136
State of the Union, 17, 20, 22, 61, 104, 106, 160, 162, 173, 184, 266
Supreme Court, 13, 14, 16, 39, 48, 51, 54, 110, 118, 119, 122-124, 224, 231, 256, 259, 266

T

Taft, William Howard, 82, 83, 84, 135, 139, 140, 145, 148, 211, 212, 224, 250, 252, 254, 256, 257, 263

tax increases, 190, 191, 192, 193, 196, 197
territorial expansion, 133
Treasury Department, 30, 40, 59, 61
Truman, Harry S., x, 14, 84, 89, 106, 140, 148, 208, 209, 219, 221, 230, 236, 237, 239, 245, 259, 263, 276
Tyler, John, 74, 148, 249, 255, 257, 258, 263

U

U.S. Navy, 136, 137
unilateralism, 132, 133

V

Van Buren, Martin, 148, 251, 252, 257, 259, 263
Vance, Cyrus, 64, 70
Venezuela, 137, 144, 257
veto message(s), 73-80, 82-86, 90, 91
veto power, 73, 74, 78, 79, 94, 97, 103, 104
veto threats, 74, 94, 97, 101, 103
Vietnam syndrome, 150, 152, 156, 159
Vietnam War, x, xiii, 150
voting behavior, xii, 221

W

War Department, 17, 41
War of 1812, x, 134, 258
war on terror, xiv
war powers, xiii
Washington Monument, 3
Washington politics, 166, 167
Washington, George, v, ix, x, xi, 3, 4, 9-12, 33, 73, 75, 76, 86, 90, 132, 208, 214, 237, 262-264, 281, 283
Washington's character, 3, 8, 9
Watergate, x, 58, 68, 69, 234
Williams, Roger, 6
Wilson, Woodrow, xiv, 16, 74, 79, 132, 141, 208, 211, 213, 218, 227, 234-239, 245-247, 252, 256, 257, 262, 263
World Trade Center, 51, 260
World Trade Organization, 129
World War I, 141, 212
World War II, 23, 78, 130, 140, 141, 282
writing staff, 58, 60-63, 66, 68, 69